Beginning ASP.NET 1.1 Databases: From Novice to Professional

DAMIEN FOGGON AND DANIEL MAHARRY

Apress®

Beginning ASP.NET 1.1 Databases: From Novice to Professional

Copyright © 2004 by Damien Foggon and Daniel Maharry

ISBN (pbk): 1-59059-369-3

Printed and bound in the United States of America 9 8 7 6 5 4 3 2 1

Lead Editors: John Franklin, Dominic Shakeshaft
Technical Reviewer: Chris Ullman
Editorial Board: Steve Anglin, Dan Appleman, Ewan Buckingham, Gary Cornell, Tony Davis, Chris Mills, Steve Rycroft, Dominic Shakeshaft, Jim Sumser, Karen Watterson, Gavin Wray, John Zukowski
Project Manager: Kylie Johnston
Copy Edit Manager: Nicole LeClerc
Copy Editor: Kim Wimpsett
Production Manager: Kari Brooks
Production Editor: Katie Stence
Compositor: Diana Van Winkle, Van Winkle Design Group
Proofreader: Patrick Vincent
Indexer: Kevin Broccoli
Artist: Diana Van Winkle, Van Winkle Design Group
Cover Designer: Kurt Krames
Manufacturing Manager: Tom Debolski

Distributed to the book trade in the United States by Springer-Verlag New York, Inc., 175 Fifth Avenue, New York, NY 10010 and outside the United States by Springer-Verlag GmbH & Co. KG, Tiergartenstr. 17, 69112 Heidelberg, Germany.

In the United States: phone 1-800-SPRINGER, e-mail orders@springer-ny.com, or visit http://www.springer-ny.com. Outside the United States: fax +49 6221 345229, e-mail orders@springer.de, or visit http://www.springer.de.

For information on translations, please contact Apress directly at 2560 Ninth Street, Suite 219, Berkeley, CA 94710. Phone 510-549-5930, fax 510-549-5939, e-mail info@apress.com, or visit http://www.apress.com.

The source code for this book is available to readers at http://www.apress.com in the Downloads section.

For the four little ones. Adam, Owen, Kate, and Drew—
last but by no means least.
—Damien Foggon

This book is for Jane. Have I ever told you that I love you?
Well, I do.
—Dan Maharry

Contents at a Glance

Contents

Part Two
Core Skills

Chapter 3 Connecting to Data Sources

About the Authors

Damien Foggon has a day job working for Energise-IT in Newcastle, England, and spends most of his spare time as technical director and lead developer for Thing-E Ltd., a company specializing in the development of dynamic Web solutions for the education sector. He was responsible for the development of several ASP and ColdFusion Web sites, and he's now in the process of moving most of them to ASP.NET. Before coauthoring this book, Damien coauthored *Programming Microsoft .NET XML Web Services* (Microsoft Press, 2003), which taught him more about Web services than any sane person should really have to know. After several false starts, he's busy assembling his personal site at http://www.littlepond.co.uk.

Dan Maharry was born in a small seaside town notable only for the BBC blowing up a bus in its harbor and for being the birthplace of artist and enfant terrible Tracy Emin. While this may have hindered others, Dan used this foundation to come to Birmingham, England, home to the industrial revolution, several parks, and the now-defunct Wrox Press, where he worked for five years. He now splits his time between working as a developer for 3Form Ltd. and as a writer/reviewer for *.NET Developers Journal* and several book publishers. His most recent title, *Beginning ASP.NET 1.1 with Visual C# .NET 2003* (Wiley & Sons, 2004), adds to his line-up of other Windows titles about Visual Studio .NET, Web services, classic ASP, and HTML. Contact him at danm@hmobius.com.

About the
Technical Reviewer

Chris Ullman is a freelance programmer and technical author who gravitated toward Microsoft technologies during the summer of ASP (1997). He cut his teeth on Wrox Press ASP guides, and since then he has contributed to more than 20 books, most notably as lead author for Wrox's best-selling *Beginning ASP/ASP.NET* series. He has also contributed chapters to books on PHP, ColdFusion, JavaScript, Web services, C#, XML, and other Internet-related technologies.

Since quitting Wrox as a full-time employee in August 2001, he has branched out into VB .NET, C# programming, and ASP.NET development, maintaining a multitude of sites from `http://www.cuasp.co.uk`, which is his "work" site, to `http://www.atomicwise.com`, which is a selection of his writings on music and art.

Acknowledgments

THEY SAY THE second is easier than the first, but I'm not so sure! Thanks to Kylie, Dominic, John, Kim, and Katie for knocking my inane babblings into something that makes sense.

Thanks again to Mum who supported me no matter what mad decisions I've made.

Jill, Andy, and, since April 7th, Drew.

Granddad for supporting me in everything I ever did.

And to Gran. Always missed.

—*Damien Foggon*

A BIG SHOUT OUT to John F., Dominic, and Kylie at Apress for letting me write this book and to Damien for agreeing to write half of it. Special thanks to Dave Sussman for being a nice landlord and helping out when I got stuck.

—*Dan Maharry*

Introduction

WELCOME TO THE INTRODUCTION. From this point on, you'll be transported into an amazing world of teenage wizards, magical furniture, creepy crawlies, evil geniuses, thrills, spills, and laughter. Oh, hang on. Sorry, that's the other book. . . .

Welcome to the introduction. From this point on, you'll discover the amazing world of ADO.NET, inanimate computer desks, late-night coding sessions, evil bugs, functions, methods, properties, and data. That's a bit better.

The idea for this kind of book isn't new, but if you're trying to learn something for the first time, having it constantly spelled out to you in a stodgy, primary-school-history-teacher-learn-these-dates-by-rote style probably won't help. Therefore, we've added one joke per 50 pages to this book to break up the monotony. :-)

Actually, a confession here: Dan studiously spent four years avoiding anything to do with databases because, despite his love of things techie, he always perceived them to be even more techie than other server products and operating systems. Come on, system administrators defer to database administrators—they've gotta wear white lab coats, have foreheads the size of Mount Rushmore to hold their huge brains, and speak in some additional language only they understand to commune directly with their charges, don't they? Of course not. That's probably the same image his mum had of him because he could program the video recorder when he was eight. Thanks to a little nudging and handholding, his mum can now record her Mel Gibson movies without any help from Dan. Likewise, he can now build *data-driven Web sites* that use databases and other sources of information to define what they present to a user and how they present it and to learn how the user would like to it to work.

With any luck, by the time you've worked through this book, you'll be able to do the same (without the need to stand stubbornly in the corner for four years muttering something about databases being scary and too techie).

How to Use This Book

This book is designed as your introduction to the world of building data-driven databases using ASP.NET and ADO.NET. It's to be read from beginning to end rather than by dipping at random points as you may do with other more reference-type books. You may have come across databases already in other books, but this one assumes you really have been sitting at the bottom of a well for the last five years and know nothing at all about databases. It does, however, assume that while you were in your well, you had a book teaching you some ASP.NET and a computer on which to write your first ASP.NET pages.

You can download all the code and example databases for this book from the Downloads section of the Apress Web site at http://www.apress.com; however, most of the examples are short enough that they can easily be typed in, and we hope you decide to do this. It'll help you learn and remember what we show here that much quicker.

The only other things you'll need are a computer that works running Windows 2000, Windows XP, or Windows 2003 and a fast-*ish* connection to the Internet. You may need to download several things to work through this book, as follows:

- .NET 1.1 (24MB)

- Web Matrix (1.3MB)

- Microsoft SQL Server Desktop Engine (MSDE) (68MB)

- MySQL and associated software (26MB)

We also cover using stand-alone Microsoft DataBase (MDB) files. These need only .NET installed to use them, but they're also often associated with Microsoft Access. But unless you have a MSDN subscription, you'll need to buy this as part of Microsoft Office.

> **NOTE** *Note that working through the book with just one database—MSDE, for instance—is fine. We're just covering our bases by presenting them all.*

If you do get truly stuck or find errors in the book, please let us know via support@apress.com, quoting this book's ISBN (369-3) to make sure the Apress peeps don't mix it up with something else. We'll get back to you.

Summarizing the Chapters

The chapters in the book are broadly divided into three sections: introductory stuff (Chapters 1 and 2), theory (Chapters 3–10) and real-world practice (Chapters 11–13).

Chapter 1 takes a high-level overview of how data-driven Web sites work, how ASP.NET and ADO.NET let them work, and what you can use as sources of data for your Web sites.

Chapter 2 takes a similarly high-level overview at just databases, which are the typical data source for a Web site. We'll cover the components that make up a database, how it stores and gives meaning to data, and a few basic rules for storing data well in a database.

Chapter 3 describes how to connect your ASP.NET page to a data source, be it a database or something else.

Chapter 4 covers the common variations of query you can send to your data source that will return data for display on a page. It also looks at how you actually send that query to the data source as well.

Chapter 5 picks up from Chapter 4 and looks at the different queries you use to add, alter, and delete from your data sources.

Chapter 6 discovers how you handle the results of your query in the Web page using a DataReader object, which is fast and direct but has drawbacks. It compares the DataReader with a DataSet object. This gives you a lot more flexibility with the results of your data but is in turn somewhat slower and bulkier than a DataReader.

Chapter 7 teaches you how to "bind" data from either a DataReader or a DataSet to any control on a page and that there are three different ways to do it depending on what control you're trying to use.

Chapter 8 shows how you can use form controls and DataSets to create, update, and delete data from a data source.

Chapter 9 describes stored procedures and how to use them. These are queries precompiled and stored in a database that will run faster than queries sent over a connection to a database from the ASP.NET page.

Chapter 10 looks at the Data Definition Language (DDL), which allows you to create, modify, and delete data sources themselves. It also shows how to use DDL from a Web page.

Chapter 11 presents an overview of designing a database-driven Web site from scratch. In particular, it covers picking the right data source for your application, the right design for your database if that's what you're using, code style, performance, error handling, debugging, and maintenance.

Chapter 12 looks at the issues involved in writing data-driven classes and then builds some as the first half of a case study. In particular, we cover code separation, class libraries, connection pooling, handling database errors, transactions, and security.

Chapter 13 finishes off the case study using the techniques you've seen in the book to build a fully operational online application.

Finally, we have four appendixes for your reference. In order, they cover the installation of the software used, the syntax for all the SQL queries written, the contents of the sample databases used, and the Web sites referred to throughout the course of this book.

And that's about it really. We hope you enjoy the book and get as much out of reading it as we did out of it writing it. Maybe we'll hear from you in the not-too-distant future.

—Damien Foggon and Dan Maharry, August 2004

Part One

Introductions

CHAPTER 1

Data Sources and the Web

LOOK AROUND YOU. No really, look around you. In the past 30 years, computers have taken over from the filing cabinets of the world to become the (almost) universal way people store and look up information. Would you rather spend five minutes rifling through some badly organized stack of paper for the name of a client or the price of a book or spend ten seconds typing in a search query on a computer and getting the desired information back immediately? We thought so—the computer wins every time.

It's not just in the office that database-powered applications have proven popular. The development of server-side technologies that allow people to hook electronic data sources—databases, spreadsheets, Extensible Markup Language (XML) files, Windows services, and more—to Web pages means that the World Wide Web is now a place of dynamic data-driven Web applications rather than the collections of static Hypertext Markup Language (HTML) pages it began as. Regardless of whether you develop your sites with ASP.NET, PHP, or JavaServer Pages (although for this book we prefer ASP.NET), you can use databases to interact with your users, giving them the information they want to see and safely storing how they want to see it for next time. E-commerce sites such as Amazon and eBay use databases to provide customers with product information, recommendations, and wish lists, and to store feedback and orders. Portal sites use them to store articles and user settings so users don't need to reset them each time they visit the site. How you choose to use data in your site is up to you, but we'll give you the tools you'll need to do it.

In this chapter, you'll look at the world of data-driven Web applications from 50,000 feet so that by the time you finish this chapter, you'll at least have a rough knowledge of how things hook together. You'll spend the rest of the book parachuting down to the ground, espying the exact details as you get closer.

Up here in the blue sky of Chapter 1 then, you'll learn the following:

- Why data-driven Web sites are such a good idea

- How a data-driven Web page actually works

- The different sources of data you can use with a .NET Web application

- How ADO.NET is the glue that joins data sources and Web applications

- What exactly you find inside ADO.NET

- How to build your first data-driven Web page

If you've already read a beginner's book on ASP.NET, such as *Beginning ASP.NET in VB .NET: From Novice to Professional* by Matthew MacDonald (Apress, 2004), you're probably familiar with some of the material in this chapter already, so you could skip forward to the next chapter. Still, we encourage you at least to browse through this chapter. You never know what nuggets of information you may find.

Are Data-Driven Web Sites a Good Idea?

That's the $64,000 question, isn't it really? If you're reading this book, we'll assume you've already come to the conclusion that using databases and other sources of data to turn static Web sites into *dynamic data-driven Web applications* is a good thing. However, we'd be lying if we said there weren't any disadvantages to using databases—there are. This section, then, covers the pros and cons of creating data-driven Web sites.

On the plus side, you have the following:

Quality and timeliness of content: Databases are optimized for the storage and retrieval of data and nothing else. They allow you to use and update information on a live site almost in real time—something that isn't possible in real time with a Web site consisting of just static HTML pages with forms on them.

For example, consider what happens when an e-commerce site receives an order for some goods. The code running behind the page knows to store the new order in a database and to reduce the inventory count for each item in the order once payment has been received. If the customer wants to change the order, it's still available in the database to be changed. The inventory also can be changed, depending on what the customer does. Say the customer cancels the order. The system can simply reinstate inventory levels and delete the record of that order.

Now consider what happens if the e-commerce site has a human on the other side instead of a database and the customer wants to change the order. For a start, the human needs to find the order, check the stock, and so on. This process wouldn't be immediate, and it would be prone to errors. What if the order was lost or incorrectly written down?

Maintenance: Using a database makes it a lot easier to maintain your data and keep it up-to-date. Take the example of a bank site that contains lists of customers by name and by branch and contains profiles for each customer. Each time the customer is mentioned in a list, their account number is also present. If for some reason that account number changed, the site owner would need to change it accordingly on all the lists, which could lead to errors; after all, account numbers aren't the easiest things to remember. A well-designed database usually ensures that easily mistyped data such as Social Security numbers (SSNs), credit card numbers, International Standard Book Numbers (ISBNs), and so on, be entered or modified in only one place rather than several. The data-driven Web site would then just generate the lists by querying the database.

Data-driven sites are also easier to maintain as they typically have fewer actual pages than static HTML sites. The pages they do have act as templates that are filled on the fly from a database rather than the complete, individual pages that static sites contain. You can find more on this in the next section, "How Do Web Sites Use Data Sources?"

Portability: Information in data sources can easily be backed up and reused elsewhere as required. Compare this to static Web sites where the information can't easily be retrieved from the surrounding HTML and layout instructions.

Data context: Databases allow you to define relationships and rules for the data in your database. For example, you can create a rule in your database that says if you store some information about a book, you must include an author and an ISBN, which must in turn be valid. In turn, this means that rather than querying the database for information by a simple index such as the one in the back of this book, you can specify what to search for as well as the order in which the information should be returned. A great example of this is the search engine. Can you imagine Google (http://www.google.com) as a table of contents for the Web?

On the downside, you have the following:

Development time: It takes a little more time to write code to access the database containing information and to populate the database with the information you require. Likewise, it may take a little more planning initially to accommodate a database in the architecture of an application. Sometimes the data may not lend itself to being used as a data source, which means more code to change it into something more appropriate. More code means more bugs.

Performance: When a user requests a static HTML page from a Web server, that Web server immediately sends the page back to the client. When a user requests a dynamic page from a Web server that requires data from a database, the server must first make a request to (or *query*) the database for the necessary data and wait for it to arrive before it can assemble the page the user requested and send it. This extra round-trip means a slight reduction in performance levels from the Web server that may be unnoticeable on small sites but that becomes more obvious on enterprise sites when maybe thousands of pages are requested per minute from the Web server.

Although you can't ever completely compensate for the additional round-trips that are made between Web server and database, you can try to minimize the number of trips made by caching pages when they're created. After all, if the data in a page hasn't changed, why does it need to be retrieved from the database again? You'll look at improving the performance of a data-driven Web site with caching and other techniques in Chapters 11–13 of this book.

Dependence on the database: Using a database in a Web application means that should the database fail for some reason, the whole application will fail. The solution may be to run multiple servers with synchronized databases, but as you can see from the next point, that could put quite a large dent in your pocket.

Cost: Full enterprise-level database solutions don't come cheap. At the top end of the market, Oracle Enterprise Edition starts at $40,000 and SQL Server Enterprise Edition at $20,000 for installation on *one* computer. Obviously, not everything costs that much, and indeed the databases used in this book are free, but things can get quite pricey quickly.

Even at grassroots level, Internet service providers (ISPs) will offer some sort of database use in their hosting packages—typically MySQL or SQL Server—but charge an additional fee per month. Don't forget to check exactly how much even if you aren't planning to deploy a database-driven site straightaway. Having the facility in place is always a plus, even if it costs a little more. Of course, hosting your own Web site would solve that problem, but then that costs money to set up as well.

All in all, the decision comes down to how big your site is likely to be and whether you'd be happy tweaking HTML all day for the rest of your nonexistent life rather than putting the effort in initially, letting the database do most of the tweaking for you, and generally enjoying the social scene. You're still a database fan, aren't you? Thought so.

How Do Web Sites Use Data Sources?

So then, you have a database or some other data source, and you have an ASP.NET page. What does the page do to use the data source?

As you know, a static HTML page doesn't do a great deal. It's static. It has a pretty simple structure: a <head>, a <body>, and probably some headings and paragraphs. When you add ASP.NET, that page becomes dynamic and can be generated in many ways depending on what code you add. However, it still ends up with the same basic HTML structure. The difference is generally the content.

At its simplest, using a data source in a Web site means getting it to store and then provide the content for a page. You can define a page whose structure and layout don't change but whose contents do. It becomes a template, or a master page, for you to fill in the gap with information from the database. For example, the successful Amazon Web site (http://www.amazon.com) uses databases to store all the information and feedback for every product it sells, and yet, as Figure 1-1 demonstrates, the basic product page has the same layout regardless of the item you're viewing.

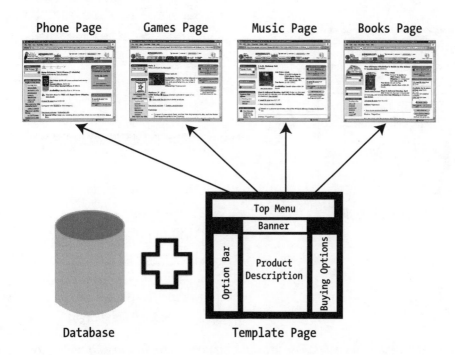

Figure 1-1. Amazon.com: One template page and many product pages

Amazon is also a good example of using a database to store layout and preferences information that changes depending on the page being requested. In Amazon's case, the basic banner changes color according to the type of product you're browsing, and a combination of cookies and database access stores information on the items you've browsed and bought in the past so as to suggest other content you may like in its recommendation pages.

In portal sites such as Slashdot (http://www.slashdot.org), a cookie on your machine identifies who you are to the site, and user preferences stored in the site's database allow for more radical changes to the site's user interface (UI), keeping track of which article groups you're interested in and whether the UI should be text only or full graphics, as Figure 1-2 demonstrates.

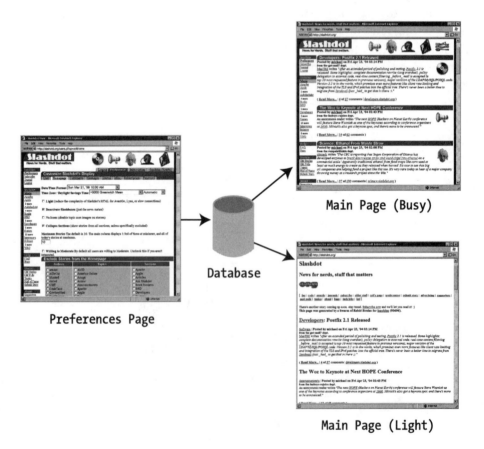

Figure 1-2. Slashdot uses a database to display its pages according to your preferences.

Delivering content and keeping track of user preferences aren't the only uses for a database in the Web environment, but they give you the idea. What about site maps, login systems, shopping carts, search engines, and bug-tracking systems? They're all variations on a theme, implemented as a database with a Web front end.

It's time to get a little more technical. What actually happens when a data-driven page is requested by a Web server? Does the code need to pray to the database gods for enlightenment and a source of knowledge? Of course not. Aside from anything else that ASP.NET may be doing in a page, the task of communicating with a data source takes just three steps, as shown in Figure 1-3.

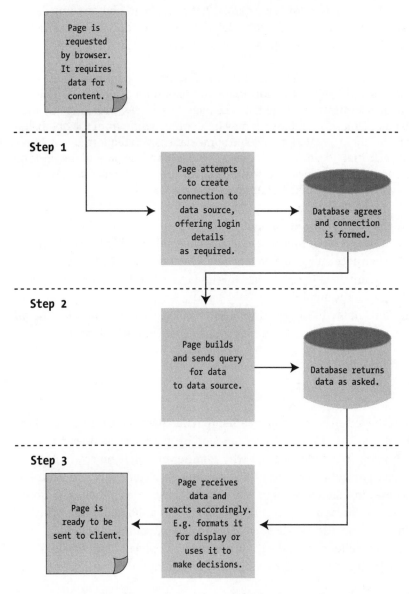

Figure 1-3. It takes three simple steps to retrieve data and use it in a page.

The steps are as follows:

1. The page tries to open a connection to a database. The code tells it which database and where it can be found. In this book, the databases will be stored on the same machine as the Web server, but this doesn't have to be the case. You'll look at creating connections in Chapter 3.

2. The page sends a command (also known as a *query*) to the database. Usually, it's a request for some data, but it could be to update some data, to add some new data, or even to delete some. The point is, it's a command. You'll look at creating and sending commands in Chapter 4.

3. The database sends back some information that the page must then handle accordingly. If it's information for display on the page, you use Web form controls to render it on the page, as you saw with Amazon and Slashdot. On the other hand, it may be a confirmation from the database that it updated, created, or deleted some data as you requested—or something else that doesn't directly affect the display of the page. It depends on the command sent in step 2. You'll discover some of the many ways to deal with query results in Chapters 5–8.

These three steps are simple, and, as you'll learn in Chapter 9, a lot of the design of a data-driven Web application revolves around that these steps are also the only way to connect a page to a data source. The design and code laid on top of the application are there to emphasize this and make as efficient use of the connection while it exists as possible.

Now that you know what a page does when it talks to a data source, it's time to look at what you can actually use as a data source to drive your Web pages.

Looking for Information

Oranges aren't the only fruit. We noted earlier that databases aren't the only source of data you can use in your Web applications, and it's good to remember this as you start to develop your code. After all, why confine yourself to one central source if it doesn't make sense to do so? For example, you could put your lists of things to do today in a database, but it makes more sense to keep them as a group of Outlook to-do items, as a note in OneNote, or even as a simple text file. With a little tweaking, you can also use these as data sources for your Web pages.

The following sections cover the three general types of data sources you'll most likely use from time to time for your Web applications.

Database Servers

Hang on. They're just called *databases*, aren't they? Where do the servers come into it? Well, strictly speaking, the database software you install—such as SQL Server, Oracle, MySQL, and so on—is a database server, or a database management server, depending on the product you're using. The database itself is just the collection of data you're using to fill your Web site with, and the server software is what hosts and manages it for you. A server may host many databases at a time, or just one, depending on the application of the server and how big the database is. The one you'll look at is a few hundred kilobytes (10^5 bytes). One of the largest databases in the world is that of the U.S. Army logistics division, which is almost a couple of hundred terabytes (10^{14} bytes)!

The following are several different types of database server (and therefore database), and each works in its own way:

Relational databases: A relational database is the most common type and the one you'll use for the duration of this book. Information about an object or an event is strongly typed (just as .NET variables are) and stored in tables. Each table is given a set of rules as to how it relates to other tables in the database. For example, if you wanted to store some contact information in a database, you could create a table called ContactInfo and include items in it such as your contacts' first names, last names, e-mail addresses, work phone numbers, and Web site URLs. You'll spend Chapter 2 looking at what makes up a relational database, how you store data in it, and how you define relations and rules on that data.

Object-oriented databases: Information about objects and events are stored as objects and manipulated using methods attached to that object's class. This mimics the way you work with objects in .NET.

Object-relational databases: Almost a superset of relational databases, object-relational databases store information in tables, but the tables themselves are given a type and allowed to be operated on in a pseudo-object-oriented fashion.

Native XML databases: These store information about an object or event as an XML document rather than an object or row in a table, reading in and offering information as XML documents only. This kind of database has come into being only recently following the development of XML as a popular technology.

A lot of commercial database servers are available; more relational and object-oriented databases exist than the others, but XML is gaining a great deal of popularity, so the balance is swiftly being redressed. However, the underlying query technology for XML has yet to be developed fully, so it'll be a while before native XML databases are truly as powerful as relational and object-oriented databases. You can find the URLs of many database Web sites in Appendix D.

Flat Files

The information stored in a database is often interrelated. "The information about cats is related to the information about their owners," for example. You design it that way, and database servers ensure that the relationship is maintained. On the other hand, the information in a flat file doesn't have a "flat file server" to keep track of a relationship between data in two flat files. "The information about cats in one flat file may be related to the information about people who own cats in another flat file, but there is nothing to enforce that relationship." If an owner moved house, a database server would note that the owner's cat's address also changes. In the flat file, the cat would still be living at the old address.

A flat file lives in its own world and is unaware of any events related to the information it contains. That doesn't mean you can't use it as a source of data, though. Information is usually stored in lists or as comma-separated values such as the following, with each line storing data for one item:

```
Judy, tabby, 12, kitekat
Fred, ginger tom, 2, cat chow
Gene, siamese, 5, live mice
Ann, albino, 8, dog food
```

For example, you can use any of the following in a Web application:

- Text files containing information written in a uniform way—perhaps as comma-separated values (a CSV file) or as a list of items, each on its own line. This could be a simple phone list perhaps or a shopping list.

- Spreadsheet files generated by applications such as Excel and Lotus 1-2-3.

- XML files.

You'll see how to use text and spreadsheet files with your Web pages in Chapter 3.

Services

Your computer maintains a lot of information about itself, even if you never use it. There are user profiles, hardware profiles, e-mail archives, and more. They can all be used as data sources if you know where to look and how to do it. For example, you can use the following in your Web applications:

- **Exchange**: You can tap into an exchange server and search for e-mail, contacts, and calendar information.

- **The Windows Registry**: You can tap into the registry, search for system settings, and tweak them a bit if you like.

- **Active Directory**: You can tap into a network's active directory and work with users, groups, and other network resources.

Please be careful if you decide to start working with these kinds of data sources. A lot of security measures guard these services and with good reason. Even with the best intentions, altering and deleting pieces of the registry, for example, can render Windows inert.

An enterprise-level Web application may use one or several of these data sources during the course of its operation, but because you're just learning here, you'll confine yourself to relational databases. These aren't critical to a computer's day-to-day running, and you can learn everything you need to start writing useful Web applications with them.

Introducing ADO.NET

So, you have a set of pages that need information and a data source to provide it. You know that the Web server will use the information to provide the page's content and influence the way it displays. All you need to know now is how to tell the page how to retrieve the content from the data source and what to do with it afterward. Does this look like a job for ASP.NET?

Not quite. While it's true that you'll use ASP.NET to react and work with the information once it has been pulled from a data source, you actually use its sibling technology, ADO.NET, to work directly with the database. If you've worked with classic ASP, the relationship between ASP.NET and ADO.NET is the same as ASP and ADO: the former deals only with the creation of Web pages, and the latter deals solely with retrieving information from data sources.

Data Access Technology: A Brief History

ADO.NET is the latest in a long line of Microsoft data access technologies spanning a good ten years with the same aim in mind—to make database access as easy and as painless as possible for anyone who needs that facility.

Back in the late 1980s and beginning of the 1990s, database server vendors all faced the same problem. A lot of third-party vendors wanted to build products backed by a database but didn't want to be limited to using just one database. That is, they wanted to keep the product as generic as possible so customers could use their application backed by their database of choice. The problem was that every database had its own way to access data inside it, so a third-party vendor had to write new code each time it wanted to support a new database.

The solution the database vendors came up with was called Open DataBase Connectivity (ODBC). This is a common set of functions and interfaces agreed upon by all the major database vendors at that time to be implemented by all their servers. Third-party vendors needed only to write code against ODBC methods to access a database, and it would now work against any database that supported ODBC, which they all did. The third-party vendors were happy because the size of their products was reduced quite dramatically, and they all worked against every ODBC database. The database vendors were happy because third-party products worked against their database servers, and they could charge the third parties license fees. Everyone's customers were happy because of the increase in competition, product, and, well, wasn't it nice when everyone played happily with everyone else?

ODBC was extremely successful and is still supported by all the major database servers in use today. However, one thing you can't call it is simple to use. ODBC works at quite a low level; in context, if your program spoke English, then you'd have to train yourself to write code in the Swahili that ODBC spoke when you wanted to access a database. Microsoft saw this problem and attempted to fix it by creating OLE DB, a set of Component Object Model (COM) components designed for Windows application developers that makes accessing data a bit simpler—more Spanish than Swahili, so still not English but easier to learn—and that also doesn't presuppose like ODBC does that the data source was a database. OLE DB was pretty successful and is still supported by several vendors including Microsoft, which decided that OLE DB would be the cornerstone for its Universal Data Access (UDA) strategy.

One of the aims of UDA was to bring an object-oriented interface to ODBC and OLE DB, which were procedural in nature—more C than C++ or VB. Its first attempts—Data Access Objects (DAO) and Remote Data Objects (RDO)—were designed to work against Access and larger databases such as SQL Server and Oracle, respectively. However, ADO v2.0 superseded both of these in 1998. ADO is a technology originally designed to give classic ASP pages a way to access databases.

ADO.NET now takes over from ADO. Like its predecessor, ADO.NET gives you the ability to work with a data source through a common set of methods and interfaces regardless of whether it supports ODBC, OLE DB, or its own proprietary access solution. This is achieved through a set of data providers, details of which you'll come to in the next section, "Data Providers." In addition to this, ADO.NET also provides better support for the following:

- Working with data away from the database itself or, rather, pulling information onto the Web server and working with it there instead of on the database server. This method of using *disconnected data* can improve performance if used wisely. To read more on this subject, look out for details of the DataSet object in Chapter 6. It's this object that you use to store disconnected data on the Web server.

- The database when it is under attack from a large number of simultaneous queries. Stability and performance have been significantly improved in ADO.NET compared to ADO.

- Binding information to any control on the page, as you'll see in Chapters 7 and 8. Strictly speaking, this is more an ASP.NET feature than ADO.NET, but in the context of this book, this is important.

In short, ADO.NET is a lot better than ADO ever was, and it's part of the .NET Framework, so it also has the development benefits that that provides. Developing data-driven Web sites has never been so straightforward. It's not quite child's play just yet, but it's certainly a lot more idiot-proof than it used to be.

Data Providers

You know now from our brief history lesson that the hard part to retrieving data from a data source has always been trying to talk to it. That's why ODBC, OLE DB, ADO.NET, and the rest were created in the first place. Ironically, as you saw in an earlier section, "How Do Web Sites Use Data Sources?" all you ever need to do with the data source for a Web site can be reduced into three steps: creating a connection, sending a command, and dealing with the result of the command. What ADO.NET provides is a common interface for performing those three steps regardless of whether you're using ODBC, OLE DB, or some other method to access it, and it does this with *data providers*.

We'll now present an example to show what this means. In this book, we'll use three different data sources so there's a bit of choice when it comes to working on your own sites. MySQL has an ODBC interface, an MDB database file has an OLE DB interface, and MSDE has both ODBC and OLE DB interfaces as well as its own optimized set of access methods.

Suppose you're going to use MySQL. Writing a bit of pseudo-code for talking to this database, your three steps may look like this:

```
<%@ import Namespace="System.Data" %>
<%@ import Namespace="System.Data.Odbc" %>
<html>
  <script>
    create OdbcConnection object to link to MySQL
    create OdbcCommand object to set up and send a command to MySQL
    get returned an OdbcDataReader object containing the results of the command
    deal with the results....
  </script>
...
</html>
```

Now we'll present the following pseudo-code for using an MDB database file, which has an OLE DB interface:

```
<%@ import Namespace="System.Data" %>
<%@ import Namespace="System.Data.OleDb" %>
<html>
  <script>
    create OleDbConnection object to link to MDB file
    create OleDbCommand object to set up and send a command to MDB file
    get returned an OleDbDataReader object containing the results of the command
    deal with the results....
  </script>
...
</html>
```

The two pieces of pseudo-code are almost identical. The only difference is that the names of the objects are slightly different to correspond to the interface being used. So, for example, it's OdbcConnection for the ODBC database and OleDbConnection for the OLE DB database. As you'll see in Chapter 3, if you look at the real code, the actual calls you make are identical, which means the only things that change between different interfaces are the namespace to use and the names of the objects being used. The same is true if you want to use the native access method for SQL Server: the same method calls and steps are taken, but slightly different namespace and objects are used.

For example:

```
<%@ import Namespace="System.Data" %>
<%@ import Namespace="System.Data.SqlClient" %>
<html>
  <script>
    create SqlConnection object to link to SQL Server
    create SqlCommand object to set up and send a command to SQl Server
    get returned an SqlDataReader object containing the results of the command
    deal with the results....
  </script>
...
</html>
```

What you're seeing is the common interface for data access operations provided by ADO.NET. A common set of interfaces (one for a Connection object, one for a Command object, and so on) are implemented *and optimized* for each data access method you may need to use—ODBC, OLE DB, SQL Server native, and so on. Each group of objects is called a *data provider* and is housed in its own namespace. For example:

- System.Data.OleDb is the .NET Data Provider for OLE DB–based databases such as Access. You can also use it to access flat files.

- System.Data.OracleClient is the .NET Data Provider for Oracle databases.

- System.Data.SqlClient is the .NET Data Provider for SQL Server and MSDE.

- System.Data.SqlServerCe is the .NET Compact Framework Data Provider for SQL Server CE. As you may imagine, its use is limited to applications running on personal digital assistants (PDAs) hosting an instance of SQL Server CE.

- System.Data.Odbc is the .NET Data Provider for ODBC-based databases. It's not part of .NET 1.1 by default, but you can easily install it by following the instructions in Appendix A.

And that's one of the beauties of ADO.NET. As long as you know which data provider to use, you need to learn only one set of calls, and every data provider supports them. Figure 1-4 shows this diagrammatically.

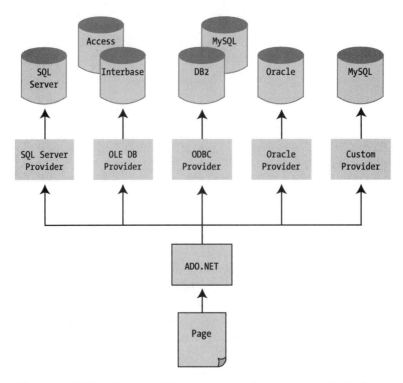

Figure 1-4. Using data providers means you have easy, optimized access to all databases.

Going one step further, if a vendor would rather .NET developers use a data provider specifically designed for their database server instead of the generic OLE DB or ODBC ones, all they have to do is implement the same common set of objects that every other data provider includes. An extra method or property here and there may take advantage of a particular feature unique to the data access technology being modeled by the data provider, but unless noted otherwise, for the purposes of this book, all the objects have the same methods and properties.

Every data provider contains implementations of the following:

- A Connection object used to represent the connection between the page and the data source. You'll learn more about this in Chapter 3.

- A Command object used to represent the query to be sent to the database. Queries are much like functions and may use parameters to be filled at runtime rather than hard-coding values at compile time. To represent the parameters in a query, a data provider also includes Parameter objects. You'll learn more about them in Chapter 4.

- A DataReader object that represents the data returned by the data source as the result of a query. For more on this, see Chapter 6.

- An Exception object and Error collection that allows your page to fall over gracefully if something untoward happens and lets you know (in detail) exactly what it was that went wrong.

Figure 1-5 demonstrates how these objects fit into the grand three-step data access scheme you saw in Figure 1-3.

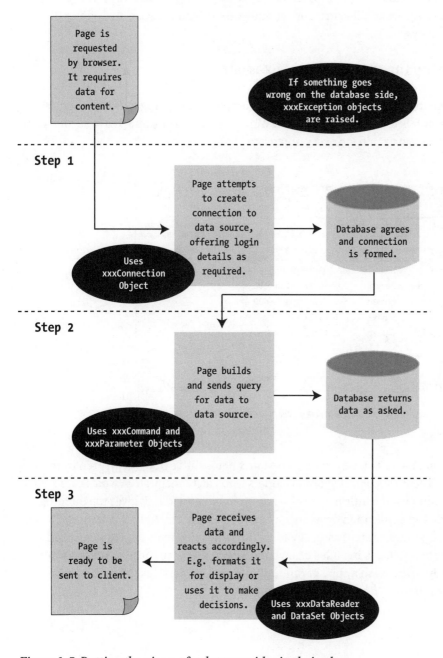

Figure 1-5. Putting the pieces of a data provider in their place

It may look as though there's an error in Figure 1-5. The lowermost bubble refers to xxxDataReaders and DataSets, but not xxxDataSets. In fact, the DataSet isn't part of any data provider. We noted earlier that a DataSet stores disconnected data on the Web server; in effect, it's a mini-relational database in memory. It never directly works with a data source and doesn't need to be part of a data provider. There's one generic DataSet class, and it's optimized for working in memory. Again, you'll learn more about working with DataSets in Chapter 6.

Developing Your First Example

Enough theory—it's time for your first example. You're going to discover exactly how easy it is to create a data-driven Web page by creating one in five seconds flat with Web Matrix. It'll look very much like Figure 1-6.

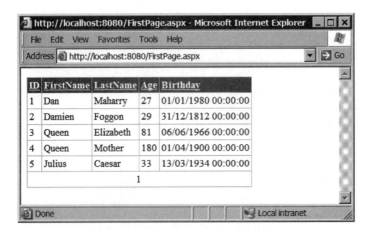

Figure 1-6. Your first data-driven Web page in action

If you haven't come across Web Matrix before, it's a free tool written by the ASP.NET team specifically for developers who can't fork out for Visual Studio .NET just yet but want a little more help than Notepad provides. It gives the budding data-driven application developer a head start, and it includes a number of head start pages that contain code already written and shortcuts to provide certain functionality. It also includes its own mini–Web server so those of you without immediate access to a copy of Internet Information Services (IIS) can carry on with this book.

CAUTION *If you're going to run this example and indeed the rest of the examples in this book, you'll need to install .NET 1.1 and Web Matrix, if you haven't already done so. Refer to Appendix A for full installation instructions and come back here when you're ready to continue.*

Try It Out: Data-Driven Web Page No. 1

In this example, you'll create a simple data-driven Web page that pulls some information from a data source and displays it in a table on the page. In this case, the data source is a small MDB database file that you can find in the Chapter01 directory of the code download for this book. It's called simple.mdb. Create a new directory called C:\BAND\Chapter01, and copy simple.mdb there.

TIP *You can download all the sample code and databases for this book from the Downloads section of the Apress Web site at* http://www.apress.com.

To create the data-driven Web page, follow these steps:

1. Start Web Matrix and create a new file called firstpage.aspx in C:\BAND\ Chapter01.

2. On the right side of the Web Matrix window, you'll see a column shared between the Properties panel in the bottom half and the Workspace pane in the top half. At the bottom of the Workspace pane is a Data tab, as shown in Figure 1-7. Click this tab to reveal the Data pane.

Figure 1-7. You can find the Data pane under the Workspace pane.

3. At the top of the Data pane, click the second icon from the right—a circular container with a green plus sign on it, as shown in Figure 1-8. Click it to start Web Matrix's Add Database wizard.

Figure 1-8. Locating the Add Database wizard icon

4. The Add Database wizard lets you search for the database you want to use in your page. It's an MDB file often used in Microsoft Access, so in the first screen of the wizard as shown in Figure 1-9, select Access Database and click OK.

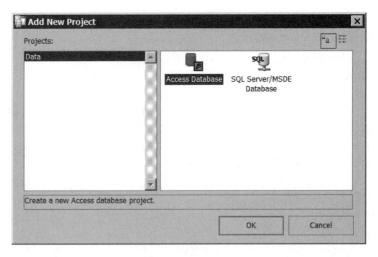

Figure 1-9. The Add Database wizard

5. The second screen of the wizard asks you to locate your sample database. Either you can type in its location directly (C:\BAND\Chapter01\simple.mdb) or you can click the button containing an ellipsis (three dots) and browse to it. Now click OK. The wizard disappears, and an entry for the database appears in the Data pane.

6. Expand the entry for simple.mdb in the Data pane by either double-clicking it or clicking the plus sign next to it. Do the same for the Tables folder underneath it. You should see another entry appear underneath called People, as shown in Figure 1-10.

Figure 1-10. The contents of a database as viewed in Web Matrix's Data pane

7. Make sure Web Matrix has FirstPage.aspx in Design view and then click and drag the People table onto the page. You'll see a large control appear on the page much like the one in Figure 1-11. This is a representation of how the People table in simple.mdb will be displayed in FirstPage.aspx when it's run.

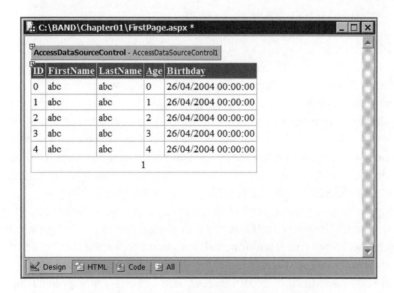

Figure 1-11. The first view of a database table on a page

8. Save `FirstPage.aspx`, and press F5. A dialog box, as shown in Figure 1-12, appears and asks you whether you want to run the page using Web Matrix's own Web server, Cassini. Say OK by clicking Start. This will start Cassini—by default as `http://localhost:8080`—and open an instance of Internet Explorer to your Web page. All being well, you'll see a page looking none too dissimilar from Figure 1-6. Congratulations. You've just made your first data-driven Web page!

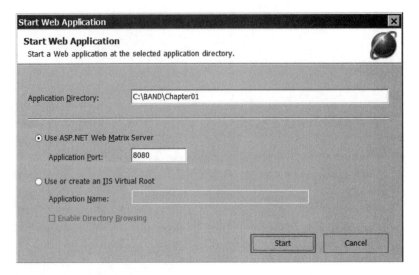

Figure 1-12. Starting your Web page in the Cassini Web server

How It Works

Web Matrix allows you to automate a lot of simple tasks when you use it, but one of the most valuable features is the Data pane. This gives you a graphical view of the database you're using and allows you to change its contents and its structure if you need to do so. This is probably less of a boon if you have a copy of Microsoft Access or SQL Server, which have their own graphical user interface (GUI) and are very good, but for MDB file and MSDE users, it's fantastic because by default they come with no administration tools at all.

If you go back to the connection to your simple database file in the Data pane and double-click the People table rather than dragging it to the Design window, Web Matrix will open a new window and show you the current contents of the table, as shown in Figure 1-13.

If you compare this screen with the contents of `firstpage.aspx` in a browser, it's clear to see that the contents are the same. Now alter the contents of the database—you can edit the raw data by hand in this screen, save it, and refresh the view of `firstpage.aspx`. The page will reflect the changes made in the database.

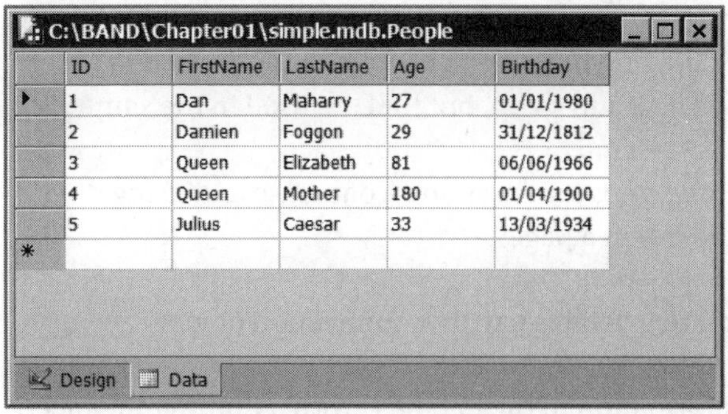

Figure 1-13. Viewing the raw data in a table

When you dragged the People table from the Data pane over to firstpage.aspx, Web Matrix automatically created an mxDataGrid object on the page and wrote the code that displays the contents of the People table in that object. All three steps to work with a database—connection, command, and result—have been dealt with for you.

If you look at the code for the page, you can see that Web Matrix uses its own Web form objects, mxDataGrid and AccessDataSourceControl, to get things working rather than their counterpart objects in the standard installation of .NET 1.1. We won't touch on these two objects again for that reason, but it's interesting to note in passing that these two objects reflect how things will be done in .NET 2.0 when it's released some time in 2005.

What more could you want from an example? You saw how to use Web Matrix's Add Database wizard, saw how easy it is to generate a simple data-driven Web page, and got a taste of ADO.NET 2.0 to boot. Time to finish this chapter before a bug crops up.

Summary

In this chapter, you took a bird's eye view of the world of data-driven Web sites and learned about the following:

- You learned how a page interacts with a data source and the different types of data source that interact with pages.

- Databases in general support at least one of the ODBC and OLE DB common database interfaces although some also support their own, optimized data access methods for speedier results.

- ADO.NET is a new technology—part of the .NET Framework. It presents the developer with a set of data providers, each of which is optimized to access data through OLE DB, ODBC, and so on, but that are used in the same way.

- The following are the three steps for accessing a database and using the information retrieved from it in a page:

  1. Create a connection to a database with a Connection object.

  2. Send a query for information to the database with a Command object.

  3. Handle the data appropriately depending on what you want it to do. Data is returned from the database in a DataReader object and may be stored on the Web server in a DataSet object, which is generic and not specific to any data provider.

Finally, you created your first data-driven ASP.NET page using a simple MDB database file and Web Matrix. You saw how you can register the database with Web Matrix and how it lets you create such a page in one easy step.

In the next chapter, you'll start coming down from the crow's nest and investigate what makes a database, and in particular a relational database, tick.

CHAPTER 2

Introducing Relational Databases

IN CHAPTER 1, you learned that you can use almost any kind of data source to drive your dynamic Web pages. You also learned that the relational database is the most commonly used type of data source for this purpose. In this chapter, you'll take a closer look at how relational databases actually work. You'll see how data is organized inside a database, and to make sure you understand it, you'll build your own sample database from scratch for use in Chapters 3–8.

We'll show how to work with three databases, each of which works a little differently. We've chosen them deliberately because they're free to download and use and also because they illustrate a good cross-section of issues that crop up when you're working with databases. The following are the three databases used in this chapter:

MDB: The Microsoft DataBase (MDB) file is the simplest relational database to get started using. It's often associated with Microsoft Access, but it runs under Microsoft's Jet database engine, which is installed with .NET, so it's in fact a stand-alone file. In this book, we'll show how to use Web Matrix as the graphical front end to the sample MDB database as far as possible and the OLE DB data provider to access it programmatically.

MSDE: The Microsoft SQL Server 2000 Desktop Engine (MSDE) is the free version of Microsoft's full SQL Server database server. Its main difference is that the number of clients that can access it at the same time is limited to 25, and the numerous administration tools SQL Server comes with aren't included. Beyond that, it's the same powerful product. MSDE is a database server, as mentioned in Chapter 1, which means that once installed, it can host as many different databases as required and keep tabs on them all for you. In this book, we'll show how to use SQL Server Web Data Administrator (or *MSDE Administrator*, as we'll call it) as the graphical front end for the MSDE database and the SqlClient data provider to access it programmatically.

MySQL: MySQL is the best open source relational database server in existence at the moment, and it's well regarded for its speed and robustness. Like all open source software, MySQL is a work in progress, and a few of the features you'll see in this chapter aren't implemented in the current stable version, 4.0, but they're in the unstable versions, 4.1 and 5.0. You'll use MySQL Control Center and MySQL Administrator as the graphical front ends for the MySQL database. Both of these programs are early beta versions of a final product but fine for these purposes. In this book, we'll show how to use the MySQL ODBC connector and the ODBC data provider to access it programmatically.

You can find the instructions for installing MSDE and MySQL in Appendix A, and you can find the complete details of the sample database you'll be building in this chapter in Appendix C. It's a simple database carrying the details of 30 books, their authors, and their publishers.

> **NOTE** *Readers who fancy using MDB files should be aware that Web Matrix allows you to create only some of the features of the sample database. We'll make it clear which those are. However, if you have a copy of Access, you'll able to work through all the examples in this chapter. Those without Access will find a completed MDB file in the Database folder of the code download for this book.*

If you're wondering why this whole chapter focuses on the theory and setup of a database, it's because badly designed and badly built databases often come back to bite you once you start to build Web sites against them. They become harder to expand and slower to run as you spot-fix individual problems that wouldn't have come up if you had thought about them in the first place. A data-driven Web application totally relies on its data source for content, so having it drag its heels because you built it wrong wouldn't be a good thing. You'll look further at the actual designing of a database in Chapter 11, but you need to be familiar with the basics before you can go there.

Introducing Tables, Rows, and Fields

The first thing to know and be comfortable with is that relational databases store all data as *tables*. Each of these tables represents a single, distinct subject: an object or an event. For example, a table may contain details of book publishers (as in Figure 2-1), fish, or compact discs. Equally, it may keep data on appointments, deliveries, or customer service enquiries.

In general, databases shouldn't store information about several types of objects or events—say, cats and fish—in the same table unless the application of the database says otherwise. Biologists, for example, will want to keep details on cats and on fish separate. More than likely the details they keep for the two species of animal will be quite different. On the other hand, an online pet store may use a single table to keep a record of all the pets it has in stock. Cats and fish would be grouped together as "pets" in one table.

Table Name: **Publisher**

PublisherID	Name	City	Contact_Email	Website
1	Apress	Berkeley	someguy@apress.com	http://www.apress.com
2	Friends of Ed	Birmingham	aneditor@friendsofed.com	http://www.friendsofed.com
3	SAMS	Indianapolis	helper@samspublishing.com	http://www.samspublishing.com
4	Addison-Wesley	Boston	manager@aw.com	http://www.awprofessional.com
5	Manning	Greenwich	theboss@manning.com	http://www.manning.com
more rows . . .				

Figure 2-1. A simple table

When you create a table in a database, you give it a name to reflect its contents—Book, Compact_Disc, Customer_Service_Enquiry, and so on. In Figure 2-1, the table is called Publisher. If you start calling a table Cats_And_Fish, for example, chances are you actually want to be creating two tables—one for cats and one for fish.

Every table contains a number of *rows*, or *records* if you prefer (or even *tuples*, if you're a mathematician). Each row represents exactly one instance of the object or event the table holds details about. So in Figure 2-1, each row in the Publisher table holds the details for exactly one book publisher. These details aren't duplicated or carried on elsewhere in the table, so when you locate that particular row, it contains all the information you have on that publisher. In Figure 2-2, for example, the row containing all the information you have on the publisher SAMS has been highlighted.

Table Name: **Publisher**

PublisherID	Name	City	Contact_Email	Website
1	Apress	Berkeley	someguy@apress.com	http://www.apress.com
2	Friends of Ed	Birmingham	aneditor@friendsofed.com	http://www.friendsofed.com
3	*SAMS*	*Indianapolis*	*helper@samspublishing.com*	*http://www.samspublishing.com*
4	Addison-Wesley	Boston	manager@aw.com	http://www.awprofessional.com
5	Manning	Greenwich	theboss@manning.com	http://www.manning.com
more rows . . .				

Figure 2-2. A row in a table contains data about one object instance.

Every row contains a number of *fields*—also called *attributes* or *columns*. Each field contains a single piece of information indicated by the field's name. Like the name for a table, the name for a field should be as unambiguous as possible. So if you look at the example in Figure 2-2, it's apparent that you need to rename the fields for the Publisher table. Take the field you've called Name—that could refer to a person's name, a Web site's name, or any name you like if you take it out of context. On the other hand, if you call it PublisherName, it's pretty clear what this field will contain. If you can change the other field names to suit this idea, you end up with the table in Figure 2-3.

Table Name: **Publisher**

PublisherID	PublisherName	PublisherCity	PublisherContact_Email	PublisherWebsite
1	Apress	Berkeley	someguy@apress.com	http://www.apress.com
2	Friends of Ed	Birmingham	aneditor@friendsofed.com	http://www.friendsofed.com
3	SAMS	Indianapolis	helper@samspublishing.com	http://www.samspublishing.com
4	Addison-Wesley	Boston	manager@aw.com	http://www.awprofessional.com
5	Manning	Greenwich	theboss@manning.com	http://www.manning.com
more rows . . .				

Figure 2-3. Field names should be as unambiguous as possible.

On the Subject of Names

You've been shown what to call tables, rows, and fields in the main text, but you need to remember that all names should start with a letter and be followed only by more letters, numbers, or an underscore—never a space. Some, but not all, databases permit using a few punctuation characters in names, but it's easier to stay clear of them altogether. Note also that these names are case sensitive. Thus, a table called BookPublisher is different from one called Bookpublisher or bookPublisher.

Retrieving information from a table is reasonably simple because every table *must* contain a field or a combination of fields that uniquely identifies any piece of data in the table. This means that it doesn't matter in what order you add rows to the table because you'll still be able to identify them individually. When you're building a database table, you identify this field or combination of fields as the table's *primary key*. In Figure 2-3, for example, the PublisherID field does this job nicely. Because of this primary key, you can access any field in a database with relative ease, as long as you know the field name, the value of the primary key for the row it's in, and the name of the table. For example, say you need a contact e-mail for Addison-Wesley (see Figure 2-4). You'd need to find the Publisher table, then the row for Addison-Wesley, and then the value in the PublisherContact_Email field on that row.

Table Name: **Publisher**

PublisherID	PublisherName	PublisherCity	PublisherContact_Email	PublisherWebsite
1	Apress	Berkeley	someguy@apress.com	http://www.apress.com
2	Friends of Ed	Birmingham	aneditor@friendsofed.com	http://www.friendsofed.com
3	SAMS	Indianapolis	helper@samspublishing.com	http://www.samspublishing.com
4	Addison-Wesley	Boston	*manager@aw.com*	http://www.awprofessional.com
5	Manning	Greenwich	theboss@manning.com	http://www.manning.com
more rows . . .				

Figure 2-4. Pinpointing data in a database

Every table must have a primary key. It doesn't have to be an ID number (although that's the norm in a simple table such as this one) as in this example, but you must be able to guarantee that each value for that primary key field will be unique. A person's last name then or an appointment date won't do for a primary key, but a global unique identifier (GUID) or a product's Amazon standard identification number (ASIN) should do fine. Consider the situation where a table doesn't have a primary key. The database server may not be able to identify a specific row in a table and either return the wrong one or indeed return many. This wouldn't help much if a Web site were trying to retrieve a user's preferences and presented them with the wrong set of options. Likewise, what if credit card numbers weren't unique but were used as primary keys? You could get sent the wrong bill or be charged with someone else's transactions. No, primary keys must be unique.

NOTE *A database will return an error if you try to add a duplicate value to a primary key field, so make sure you never need to by choosing the key wisely.*

You can also use a combination of fields as a primary key instead of just one. If a primary key is a single field, it's a *simple primary key*. If it consists of two or more fields, it's a *composite primary key*. For example, you couldn't uniquely identify an album in a table by its name alone (consider *4*—the name of albums by Peter Gabriel, Led Zeppelin, and Black Sabbath, no less), but you could by setting the table's primary key to contain both the band and title. You'll see further examples in the forthcoming "Many-to-Many Relationships" section.

Creating a New Table

You can create a new table in a database in many ways depending on which database server software and which development environment you're using. In the following sections, you'll investigate how to do this using the graphical tools you have available. So then, you'll be using the following:

- Web Matrix for MDB files

- SQL Web Data Administrator for MSDE

- MySQL Control Center for MySQL

If you have a copy of Access, feel free to use that to create a new database and the Publisher table within it.

Try It Out: Creating a New Table with Web Matrix

In this example, you'll create the Publisher table shown in Figure 2-3 inside a new MDB file using Web Matrix. Follow these steps:

1. Start Web Matrix, and close the Add New File dialog box if it appears. Now switch the Workspace pane in the top-right corner of the window to the Data pane, and hit the Add Database Connection button, as demonstrated in Chapter 1 in the section "Try It Out: Data-Driven Web Page No. 1."

2. When the Add New Project dialog box appears, as shown in Figure 2-5, choose an Access Database file and click OK. Note that you can also use Web Matrix to work with SQL Server databases, although you won't do this in this example.

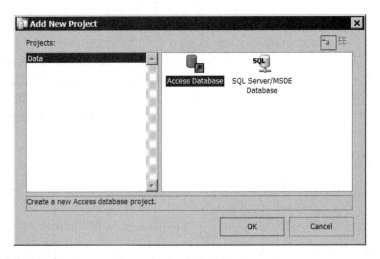

Figure 2-5. The Add New Project dialog box

3. The next dialog box asks you to connect to the database you want to use. The example database doesn't exist yet, so click the Create a New Database hyperlink in the bottom left of the dialog box.

4. You're asked next where you want to create the new database. Create it as
   `C:\BAND\Database\books.mdb`.

5. Click OK. The database will be created, and an entry for it will be displayed
   in Web Matrix's Data pane, as shown in Figure 2-6.

Figure 2-6. The new MDB file in the Data pane

6. Double-click the entry for your new database, and select the Tables subfolder that appears. Now click the New Database Object icon from the top of
   the data panel. This is the second icon from the left, as shown in Figure 2-7.

Figure 2-7. The New Database Object icon

7. A new dialog box appears and asks you for the name of the table to create.
   Type **Publisher**, and click OK. A new window appears in Web Matrix
   showing you the details of the new Publisher table. You'll need to add
   some fields (or *columns* as they're referred to here) to the table.

8. The first task is to create the PublisherID field that's the primary key field for this table. A new, blank field called *Column0* is already selected, so you just need to alter a few values. In the bottom half of the Publisher table window (the Properties half), set Name to PublisherID, DataType to Integer, and InPrimaryKey and IsUniqueKey to True, as shown in Figure 2-8.

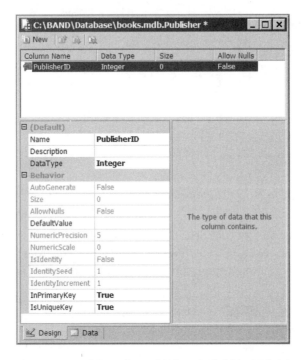

Figure 2-8. Adding the PublisherID field in Web Matrix

9. Now add the four remaining fields to the Publisher table. Hit New in the top left of the Publisher table window to add another field to the table and change the properties given in Table 2-1 before adding the next one. Leave everything else as the default.

Table 2-1. Field Properties for the Publisher Table (MDB Version)

Field Name	Properties to Change
PublisherName	DataType: Text
PublisherCity	DataType: Text
PublisherContact_Email	DataType: Text, Size: 100
PublisherWebsite	DataType: Text, Size: 100

10. When all five columns have been added, the page for the Publisher table should look like Figure 2-9. Finally, select File ➤ Save (Ctrl+S) in Web Matrix to save the table layout and close the window.

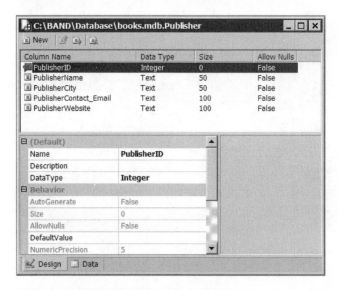

Figure 2-9. The Publisher table in full

Try It Out: Creating a New Table with MSDE Administrator

In this example, you'll create the Publisher table shown in Figure 2-3 inside a new database hosted by MSDE. You'll use MSDE Administrator to create the database and table. Follow these steps:

1. Start MSDE Administrator. When the Web Server Configuration dialog appears, click Start if you have Information Internet Services (IIS) installed. If not, check Cassini Personal Web Server and then click Start. Cassini is installed with Web Matrix.

2. Now you have to log into MSDE. Use the system administrator account to log in here. Check the SQL Login authentication method, and then set the Username to sa, Password to secpas, and Server to (local)\BAND, as shown in Figure 2-10. Then click Login.

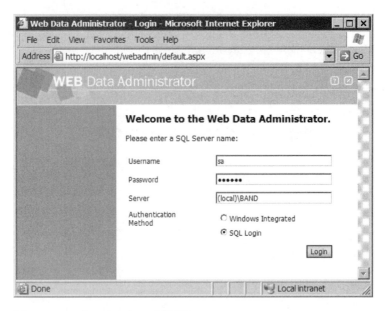

Figure 2-10. Logging into MSDE

3. MSDE Administrator now displays its main screen (see Figure 2-11). Your first job is to create the Books database. Click the Create New Database link, and when asked for the new database's name, type **Books** and then click Create.

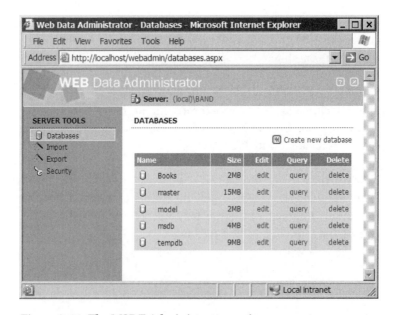

Figure 2-11. The MSDE Administrator main screen

4. The Books database is created in the background, and MSDE Administrator presents you with a list of the tables it contains, which is zero at the moment. To start building the Publisher table, click the Create New Table link. When asked for the new table's name, type **Publisher** and then click Create.

5. Now you need to create the five fields in the table, starting with the PublisherID field, which is the primary key for this table. MSDE Administrator has already opened the Edit Column screen for you, so you just need to change a few things. Check the Primary Key box, set Column Name to PublisherID, Data Type to int, Length to 4, and uncheck Allow Null. Finally, check the Identity box, and leave everything else as is. The page should look like Figure 2-12. Now hit Add.

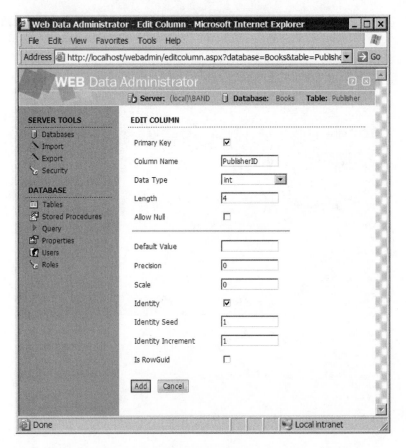

Figure 2-12. Adding the PublisherID field

6. Next, add the four remaining fields to the Publisher table. Click the Create New Column link to add another field to the table and change the properties given in Table 2-2 before hitting Add and going onto the next one. Leave everything else as the default.

Table 2-2. Field Properties for the Publisher Table (MSDE Version)

Field Name	Properties to Change
PublisherName	DataType: varchar, Length: 50
PublisherCity	DataType: varchar, Length: 50
PublisherContact_Email	DataType: varchar, Length: 100
PublisherWebsite	DataType: varchar, Length: 100

7. When all five columns have been added, the page for the Publisher table should look like Figure 2-13. The table is saved automatically.

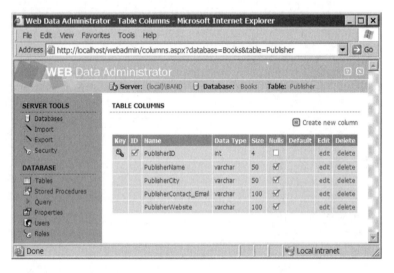

Figure 2-13. The full Publisher table

Try It Out: Creating a New Table with MySQL Control Center

In this example, you'll create the Publisher table shown in Figure 2-3 inside a new MySQL database using MySQL Control Center. Follow these steps:

1. Start MySQL Control Center, and right-click the Databases folder in the MySQL Servers pane on the left of the Console Manager window. Select New Database from the menu that appears, as shown in Figure 2-14.

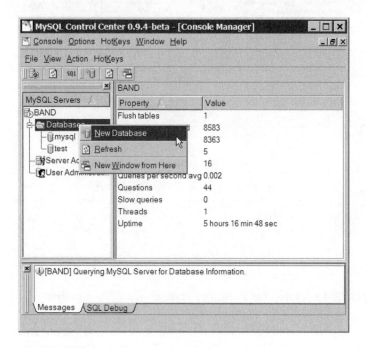

Figure 2-14. Adding a new database to MySQL

2. In the dialog box that appears, enter **Books** for the new database and click OK. An entry for the new database now appears under the Databases folder.

3. Right-click the Books database icon, and select Connect from the menu that appears. A new subfolder appears called *Tables*.

4. Right-click Tables, and select New Table. MySQL Control Center now displays its table design window, where you add fields to the table.

5. The first task is to create the PublisherID field that's the primary key field for this table. A new, blank field is already selected, so you just need to alter a few values. Set Field Name to PublisherID and Data Type to int. Now check the AUTO_INCREMENT box and the golden key icon above the Field Name column. This sets the field as the primary key for this table. (Pressing Ctrl+K also does this.) With that done, the table designer should look like Figure 2-15.

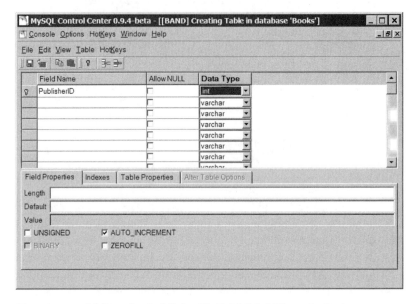

Figure 2-15. Adding the PublisherID field (MySQL variation)

6. Now add the rest of the fields for this table by clicking the empty rows under PublisherID. You have four more fields to add besides PublisherID. Table 2-3 lists their names and the properties you need to change from their default.

Table 2-3. Field Properties for the Publisher Table (MySQL Variation)

Field Name	Properties to Change
PublisherName	DataType: varchar, Length: 50
PublisherCity	DataType: varchar, Length: 50
PublisherContact_Email	DataType: varchar, Length: 100
PublisherWebsite	DataType: varchar, Length: 100

7. When all five columns have been added, the page for the Publisher table should look like Figure 2-16. The table is saved automatically.

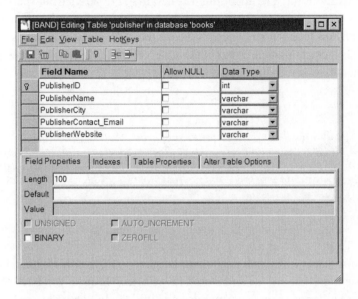

Figure 2-16. The full Publisher table

8. Now click the Table Properties tab. You need to give the table a name—Publisher—and change its table type from MyISAM to InnoDB. You do this because MyISAM tables don't support all the features required in the database but InnoDB does.

9. Select File ➤ Save to finish editing the table.

How It Works

Even though all three examples do the same thing, it's interesting to note how the different graphical tools approach the following three tasks:

- Creating a new database

- Creating a new table in the database

- Creating new fields in the table

For example, you set the primary key field in MySQL Control Center by hitting a button or keyboard shortcut (Ctrl+K) rather than setting a property as you do in MSDE Administrator. You also encounter the first major difference between the three databases—the data types you give to the fields are slightly different across them all. You'll look at this further in the next section, "Properties and Constraints." Also, Appendix B contains a complete breakdown on which data type corresponds to which other types across the databases.

> **NOTE** *Be sure that the fields in the Publisher table have been created correctly. Once data has been added to the table, as you'll do later in this chapter, you can't change a field's properties. You can add only a new field or delete an existing one. This applies to any database table and not just MSDE, MySQL, and MDB files.*

All three graphical tools actually interpret your wishes to create databases and fields into commands in the database's own language—SQL—which you'll look at later in the section "Statements and Stored Procedures." Indeed, you have several other ways to send these same commands and build the Publisher table. They include the following:

- Using Access to build the MDB file, which has the added advantage that Access lets you specify more data types for a field than Web Matrix does. Access can also act as a front end for MSDE databases.

- Using Visual Studio .NET or SQL Server client tools to work with MSDE.

- Using Web Matrix to build the MSDE database.

- Using a database's command-line utility, such as `osql.exe` for MSDE or `mysql.exe` for MySQL, as you'll see in Chapter 10.

- Using a stored procedure, which we'll cover in Chapter 9.

- Building your own application to send the command to the database.

Many other third-party utilities allow you to work with a database that are more appealing.

Properties and Constraints

One thing you learn from building even a simple table such as Publisher is that you can do a lot more than give the fields in a row a name. You can give each one a series of properties that strongly types and then further restricts the range of values that it can hold. This is akin to the way you give every variable in C# a simple type, or perhaps even a complex type if you want to restrict its values further.

Strictly speaking, you actually give each field a set of *properties* and then apply zero or more *constraints* to it that restrict the values it can hold.

The following are the field properties you've seen:

Name: This is the name of the field.

Data Type: This is the data type of the field. You can find a complete list of data types you can give to a field in Appendix B. Note that most of the data types have different names for MDB files, MSDE, and MySQL, as you saw in the examples. This is the first major difference between the three databases.

Length: This is the number of bytes each instance of that field will be stored in by the database server. This effectively restricts the length of the field. Some data types have a fixed length. For example, byte has a fixed length.

InPrimaryKey: This sets whether the field is part of the primary key for its table.

As you saw in the previous examples, setting a field to automatically generate an integer also enables two more properties you can choose to change from their defaults if you so want. They're as follows:

- **IdentitySeed**: Sets the value given to the first row entered into the table. The default is 1.

- **IdentityIncrement**: Sets the number added to the most recently created row in the table to produce the next value of the field for a new row yet to come. The default is 1.

By default then, an automatically generated integer field will be set to 1 for the first row created in the table, then 2 for the second, 3 for the third, and so on. If you set IdentitySeed to 10 and IdentityIncrement to 2, the first row would get 10, the second 12, the third 14, and so on.

Once you've set the general possibilities for a field, you can narrow them down by applying constraints. When a constraint is applied to a field, all the values for that field in a table must adhere to it. The following are four basic constraints and what they imply:

- **Not Null**: A field may not equal NULL. That is, it must have a value assigned to it when a row is created. So either the column must have a default value or you must force a user to give the field a value.

- **Unique**: Values in this field must be unique across all the rows in the table. Apply this constraint to fields that aren't part of the primary key. Primary key fields must be unique by definition, so the constraint isn't necessary.

- **Default**: Specifies a default value for a field if one isn't supplied.

- **Check**: Checks that the value of the field obeys a certain condition.

Looking back at the previous examples, it's clear that the way in which you apply these constraints to a table also depends on the tool you're using. In Web Matrix, the Unique constraint is set as a property. In MySQL Control Center, a whole dialog box is devoted to setting it and other constraints on a table, which you shall come to in the next set of examples.

> **NOTE** *You'll learn about one more type of constraint in this chapter. It has two names—*foreign key constraint *and* referential integrity constraint—*and is concerned with maintaining the validity of data between two tables that are related. Of course, this doesn't make much sense until you understand how tables can be related, so you'll come back to this topic after the section "Building Relationships Between Tables."*

Statements and Stored Procedures

Lots of parallels exist between the way you program in .NET and the way you set up a relational database. You've already come across the idea of strongly typing fields and giving them properties. It shouldn't be a surprise then to learn that relational databases also allow you to perform actions (methods, if you like) on rows, fields, tables, and even the database itself.

As we noted at the end of the previous examples, these actions are written in Structured Query Language (SQL), and knowing how to write commands in SQL is as fundamental to working with a database as knowing how tables, rows, and fields fit together. Recall from the section "How Does a Data-Driven Page Work?" in Chapter 1 that the second step of talking to a database is to send it a command to retrieve, create, modify, or delete some data. This command needs to be defined and called explicitly, much like a method in .NET, and you use SQL to do this.

Introducing Structured Query Language (SQL)

So, what the hell is SQL, and why do you need to use it? Why can't you just use C# instead? SQL (pronounced *sequel*) is the de facto standard language for talking to relational databases. Invented by IBM alongside the original idea of relational databases, SQL was designed to fit the mathematical concepts that relational databases were built upon while being straightforward to write and prove commands in. Interestingly, the man who first published the rules for relational databases (Dr. E. F. Codd) disliked SQL quite a lot and preferred another query language, but that's by the by.

SQL is now in its second version as an International Organization for Standardization (ISO) and an American National Standards Institute (ANSI) standard and essentially works like Open DataBase Connectivity (ODBC) as a common interface to a database that all vendors implement and everyone uses. One key difference between it and ODBC, though, is that although every vendor implements all the basic elements of the SQL standard, they then add their own proprietary commands to it and badge the whole as their version of SQL. Microsoft products—SQL Server, MSDE, and MDB files—use Transact-SQL (T-SQL), and Oracle uses pl\SQL. MySQL meanwhile aims to implement straight ANSI-standard SQL although it hasn't managed all of it just yet.

> **NOTE** *At the beginner level, the only differences between the flavors of SQL used by Microsoft and MySQL are a point or two of syntax, but we'll note them as we go along. Ninety-five percent of the time, one SQL statement will work equally across MDB, MSDE, and MySQL databases.*

SQL statements are at the heart of what you'll be doing in the rest of this book. They're the commands the page gives the database. They can be sent individually or in groups with each statement separated by a semicolon (like C#) or a line break (like VB .NET). What you need to learn is how to write those statements correctly, what kind of result they will return, and how to handle those results (see Chapters 4 and 5 for more on this). You can't just use C# instead of SQL because no database understands C# (yet).

SQL can be divided up into two main parts—a Data Manipulation Language (DML) and a Data Definition Language (DDL)—and over the next few pages, you'll take a whirlwind tour through the key instructions that you'll use through this book. Chapters 3–8 and 10 will expand upon the syntax for each instruction as you use them, and Appendix B at the back of the book sums them all up into a syntax reference.

NOTE *Keywords in SQL aren't case sensitive. However, we'll continue to write them in caps to make them easily distinguishable from the values you add to statements.*

DML Commands

SQL's DML contains instructions that let you create, retrieve, update, and delete data from a database. It has the following four basic commands:

INSERT: INSERT creates a new row in a table and then adds some new data to it. For example, if you needed to add a new row to the Publisher table, you'd issue an INSERT command, like so:

```
INSERT INTO Publisher ⤶
    (PublisherName, PublisherCity, ⤶
        PublisherContact_Email, PublisherWebsite)
VALUES ('Springer', 'Berlin', ⤶
    'cto@springer.de', 'http://www.springer.de')
```

where each field in the row you want to give a value to is named in the first list and the values they will be given are in the second list, respectively.

UPDATE: UPDATE changes the values of one or more fields in a table row. For example, if you need to change the name of publisher, say *Friends Of Ed* to *Friends Of Gary*, you'd issue the following command:

```
UPDATE Publisher SET PublisherName = 'Friends Of Gary'
WHERE PublisherName = 'Friends Of Ed'
```

As mentioned in the earlier "Tables, Rows, and Fields" section, every field can be identified uniquely using table name, primary key value, and field name. UPDATE statements can use all three to pinpoint exactly which piece of data to change but can also effect more sweeping changes, modifying several rows at a time by being less specific.

DELETE: DELETE removes rows from a table. For example, if you needed to remove the entry in the Publisher table for Manning, you'd issue the following command:

```
DELETE FROM Publisher WHERE PublisherName = 'Manning'
```

Like UPDATE, DELETE can target many rows in a table at a time. You need to be careful using DELETE. One false step and you might delete *all* the data in a table by accident.

SELECT: SELECT fetches data from the database and returns it to the waiting page. For example, if you wanted a list of all publishers and their contact e-mail addresses, you'd issue the following command:

```
SELECT PublisherName, PublisherContact_Email WHERE PublisherID = *
```

The SELECT statement is incredibly powerful, and we'll only touch on some of its capabilities in this book. You can use it to preprocess data, retrieve data across several tables at once, and then work on that data again before the page gets it. You can return tables of data or single values. You can present data using aliases or using a field's name as it is in the table. There are books dedicated to just this statement so don't be disheartened if you don't get your SELECT statements working first time round.

> **NOTE** *One of the best books about SELECT statements is* SQL Queries for Mere Mortals *by Michael J. Hernandez and John L. Viescas (Addison-Wesley, 2000).*

The basic syntax is pretty straightforward for all four statements. To begin with, you'll just plug in values to those simple statements and go. Then you'll start to vary and tweak. You can already see that the WHERE keyword is used in UPDATE, DELETE, and SELECT statements. They work much like if statements in C#. They can match more than one row if you want to affect more than one row (for example, by using the * wildcard) and can concatenate conditions together with boolean operators (AND, NOT, OR) to create specific clauses that may not match any rows at all.

DDL Commands

A DDL command contains instructions that let you build, alter, and remove databases, tables, relationships, constraints, indexes, and more. For example, the sample database that you'll build in this chapter can also be built using a mixture of DDL to create the Books database construct, the tables within it, and the fields within the tables, and some DML to add the values to the tables.

DDL has three basic commands:

CREATE: CREATE allows you to create a new database or object within the database. For example, if you wanted to add a new table called BookSeries with an ID field and a Name field, you'd issue the following command:

```
CREATE TABLE BookSeries (ID INT, Name VARCHAR(100))
```

The CREATE TABLE command is quite powerful—you can create as many strongly typed fields for the table as you like, specify a primary key, and set some of the field properties and constraints you saw earlier.

ALTER: ALTER allows you to modify a database object that already exists. For example, if you wanted to add a new field called PublisherContact_Phone to the Publisher table, you'd issue the following command:

```
ALTER TABLE Publisher ADD PublisherContact_Phone VARCHAR(15)
```

Both ALTER and DROP (to come) can be awkward as databases can refuse to execute these commands and return an error. This is usually because in altering the table, constraint, and so on, the altered version of the database will violate the rules still holding over the database and violate its integrity. Or rather, it will render the data invalid. For example, changing the type of the PublisherName field to integer isn't allowed.

DROP: DROP allows you to delete any object in a database. For example, if you wanted to delete the Publisher table from the database, you'd issue the following command:

```
DROP TABLE Publisher
```

CAUTION *As long as your page has the right privileges to delete a database, the server will go ahead and delete anything you tell it to if it doesn't violate a constraint, regardless of whether you've backed anything up or there's anything still in it. Database servers have no concept of a recycle bin either, so once you say delete, it's gone. Finito. Be very careful using DROP. It can kill anything—database, table, constraint, and so on—just as CREATE and ALTER can create and modify anything.*

Emphasis is more obviously placed on security if you're working with DDL statements, but every statement is subject to a security check before it can be performed. As you learned earlier, when a page connects to a database, it also identifies the user it's attempting to run the statement as. If the user hasn't got clearance, the statement doesn't get run.

All database servers can also restrict which of the previous SQL instructions a user may execute. You can administer those permissions with three further DDL commands:

GRANT: GRANT allows you to give a user account the permission to run a certain kind of SQL statement. For example, if you wanted to let the user account Bob INSERT and SELECT data from a database, you'd issue the following command:

```
GRANT INSERT, SELECT TO Bob
```

DENY: DENY allows you to prevent a user account from running a certain SQL statement that it already has permission to run indirectly, say, because the permission was given to a group or role the user was part of. For example, if you wanted to prevent the user account Mary from running DELETE and DROP statements, you'd issue the following command:

```
DENY DELETE, DROP TO Mary
```

REVOKE: REVOKE completely removes the permission to run a certain SQL statement from a user account. For example, if you wanted to remove all permissions from an exEmployee user, you'd issue the following command:

```
REVOKE ALL FROM exEmployee
```

Replacing SQL

Now, SQL won't be going anywhere for quite some time to come because it's too well established and because it's the de facto standard language that all database servers use—indeed, millions of lines of SQL run every day—but that doesn't mean you'll always have to use it. For example, the next version of Microsoft's SQL Server, code name Yukon, will allow you to write the equivalent of SQL statements in any .NET language: C#, VB .NET, and so on, as well as in SQL. Don't expect to see it released until at least the first half of 2005, though. And as to whether this functionality will filter down into MSDE and Access? Who knows. For more on Yukon's .NET support, refer to http://www.microsoft.com/sql/yukon/productinfo/top30features.asp#B.

If you think Extensible Markup Language (XML) may be your calling, then you also have a third option. The World Wide Web Commission (W3C, http://www.w3.org) has been working on an XML-based database querying language for some time. XQuery is still a working draft—the biggest they've ever created, too—but will be pretty solid when it's finished. The big companies such as Microsoft, IBM, and Oracle are all working on this with the W3C so it will be well supported, too. For more details, go to http://www.w3.org/XML/Query.

Stored Procedures

When you write an ASP.NET page, you know that it will always take a little while longer to display on screen the first time it's accessed. This is because the .NET runtime must compile the code inside the page before that code can be run and the page displayed. The next time the page is requested, the code is already compiled in memory so the server can skip the compilation step and produce the page faster. In the same fashion, most relational database servers allow you to store precompiled SQL statements alongside the databases they query. These *stored procedures*, as they're known, thus execute faster than queries that must be compiled once they're sent to the server by the database and increase the performance of the application using them. Of course, you have to set up these stored procedures on the database before you make the application live, but the performance benefit justifies that extra bit of setup. Rather than the statement itself, the page now sends a call to a stored procedure on the database along with any parameter values it may require, just like you call a method on an object.

You'll look at using stored procedures in much greater detail in Chapter 9.

Indexes

While constraints help ensure that any modifications to the database don't disturb the validity of the data it contains and so potentially slow down the rate at which you interact with a database, the aim of indexes is to increase the rate at which you can retrieve information. Consider a situation where you want to find all the references to *MSDE* in this book. You could read this book from cover to cover and write them all down, or (if the publisher has done a particularly good job) you could turn to the back of the book, look in the index under MSDE, and turn to the pages listed under that entry. The second method—using an index—is obviously a lot faster, and a database index works in the same way for the same reason.

Consider a situation where you want to retrieve information on all the books whose titles begin with the word *Beginning*. Even with just the 30 books outlined in Appendix C, the database must work through all 30 rows to make sure it has found all the books that fit the criteria before returning them to the page, as shown in Figure 2-17, even though there are only three books to return.

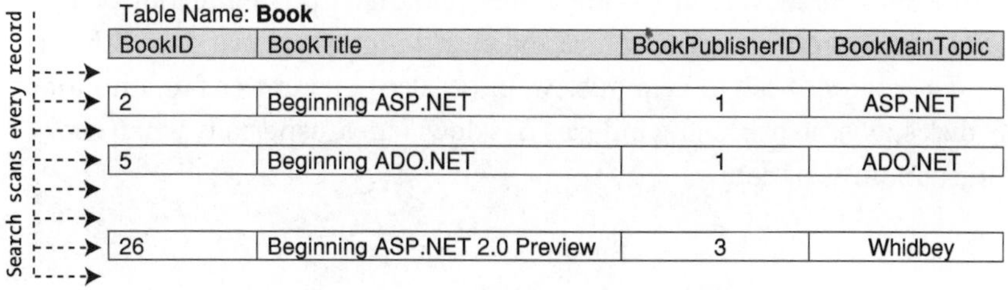

Figure 2-17. Scanning through a table without an index

By asking it to create an index on the BookTitle field of the Book table (referred to as the *index key* in this context), the database server makes available an ordered list of the values in the BookTitle field to any searches. Essentially, this works in the same way the index in the back of a book works. When it needs to look up a book title, the search knows that titles are ordered alphabetically in the index you've created, so it just looks under 'B', finds the titles that start with *Beginning*, and follows the index links to the correct rows. Rather than search through 30 rows in the Book table, it looks through three, as shown in Figure 2-18.

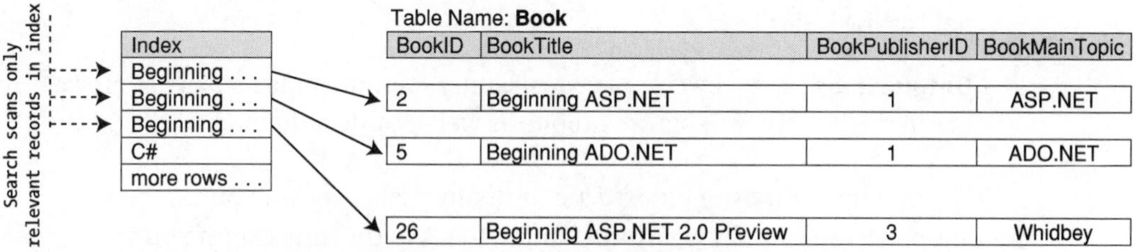

Figure 2-18. Scanning through a table with an index

Database indexes work exclusively behind the scenes, and aside from adding and removing indexes in the first place, you never need to reference them in your code. If it exists, a search will know to use it, and if it doesn't, the search won't. Indeed, it can significantly improve performance if you add the right indexes to the right tables. If a query is commonly made that requests information to be ordered on or grouped by a certain field, it makes sense to add an index to the database based on that field.

Of course, there are always downsides. The database server must maintain every index added to the database, which means a performance hit if items are frequently added, deleted, or changed. With each modification, the server must first make that change, see if it affects any index, and then update the index if it does. That's three operations per modification with an index against one without an index and a judgment call to be made. An index also consumes a fair amount of additional disk space, so overusing indexes has downsides, especially when they contain large amounts of data.

Adding Indexes to a Database

You can add several kinds of indexes to a database:

Simple index: A simple index uses only one field as the index key.

Composite index: A composite index uses two or more fields in its index key.

Clustered index: This is the most important kind of index in a database. It determines the actual order that fields in a table are stored in the database. Compare this against the previous example (Figure 2-18) where the index contained purely a list of index key fields in the right order with links to the actual rows in the table. This example is known as an *unclustered index*. A database allows only one clustered index per table. Creating a primary key field in a table automatically creates a simple clustered index using the primary key field as the index key.

Unique index: Used by Unique constraints, a unique index ensures that values in the index key fields are unique as well as orders them.

Simple and composite indexes are mutually exclusive, but you can create unique, clustered indexes with one or more fields in the index key if you so choose. The power of indexes is in creating them wisely—for example, the effectiveness of an index whose index key field contains values that are usually the same will be much less than one where the values are unique. Consider also that as a database server silently copies all the values in an unclustered index key field in order to sort them and maintain the index, choosing a field for the index key that contains sizable values (in other words, values that require a lot of storage) will increase the resources needed by the database and make it slower to use. Where possible, choose integer fields as indexes over those that are text-based.

In the sample database, you'll add a simple index to the Book table using the BookMainTopic field as the index key. With only 30 records in the table itself, this will have only a small effect on performance, but it's important to know how to add indexes to your databases.

NOTE *You can add indexes to MDB files only with Microsoft Access. Web Matrix doesn't support this.*

Try It Out: Adding Indexes with MSDE Administrator

In this example, you'll add a simple index to the BookMainTopic field in the Book table of the MSDE database using MSDE Administrator. Follow these steps:

1. Start MSDE Administrator if it isn't already running, and select the Books database. Now click Query in the left blue column of the window under DATABASE. This will open the database query page, as shown in Figure 2-19.

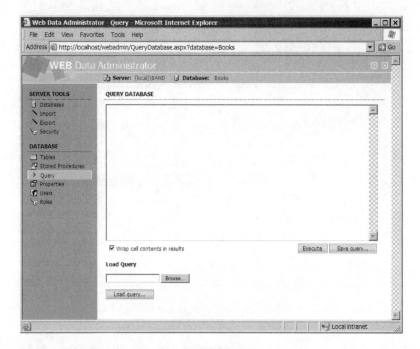

Figure 2-19. The database query window

2. To add the index, type the following command into the query window and click Execute.

```
CREATE INDEX IX_BookMainTopic ON Book (BookMainTopic)
```

3. To confirm that the index has been added to the database, execute the query again. You'll get an error saying that the index already exists.

Try It Out: Adding Indexes to MySQL

In this example, you'll add a simple index to the BookMainTopic field in the Book table of the MySQL database. To do this, you shall use MySQL's Table Designer. Follow these steps:

1. Start MySQL Control Center if it isn't already running, and right-click the Book table from the tree view in the left pane of the Console Manager window. Select Edit Table to open the Table Designer window.

2. Now select the Indexes tab in the lower half of the window. This tab allows you to create, edit, and delete any indexes on this table. Initially, it displays the primary key index created automatically when you first built the table (see Figure 2-20).

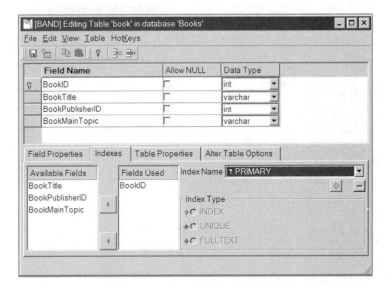

Figure 2-20. The Indexes tab in MySQL Control Center

3. To add the index, click the green plus sign to the right of the window under the Index Name list. A dialog box pops up and asks for the name of the new index. Type **IX_BookMainTopic,** and click OK.

4. The new name now appears in the Index Name field. This index contains only the BookMainTopic field, so select it from the Available Fields box and hit the blue arrow to its right to place it in the Fields Used box. You're creating a simple index here so you can leave the Index Type set to INDEX. The Index tab should look like Figure 2-21.

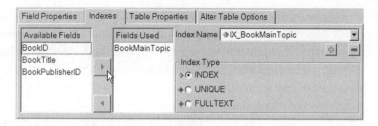

Figure 2-21. Building an index for MySQL

5.   Now save the table, and close the Table Designer window.

How It Works

The distinctly different methods with which you created this simple index in the two databases demonstrates nicely that, although you may use a graphical tool to work with the database, all the tool actually does is generate some SQL in the background to send to the database. Using the MSDE Administrator's query window is just that bit more blatant about it. You could've used the same SQL command in MySQL Command Center's query window, but the index editor is that much more convenient.

The CREATE INDEX command that gets sent onto the database has a simple syntax, as follows:

```
CREATE INDEX name_of_index ON table_name (field_name)
```

You could use the commands CREATE UNIQUE INDEX or CREATE CLUSTERED INDEX as well in this situation to create those kinds of indexes, but that wasn't necessary here.

Building Relationships Between Tables

Ironically, the term *relational databases* was coined because this kind of database was developed using mathematical set theory—a *relation* is a part of set theory—rather than because you can create relationships between tables. Regardless, it's this ability that's one of the core concepts in relational databases. Tables are said to have a relationship between them if the records they contain are somehow associated with each other. For example, a book is "released by" a publisher and "written by" authors. Thus, in a database, a book table would have a relationship with a publisher table and an author table.

When you design databases to drive an application, you look to build relationships between the objects and events modelled by the various tables you've established. This allows you to bind the data closer together, make it easier to update, and allow the computer to help you establish whether new changes are valid. You'll see how in the following example and then learn how to model different types of relationships in a relational database.

Say your database includes a second table called Book (see Figure 2-22). It contains details of some programming books due to be released in the near future by the publishers listed in the Publisher table.

Table Name: **Book**

BookID	BookTitle	BookPublisher	BookAuthors	BookMainTopic
1	Starting Up C#	Friends of Ed	Dan Maharry	C#
2	Beginning ASP.NET	Apress	Damien Foggon	ASP.NET
3	Waking Up to .NET	SAMS	Jane Randall	.NET Framework
4	Starting Up VB.NET	Manning	Dave Sussman	VB.NET
5	Beginning ADO.NET	Apress	Dominic Briffa	ADO.NET
more rows . . .				

Figure 2-22. The Book table

The books detailed in this table have "a relationship" to the publishers in the Publisher table in that every book needs a publisher to publish them. The BookPublisher field details which book is published by which publisher. This looks OK, but hang on a minute; it's not terribly efficient. The following two problems spring to mind:

What happens if a publisher changes its name, say from Apress to Bpress? Potentially, you have to look through every row in this Book table and any others in the database that are related to the Publisher table and change any reference to Apress. If you miss an entry and then code a page to look up details for Apress, it won't exist according to the database because it has changed its name. Things could easily start to go wrong.

What happens if a publisher files for bankruptcy or gets bought by someone else? You might delete the row in the Publisher table while books in the Book table still have references to the publisher. This doesn't make sense.

Fortunately, it's easy to fix this so that if a publisher changes its name, all you need to do is change the name in the Publisher table. Likewise, it's easy to make sure that the computer checks whether it's valid to delete data still used by other tables. It's just a matter of creating the right relationship between the two tables and creating the right foreign key constraint over the relationship.

Three types of relationships exist, and it's quite important that you get them right in your head.

One-to-One Relationships

When a row in one table can be associated with just one row in another table and a row in that table can only be associated with one row in the first table, those two tables are said to have a *one-to-one (1:1) relationship*. For example, a book can only ever have one budget, and a budget only ever applies to one book project. Thus, a table containing books has a one-to-one relationship to a table containing budgets.

To establish this relationship in a relational database, the primary key in one table is copied across to the second to become the primary key of the second table, as shown in Figure 2-23. To determine which budget belongs to which book, you just use the value of the primary key as a reference.

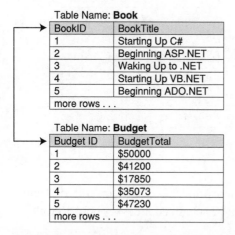

Table Name: **Book**

BookID	BookTitle
1	Starting Up C#
2	Beginning ASP.NET
3	Waking Up to .NET
4	Starting Up VB.NET
5	Beginning ADO.NET
more rows . . .	

Table Name: **Budget**

Budget ID	BudgetTotal
1	$50000
2	$41200
3	$17850
4	$35073
5	$47230
more rows . . .	

Figure 2-23. Book and Budget tables in a one-to-one relationship

NOTE *Establishing a relationship between tables usually means taking a copy of one table's primary key field and copying it into the second table. At this point, it becomes a foreign key—foreign because it isn't directly relevant to the object or event the second table models. Values of a foreign key must be drawn from the table where it's the primary key. It makes no sense for a foreign key to contain a value that doesn't identify a row in the other table.*

One-to-Many Relationships

When a single row in one table can be associated with many rows in another table, but a single row in that table can be associated with only a single row in the first table, you have a *one-to-many (1:m) relationship*. This fits in with the Book and Publisher example from earlier. A publisher can publish many books, but a book can be published by only one publisher at a time.

To establish this relationship, you need to copy the primary key from the table on the "one" side—in this example, the Publisher table—and use it as a foreign key in the "many" table—the Book table, as shown in Figure 2-24. To determine who published the book, you use the ID in the Book table to look up the name in the Publisher table.

Table Name: **Publisher**

PublisherID	PublisherName	PublisherCity	PublisherContact_Email	PublisherWebsite
1	Apress	Berkeley	someguy@apress.com	http://www.apress.com
2	Friends of Ed	Birmingham	aneditor@friendsofed.com	http://www.friendsofed.com
3	SAMS	Indianapolis	helper@samspublishing.com	http://www.samspublishing.com
4	Addison-Wesley	Boston	manager@aw.com	http://www.awprofessional.com
5	Manning	Greenwich	theboss@manning.com	http://www.manning.com
more rows . . .				

Table Name: **Book**

BookID	BookTitle	BookPublisherID	BookAuthors	BookMainTopic
1	Starting Up C#	2	Dan Maharry	C#
2	Beginning ASP.NET	1	Damien Foggon	ASP.NET
3	Waking Up to .NET	3	Jane Randall	.NET Framework
4	Starting Up VB.NET	5	Dave Sussman	VB.NET
5	Beginning ADO.NET	2	Dominic Briffa	ADO.NET
more rows . . .				

Figure 2-24. Establishing a one-to-many relationship

Every book now points to one place where publisher details are stored. If you change the details in the Publisher table, they're changed for every book as well.

Many-to-Many Relationships

The last type of relationship between tables occurs when rows in one table can be associated with many rows in another and when rows in that one can be associated with many rows in the first table. In this case, the two tables are said to have a *many-to-many (m:n) relationship*. In the book example, this is certainly the case of the relationship between books and authors. A book can have many authors, and authors often contribute to more than one book.

In Figure 2-22, the Book table contains a column called BookAuthors. The alarm should already be ringing because the field name is plural—fields should contain single pieces of information rather than several. So then, say that every book has only one author. If that was the case, you should create a new table called Author, which is in a many-to-one relationship with the Book table, much as in Figure 2-25.

Table Name: **Author**

Author ID	AuthorFirstname	AuthorSurname	AuthorSSN	AuthorLastContact
1	Dan	Maharry	123-55-6254	01/02/2004
2	Damien	Foggon	123-55-7651	12/02/2004
3	Dave	Sussman	123-55-9164	3/12/2003
4	Jane	Randall	123-55-1753	14/02/2004
5	Dominic	Briffa	123-55-8632	24/04/2003
more rows . . .				

Table Name: **Book**

BookID	BookTitle	BookPublisherID	BookAuthor	BookMainTopic
1	Starting Up C#	2	1	C#
2	Beginning ASP.NET	1	2	ASP.NET
3	Waking Up to .NET	3	4	.NET Framework
4	Starting Up VB.NET	5	3	VB.NET
5	Beginning ADO.NET	2	5	ADO.NET
more rows . . .				

Figure 2-25. If books had only one author, this would be correct.

Of course, not every book has a single author. Quite often they have many. But how many? You could add a couple more columns to the Book table to account for a book having two or three authors, but what happens when you have a fourth? This relationship is still *unresolved*. Logic dictates there has to be a better solution than this, and there is.

To express this many-to-many relationship properly, you remove Author fields from the Book table entirely, and create a linking table (with its own name—for example, WhoWroteWhat) that contains at least two columns—one for each of the two table's primary keys, as shown in Figure 2-26.

Table Name: **Book**

BookID	BookTitle	BookPublisherID	BookMainTopic
1	Starting Up C#	2	C#
2	Beginning ASP.NET	1	ASP.NET
3	Waking Up to .NET	3	.NET Framework
4	Starting Up VB.NET	4	VB.NET
5	Beginning ADO.NET	1	ADO.NET
more rows . . .			

Table Name: **WhoWroteWhat**

WWWBookID	WWWAuthorID
1	1
1	2
2	3
3	1
3	4
3	3
4	5
5	3

Table Name: **Author**

Author ID	AuthorFirstname	AuthorSurname	AuthorSSN	AuthorLastContact
1	Dan	Maharry	123-55-6254	01/02/2004
2	Damien	Foggon	123-55-7651	12/02/2004
3	Dave	Sussman	123-55-9164	13/12/2003
4	Jane	Randall	123-55-1743	14/02/2004
5	Dominic	Briffa	123-55-8632	24/04/2003
more rows . . .				

Figure 2-26. Using a link table to model a many-to-many relationship

To discover who wrote a book, you now look up the BookID in the link table and follow all the AuthorIDs associated to the book for their details. You just need to be aware that the BookID will occur in several rows in the link table—one for each author. The combination of the two foreign keys, WWWBookID and WWW AuthorID, is then used as the primary key for the table. (Note that while WhoWrote-What makes sense as the table name here, it's usually a good idea to include the names of the tables that the link table links and make its purpose clear—for example, Book_Author or WhoWroteWhat_Book_Author.)

Foreign Keys and Foreign Key Constraints

To model any of the three kinds of relationship between two tables, you create a column in one table that contains only the values from the primary key in another. For example, in Figure 2-26 you reference the primary key field AuthorID in the Author table in the WWWAuthorID field in the WhoWroteWhat table. WWWAuthorID is known as a *foreign key field*.

> **TIP** A foreign key *is a field that references values of a primary key in another table. If the primary key is a composite one, the foreign key may also consist of more than one field.*

This all makes sense, but what keeps track of these relationships as you build them? After all, the foreign key field is just another field. When you start adding, changing, and deleting data to and from those related tables, do *you* have to keep making sure that the data makes sense according to those relationships, or can you get the database to do it for you? Say, for example, you delete an author from the Author table. What happens to the entries relating to that author in the WhoWroteWhat table? They don't reference an author anymore, so do you delete those entries, too? Do you set them to NULL?

We'll rephrase that question in a minute. If the data in a database remains *valid* and obeys the rules and relationships set out over the tables containing it, then the *integrity* of the database is intact. If you delete an author, that integrity isn't intact because the WhoWroteWhat table now references an author that has been deleted. How do you manage this and restore the (referential) integrity of the database?

The answer lies in the fifth type of constraint we alluded to in the earlier section "Properties and Constraints"—*a foreign key*, or *referential integrity, constraint*. By applying this kind of constraint to the two fields concerned, you can lay out exactly how the database will react when you delete an entry from the table containing the primary key in a relationship. Indeed, this kind of constraint lets you define three particular things.

- Which fields are the primary key and the foreign key

- If the database should check newly entered data against this constraint

- If the database should enforce this constraint when data in either field is modified or deleted, and if so, what the database should do about it

By default, the database won't allow you to violate the integrity of the database by modifying or deleting information, but you can reverse this so that either the action is just allowed (and the database's integrity is violated) or the database updates/deletes the appropriate rows in the corresponding tables. This is known as *cascading* the changes between the tables in the relationship.

You'll look at this in practice by building some more sample database and creating some constraints to enforce the relationships between the tables.

> **NOTE** *You have other ways to enforce a relationship between tables, but adding foreign key constraints to a database is the most convenient.*

Enforcing Relationships with Foreign Key Constraints

In the previous set of examples, you saw how to build a single table—the Publisher table—and add some data to it. The next step is to build the remaining three tables—Book, Author, and WhoWroteWhat—and then add the appropriate foreign key constraints that ensure their relationships are maintained and the integrity of the data within them stays intact.

> **NOTE** *To create the remaining three tables, follow the steps again in the "Try It Out: Creating a Table..." sections but use the table information for the other tables as listed in Appendix C.*

You'll add three foreign key constraints to your database. The first is between the Publisher and Book table and will strengthen the one-to-many relationship between books and their publishers. The second and third will strengthen the many-to-many relationship between books and their authors using the WhoWroteWhat table as the middleman.

Try It Out: Adding Foreign Key Constraints with Web Matrix

In this example, you'll add three foreign key constraints to the MDB file Books database. To do this, you shall use Web Matrix's Foreign Key Editor. Follow these steps:

1. Start Web Matrix if it isn't already running, and expand the list of tables in the Books database in Web Matrix's Data pane.

2. The first constraint to add is between the Book table and the Publisher table. Double-click the Book table entry in the Data pane to open its table design window and then select Tools ➤ Db Foreign Key Editor from the main menu, or press Ctrl+Shift+F2.

3. The Foreign Key Editor appears. Click New to start building a new constraint. The relationship between the Book and Publisher tables uses the PublisherID field in the Publisher table as the primary key field replicated in the Book table as the BookPublisherID field, so you need to tell the editor this. In the Foreign Key Properties section of the screen, change Foreign Key Field to BookPublisherID, change Primary Table to Publisher, and change Primary Table Field to PublisherID, as in Figure 2-27.

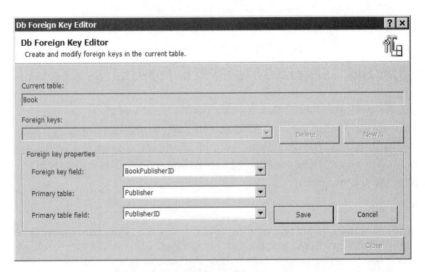

Figure 2-27. Using Web Matrix's Foreign Key Editor

4. Now hit the Save button. The editor will create the constraint and give it a unique name. Hit Close. That's one constraint down, two to go.

5. The two other constraints both use foreign key fields in the WhoWroteWhat table, so double-click the WhoWroteWhat table in the Data pane to open its table design window and start the Foreign Key editor again.

6. First, create the constraint between WhoWroteWhat and Author. Click New and set Foreign Key Field to WWWAuthorID, Primary Table to Author, and Primary Table Field to AuthorID. Now hit Save.

7. Hit New again to create the final constraint between WhoWroteWhat and BookID. Set Foreign Key Field to WWWBookID, Primary Table to Book, and Primary Table Field to BookID. Now hit Save, and then Close to end the editor session.

Try It Out: Adding Foreign Key Constraints with MSDE Administrator

In this example, you'll add three foreign key constraints to the MSDE Books database. To do this, you shall use MSDE Administrator's Database Query page as you did for the "Try It Out: Adding Indexes..." example. Follow these steps:

1. Start MSDE Administrator if it isn't already running, and select the Books database. Now click Query in the left blue column of the window under the DATABASE heading to open the database query page, as shown in Figure 2-19.

2. The first constraint to add is between the Book table and the Publisher table. Type the command shown in Figure 2-28 into the query window, and then click Execute.

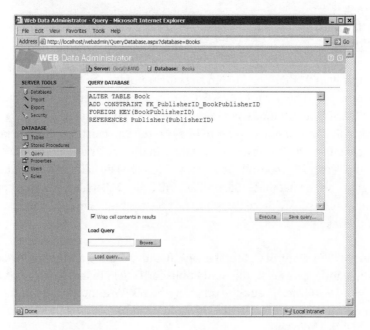

Figure 2-28. Adding a foreign key constraint to MSDE

3. MSDE now adds the constraint to the Books database, but unfortunately you don't get any acknowledgment of this. One way to confirm it, however, is to run the command again. This time, you'll get an error saying the constraint already exists in the database.

4. You have two more constraints to add. The first is between the WhoWrote-What table and the Author table. Run the following command in the query window:

```
ALTER TABLE WhoWroteWhat
ADD CONSTRAINT FK_AuthorID_WWWAuthorID
FOREIGN KEY (WWWAuthorID)
REFERENCES Author (AuthorID)
```

5. The last constraint to add is between the WhoWroteWhat table and the Book table. Run the following command in the query window:

```
ALTER TABLE WhoWroteWhat
ADD CONSTRAINT FK_BookID_WWWBookID
FOREIGN KEY (WWWBookID)
REFERENCES Book (BookID)
```

6. All three constraints have now been constructed.

Try It Out: Adding Foreign Key Constraints with MySQL Control Center

In this example, you'll add three foreign key constraints to the MySQL Books database. To do this, you shall use the MySQL Control Center's query window and the same ALTER TABLE commands used in the previous MSDE example.

Now, MySQL has a couple of rules to obey before you can add a foreign key constraint to a table. The first is that both tables in the constraint are InnoDB tables, and the second is that both primary and foreign key fields must be the first field in an index on the database. So, unlike MSDE and MDB files, you must create two extra indexes to satisfy these rules and be able to create the constraints.

Follow these steps:

1. Start MySQL Control Center if it isn't already running and create two new simple indexes, one on the BookPublisherID field in the Book table called IX_BookPublisherID and the other on the WWWAuthorID field in the WhoWroteWhat table. Use the previous example "Adding Indexes to MySQL" to help you.

2. Now select the Books database from the tree view in the left hand pane of the Console Manager window. Now choose File ➤ Query or press Ctrl+Q to bring up the Query Window, as shown in Figure 2-29.

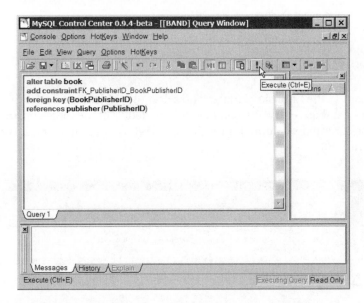

Figure 2-29. The MySQL Control Center Query Window

3. The first constraint to add is between BookPublisherID in the Book table and PublisherID in the Publisher table. Type the following command into the query window, as shown in Figure 2-29, and then click Execute:

```
ALTER TABLE Book
ADD CONSTRAINT FK_PublisherID_BookPublisherID
FOREIGN KEY (BookPublisherID)
REFERENCES Publisher (PublisherID)
```

The Messages pane of the Query Window acknowledges the query and tells you the constraint was added successfully.

4. You have two more constraints to add. The first is between the WWWAuthorID in the WhoWroteWhat table and AuthorID in the Author table. Type and run the following command in the Query Window:

```
ALTER TABLE WhoWroteWhat
ADD CONSTRAINT FK_AuthorID_WWWAuthorID
FOREIGN KEY (WWWAuthorID)
REFERENCES Author (AuthorID)
```

5. The last constraint to add is between WWWBookID in the WhoWroteWhat table and BookID in the Book table. Type and run the following command in the Query Window:

```
ALTER TABLE WhoWroteWhat
ADD CONSTRAINT FK_BookID_WWWBookID
FOREIGN KEY (WWWBookID)
REFERENCES Book (BookID)
```

6. Go back to the Console Manager and select the Tables icon under the Books database entry. You can now see the details of the three constraints in the comments column for the Book and WhoWroteWhat tables (see Figure 2-30).

Table	Records	Size (bytes)	Created	Type	Comments
author	0	16384		InnoDB	InnoDB free: 4096 kB
book	0	16384		InnoDB	InnoDB free: 4096 kB; (BookPublisherID) REFER books/publisher(PublisherID)
publisher	0	16384		InnoDB	InnoDB free: 4096 kB
whowrotewhat	0	16384		InnoDB	InnoDB free: 4096 kB; (WWWAuthorID) REFER books/author(AuthorID); (WWWBookID) REFER books/book(BookID)

Figure 2-30. Details of a table's relationships are given in the Console Manager's table view.

How It Works

As with all the examples in this chapter, your tools are actually sending a SQL command to the database in the background. In this case, they all send the three ALTER TABLE commands you sent explicitly to MSDE and MySQL. You'll look further at ALTER TABLE in Chapter 10, but for now the following is the syntax for the command to add a foreign key constraint to a table:

```
ALTER TABLE table_with_foreign_key
ADD CONSTRAINT name_of_restraint
FOREIGN KEY (name_of_foreign_key_column)
REFERENCES table_with_primary_key (name_of_primary_key_column)
```

Eagle-eyed readers may have noticed a contradiction between this chapter and the design of this database. You didn't? Go back and look again. See if you can find what they are before you continue. You can find the answer at the end of the next section, "Relationship Diagrams."

Relationship Diagrams

It's time for a quick aside before leaving the topic of relationships. This isn't a problem, but consider a situation where you want to share with others how you've designed the structure of the tables in your database and how they relate. You could write a document containing descriptions of each table, the fields they contain, and the relationships you've established between them, but that's a bit long-winded. Alternatively, you can prepare a *relationship diagram* for the database.

It's said that pictures are worth a thousand words, and in this case, that's true. A relationship diagram allows you to capture all this information in one fell swoop, and it can be handy to know how to use them. Proprietary databases such as Microsoft SQL Server, Oracle, and even Access allow you to build tables in a database and then create relationship diagrams for those tables. As you do so, the relationships you draw are then enforced by the databases as they generate the appropriate constraints to match your diagram.

Take, for example, Figure 2-31 (from Microsoft Access), which shows the four tables in your database.

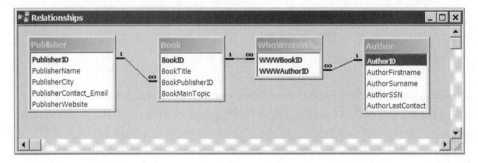

Figure 2-31. The relationship diagram for the Books sample database

This tells you the following:

- Each table's name is clearly given.

- The name of each field in a table is given.

Relationships between tables are drawn as lines between tables. At the ends of each line are a 1 and a chain (or an infinity symbol if you prefer). The table on the number side contains the primary key being used as a foreign key in the table on the chain side. The relationship lines point at the fields involved in the relationship.

It doesn't tell you the following:

- The data type of each field in a table

- Which fields are the primary keys in their table

Neither Web Matrix nor MySQL Command Center support the creation of relationship diagrams, but if you continue to work with databases, you're bound to see them soon because they're quite commonplace. For example, SQL Server, Oracle, and Access all support their creation, albeit producing relationship diagrams with slightly different information on them.

> **TIP** *For those looking here to discover the contradiction between the sample database and what you've learned in the book, you'll find it here. You haven't branched out the BookMainTopic field into its own table and created a many-to-one relationship with the Book table as you should have done. This has been done deliberately to demonstrate the extra programming work even this small omission may cause.*

Users, Roles, and Permissions

Just like any other modern server product or operating system, database servers have a security layer that restricts access to their contents based on the credentials a user or program supplies logging on. A database server maintains a list of all user accounts that can log into a specific database and then exactly what those users can do to the contents of that database. All databases are installed with one user already set up—the system administrator. This account, called *sa* in MSDE and MDB files and *root* in MySQL, has the complete run of the system. When logged in as the system administrator, a user or program can back up the system, add data, delete everything, and do whatever, so it's vital that this account is secured properly.

> **CAUTION** *By default, neither the sa account in MSDE nor the root account in MySQL have a password when installed. Appendix A demonstrates how to create these passwords during installation of the server.*

Now it won't come as a surprise to learn that connecting to the database from a page using the system administrator account isn't a good idea. Any malcontents might find a way to hijack the connection to the database through a page, and if you used the system administrator account to make the connection, they'd have the run of the system. Instead, you must create your own user accounts for use by your applications. This process has the following three steps:

1. **Adding a user account to the server's user table**: You need to give the account a user ID and a password.

2. **Giving the account the right permissions on the application's database**: You need to tell the server whether the account is restricted to just retrieving data from the database and whether it can modify data, add it, delete, or even modify the structure of the database itself.

3. **Giving the account any server permissions if appropriate**: An account can also be given varying levels of permission to work with all the databases being hosted by the server. For example, an account can be given permissions for backing up, securing, and optimizing the databases on the server. Unless you're writing a Web-based data administration application, though, there's no reason to give a user account any of these permissions.

The best rule of thumb when it comes to adding users is to give them the fewest permissions possible to do the job they need to do and to create a different user account for the different roles users may have within your application. For example, there's no need to use an account with write permissions on a page that just displays the current threads in a forum, but if someone has logged into the forum as a moderator, then they should have the privilege when they navigate to the forum admin pages. In the main then, you just need to use your common sense, evaluate exactly what may need to be done to the database on a given page, and connect to a database with a user account with permissions for those specific actions. Any more is wasteful.

NOTE *MSDE also allows users to log in using their Windows domain accounts, giving them permissions according to their Windows user roles. This Windows login mode may well suit intranet-based applications, but for this sample database, you've used SQL login mode to keep things simple. Neither MySQL nor Access supports this.*

Adding a New User Account

You'll now follow this advice and add a new user account called *BAND* to access the sample database during the course of the book. In the next few chapters, you'll see how to add, modify, retrieve, and delete information from the database, so those are the permissions you shall give it, along with the password *letmein*.

> **NOTE** *Web Matrix doesn't support the creation of users for MDB files. You must do this using Access.*

Try It Out: Adding a User to MSDE

In this example, you'll create a user account (ID: BAND, password: letmein) that you'll use in the next few chapters to access your MSDE database. Follow these steps:

1. Start MSDE Administrator if it isn't already running, and click Security under the SERVER TOOLS heading on the left side of the window. On the next screen, click Logins. The resulting screen (see Figure 2-32) lists all the current logins allowed into this instance of MSDE.

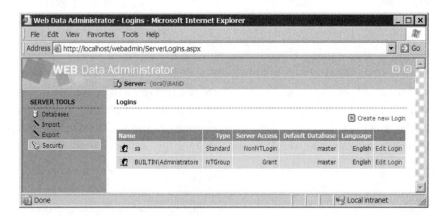

Figure 2-32. Listing the MSDE login accounts

2. To add a new account, click the Create New Login link. You're using a SQL Login account, so change the authentication method accordingly on the next page. Also, set Login Name to BAND and Password to letmein, as shown in Figure 2-33, and click Create Login.

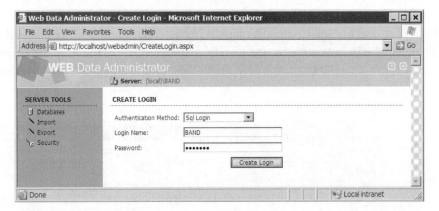

Figure 2-33. Adding a new login account

3. In the next screen, you set which databases hosted by MSDE the new login account can access. In the Defaults section, set the Database entry to the Books database. This ensures that unless you state otherwise, an ASP.NET page logging in as BAND will be connected to Books rather than any other database being hosted by MSDE.

4. Now switch the Sections drop-down box to Database Access, and click Books. This gives the BAND account permission to access the Books database. Click Save Changes to finish creating the new login account.

5. Open the MSDE Administrator's database query page by clicking Query in the left blue column of the window under the DATABASE heading. Type the following command and then click Execute.

```
GRANT SELECT, INSERT, DELETE, UDPATE To BAND
```

Try It Out: Adding a User to MySQL

In this example, you'll create a user account (ID: BAND, password: letmein) that you'll use in the next few chapters to access your MySQL database. To do this, you'll use MySQL Control Center's user administration window. Follow these steps:

1. Start MySQL Control Center if it isn't already running, and right-click the User Administration icon from the tree view in the left pane of the Console Manager window. Select New User to bring up the user administration window (see Figure 2-34).

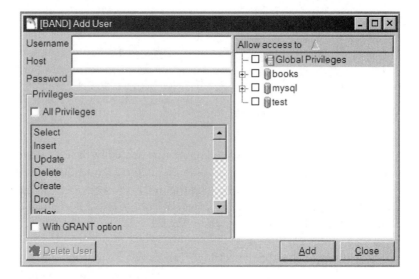

Figure 2-34. The user administration window in MySQL Control Center

2. To add the user, set Username to BAND, Host to %, and Password to letmein. In the Privileges box, check With GRANT Option and make sure only Select, Insert, Delete, and Update are selected in the box. Finally, check the box against Books in the Allow Access To pane. The window should now look like Figure 2-35.

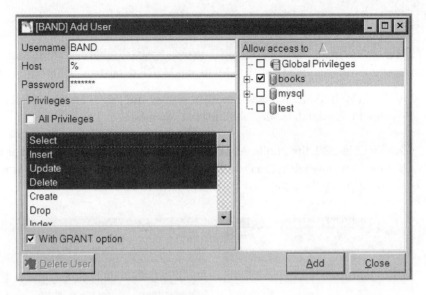

Figure 2-35. Adding a user to MySQL

3. Now click Add and then Close. The new user account now appears in the Console Window under the User Administration node.

Completing the Sample Database

Now that you've learned a little about relational databases and the SQL statements your ASP.NET pages will be sending it, you've learned about everything the sample database needs to use. A SQL database has a few other pieces that the "Views and Triggers" section covers briefly but that aren't a part of the rest of this book, so it makes sense to finish building the sample database before moving on.

Indeed, you've done all the hard work building the thing. All you have left to do is put some data in it. You'll spend a lot of Chapter 8 learning how to add, alter, and delete data through a page, so we'll save that until then. Right now, you'll fill the database using the same tools you built it with.

Try It Out: Filling the Database with Web Matrix

In this exercise, you'll learn how to add data to a database table using Web Matrix. This method works equally well with MDB and MSDE databases. Follow these steps:

1. Start Web Matrix if it isn't already running, and expand the list of tables in the Books database in Web Matrix's Data pane.

2. Double-click the Publisher table entry to bring up the table designer dialog box. Now select the Data tab in the bottom-left corner of this window to bring up the data entry pane, as shown in Figure 2-36.

Figure 2-36. A data entry dialog in Web Matrix

3. A reminder box appears and asks you to save the table design first. Click Yes, and fill in the data as given in Appendix C. The data is saved automatically, so you can close the window when you're ready.

4. Repeat this for the three other tables in the sample database, Book, Author, and WhoWroteWhat. The data for each is in Appendix C.

Try It Out: Filling the Database with MSDE Administrator

In this exercise, you'll learn how to add data to a MSDE database table using MSDE Administrator and its Database Query page. Follow these steps:

1. Start MSDE Administrator if it isn't already running, and select the Books database. Now click Query in the left blue column of the window under the DATABASE heading to open the database query page, as shown in Figure 2-19.

2. As you learned earlier, the SQL command to add a row of data to a table is INSERT, so you'll need to run an INSERT command for every row of data in each table. For example, the INSERT command for the first row in the Publisher table is as follows:

```
INSERT INTO publisher ⏎
(PublisherID, PublisherName, PublisherCity, ⏎
    PublisherContact_Email, PublisherWebsite) ⏎
VALUES (1, 'Apress', 'Berkeley', ⏎
    'someguy@apress.com', 'http://www.apress.com')
```

3. Type this command into the query window, click Execute, and repeat for the remaining rows.

Note that this method is particularly long-winded. We suggest using Web Matrix to create this database. Simply add a connection to the MSDE database in Web Matrix as demonstrated in steps 1 and 2 of "Try It Out: Creating a Table with Web Matrix" and then choose the established MSDE database rather than creating an Access database. Then see the previous exercise for instructions on adding data to the database.

Try It Out: Filling the Database with MySQL Control Center

In this exercise, you'll learn how to add data to a MySQL database table using MySQL Control Center. Follow these steps:

1. Start MySQL Control Center if it isn't already running and double-click the Publisher table icon from the tree view in the left pane of the Console Manager window.

2. This opens a new window that displays the contents of the table. At the moment, of course, this is empty. To add a new row to the table, choose Query ➤ Insert Record or press Ctrl+I.

3. Fill in the data as shown in Figure 2-37. You can tab between each field in the row to add values in each. When you finish a row, you'll have to press Return and then Ctrl+I to add another row to fill in. When you're finished, hit Save and close the window.

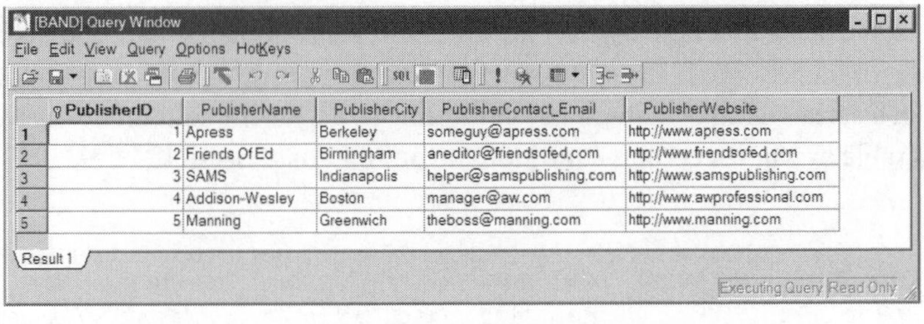

	⏚ PublisherID	PublisherName	PublisherCity	PublisherContact_Email	PublisherWebsite
1	1	Apress	Berkeley	someguy@apress.com	http://www.apress.com
2	2	Friends Of Ed	Birmingham	aneditor@friendsofed.com	http://www.friendsofed.com
3	3	SAMS	Indianapolis	helper@samspublishing.com	http://www.samspublishing.com
4	4	Addison-Wesley	Boston	manager@aw.com	http://www.awprofessional.com
5	5	Manning	Greenwich	theboss@manning.com	http://www.manning.com

Figure 2-37. Adding data in MySQL Control Center

How It Works

It's not difficult to figure out that while the graphical options to add data given by Web Matrix and MySQL Control Center are much quicker than the drawn-out writing of INSERT statements by MSDE Administrator, both Matrix and Center actually send those same INSERT commands to their databases in the background. When it gets down to it, though, it's much nicer to use the tools than the "honest" method offered by MSDE Administrator.

Views and Triggers

Before you start actually coding some pages in Chapter 3, you may find that two other facets to a relational database server are handy in future projects.

One drawback of the "one object or event per table" rule is that quite often the information you actually need for a page is spread across several tables. For example, it wouldn't be a stretch to imagine an ASP.NET page displaying a book's title, the name of its publisher, and its main author, too. This means pulling information from four different tables and means quite a complex SELECT statement to boot. Like indexes, *views* are designed to save you some time. They're virtual tables containing related fields from many tables in one place. You could, for example, create a view on your sample database containing BookTitle, PublisherName, and the name of one of the authors who wrote it. All you do then is write a SELECT statement on this view, and the database server would do the complex part of pulling all the information together without you knowing.

> **NOTE** *If you'd like to learn more about SQL views, check out this MSDN tutorial about them at* http://msdn.microsoft.com/library/en-us/architec/8_ar_da_2d9v.asp.

You can also set up *triggers*—the database equivalent of an event in .NET. These triggers monitor the state of a database table or group of tables and are fired when a certain kind of statement—for example, a CREATE statement—is run on that table or when a certain condition in your database occurs.

> **NOTE** *If you'd like to learn more about SQL triggers, check out this two-part article from MSDN Magazine at* http://msdn.microsoft.com/msdnmag/issues/03/12/DataPoints/default.aspx *and* http://msdn.microsoft.com/msdnmag/issues/04/01/DataPoints/default.aspx.

Summary

In this chapter, you've taken a crash course in what makes a relational database (and its server) tick. You've also used some of that theory to build your own database for use in Chapters 3–8. This chapter has covered a lot of ground, so the following is a recap of what you've seen:

- You've learned that all relational database management systems use tables to store information about a *single* type of object or event. Each row in a table represents *one* instance of that object or event, and every field in the row contains a *single* piece of information about that instance.

- Every field has a number of properties and constraints that determine the range of values the field may contain.

- Every table must contain a field or a combination of fields that *uniquely identifies* that row in the table. This (combination of) field(s) is designated as the *primary* key for the table. Together, the table name, primary key value for the row, and field name allow you to pinpoint any single piece of information in the database.

- You can model three kinds of relationship between a pair of tables in a database. They are one-to-one, many-to-one, and many-to-many. Each type of relationship is realized by using one table's primary key as a foreign key in another. Each relationship should be enforced with a foreign key constraint on the tables.

- You use statements written in SQL to convey your wishes to the database.

- You can use stored procedures, indexes, views, and triggers to improve the performance of the database.

In Chapter 3, you'll start building data-driven ASP.NET pages and discover how to create a connection to a data source—not just relational databases but flat files and a few others too. If you'll recall from Chapter 1, this is stage one of three in an ASP.NET's dialogue with a data source, and much as you may want it, this isn't a case of "one connection fits all." It all depends on the data provider you have to use and the data source you're trying to contact.

One final note: Congratulations for building the sample database for this book. It would be a bit unfair of us to let you rebuild it each time something went wrong, so we've included a clean MDB file and SQL scripts that will rebuild the MySQL and MSDE versions of the database in the code downloads for this book. You can find instructions on how to run the scripts in Appendix C. You can download the scripts and MDB file from `http://www.apress.com/book/bookDisplay.html?bID=297`.

Part Two

Core Skills

CHAPTER 3

Connecting to Data Sources

THE PREVIOUS TWO CHAPTERS covered the fundamentals required to start using databases. Chapter 1 showed the various types of data sources available, and you saw how you can use text files, Extensible Markup Language (XML) files, spreadsheets, and the Active Directory store, not to mention *real* databases as data sources. Chapter 2 then moved on to talk about relational databases, and by the end of the chapter you had fundamentally the same database in three different flavors: MSDE, Access, and MySQL.

We've covered an awful lot of theory so far, so now we'll actually show how to put some of this into practice. In this chapter, you'll concentrate on connecting to some of the different data sources that are available, and in the following two chapters you'll work with the data in the data source.

Connection Objects

As you saw in Chapter 1, the data provider for a particular data source contains implementations of several objects. Each of these objects handles a specific task, and a Connection object, unsurprisingly, handles a connection to a data source. The Connection object (as was the case with traditional ADO) is the basis for all interactions with the data source you want to use—you must open the connection before you access the data source, and you must close it when you're finished.

> **NOTE** *Unlike traditional ADO, you must always create a Connection object when talking to a data source. With ADO, you could pass an ADODB.Connection object or a connection string to an ADODB.Command object, but when using ADO.NET, you must create an instance of a Connection object and pass this to the Command object.*

Again, as you saw in Chapter 1, the data provider architecture allows a data provider to be specifically designed for a data source; several data providers are available. It'd be impossible to look at every combination of data provider and data source, so you'll concentrate on the following three implementations of the Connection object in this chapter:

- The SqlConnection object to connect to a SQL Server/MSDE database

- The OdbcConnection object to connect to a data source using an ODBC driver

- The OleDbConnection object to connect to a data source using an OLE DB provider

Connection Strings

Irrespective of which implementation of the Connection object you use, you must specify the data source to which you want to connect. Although any choice of Connection object limits the data sources you can talk to (you can't, for instance, use the SqlConnection object to connect to a MySQL database), all the Connection objects use the connection string to specify the data source.

So, what sort of things does a connection string contain? This depends upon the Connection object you're using as well as, in the case of OLE DB and ODBC, the underlying provider/driver you're using.

If you're using the OleDbConnection or OdbcConnection objects, the connection string you use is the same as the connection string you'd use in ADO when using the corresponding OLE DB provider or ODBC driver.

The SqlConnection object uses a slightly simpler connection string than OleDbConnection or OdbcConnection because you don't need to specify the type of data source you're connecting to—it's implicit in your choice of the SqlConnection object.

The one thing that all connection strings have in common is that they must always contain details of the data source to which they're connecting. Whether this is a Microsoft SQL Server 2000 Desktop Engine (MSDE) database, an Access database, or a Comma-Separated Value (CSV) file, you must always specify the data source.

In most cases, you should also provide security information such as username and password. The data source you're connecting to determines this.

> **NOTE** *You have a multitude of options for connecting to data sources—far too many to list or discuss in any detail. In the examples that follow, you'll see several instances that give the general flavor. For a comprehensive list, see* `http://www.able-consulting.com/ADO_Conn.htm`.

Connecting to the Data Source

Enough of the theory! You'll now concentrate on connecting to the three databases supplied in the code download for the book (MSDE, Access, and MySQL), but you'll also briefly see how you connect to older versions of SQL Server and to a couple of flat-file data sources—namely, an Excel spreadsheet and a CSV file.

Rather than typing a lot of code and having to explain bits of code that are covered in subsequent chapters, we'll use one of the wizards in Web Matrix to create the basis for all of the examples and modify the bits. This will allow you to create examples that actually do something swiftly; these examples not only connect to the data source but also retrieve data and display it in a DataGrid.

Connecting to MSDE Using the SqlConnection Object

To connect to an MSDE database, you use the `SqlConnection` object. As this is a specific provider for MSDE, you can assume that it's the quickest way of accessing the database.

> **NOTE** *If you're trying to connect to SQL Server version 6.5 (or earlier), you can't use the* `SqlConnection` *object; it'll work only with SQL Server version 7.0 and newer. With SQL Server 6.5, use the* `OleDbConnection` *object and the OLE DB provider for SQL Server, which we'll discuss later in the "Connecting to SQL Server 6.5" section.*

Try It Out: Connecting to MSDE

In this example, you'll use of one of the wizards provided by Web Matrix to generate the code needed to connect to an MSDE database. Because you're interested in only the connection to the database, you'll see some code here that we'll explain in later chapters. Follow these steps:

1. Start Web Matrix, and navigate to the C:\BAND\Chapter03 folder. If this folder doesn't exist, then create it.

2. Select File ➤ New, and you'll be presented with the Add New File dialog box. Select Data Pages from the templates list and Simple Data Report from the list of available pages. Enter a filename of **msde.aspx**, as shown in Figure 3-1.

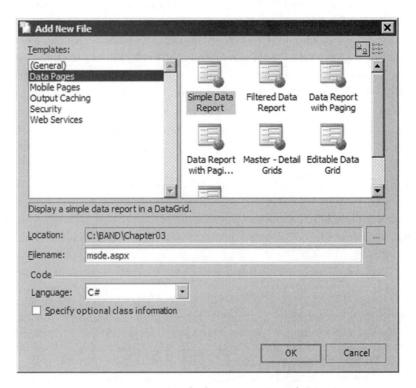

Figure 3-1. Creating a new simple data report in Web Matrix

3. Click OK to create the new report. As you'll see from the page that's created, shown in Figure 3-2, the wizard has created the bare bones of the page for you.

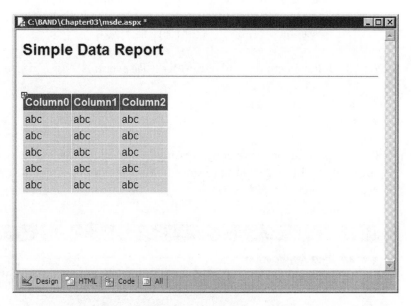

Figure 3-2. Design view of autogenerated data report

4. Switch to the Code view of the page, as shown in Figure 3-3, by selecting the Code tab at the bottom.

```
void Page_Load(object sender, EventArgs e) {

    // TODO: update the ConnectionString and CommandText values for your applicati
    string ConnectionString = "server=(local);database=pubs;trusted_connection=tru
    string CommandText = "select au_lname as [Last Name], au_fname as [First Name]

    SqlConnection myConnection = new SqlConnection(ConnectionString);
    SqlCommand myCommand = new SqlCommand(CommandText, myConnection);

    myConnection.Open();

    DataGrid1.DataSource = myCommand.ExecuteReader(CommandBehavior.CloseConnection
    DataGrid1.DataBind();
}
```

Figure 3-3. Code view of autogenerated data report

5. Change the first two lines of code within the Page_Load event to the following:

```
string ConnectionString = ⤶
  @"server=(local)\BAND; database=Books; uid=band; pwd=letmein";
string CommandText = "select * from Publisher";
```

6. Add the following to the end of the Page_Load event:

```
// close the connection
myConnection.Close();
```

7. Run the page in the browser by pressing F5 or clicking the start icon in the toolbar. This will prompt to start the Web server that ships with Web Matrix, as shown in Figure 3-4.

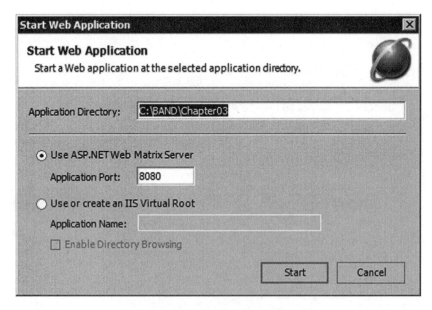

Figure 3-4. Starting the Web Matrix built-in Web server

8. Once the browser has opened, the page will be executed and the results of the query will be returned, as shown in Figure 3-5.

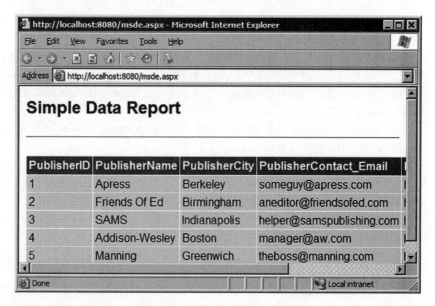

Figure 3-5. Results of the simple query using the SqlConnection *object*

How It Works

That wasn't too hard, was it? All of the code was generated for you, and you simply had to change two strings to connect to the correct MSDE database. You don't need to examine some of the code just yet, so you'll just concentrate on code for the connection itself.

Before you can use any of the database objects, you must reference the namespaces that contain those objects. You could use fully referenced names to refer to them, but this leads to lots of typing and some unwieldy lines of code. As you saw in Chapter 1, a general namespace exists for all the data objects, and you include a reference to this in the .aspx file, which allows you to refer to the objects using much shorter names. If you look at the top of the All view in Web Matrix, you'll see that the wizard has already added the following reference to this namespace:

```
<%@ import Namespace="System.Data" %>
```

You'll also see the following reference to the namespace that contains the SQL Server–specific objects:

```
<%@ import Namespace="System.Data.SqlClient" %>
```

Because you want the page to be populated every time the page loads, you need to use the page's Page_Load event. This executes every time the page loads, and you'll place all of the code you want to run here, much like the Web Matrix wizard has done.

As we pointed out earlier, you need to modify only two lines of code; these are the first two in the Page_Load event.

The first line of code you change contains a definition of the connection string to the database. This is stored in the ConnectionString variable, as follows, and specifies the database you want to connect to as well as the security information:

```
string ConnectionString = ⤸
  @"server=(local)\BAND; database=Books; uid=band; pwd=letmein";
```

The first property of the connection string, server, specifies which database server you want to connect to—in this case, the BAND server instance on the local machine. You could have also used Data Source instead of server if you had wanted.

The database property specifies which database you want to connect to—in this case, the Books database. You could also have used Initial Catalog to specify which database you wanted to connect to, and you can use the two property names interchangeably.

The uid and pwd properties specify the login that the connection is to use when connecting to the database. You can also set these using User ID and Password.

The second line of code you change defines the queries, in the CommandText string, that you want to execute against the database, like so:

```
string CommandText = "select * from Publisher";
```

This, as the name of the variable suggests, is a variable used by the Command object; you'll look at this in more detail in Chapter 4. For now all you need to know about it is that it will return all of the information in the database for the publishers.

Once the connection string has been populated, it's time to create the SqlConnection object and point it at the correct database. You do this by passing the connection string into the constructor, like so:

```
SqlConnection myConnection = new SqlConnection(ConnectionString);
```

> **NOTE** *Although you pass the connection string into the constructor to initialize it, you can create a connection without passing in a connection string. In this case, you must set the* ConnectionString *property of the Connection object to the correct connection string* before *you attempt to open the connection.*

Although you've now created a SqlConnection object, you still haven't made the connection to the database. You do this by calling the Open() method, like so:

```
myConnection.Open();
```

Once the connection is opened, you can carry out tasks on the data (in this case, some data binding that you'll look at in later chapters), like so:

```
DataGrid1.DataSource = myCommand.ExecuteReader(CommandBehavior.CloseConnection);
DataGrid1.DataBind();
```

You should always close the connection to the database when you're finished with it, but the wizard-generated code doesn't do this. To close the database connection once you're finished with it, you use the Close() method of the Connection object:

```
myConnection.Close();
```

You may be wondering why the wizard doesn't add the Close() method for the database connection. This is because the data binding code that's generated automatically specifies that the connection to the database should be closed when it's no longer required. Leaving the connection to be closed automatically can lead to it being open for longer than required, so you should always explicitly close the connection. You'll take another look at this in the "Error Handling" section at the end of the chapter.

That's all there is to it. You've created a connection to the database, opened the connection, and then closed the connection. It doesn't get any more complex than that.

Trusted Connections

Specifying a username and password in the connection string causes the connection to use SQL Server Authentication. There may be cases when you don't want to use SQL Server Authentication but instead want to use Windows Authentication (although for an ASP.NET application, the opportunities to use this are rare).

To use Windows Authentication, the database and the Web server must be on the same machine. To configure the connection to use Windows Authentication, remove the `uid` and `pwd` properties and add `Integrated Security=Yes`, as shown:

```
string ConnectionString = ↩
  @"server=(local)\BAND;database=Books;Integrated Security=Yes";
```

When using Windows Authentication, you make the connection to the database using the account of the user that's executing the page.

If you're using the Web Matrix server, as you are here, then the server runs with the same permissions as the currently logged-in user, and it's this account that's used.

If the page is running under Internet Information Services (IIS), the account that's used isn't the user that's viewing the page but is a specific account for the ASP.NET process.

Irrespective of which account is used to make the connection, the database must be configured to allow the required level of access for that user.

> **NOTE** *This isn't the end of the Windows Authentication story. By configuring IIS to disable anonymous access to the Web site, you can force users to log in using a valid Windows account and use this when accessing the database. However, this is beyond the scope of this book; for more information, refer to* `http://msdn.microsoft.com/library/en-us/vbcon/html/vbtskaccessing-sqlserverusingwindowsintegratedsecurity.asp`.

Connecting to MySQL Using the OdbcConnection Object

For some data sources, such as MSDE, you'll have a specific data provider to use. For others, you may not have a specific data provider, and you'll have to use an ODBC driver or OLE DB provider to connect to the data source.

As you saw in Chapter 1, OLE DB was a replacement for ODBC, and in most cases if there's an ODBC driver and an OLE DB provider for a data source, the ODBC driver will be slightly quicker. So if you have a choice between using an ODBC driver and an OLE DB provider, pick the ODBC driver and use the `OdbcConnection` object to connect to the database.

Using the `OdbcConnection` object to connect to a MySQL database is no different from using the `SqlConnection` object to talk to an MSDE database. Although you use different objects, the methodology remains the same.

Try It Out: Connecting to MySQL

In this example, you'll build the same page as in the previous example but this time use the `OdbcConnection` object to talk to a MySQL database. Follow these steps:

1. Start Web Matrix, and navigate to the `C:\BAND\Chapter03` folder.

2. Select File ➤ New, and create a new simple data report with a filename of `mysql.aspx`.

3. Switch to the All view of the document, and replace the `import` statement for `SqlClient` with the following:

   ```
   <%@ import Namespace="System.Data.Odbc" %>
   ```

4. Switch to the Code view, and change the connection string and command text for the database connection to the following:

   ```
   string ConnectionString = @"driver={MySQL ODBC 3.51 Driver}; ↵
     server=localhost; database=books; uid=band; pwd=letmein;";
   string CommandText = "select * from Publisher";
   ```

5. Replace the `SqlCommand` and `SqlConnection` objects with their ODBC equivalents as follows:

   ```
   OdbcConnection myConnection = new OdbcConnection(ConnectionString);
   OdbcCommand myCommand = new OdbcCommand(CommandText, myConnection);
   ```

6. Add the code to close the connection at the end of the `Page_Load` event:

   ```
   // close the connection
   myConnection.Close();
   ```

7. Run the page in the browser by pressing F5 or clicking the start icon in the toolbar. If the Web Matrix Web Server is already running, then the browser window will open immediately. If it isn't running, then click the Start button on the pop-up window to start it.

8. The query will be executed against the database, and the results will be returned, as shown in Figure 3-6.

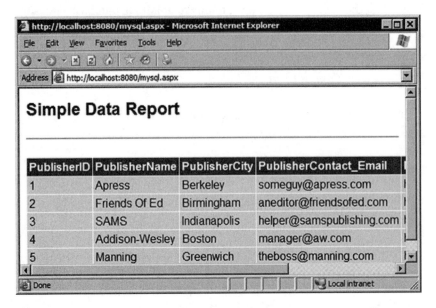

Figure 3-6. Results of the simple query using the `OdbcConnection` *object*

How It Works

If you compare the code for the MSDE example and this one, you'll see they're similar, and you should be able to follow what's going on without any problems.

The first thing you do is include the correct namespaces in the page. The wizards in Web Matrix assume you're going to be connecting to MSDE using the `SqlConnection` object and you need to change both the namespace and, as you'll see shortly, the objects that are used to interact with the data source.

You again use `System.Data` to allow access to the base data objects, but instead of the `System.Data.SqlClient` namespace specified by the wizard, you use the `System.Data.Odbc` namespace instead, like so:

```
<%@ import Namespace="System.Data" %>
<%@ import Namespace="System.Data.Odbc" %>
```

You then specify the correct connection string for connecting to a MySQL database, as follows:

```
string ConnectionString = @"driver={MySQL ODBC 3.51 Driver};
  server=localhost;database=books;uid=band;pwd=letmein;";
```

To connect to a data source using an ODBC driver, you must specify the ODBC driver you want to use. This example uses the MySQL ODBC 3.51 driver. The rest of the connection string is specific to the ODBC driver you're using, and for MySQL you need to specify the server, database, uid, and pwd you want to use.

As the three databases that you're using have the same structure, it will come as no surprise that the query to retrieve the publishers from the database is identical to the one you used in the previous example.

Before you can run the page, you need to change the objects that you're using from the wizard-assumed MSDE versions. You use the OdbcConnection object to make connections to a data source using an ODBC driver, and you use the OdbcCommand object to execute queries against that data source, like so:

```
OdbcConnection myConnection = new OdbcConnection(ConnectionString);
OdbcCommand myCommand = new OdbcCommand(CommandText, myConnection);
```

The results of executing this page are identical to those of the previous example, as you'll see if you compare Figure 3-6 with Figure 3-5.

Using DSNs

Although the example you've seen uses a connection string that contains all the data required to connect to the data source within the connection string itself, ODBC provides another way to store this data: data source names (DSNs).

You can quite easily use an existing DSN by specifying the DSN in the connection string rather than the details to connect directly. If you've created a System DSN called BAND, containing all of the details required to connect to the database, you can use this by setting the connection string as follows:

```
string ConnectionString = "DSN=BAND;";
```

> **NOTE** *It's also possible to use User DSNs instead of System DSNs in this manner. However, as the User DSN is available only to the user who created the DSN, it's advisable to use only System DSNs.*

ODBC also allows the connection details to be stored in a File DSN, and you can also use this as the basis for this connection string:

```
string ConnectionString = "FILEDSN=C:\BAND\band.dsn;";
```

Although it's possible to use DSNs to store connection information, the use of these has been slowly fading for some time, and it's better to use a connection string to specify the data source connections details. Two of the main reasons for this are as follows:

- System DSNs are stored in the registry; every time you use them to connect to the database, a registry lookup has to occur to get the details. This introduces an overhead into the database connection that you can remove if you use a connection string directly.

- As the DSN is stored in the registry, it must be re-created on the new machine if the page is moved to a different server. By having the connection string specified with the page, the connection string will move with the page.

Connecting to Access Using the OleDbConnection Object

The third database you'll look at connecting to is Access. The easiest way to connect to an Access database is by using the Microsoft Jet database engine, more commonly known as the Jet engine; this is an OLE DB provider. You can access this provider using the last of the Connection objects—OleDbConnection.

Rather than being specific to Access, the Jet engine allows you to connect to various sources, not just Microsoft products. The Jet engine allows you to connect, among others, to dBASE and Paradox databases, Excel spreadsheets, and text files. You'll look at connecting to Excel spreadsheets and text files shortly, but for now you'll just concentrate on connecting to an Access database.

> **NOTE** *Since the release of MDAC 2.6, the Jet engine isn't installed as standard. Therefore, if you don't have Access installed, you may not have it. You can download the latest version of the Jet engine—service pack 8—from* http://support.microsoft.com/?kbid=239114.

Try It Out: Connecting to Access

In this example, you'll build the same page as in the previous two examples but this time use the OleDbConnection object to talk to an Access database. Follow these steps:

1. Start Web Matrix, and navigate to the C:\BAND\Chapter03 folder.

2. Select File ➤ New, and create a new simple data report with a filename of access.aspx.

3. Switch to the All view of the document, and replace the import statement for SqlClient with the following:

   ```
   <%@ import Namespace="System.Data.OleDb" %>
   ```

4. Switch to the Code view, and change the connection string and command text for the database connection, like so:

   ```
   string ConnectionString = @"Provider=Microsoft.Jet.OLEDB.4.0; ↵
     Data Source=C:\BAND\Database\books.mdb;";
   string CommandText = "select * from Publisher";
   ```

5. Replace the SqlCommand and SqlConnection objects with their OLE DB equivalents, as follows:

   ```
   OleDbConnection myConnection = new OleDbConnection(ConnectionString);
   OleDbCommand myCommand = new OleDbCommand(CommandText, myConnection);
   ```

6. Add the following code to close the connection at the end of the Page_Load event:

   ```
   // close the connection
   myConnection.Close();
   ```

7. Run the page in the browser by pressing F5 or clicking the start icon in the toolbar. If the Web Matrix Web Server is already running, then the browser window will open immediately. If it isn't running, then click the Start button on the pop-up window to start it.

8. The query will be executed against the database, and the results will be returned, as shown in Figure 3-7.

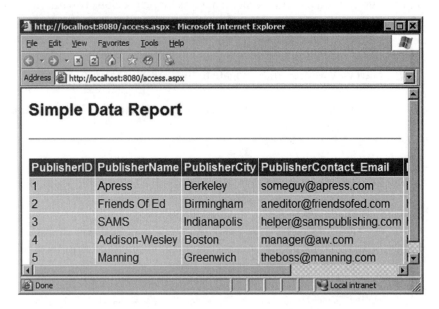

Figure 3-7. Results of the simple query using the OleDbConnection object

How It Works

If you compare the code for the previous two examples and this one, you'll see that they're all similar, and you should, by now, be able to follow what's going on without any problems.

The first thing you do is include the correct namespaces in the page. You again use System.Data to allow access to the base data objects and System.Data.OleDb to access the provider-specific objects, like so:

```
<%@ import Namespace="System.Data" %>
<%@ import Namespace="System.Data.OleDb" %>
```

You then specify the correct connection string for connecting to an Access database:

```
string ConnectionString = @"Provider=Microsoft.Jet.OLEDB.4.0; ⤶
  Data Source=C:\BAND\Database\database.mdb;";
```

To connect to an Access database, you specify the Jet engine and the full path of the database to which you want to connect. Although the Jet engine can connect to various data sources, it assumes you're connecting to an Access database, and you therefore don't have to specify the source to which you're connecting.

Because the three databases you're using have the same structure, it will come as no surprise that the query to retrieve the publishers from the database is identical to the one you used in the previous example.

You again need to change the objects you're using. You use the `OleDbConnection` object to make connections to a data source using OLE DB, and you use the `OleDbCommand` object to execute queries against that data source.

The results of executing this page are identical to those of the previous example, as you'll see if you compare Figure 3-7 with Figure 3-5 and Figure 3-6.

Security

It's also possible to secure Access databases—either by setting a database password or going further and creating users and groups. In these cases, you need to specify this extra information when creating the connection string.

If the database has a password, you must attach this to a connection string using the `Jet OLEDB:Database Password` property, like so:

```
string ConnectionString = @"Provider=Microsoft.Jet.OLEDB.4.0; 
  Data Source=C:\BAND\Database\database.mdb; 
  Jet OLEDB:Database Password=letmein";
```

If the database requires a specific user account to be used, then you can specify this using the `User ID` and `Password` properties, like so:

```
string ConnectionString = @"Provider=Microsoft.Jet.OLEDB.4.0; 
  Data Source=C:\BAND\Database\database.mdb; 
  User ID=band;Password=letmein";
```

Connecting to Other Data Sources

Although you've seen how to connect to the three main databases, these aren't the only data sources you'll ever use. You'll now see the following three examples of using the `OleDbConnection` object:

- Connecting to SQL Server 6.5

- Connecting to an Excel spreadsheet

- Connecting to a CSV file

Connecting to SQL Server 6.5

Although you have a native data provider that you can use when connecting to
SQL Server or MSDE, you can't use it in one instance. If you're trying to connect
to a version of SQL Server before version 7, then you can't use the `SqlConnection`
object. Instead, you must use the SQL Server OLE DB provider to connect to the
database.

> **NOTE** *You can also use this connection method for all versions of SQL Server, but
> the native data provider performs more quickly and should always be used if
> possible.*

Try It Out: Connecting to SQL Server 6.5

This example simulates connecting to a version of SQL Server that's 6.5 or earlier.
You can use the `OleDbConnection` object to connect to all versions of SQL Server and
MSDE, and you'll simulate a SQL Server 6.5 database by using an MSDE database.
Follow these steps:

1. Start Web Matrix, and navigate to the `C:\BAND\Chapter03` folder.

2. Select File ➤ New, and create a new simple data report called
   `msde_oledb.aspx`.

3. Switch to the All view of the document, and replace the second `<%@ import
   %>` statement with the following:

   ```
   <%@ import Namespace="System.Data.OleDb" %>
   ```

4. Switch to the Code view, and replace the code within the `Page_Load` event
   with the following:

   ```
   string ConnectionString = @"provider=sqloledb; ⏎
     server=(local)\BAND; database=Books; uid=band; pwd=letmein;";
   string CommandText = "select * from Book";
   ```

```
OleDbConnection myConnection = new OleDbConnection(ConnectionString);
OleDbCommand myCommand = new OleDbCommand(CommandText, myConnection);

myConnection.Open();

DataGrid1.DataSource = ↵
  myCommand.ExecuteReader(CommandBehavior.CloseConnection);
DataGrid1.DataBind();

myConnection.Close();
```

5.   Run the page in the browser by pressing F5 or clicking the start icon in the toolbar. If the Web Matrix Web Server is already running, then the browser window will open immediately. If it isn't running, then click the Start button on the pop-up window to start it.

6   The query will be executed against the database, and the results will be returned. As shown in Figure 3-8, you'll see that you've returned all the books in the database.

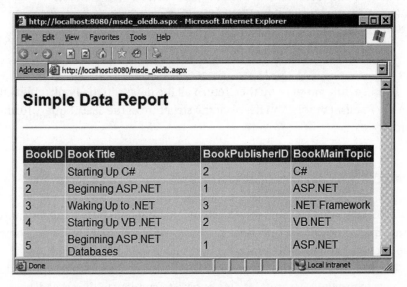

Figure 3-8. Connecting to SQL Server using the OLE DB provider for SQL Server

How It Works

You've already seen how to query a data source using the `OleDbConnection` object when you looked at connecting to Access, and if you compare the `Page_Load` event in the two pages, you'll see that the main difference is in the following connection string, which you're using to connect to the data source:

```
string ConnectionString = @"provider=sqloledb; ↩
   server=(local)\BAND; database=Books; uid=band; pwd=letmein;";
```

The first thing you need to specify in the connection string is that you want to use `sqloledb`, the Microsoft OLE DB Provider for SQL Server. You then specify the details you need to connect to the database—namely, the `server`, `database`, `uid`, and `pwd`.

If you're wondering where you've seen the rest of the connection string before, it's the same as the connection string used for the `SqlConnection` example.

> **NOTE** *If you want to use Windows Authentication with the* `OleDbConnection` *object, you can. Simply add the* `Integrated Security=Yes` *property to the connection string, as you saw when you looked at the* `SqlConnection` *object earlier.*

To add a little variety, you then return all the details in the Book table rather than the Publisher table. You'll look at the structure of the `SELECT` query further in Chapter 4.

Connecting to an Excel Spreadsheet

Although databases are ideal ways to store data, they can be overkill for simple storage and retrieval. Not only does a database add a file size overhead, sometimes simply looking at data in a tabular format, such a spreadsheet, is far easier.

There's no specific OLE DB provider for connecting to an Excel spreadsheet; you have to use the Microsoft Jet data engine to connect to the spreadsheet.

Try It Out: Connecting to an Excel Spreadsheet

In this example, you'll look at retrieving data from an Excel spreadsheet by using the stock levels from an imaginary warehouse. Every week you receive a spreadsheet that details all the stock currently at the warehouse. To use this data in your application, you could enter this manually into the database. However, if you get past the 30 books you currently have, this can quickly become a repetitive and time-consuming task.

In this example, you'll read the data from the spreadsheet and display it on the screen, but as you'll see in later chapters, you could just as easily insert this data into a database. Follow these steps:

1. Start Web Matrix, and navigate to the `C:\BAND\Chapter03` folder.

2. Select File ➤ New, and create a new simple data report with a filename of `excel.aspx`.

3. Switch to the All view of the document, and replace the second `<%@ import %>` statement with the following:

   ```
   <%@ import Namespace="System.Data.OleDb" %>
   ```

4. Switch to the Code view, and replace the contents of the `Page_Load` event with the following:

   ```
   string ConnectionString = @"Provider=Microsoft.Jet.OLEDB.4.0; ⤴
     Data Source=C:\BAND\Database\spreadsheet.xls; ⤴
     Extended Properties=""Excel 8.0;HDR=Yes""";
   string CommandText = "select * from [Book$]";

   OleDbConnection myConnection = new OleDbConnection(ConnectionString);
   OleDbCommand myCommand = new OleDbCommand(CommandText, myConnection);

   myConnection.Open();

   DataGrid1.DataSource = ⤴
     myCommand.ExecuteReader(CommandBehavior.CloseConnection);
   DataGrid1.DataBind();

   myConnection.Close();
   ```

5. Run the page in the browser by pressing F5 or clicking the start icon in the toolbar. If the Web Matrix Web Server is already running, then the browser window will open immediately. If it isn't running, then click the Start button on the pop-up window to start it.

6. The query will be executed against the spreadsheet and the results returned, as shown in Figure 3-9.

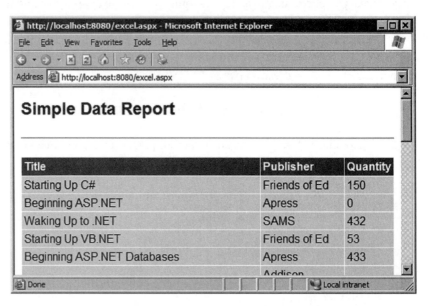

Figure 3-9. Connecting to an Excel spreadsheet

How It Works

As with the Access database version of this page, there isn't an awful lot of difference between connecting to an Excel spreadsheet and connecting to any other data source. The only thing you have to change is the connection string. This is the string for connecting to an Excel spreadsheet:

```
string ConnectionString = @"Provider=Microsoft.Jet.OLEDB.4.0;
  Data Source=C:\BAND\Database\spreadsheet.xls;
  Extended Properties=""Excel 8.0;HDR=Yes"";
```

As you can see, you've specified the provider and file you want to connect to in the same way as you did when you connected to an Access database. What's different is the addition of the Extended Properties property.

The Extended Properties property allows you to specify, as the name suggests, any properties for the provider, with multiple properties separated by semicolons.

Because the default connection type for the Jet engine is Access, the first thing you specify is that you're connecting to an Excel spreadsheet. For Excel, you have four strings you can use depending upon the version of Excel the spreadsheet was created in, as shown in Table 3-1.

Table 3-1. Extended Property Values for Versions of Excel

Extended Property Value	Excel Versions
Excel 3.0	Excel 3
Excel 4.0	Excel 4
Excel 5.0	Excel 5 and Excel 95
Excel 8.0	Excel 97 onward

You can pass another property to the Jet engine—namely, HDR. The HDR property stands for *header*, and setting this to Yes, which is the default, will tell the Jet engine to use the first row of the worksheet as a list of columns; this allows the query you generate to use this as field names. If you set HDR to No, then the entire worksheet becomes the data, and the fields must be referred to as F1, F2, and so on.

> **NOTE** *You'll notice that the query is slightly different for selecting from spreadsheets. Within the spreadsheet, there's a workbook called Book, and you can use this as a table source provided you use it in the correct format—namely, the worksheet name followed by a dollar sign, with all of it surrounded by square brackets (in this case, [Book$]).*

Connecting to a CSV File

As you've seen, connecting to an Excel spreadsheet is no harder than connecting to any other data source. The same is also true of CSV files.

Try It Out: Connecting to a CSV File

In this example, you'll assume that the stock levels are sent to you in a CSV file rather than a spreadsheet. The warehouse may have an archaic system that still outputs information as a CSV file, and you have to use it in your application. Again, you're displaying the information only on the screen, but in a real application you're likely to do something more meaningful with the data in the CSV file. Follow these steps:

1. Start Web Matrix, and navigate to the C:\BAND\Chapter03 folder.

2. Select File ➤ New, and create a new simple data report called text.aspx.

3. Switch to the All view of the document, and replace the second <%@ import %> statement with the following:

```
<%@ import Namespace="System.Data.OleDb" %>
```

4. Switch to the Code view, and replace the content of the Page_Load event with the following:

```
string ConnectionString = @"Provider=Microsoft.Jet.OLEDB.4.0; ↵
  Data Source=C:\BAND\Database; Extended Properties=""text;HDR=YES;"";";
string CommandText = "select * from csv.txt";

OleDbConnection myConnection = new OleDbConnection(ConnectionString);
OleDbCommand myCommand = new OleDbCommand(CommandText, myConnection);

myConnection.Open();

DataGrid1.DataSource = ↵
  myCommand.ExecuteReader(CommandBehavior.CloseConnection);
DataGrid1.DataBind();

myConnection.Close();
```

5. Run the page in the browser by pressing F5 or clicking the start icon in the toolbar. If the Web Matrix Web Server is already running, then the browser window will open immediately. If it isn't running, then click the Start button on the pop-up window to start it.

6. The query will be executed against the text file, and the results will be returned, as shown in Figure 3-10.

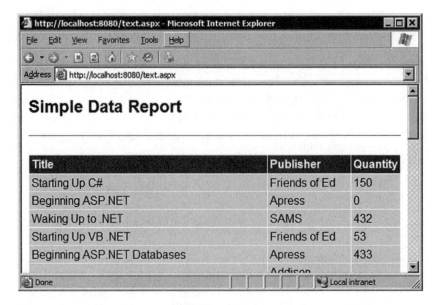

Figure 3-10. Connecting to a CSV file

How It Works

As with the connection to the Excel spreadsheet, you use the Jet engine to connect to a text file. If you take a look at the connection string, you'll see that the string is similar to that when you connect to a spreadsheet:

```
string ConnectionString = @"Provider=Microsoft.Jet.OLEDB.4.0; ⏎
  Data Source=C:\BAND\Database; Extended Properties=""text;HDR=YES;"";";
```

The first thing to notice is that you don't specify a physical file to connect to but only give the directory that contains the file. The provider connects to the directory, allowing you to select the different files in the directory as though they were tables.

As with the Excel spreadsheet connection, you must specify in the Extended Properties that you're using a text file, and you do this using text.

You'll see there's also an HDR extended property that allows you to say whether the file contains a header row that will be used as field names for queries or whether the fields are called F1, F2, and so on.

> **NOTE** *You'll notice that the query is again slightly different from standard SQL for selecting from a text file instead of a database. You specify the directory that contains the files you want to use within the connection string and in the query use the name of the file you want as the table source—in this case,* csv.txt.

The Connection Object in More Detail

Although you've looked at connecting to data sources using three different Connection objects, a few properties and methods that, whilst not essential for connecting to data sources, allow you greater control over the connection to the data source.

You've already seen two of the methods of the Connection object, Open() and Close(), and you'll now look at some of the methods and properties that are available.

> **NOTE** *We won't cover every property and method that's available on every implementation of the Connection object. Several are rarely used, and others will never be used except in advanced situations.*

The ConnectionString Property

In the examples you've looked at so far, you've always created the Connection object by passing the connection string to the constructor. The Connection object also exposes the ConnectionString property, which you can use instead to specify the connection string after you've created the Connection object. So, for the first example you looked at, you could have used the alternative method of setting the connection string, like so:

```
SqlConnection myConnection = new SqlConnection();
myConnection.ConnectionString = ⤶
  @"server=(local)\BAND; database=Books; uid=band; pwd=letmein";
```

The State Property

One of the more useful properties of the Connection object is the State property. This allows you to check what state the connection to the data source is in.

The State property is read-only and may take, in the current release of the .NET runtime, a value of ConnectionState.Open or ConnectionState.Closed.

Although it may not be immediately obvious why you'd need these, when you get to the "Error Handling" section shortly, you'll see where they can be useful.

SQL Server and the PacketSize Property

When connecting to an MSDE or a SQL Server database, one of the properties you may be interested in is the PacketSize property.

> **NOTE** *The* PacketSize *property is available only on the* SqlConnection *object.*

When connecting to an MSDE database, the default packet size of the data transmitted to and from the database is 8 kilobytes (KB), or 8,192 bytes. If the query you're executing against that database is a query that doesn't return any results, then you're returning nearly 8KB worth of useless data. Conversely, if you're returning large amounts of data from the database, then a packet size of 8KB may not be the most efficient size.

The PacketSize property allows you to reduce (or increase) the size of the packets that are sent to and from the database from 512 bytes to 32KB, or 32,767 bytes.

You change the packet size by adding an extra property to the connection string. So, to change the packet size to 512 bytes, you can use the following for the connection string:

```
server=(local)\BAND; database=Books; uid=band; pwd=letmein; Packet Size=512;
```

You can retrieve the current size of the packets being used from the SqlConnection object using the read-only PacketSize property.

There's More?

We aren't going to cover several other properties and methods, so if you need further details, you can find more information on MSDN at the following locations:

- **SqlConnection**: http://msdn.microsoft.com/ library/en-us/cpref/html/ frlrfsystemdatasqlclientsqlconnectionclasstopic.asp

- **OdbcConnection**: http://msdn.microsoft.com/lbrary/en-us/cpref/html/ frlrfsystemdatasqlclientsqlconnectionclasstopic.asp

- **OleDbConnection**: http://msdn.microsoft.com/library/en-us/cpref/html/ frlrfsystemdatasqlclientsqlconnectionclasstopic.asp

To give you a flavor of what properties are available on the Connection object, the download for this chapter contains a file called properties.aspx. If you run this page, it'll open a connection to the MSDE database and output all the property values for that connection using the SqlConnection, OleDbConnection, and OdbcConnection objects—it's very simple and doesn't add anything to what you've already seen, so we won't explain what's happening. If you copy this file to the Chapter03 folder that you've been working in and run it, you'll see that an awful lot of properties are available that you can use. For the machine that this chapter was written on, some of these values are shown in Figure 3-11.

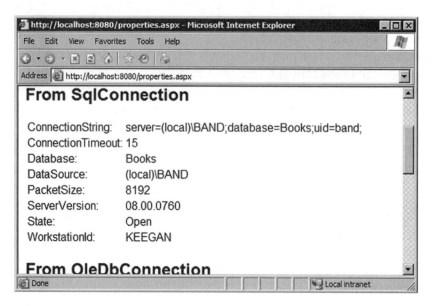

Figure 3-11. Properties for a SqlConnection *to an MSDE database*

Storing the Connection String

In all the examples you've seen so far, you've stored the connection string for the data source on each individual page. Although this works, it can quickly become a maintenance nightmare—what if the data source moves or the security details need to be changed?

You'd have to find every single instance of the connection string and change them. And if you type one of them incorrectly, you've introduced an error into the application that may not be discovered immediately.

What you need is a way to store this information in one place and have all the different pages that need to know the connection string use the same connection string. You can accomplish this easily by storing the connection string in the web.config file and using the value from here in the pages that require it.

> **NOTE** *The* web.config *file holds all the configuration details for a given application. You can control a lot of settings on an individual application basis; for more information, refer to* http://msdn.microsoft.com/library/en-us/cpguide/html/ cpconaspnetconfiguration.asp.

Try It Out: Storing the Connection String in web.config

This section moves to more robust and maintainable code by showing how you can store configuration information in web.config. You'll copy the first example in the chapter, msde.aspx, and modify it to read the required connection string from web.config.

Although the example in the code download contains the MSDE version of this example, nothing is stopping you from using any of the other examples—just remember to use the correct connection string in step 3. Follow these steps:

1. Start Web Matrix, and navigate to the C:\BAND\Chapter03 folder.

2. Select File ➤ New, and create a new web.config file from the General templates. Accept the default name of web.config.

3. Remove the entire contents of web.config, and replace it with the following:

    ```
    <configuration>
      <appSettings>
        <add key="MSDEConnectString" ⤵
          value="server=(local)\BAND;database=Books;uid=band;pwd=letmein" />
      </appSettings>
    </configuration>
    ```

4. Open Windows Explorer, and navigate to the C:\BAND\Chapter03 folder. Copy msde.aspx, and give the new file the name of config.aspx.

5. Return to Web Matrix, and refresh the file list by clicking the Chapter03 folder and selecting Refresh from the context menu.

6. Open config.aspx, and switch to the code version of the page.

7. In the Page_Load event, change the line that defines the connection string as follows:

    ```
    string ConnectionString = ⤵
      ConfigurationSettings.AppSettings["MSDEConnectString"];
    string CommandText = "select * from Publisher";
    ```

8. Run the page in the browser by pressing F5 or clicking the start icon in the toolbar. If the Web Matrix Web Server is already running, then the browser window will open immediately. If it isn't running, then click the Start button on the pop-up window to start it.

9. The query will be executed against the database using the Connection-String taken from web.config, and the results from the query will, not surprisingly, be the same as those for the original version of the page. This was shown earlier in Figure 3-5.

How It Works

As briefly mentioned, web.config can contain a plethora of settings that can control how your application functions, and Web Matrix adds a few of these (as comments) that it thinks you may need. It's always best to remove everything so that you're left with just these basics:

```
<configuration>
</configuration>
```

You can always add the configuration settings you need.

To add your own settings, you need to add an <appSettings> element, if it doesn't exist, and then each setting you want to add needs its own <add> element. Within the <add> element, you can use the key and value attributes to specify the setting, like so:

```
<appSettings>
  <add key="MSDEConnectString"
    value="server=(local)\BAND;database=Books;uid=band;pwd=letmein" />
</appSettings>
```

You've added a configuration setting called MSDEConnectString with the value being the connection string that you need to connect to the database.

To access values stored in web.config, you use the ConfigurationSettings.AppSettings property. This is a static property in the System.Configuration namespace, and you must request the setting that you require:

```
string ConnectionString =
  ConfigurationSettings.AppSettings["MSDEConnectString"];
```

In this case, you want the `MSDEConnectString` setting, and you assign this to the `ConnectionString` variable. As you've already looked at in the earlier examples, this is then used to create the connection to the database.

Be careful when modifying `web.config` because it's case sensitive. `<appSettings>` isn't the same as `<appsettings>` and will cause an exception to be thrown when `web.config` is parsed. However, the data you're storing isn't case sensitive, and you can access the `MSDEConnectString` setting using any combination of uppercase and lowercase; for example, `MSDECONNECTSTRING` and `msdeconnectstring` both all return the same value if you pass this to the `AppSettings` property or change the value of the key attribute in `web.config`.

Error Handling

As any programmer worth his or her salt will tell you, the thing you need to be careful with is error handling. You're never going to write code that doesn't fall over at some point—whether this is an error with the code or something outside of the scope of the code (such as someone unplugging the database server).

Unless you have some way of handling any errors that occur, any problems you encounter can have the side effect of leaving connections to data source open—which, if you're using connection pooling (as the `SqlConnection` object does as standard) can quickly lead to problems with no connections available.

Try It Out: Catching and Handling Errors

You should already be familiar with the `try..catch..finally` syntax for handling errors, so you'll now see how to use this syntax to handle any errors that may occur within an ASP.NET page. If an error occurs, you'll log an error in the Event log and close the open database connection.

You're again looking at error handling only in relation to one of the data sources you could use. All the information you're giving is equally applicable to any data source you may want to use. Follow these steps:

1. Start Web Matrix, and navigate to the `C:\BAND\Chapter03` folder.

2. Create a new simple data report called `error.aspx`.

3. Switch to the All view of the page, and add the following imports statement to the top of the page:

   ```
   <%@ import Namespace="System.Diagnostics" %>
   ```

4. Change the code in the Page_Load event to the following:

```
SqlConnection myConnection = new SqlConnection();

try
{
  string ConnectionString = ↵
    ConfigurationSettings.AppSettings["MSDEConnectString"];
  string CommandText = "select * from Publishers";

  myConnection.ConnectionString = ConnectionString;
  SqlCommand myCommand = new SqlCommand(CommandText, myConnection);

  myConnection.Open();

  DataGrid1.DataSource = myCommand.ExecuteReader();
  DataGrid1.DataBind();
}
catch (Exception ex)
{
  // log the error to the Application event log
  EventLog myEventLog = new EventLog("Application");
  myEventLog.Source="BANDC03";
  myEventLog.WriteEntry(ex.ToString(), EventLogEntryType.Error);

  // now rethrow the error
  throw(ex);
}
finally
{
  // close the database connection
  myConnection.Close();
}
```

5. Run the page in the browser by pressing F5 or clicking the start icon in the toolbar. If the Web Matrix Web Server is already running, then the browser window will open immediately. If it isn't running, then click the Start button on the pop-up window to start it.

6. You should immediately be presented with an error, as shown in Figure 3-12.

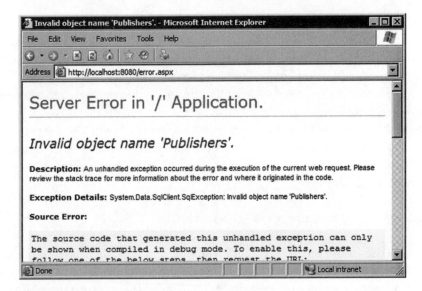

Figure 3-12. The error presented to the user

7. Open the Event Viewer, and in the Application log you'll see the error has been logged, as shown in Figure 3-13.

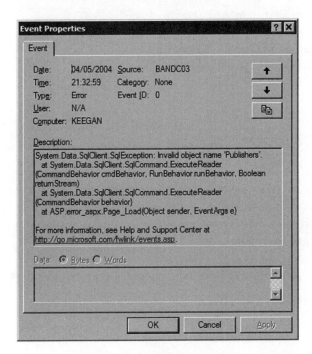

Figure 3-13. The error has been logged in the Event log.

How It Works

The code for this example is a little more complex than you've already seen, but nothing should really cause any problems. You should already be familiar with error handling in .NET, and you've moved some of the code for accessing the database around to fit within the try..catch..finally paradigm.

The first thing you need to do within the Page_Load event handler, before you get to any error handling code, is create the Connection object you need. You must do this here because the connection object needs to be "global" to the entire event handler. If you'd created it in the try block, it wouldn't be available in the catch or the finally block. You create the Connection object without specifying the connection string, like so:

```
SqlConnection myConnection = new SqlConnection();
```

You then move into the try block. The code you've got here is the same as you've seen in the previous example; the only difference is that instead of creating the Connection object with the correct connection string, you set the ConnectionString property of the existing Connection, like so:

```
string ConnectionString = 
  ConfigurationSettings.AppSettings["MSDEConnectString"];
string CommandText = "select * from Publishers";

myConnection.ConnectionString = ConnectionString;
SqlCommand myCommand = new SqlCommand(CommandText, myConnection);

myConnection.Open();

DataGrid1.DataSource = myCommand.ExecuteReader();
DataGrid1.DataBind();
```

The main point to notice in the previous code is the call that you make to execute the query against the database. In all the previous examples, you've accepted the following code that the wizard has generated for you that automatically closes the database connection:

```
DataGrid1.DataSource = myCommand.ExecuteReader(CommandBehavior.CloseConnection);
```

Now that you're handling any errors that occur correctly, you don't want to rely on the database connection being closed automatically, so you remove the specification of the CommandBehavior. This leaves the closing of the connection completely up to you. You'll look at the reasons behind this in Chapter 4.

If any of the code in the try block generates an error, then execution is automatically passed to the catch block, and it's in here that you log the error to the Event log:

```
// log the error to the Application log
EventLog myEventLog = new EventLog("Application");
myEventLog.Source="BANDC03";
myEventLog.WriteEntry(ex.ToString(), EventLogEntryType.Error);
```

To write entries to the Event log, you need to create an instance of the System.Diagnostics.EventLog class and set the Source property. You've added an import statement for the System.Diagnostics namespace to the page, and you can use the short name of EventLog. You're free to create whatever source you want; we used BAND03 to indicate that the error is from this chapter.

You then write the entire error to the Event Log, specifying that it's an error, using the WriteEntry method.

> **NOTE** *You can find more detailed information regarding the* EventLog *class at* http://msdn.microsoft.com/library/en-us/cpref/html/frlrfsystemexception-classtopic.asp.

You then reraise the error that you've handled, like so:

```
// now rethrow the error
throw(ex);
```

If you don't rethrow the error, ASP.NET will, since you've caught the error, assume that it has been handled and that any problems have been rectified. As you're only logging the error and not doing anything to fix it, you rethrow the error so that ASP.NET is aware that a problem occurred. If you don't rethrow the error, the user would be presented with a page that's equally as unhelpful as an ASP.NET error message, as shown in Figure 3-14.

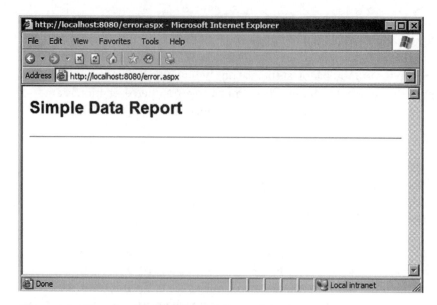

Figure 3-14. You shouldn't hide errors from ASP.NET.

Whether you have an error or not, the `finally` block then executes. All you want to do here is close the connection to the database, like so:

```
// close the database connection
myConnection.Close();
```

Although it's possible to check the state of the connection using the `State` property and close the connection only if it's open, this isn't necessary. If the connection is already closed, then calling the `Close()` method again won't have any unwanted side effects.

Summary

As you saw in Chapter 1, before you can do anything with a data source, you must make a connection to it. You've spent some time in this chapter looking at connecting to several different data sources using the following Connection objects:

- MSDE using the `SqlConnection` object

- MySQL using the `OdbcConnection` object

- Access, Excel, and CSV files using the Jet engine through the `OleDbConnection` object

- SQL Server 6.5 using the SQL Server OLE DB provider through the `OleDbConnection` object

Although you've looked at all these data sources, the beauty of the data provider architecture in ASP.NET is that the paradigm for all of the Connection objects is the same. You'll see in later chapters that this is also the case for all the objects defined in the data provider.

After looking at the different Connection objects, you then briefly looked at some of the other properties and methods of the Connection objects. While not providing a discussion of all of the properties and methods that are available, we showed some of the important ones.

You then looked at storing the connection string in an application-wide configuration setting rather than having it repeated on every page that needs it. From an application maintenance perspective, this is by far a better way to manage the connection string.

At the end of the chapter, you looked at basic error handling and wrote an error handler that ensures you never leave any connections open. We'll come back to error handling and explain it in more detail in Chapter 13 when we discuss handler errors that occur within the case study.

In the next chapter, you'll start looking at proper interactions with data sources. In this chapter, we skipped any code that wasn't directly related to connecting to data sources and concentrated solely on the connection details. You'll soon see that this is only the beginning of the story.

CHAPTER 4

Commands and SQL Queries I

IN CHAPTER 3 you looked at the first step in the data life cycle. The ASP.NET page must create a connection to the data source, open the connection, and, eventually, close it.

You saw that the procedure to do this is the same across all the data providers, and you looked at the main three Connection objects: SqlConnection, OleDbConnection, and OdbcConnection.

In this chapter, you'll look at the first part of step two of the data life cycle—creating and sending SELECT queries to the data source for processing using the ExecuteReader() method.

In Chapter 5, we'll extend this further and show how you can deal with queries that don't return a set of results and show that the ExecuteReader() method isn't the best way to execute non-SELECT queries.

Introducing the Connection and Command Life Cycle

As you saw in Chapter 3, you have a Connection object that, be it a SqlConnection, OleDbConnection, or OdbcConnection, holds the information pertaining to the connection between the page and the data source. Similarly, you have a Command object that represents the SQL query you run against the data source.

We can summarize the life cycle for connecting to a data source and executing queries against it as follows:

- Create the Connection object, and specify the data source.

- Create the Command object.

- Tell the Command object which Connection object to use.

- Specify the query to execute and pass to the Command object.

- Open the connection to the data source.

- Execute a query against the data source.

- Do something with the query results.

- Close the connection to the data source.

The examples in Chapter 3 used the Simple Data Report wizard to generate most of the code for you (shown in truncated form here):

```
string ConnectionString =
  @"server=(local)\BAND;database=Books; uid=band;pwd=letmein";
string CommandText = "select * from Publisher";
SqlConnection myConnection = new SqlConnection(ConnectionString);
SqlCommand myCommand = new SqlCommand(CommandText, myConnection);

myConnection.Open();

DataGrid1.DataSource = myCommand.ExecuteReader(CommandBehavior.CloseConnection);
DataGrid1.DataBind();

myConnection.Close();
```

You can see that the code generated matches the life cycle summarized previously, but the order of some of the steps is slightly different.

Although you must execute all of the steps in the life cycle you don't have to execute them in the order that you saw above. Almost any order will do as long as the connection to the data source is open before you try to execute any queries against it.

Having an open connection to the data source is resource intensive, and you want to keep the connection open for as short a time as possible—open it at the last possible moment and close it as soon as you're finished with it. In other words, don't have connections open for any longer than is absolutely necessary.

You can perform a multitude of different tasks through a Command object that are quite complex compared to the basic life cycle we've shown previously. Now that you have an idea of what you're looking at, it's time to dive straight in.

Introducing the Command Object

As you saw in Chapter 3, you use a different Connection object depending upon your connection choice. It probably won't come as any great surprise that there are three corresponding Command objects for executing queries against the data source.

> **NOTE** *Although you have different Command objects, you'll concentrate on query-ing Microsoft SQL Server 2000 Desktop Engine (MSDE) in both this and the next chapter, and the examples you'll look at deal solely with using* SqlConnection *and* SqlCommand *objects to query the database. However, everything that's discussed in relation to the* SqlConnection *object is equally applicable to the* OleDbCommand *and* OdbcCommand *objects. Where you prefix objects with* Sql, *you can, unless noted, replace these with an* OleDb *or* Odbc *version of the same object. In the code download for the chapter, you'll find* access *and* mysql *folders that contain the corresponding code for Microsoft DataBase (MDB) and MySQL databases.*

Creating a Command

Creating a Command object is straightforward, and in the truncated code listing you've just looked at, you saw one way of doing this by passing the query and connection to the Command object constructor.

The SqlCommand object has four constructors that allow the Command object to be configured as you require. The four constructors are as follows:

- **SqlCommand()**: This constructor creates a Command object that has nothing configured, and you must, at a minimum, specify a connection to use and the query you want to execute. You can specify these, as you'll see shortly, using the Connection and CommandText properties.

- **SqlCommand(string)**: This allows you to specify the query you want to execute, although you'll still have to provide a connection, using the Connection property.

- **SqlCommand(string, SqlConnection)**: This specifies both the query you want to execute and the connection you want to use. This is the constructor that the Simple Data Report wizard in Web Matrix uses.

- **SqlCommand(string, SqlConnection, SqlTransaction)**: This allows you to specify, along with the connection and query, the transaction you want this Command object to participate in. You'll look at transactions in more detail when you look at the case study in Chapter 13.

Although you have four different versions of the constructor to use, nothing is stopping you from using whichever version you find more comfortable—or as Microsoft likes to say, "You have a lifestyle choice."

As you've already seen, the Simple Data Report wizard uses the two-parameter version, like so:

```
SqlCommand myCommand = new SqlCommand(CommandText, myConnection);
```

This is equivalent to the following:

```
SqlCommand myCommand = new SqlCommand(CommandText);
myCommand.Connection = myConnection;
```

This is also equivalent to the following:

```
SqlCommand myCommand = new SqlCommand();
myCommand.CommandText = CommandText;
myCommand.Connection = myConnection;
```

Use whichever version you feel more comfortable with as long as you remember to set all the necessary properties before you open the connection and attempt to execute the query against the database.

The version you're most likely to use is the version that the Simple Data Report wizard uses, and this is what you'll use for the rest of this chapter.

Introducing Query Commands

The first type of command you'll see is the query command; in other words, it's a query you execute against the database that returns a set of rows that contains the data you require.

You already briefly looked at query commands when you learned how to connect to the database in Chapter 3, but, as you'll recall, we simply skipped any discussion of code that wasn't related to opening and closing the connection to the database.

To return data from a database, you use the SELECT query; the basic format of the SELECT query is as follows:

```
SELECT <select column list>
FROM <table list>
WHERE <constraints>
ORDER BY <order column list>
```

As you can see, a SELECT query has four parts, and you must provide only two of them. A SELECT query must always have a `<select column list>` and a `<table list>`, but the WHERE and ORDER BY clauses are optional and allow you to filter and sort the data you're retrieving.

> **NOTE** *Instead of listing the columns you want to retrieve with the query, it's also possible to use the* `SELECT *` *to return all the columns from the query. It's better to explicitly list the columns to return rather than relying on returning all the columns—not only is it quicker (the database doesn't have to compile a list of columns to return before it executes the query) and produces less network traffic (you're not returning columns you don't need), but it also makes the code more readable because anyone can see what the query is returning without having to look at the database structure.*

The SELECT query can get confusing quickly, so we'll start with a simple example before expanding on it to sort the results by adding an ORDER BY clause to the SELECT query. We'll then expand the example by selecting data that's in more than one table by extending the `<table list>` to include more than one table using the INNER JOIN syntax to link two tables. In the final example, we'll show how to constrain what you're returning by adding a WHERE BY clause that limits the results returned from the database.

> **NOTE** *We're not trying to teach you every little nuance of SQL here; we're showing only a small subset of what's possible. Appendix B contains more details of the various SQL commands. For a complete reference, refer to* The Programmer's Guide to SQL *(Apress, 2003).*

Querying a Single Table

The easiest form of SELECT query you can make against the database is to query for values from a single table. In this case, you'll list all the books that are in the database.

Try It Out: Querying a Single Table

This example is the basis for the rest of the SELECT examples you'll see. You'll start with a simple SELECT query that returns data from the database and presents it to the user. Follow these steps:

1. Start Web Matrix, and navigate to the `C:\BAND\Chapter04` folder.

2. Create a new `web.config` file, and replace the contents of it with the following:

```
<configuration>
  <appSettings>
    <add key="MSDEConnectString" ⤴
      value="server=(local)\BAND;database=Books;uid=band;pwd=letmein" />
  </appSettings>
</configuration>
```

3. Create a new filtered data report called `select.aspx`.

4. Switch to the Design view of the page, enter **BAND Books** for the title of the page, and enter **Select a Publisher** for the text to the left of the drop-down list, as shown in Figure 4-1.

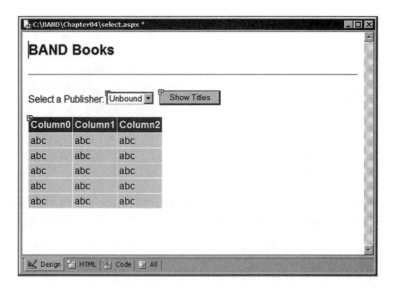

Figure 4-1. Setting the labels on the form correctly

5. Switch to the Code view of the page, and remove all of the code in the Page_Load event.

6. Replace the code within the ApplyFilter_Click event handler with the following:

```
// create the connection object
string ConnectionString = ↵
   ConfigurationSettings.AppSettings["MSDEConnectString"];
SqlConnection myConnection = new SqlConnection(ConnectionString);

// SET UP THE BOOKS
try{
   // create the Command object
   string CommandTextBooks = ↵
      "SELECT BookTitle, BookPublisherID FROM Book";
   SqlCommand myCommandBooks = ↵
      new SqlCommand(CommandTextBooks, myConnection);

   // open the database connection
   myConnection.Open();

   // do the data binding
   DataGrid1.DataSource = myCommandBooks.ExecuteReader();
   DataGrid1.DataBind();
}
catch (Exception ex){
   throw(ex);
}
finally{
   // close the database connection
   myConnection.Close();
}
```

7. Start the page by pressing F5 or clicking the start icon on the toolbar, starting the ASP.NET Web Matrix Web Server if necessary. The page will initially be unpopulated, but clicking the Show Titles button will execute the ApplyFilter_Click event handler, executing the SELECT query against the database and returning the results shown in Figure 4-2.

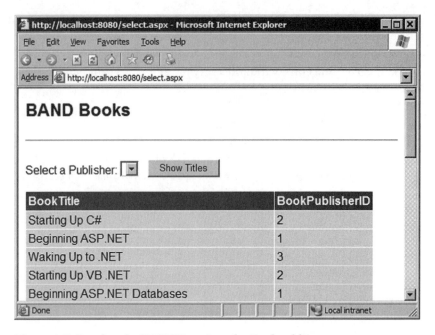

Figure 4-2. Results of a SELECT against the Book table

How It Works

Although this example looks a lot more complex than the examples you saw in Chapter 3, there isn't anything here you haven't looked at yet or you shouldn't be reasonably familiar with, since you're already familiar with ASP.NET.

The example uses one of the Web Matrix built-in templates as the basis for the page because you'll use the extra functionality it gives you shortly. You've used part of this new code by choosing to do something only when the Show Titles button is clicked. The Web Matrix template has kindly linked the click event for the button to the `ApplyFilter_Click` event handler, and it's in here that you've placed all the code. You'll look at the Select a Publisher drop-down list in a later example, so for now just forget that it's there.

The code in the `ApplyFilter_Click` event handler is the same as the code you saw at the end of Chapter 3—you have the requisite error handling in place, and you load the connection string from `web.config`.

You don't need to look again at something that's relatively fresh in your mind. What you should be really interested in with this example is the two pieces of the puzzle we skipped over in Chapter 3: the SELECT query you execute and how you actually execute the query against the database.

The SELECT query you use to select all of the books is about as simple as it can get. You specify the fields you want to retrieve and the table you want to retrieve them from, like so:

```
SELECT BookTitle, BookPublisherID
FROM Book
```

OK—it could have been simpler; you could have returned only one column, but returning two is only a little more complex. You specify the columns you want to retrieve separated by commas (in this case, BookTitle and BookPublisherID) and the table from which you want the data to be returned after the FROM statement.

> **NOTE** *Although you can refer to the columns using only the name of the column—for example, BookID—the correct name of the column is actually Book.BookID. The database allows you to use this shorthand version because there's no confusion as from which table the column is coming. There's no restriction on the names of columns, and when you join tables it's likely that columns with the same name will appear in multiple tables. The only way you can distinguish which column you're after is to use the "full name" syntax for specifying the column name.*

When you want to execute a query against the database, you need to accomplish three tasks. You must first create the Command object you need, then open the connection to the database, and finally execute the query.

You looked earlier at creating a Command object, and you can create a new Command object by passing the query to execute and connection to use to the constructor:

```
SqlCommand myCommandBooks = new SqlCommand(CommandTextBooks, myConnection);
```

You know how to open a connection to the database using the Open() method of the Connection object; once the connection is open, you can use the ExecuteReader() method to execute the query against the database and return the results in the format you require, like so:

```
DataGrid1.DataSource = myCommandBooks.ExecuteReader();
```

The ExecuteReader() method of the Command object returns a DataReader that contains the results of the query. In this example, you're using a SqlCommand object so you get a `SqlDataReader`—if you were using the `OleDbCommand` object, you'd get an `OleDbDataReader`, and for the `OdbcCommand` object you'd get an `OdbcDataReader`.

In this example, you bind the `SqlDataReader` to a DataGrid. You'll look at the DataReader objects and data binding in much more detail in Chapters 6–8.

`ExecuteReader()` is one of three Execute methods that are common across all the Command objects, and which one you'll use depends upon what you're trying to accomplish with your query. You'll take a closer look at the three `Execute()` methods in the later "Using the Execute Methods" section, but before that you'll get an introduction to the SELECT query by looking at the ORDER BY and WHERE clauses.

Ordering the Results

One of the problems with the results you've received in the previous example is that they're not ordered. You've returned all of the records in the database in whatever order the records were entered into the database. If you look at Figure 4-2, you'll see that trying to find a specific book will require a lot of work on the behalf of the reader.

What you need to do is order the results, and SQL provides this ability with the ORDER BY clause of the SELECT query.

Try It Out: Ordering by Book Title

In this example, you'll build upon the simple SELECT query of the last example and sort the books alphabetically. Follow these steps:

1. If you've closed `select.aspx` from the previous example, then reopen it.

2. Switch to the Code view of the page, and modify the query within the `ApplyFilter_Click` event handler that you're executing, like so:

   ```
   string CommandTextBooks = ⏎
     "SELECT BookTitle, BookPublisherID ⏎
     FROM Book ORDER BY BookTitle";
   ```

3. Execute the page, and start the ASP.NET Web Matrix Web Server if necessary. The results will be the same as the previous example except that the books will be in alphabetical order, as shown in Figure 4-3.

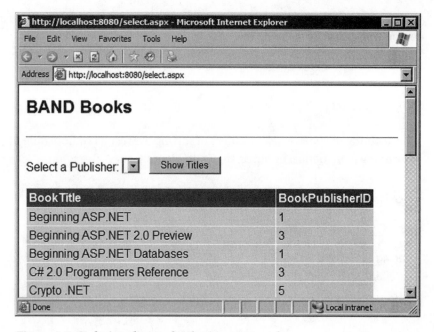

Figure 4-3. Ordering the results that are returned

How It Works

By simply appending an ORDER BY clause to the query you're executing, you've ordered the results in ascending alphabetical order, like so:

```
SELECT BookTitle, BookPublisherID
FROM Book
ORDER BY BookTitle
```

Adding the ORDER BY clause and specifying a text column sorts, as you can see in Figure 4-3, the results alphabetically on that column. Being allowed to sort alphabetically on text columns isn't the only thing the ORDER BY clause allows you to do. If it was, you wouldn't get very far.

If you specify a column for the ORDER BY clause, the sort order is, by default, ascending. The query you've used to sort the results that you get in Figure 4-3 is equivalent to specifying a sort order of ASC along with the column, like so:

```
SELECT BookTitle, BookPublisherID
FROM Book
ORDER BY BookTitle ASC
```

Ascending order isn't the only way you can sort columns; you can also sort in descending order using DESC, like so:

```
SELECT BookTitle, BookPublisherID
FROM Book
ORDER BY BookTitle DESC
```

Executing this query has the affect of sorting the results by book title in descending alphabetical order, as shown in Figure 4-4.

BookTitle	BookPublisherID
Waking Up to .NET	3
VB .NET Reflection Handbook	1
System.NET Class Library Reference	2
Starting Up VB. NET	2
Starting Up C#	2

Figure 4-4. Sorting by book title in descending alphabetical order

Although the examples you've seen sort on a text column, BookTitle, you can actually sort on any type of column no matter what the type—dates will be sorted earliest to latest if you specify an ascending order and latest to earliest if you specify descending. Numbers are sorted smallest to largest or largest to smallest. Each type of column follows its own rules, and the ordering they impose generally makes sense.

You can see how ordering applies to nontext columns if you order the results by BookPublisherID, like so:

```
SELECT BookTitle, BookPublisherID
FROM Book
ORDER BY BookPublisherID
```

Executing this query returns the results in ascending BookPublisherID order, as shown in Figure 4-5.

BookTitle	BookPublisherID
Beginning ASP.NET	1
Beginning ASP.NET Databases	1
Dive Into Databases with ASP.NET and VB .NET	1
MySQL in .NET	1
Delve Into Intermediate Language	1

Figure 4-5. Sorting by an integer column, BookPublisherID

You can also return the results in descending BookPublisherID order if you wanted, and the books that have a BookPublisherID of 5 would be at the beginning of the results rather than those shown in Figure 4-5.

The ORDER BY clause also allows you to sort the results on multiple columns. If you look at the results in Figure 4-5, you'll see that, although you've sorted by BookPublisherID, the BookTitle column is unsorted. What you really want is the results sorted by BookPublisherID and then sorted by BookTitle.

You can accomplish this relatively easily by specifying the two columns you want to order separated by commas after the ORDER BY clause, like so:

```
SELECT BookTitle, BookPublisherID
FROM Book
ORDER BY BookPublisherID, BookTitle
```

This will order the books by BookPublisherID and BookTitle. Both of the sorts will be in ascending order, as you can see from the results returned in Figure 4-6.

BookTitle	BookPublisherID
Beginning ASP.NET	1
Beginning ASP.NET Databases	1
Delve Into Intermediate Language	1
Dive Into Databases with ASP.NET and VB .NET	1
MySQL in .NET	1

Figure 4-6. Sorting on multiple columns

It's also possible to have different sort orders on different columns by specifying the sort order you want for each column, like so:

```
SELECT BookTitle, BookPublisherID
FROM Book
ORDER BY BookPublisherID DESC, BookTitle
```

You want the results by BookPublisherID in descending order and then by BookTitle in ascending order, and, as you'll see in Figure 4-7, this is exactly the order that the results are returned.

BookTitle	BookPublisherID
Crypto .NET	5
Games .NET	5
Jumping from Java to C#	5
Jumping from VB6 to VB .NET	5
Open-Source .NET	5

Figure 4-7. Sorting on multiple columns with different sort orders

Querying Multiple Tables

If you look at the results you received from the previous example (Figure 4-3), you'll see that although you return the title of the book correctly, the publisher is simply an integer. If you recall the database design from Chapter 2, you'll remember that the BookPublisherID field in the Book table corresponds to the PublisherID field in the Publisher table. Unless you're capable of remembering vast quantities of data, the integer on its own won't be a lot of use. What's needed is some way of joining the Book and Publisher tables so that, instead of returning the BookPublisherID, you can return the name of the publisher instead.

SQL allows you to return data from multiple tables by using the JOIN clause when you specify from which tables you want to return data. You'll now see a JOIN in action by building on the previous example, but instead of returning BookPublisherID, you'll return the name of the publisher instead.

Try It Out: Querying Multiple Tables

As you saw in the previous example, sometimes you need to query across more than one table—after all returning an integer identifier for the publisher is not very meaningful. In this example, you'll see table joins in action by building on the previous example and returning the name of the publisher instead of BookPublisherID. Follow these steps:

1. If you've closed `select.aspx` from the previous example, then reopen it.

2. Switch to the Code view of the page, and within the `ApplyFilter_Click` event, change the line that specifies the command text to the following:

    ```
    string CommandTextBooks =  ⤶
      "SELECT Book.BookTitle, Publisher.PublisherName ⤶
      FROM Book INNER JOIN Publisher ⤶
      ON Book.BookPublisherID = Publisher.PublisherID ⤶
      ORDER BY Book.BookTitle";
    ```

3. Start the page by pressing F5 or clicking the start icon on the toolbar. The query will be run against the database and the results returned as shown in Figure 4-8.

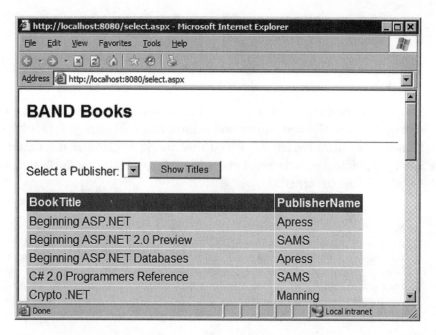

Figure 4-8. Results of a SELECT against the Book and Publisher table

How It Works

As with the previous example, the only line you've changed is the following one, which specifies the query you want to execute:

```
SELECT Book.BookTitle, Publisher.PublisherName
FROM Book
  INNER JOIN Publisher ON Book.BookPublisherID = Publisher.PublisherID
ORDER BY Book.BookTitle
```

The first thing you'll notice with the query is that you're now using the "full name" syntax to refer to the columns. Although the database doesn't have any column names that could clash, it's good practice when returning data from multiple tables to use the full name even if you don't have to do so. Not only does it make it easier to see which table a column comes from, it should also make the query a little faster—the database won't have to find the table that contains the column because you've already specified it.

The following FROM clause, and in particular the INNER JOIN you've added, is the important part of the query:

```
FROM Book
  INNER JOIN Publisher ON Book.BookPublisherID = Publisher.PublisherID
```

When joining tables using an INNER JOIN, the database combines both tables into one "supertable" and returns only records that exist on both sides of the join. It does this by using the table specified after the FROM clause as the master table and by appending matching records in the table specified after the INNER JOIN based upon the ON criteria.

> **NOTE** *Using INNER JOIN rather than simply using JOIN should give a clue that this type of join isn't the only one you have; there are in fact three other types of join. SQL also defines RIGHT JOIN, LEFT JOIN, and CROSS JOIN that allow you to change how the tables in the join are actually joined. The INNER JOIN is by far the most common type of join you'll use; we won't show the other types of join in any detail.*

The ON criterion specifies how the two tables you're joining are being joined. In this case, you specify that the BookPublisherID column in the Book table is equal to the PublisherID column in the Publisher table. This tells the database that the two columns are equal and to combine the tables based on this.

If you could see the constructed "supertable" for this join of the Book and Publisher table, you'd initially have all of the columns in both tables, as shown in truncated form in Figure 4-9.

BookID	BookTitle	BookPublisherID	BookMainTopic	PublisherID	PublisherName	PublisherCity
2	Beginning ASP.NET	1	ASP.NET	1	Apress	Berkeley
26	Beginning ASP.NET 2.0 Preview	3	Whidbey	3	SAMS	Indianapolis
5	Beginning ASP.NET Databases	1	ASP.NET	1	Apress	Berkeley
27	C# 2.0 Programmers Reference	3	Whidbey	3	SAMS	Indianapolis
23	Crypto .NET	5	C#	5	Manning	Greenwich

Figure 4-9. "Supertable" from the join of the Book and Publisher tables

As you can see, you've got the BookID, BookTitle, BookPublisherID, and BookMainTopic fields from the Book table and the PublisherID, PublisherName, and PublisherCity from the Publisher table. The super table contains a further two/three columns that we don't have the space to show. In addition, both the BookPublisherID and the PublisherID fields have the same value as these are the fields that you specified in the INNER JOIN statement.

The query actually specifies only that the Book.BookTitle and Publisher.PublisherName fields are returned from the query, and the remaining columns are ignored, as shown in Figure 4-10.

BookTitle	PublisherName
Beginning ASP .NET	Apress
Beginning ASP .NET 2.0 Preview	SAMS
Beginning ASP .NET Databases	Apress
C# 2.0 Programmers Reference	SAMS
Crypto .NET	Manning

Figure 4-10. Returning a subset of the columns from the "supertable"

When you looked at sorting columns in the previous example, you learned that you can sort of set a results by more than one column. The same is also true if you have multiple tables, and you can sort across any of the columns that are in the "supertable." So to sort by PublisherName and then by BookTitle, you'd add both of these to the ORDER BY clause in the order you wanted the sorting to take place, like so:

```
SELECT Book.BookTitle, Publisher.PublisherName
FROM Book
  INNER JOIN Publisher ON Book.BookPublisherID = Publisher.PublisherID
ORDER BY Publisher.PublisherName, Book.BookTitle
```

So, rather than having a list of books that's sorted by the title of the book, you'll now have a list of books sorted by the name of the publisher and then book title, as shown in Figure 4-11.

BookTitle	PublisherName
Deep Down ASP .NET	Addison-Wesley
Deep Down C#	Addison-Wesley
Deep Down VB. NET	Addison-Wesley
Journeyman Webforms	Addison-Wesley
Journeyman Winforms	Addison-Wesley

Figure 4-11. You can also sort using columns from different tables.

> **NOTE** *Although a simple join between two tables isn't that complex, the entire story behind joins is a lot more complex than this. It's possible to have multiple joins in the same SQL query and also to mix different join types within the same SQL query. They can pretty soon become hideously complex. To explain every possible combination of join would quickly lead into two or three chapters in itself, and that's not what we're trying to teach you here. You can find more information on joins and SQL in general in* The Programmer's Guide to SQL *(Apress, 2003).*

Filtering the Results

In the previous three examples, you've come from writing a simple query that takes data from one table to being able to order the results you get and join two tables to retrieve user-friendly data.

What we haven't yet covered is how you can constrain the queries that you're executing to return only those records that meet the criteria you specify.

In the first example, we pointed out that there was some code you weren't going to look at just yet and you'd look at a little later. You'll explore that code here and further build upon the previous example, adding the facility to filter the books by publisher.

You filter the results of a query by using a WHERE clause to constrain the records that are returned. You can do this in the following two ways:

- By modifying the query that you're executing at runtime and specifying the variables within the WHERE clause directly

- By placing parameters within the WHERE clause of the query at design time and changing the values of these parameters at runtime

You'll look at each of these methods in turn.

Try It Out: Filtering the Results

In this example, you'll again build upon the previous example and allow the user to select the publisher in which they're interested. Once a selection has been made, only the books for that publisher will be returned. Follow these steps:

1. If you've closed select.aspx from the previous example, then reopen it.

2. Add the following code to the empty Page_Load event handler:

```
// only want to populate controls on first page load
if (!Page.IsPostBack)
{
  // create the connection object that we need
  string ConnectionString = ↵
    ConfigurationSettings.AppSettings["MSDEConnectString"];
  SqlConnection myConnection = new SqlConnection(ConnectionString);
```

```
// SET UP THE PUBLISHERS
try{
  // create the Command object
  string CommandTextPublisher = ↵
   "SELECT PublisherID, PublisherName ↵
   FROM Publisher";
  SqlCommand myCommandPublishers = ↵
    new SqlCommand(CommandTextPublisher, myConnection);

  // open the database connection
  myConnection.Open();

  // do the data binding
  DropDownList1.DataSource = myCommandPublishers.ExecuteReader();
  DropDownList1.DataTextField = "PublisherName";
  DropDownList1.DataValueField = "PublisherID";
  DropDownList1.DataBind();
  DropDownList1.Items.Insert(0, ↵
    new ListItem("-- All Publishers --", "0"));
}
catch (Exception ex){
  throw(ex);
}
finally{
  // close the database connection
  myConnection.Close();
}
}
```

3. In the `ApplyFilter_Click` event handler, change the code that creates the `CommandTextBooks` string to the following:

```
string CommandTextBooks = ↵
  "SELECT Book.BookTitle, Publisher.PublisherName ↵
  FROM Book INNER JOIN Publisher ↵
  ON Book.BookPublisherID = Publisher.PublisherID";
string filterValue = DropDownList1.SelectedValue;
if (filterValue != "0")
  CommandTextBooks += " WHERE Book.BookPublisherID = " + filterValue;
CommandTextBooks+=" ORDER BY Book.BookTitle";
```

4. Execute the page. On the first load of the page, you'll see that the drop-down list is populated with the available publishers in the database, as shown in Figure 4-12.

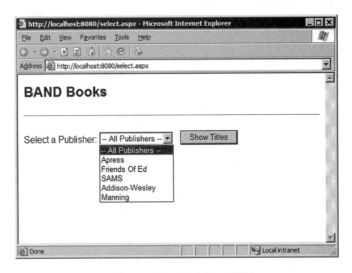

Figure 4-12. Drop-down of available publishers

5. Select -- All Publishers -- from the drop-down list, and click the Show Titles button. This will call the ApplyFilter_Click event handler and populate the DataGrid with the books for all of the publishers, as shown in Figure 4-13.

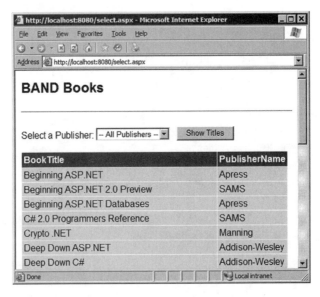

Figure 4-13. You can view the books for all publishers.

6. Select Apress from the drop-down list, and click Show Titles. This will repost the page and populate the DataGrid with only the books published by Apress, as shown in Figure 4-14.

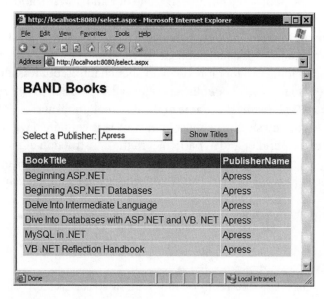

Figure 4-14. But you can also filter by publisher.

7. Select any of the other publishers, and click the Show Titles button to see that the list of books is indeed modified to display only the correct list of published books.

How It Works

Although you've looked at several different examples so far in the book, this is the first page you've seen that starts to give an idea of what's possible with data-driven pages—you've responded to a user selection to modify the results that are returned as part of the query.

If you look at the code for the page, you'll see that, as with all of the examples you've looked at so far, there's code that we don't want to talk about until later chapters. We'll briefly mention this code but not spend too long explaining it and leave the discussion until later.

The Page_Load event handler executes every time the page is loaded (whether a first view or a postback responding to a request from the user), and in data-driven applications you'll want to perform some actions only once, such as populating dynamic controls, rather than every time the page is loaded. You can check for the type of page request using the IsPostBack property of the Page object—this returns true if the page is a postback because of a user request.

On the first view of the page, checking that the Page.IsPostBack property returns false, you populate the publisher drop-down list using data binding and add a further entry for -- All Publishers --.

In the database, the publishers have an ID value of 1 and upward, and, as you'll see shortly, you'll use this to modify the query you're executing against the database. You therefore give the -- All Publishers -- a value of 0, sure in the knowledge that this won't conflict with a real publisher in the database.

We'll cover data binding in a lot more detail in later chapters, but it's worth noting that the query to retrieve the publishers is just a simple SELECT query that returns the PublisherID and PublisherName of the different publishers.

The part of the code you should be most interested in is contained within the ApplyFilter_Click event handler and in particular in the construction of the SQL query you're going to execute against the database. Unlike the previous examples, you build the string depending upon the user's selection; you'll look at each of these in turn.

The first part of the query you need to look at is as follows:

```
SELECT Book.BookTitle, Publisher.PublisherName
FROM Book
  INNER JOIN Publisher ON Book.BookPublisherID = Publisher.PublisherID
```

This is a perfectly valid query in its own right, and it'll return all the books in the database irrespective of the publisher. It's in fact the same query as you used in the previous example with the ORDER BY clause removed. If you recall the SELECT syntax from earlier in the chapter, you'll remember that the WHERE clause to constrain the query must come before the ORDER BY clause—you must filter the query before you can order it—and you have to remove the ORDER BY clause so that you can add the WHERE clause.

To constrain the query, you first retrieve the value of the user's selection from the drop-down list using the SelectedValue property. You store this in a local variable, filterValue, because you'll use it in several places, like so:

```
string filterValue = DropDownList1.SelectedValue;
```

You've stored this value because you can't simply use it to constrain the query as if you've requested all the publishers you don't want to add a constraint. You'll recall that you added an -- All Publishers -- entry to the drop-down list, and if you've selected this, you want to return all the books in the database as opposed to a list of books for a particular publisher. It's when a publisher has been selected that you want to modify the query and you can check whether a specific publisher has been selected by checking for a value that's nonzero. If it's nonzero, you want to add a WHERE clause:

```
CommandTextBooks += " WHERE Book.BookPublisherID = " + filterValue;
```

The effect of this WHERE clause is to tell the database you want only the records returned that have a BookPublisherID that's equal to the value you've specified. As you'll shortly see when you look at the WHERE clause in more detail, you're not limited to checking that values are equal, and you can use several more operators.

> **NOTE** *Although you specify that you want to constrain the query on the Book.BookPublisherID field, nothing is stopping you from using the Publisher.PublisherID field instead. As they're the fields that make the join, you can use either of them and still expect the same results.*

Regardless of whether a WHERE clause has been added to the query, you add an ORDER BY clause so that the books are ordered alphabetically, like so:

```
ORDER BY Book.BookTitle
```

Now that you know how the query is built, you can look at what's actually executed against the database. If you've selected the -- All Publishers -- option, you're not adding a WHERE clause, and the query that's executed is the query you had in the previous example. For example, the following:

```
SELECT Book.BookTitle, Publisher.PublisherName
FROM Book
  INNER JOIN Publisher on Book.BookPublisherID = Publisher.PublisherID
ORDER BY Book.BookTitle
```

will return all the books in the database because you're not constraining the query. However, if you select the Apress option, you want to add a WHERE clause, and the query you execute is as follows:

```
SELECT Book.BookTitle, Publisher.PublisherName
FROM Book
  INNER JOIN Publisher on Book.BookPublisherID = Publisher.PublisherID
WHERE Book.BookPublisherID = 1
ORDER BY Book.BookTitle
```

You constrain the query to return only the results that have a BookPublisherID equal to 1, which is the PublisherID value for Apress.

Try It Out: Using Parameters in Queries

Rather than constructing a SQL query at runtime and passing this to the database to be executed, you can instead use parameters to modify a fixed SQL query. This example will use that methodology to replicate the functionality you saw in the previous example. Follow these steps:

1. In Windows Explorer, navigate to the `C:\BAND\Chapter04` folder and copy `select.aspx`, renaming it to `parameters.aspx`.

2. Open the copied file, `parameters.aspx`, in Web Matrix.

3. Switch to the Code view of the page, and change the `try` block of the `ApplyFilter_Click` event handler to the following:

```
// create the Command object
string CommandTextBooks = ⤶
  "SELECT Book.BookTitle, Publisher.PublisherName ⤶
  FROM Book INNER JOIN Publisher ⤶
  ON Book.BookPublisherID = Publisher.PublisherID ⤶
  WHERE @publisher=0 OR Book.BookPublisherID=@publisher ⤶
  ORDER BY Book.BookTitle";
SqlCommand myCommandBooks = ⤶
  new SqlCommand(CommandTextBooks, myConnection);

// create the parameter and add it to the Command object
SqlParameter myParameter = new SqlParameter();
myParameter.ParameterName = "@publisher";
myParameter.SqlDbType = SqlDbType.Int;
myParameter.Value = DropDownList1.SelectedValue;
myCommandBooks.Parameters.Add (myParameter);

// open the database connection
myConnection.Open();

// do the data binding
DataGrid1.DataSource = myCommandBooks.ExecuteReader();
DataGrid1.DataBind();
```

4. Start the page by pressing F5 or clicking the start icon on the toolbar. Once the page has opened, select Apress from the drop-down list, and click the Show Titles button. The query will be run against the database and the results will be returned as shown in Figure 4-15.

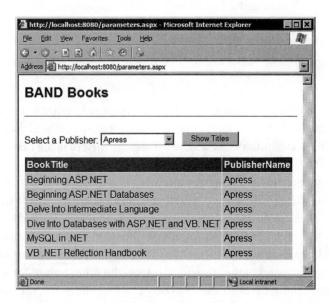

Figure 4-15. You can also use parameters to modify queries.

How It Works

As with most of the examples in this chapter, all you've changed is the query you'll execute against the database. Instead of having a query that's entirely contained within a string, you now have a combination of a string and a `SqlParameter` that you need to populate before the query will function correctly.

Parameters are the means whereby you can pass information into a query at runtime without making any changes to the query. In the previous example, you had to modify the string containing the query to include the value you selected. When you use parameters, you can use the same query string without any modifications and pass in the different parameter values.

> **NOTE** *Parameters are something you'll see a whole lot more of when you look at stored procedures in Chapter 9.*

You add parameters to a query by giving them a name preceded by an at sign (@), which is used in place of any values you may want to change. The query you're executing should become a little clearer straightaway.

```
SELECT Book.BookTitle, Publisher.PublisherName
FROM Book
  INNER JOIN Publisher on Book.BookPublisherID = Publisher.PublisherID
WHERE @publisher=0 OR Book.BookPublisherID=@publisher
ORDER BY Book.BookTitle
```

As you can see, the WHERE clause uses the @publisher parameter to constrain the results you want to return. You have two parts of the constraint, and you've used the OR statement to combine these. The second constraint is the one you'd expect that will return all books that match the value of @publisher, but you have to circumvent this when you haven't selected a specific publisher.

The value for -- All Publishers -- is 0, and if you pass a value of 0 to the query without the first part of the WHERE clause, it will return no results—a book can't have a publisher value of 0. The first part of the WHERE clause traps this and returns true if you have a value of 0 for @publisher. Because of the way the OR clause functions, if either part of the statement is true, the other part of the statement is ignored. Even though a book can't have a publisher value of 0, the overall WHERE clause will return true, and all of the books will be returned.

To add the value of @publisher to the query you use a SqlParameter object. You must first create the necessary SqlParameter object:

```
SqlParameter myParameter = new SqlParameter();
```

Before you can use this parameter, you must set various properties on it—at a bare minimum you must set the name, the data type, and the value of the parameter, like so:

```
myParameter.ParameterName = "@publisher";
myParameter.SqlDbType = SqlDbType.Int;
myParameter.Value = DropDownList1.SelectedValue;
```

The ParameterName must match the name in the query, and the value is simply the value that you want to assign to the parameter—in this case, the SelectedValue of the drop-down list.

You specify the data type using the SqlDbType property and passing in a member of the SqlDbType enumeration. There are values in the enumeration corresponding to all the data types that are available in SQL, and you can use any of them in parameters. In this case, you want a simple integer and to specify SqlDbType.Int. You'll find a full list of the values available in the SqlDbType enumeration in Appendix B along with the equivalent .NET and SQL types.

Once you've created the parameter, you must add it to the Command object before the query executes:

```
myCommandBooks.Parameters.Add (myParameter);
```

Parameters and Commands

Using parameters is one of the few instances where the query to be executed and the corresponding code changes depending upon the Command object you're using. Each of the Command objects utilizes parameters in slightly different ways and requires different queries and changes to the way parameters are added.

Recall from the previous example that the parameters were added with the ParameterName of the SqlParameter matching the name of the parameter in the query passed to the SqlCommand. The query had a parameter called @publisher, and a SqlParameter with its ParameterName set to @publisher was added to the SqlCommand. With named parameters, the SqlConnection object can determine which SqlParameter is required, and even though the parameter was used twice in the query, only one SqlParameter is required.

However, only the SqlCommand object supports named parameters, and both the OdbcCommand and OleDbCommand objects rely on the order that the Parameter objects are added to the Command object to determine how they're inserted into the query.

As named parameters are no longer used, OdbcCommand and OleDbCommand require a slightly different query than SqlCommand. You can no longer use the @ syntax to refer to a parameter; you use a question mark (?) instead, like so:

```
SELECT Book.BookTitle, Publisher.PublisherName
FROM Book
  INNER JOIN Publisher on Book.BookPublisherID = Publisher.PublisherID
WHERE ?=0 OR Book.BookPublisherID=?
ORDER BY Book.BookTitle
```

As you have two parameters (indicated by the two question marks), you must have two Parameter objects added to the Command object—even if, as in this case, the two parameters take the same value.

For the `OdbcCommand` object, you need to create two `OdbcParameter` objects and add them to the `OdbcCommand` object, like so:

```
// add the first parameter
OdbcParameter myParameter1 = new OdbcParameter();
myParameter1.ParameterName = "@pub1";
myParameter1.OdbcType = OdbcType.Int;
myParameter1.Value = DropDownList1.SelectedValue;
myCommandBooks.Parameters.Add (myParameter1);

// add the second parameter
OdbcParameter myParameter2 = new OdbcParameter();
myParameter2.ParameterName = "@pub2";
myParameter2.OdbcType = OdbcType.Int;
myParameter2.Value = DropDownList1.SelectedValue;
myCommandBooks.Parameters.Add (myParameter2);
```

For the `OleDbCommand` object, the process is the same. You create the following two `OleDbParameter` objects and add these to the `OleDbCommand` object:

```
// add the first parameter
OleDbParameter myParameter1 = new OleDbParameter();
myParameter1.ParameterName = "@pub1";
myParameter1.OleDbType = OleDbType.Integer;
myParameter1.Value = DropDownList1.SelectedValue;
myCommandBooks.Parameters.Add (myParameter1);

// add the second parameter
OleDbParameter myParameter2 = new OleDbParameter();
myParameter2.ParameterName = "@pub2";
myParameter2.OleDbType = OleDbType.Integer;
myParameter2.Value = DropDownList1.SelectedValue;
myCommandBooks.Parameters.Add (myParameter2);
```

NOTE *The code download for this chapter contains the* parameters.aspx *files in two other versions—one for each of the other two Command objects. The* Odbc-Connection *version is* mysql/parameters.aspx, *and the* OleDbConnection *version is* access/parameters.aspx.

Introducing the WHERE Clause

In the previous two examples, you've seen briefly that you can use the WHERE clause to restrict the records that you've returned based upon the criteria you specify.

Not only is the WHERE clause used with the SELECT query, it can also be used with the INSERT and UPDATE statements to restrict your actions within the database. You'll look at UPDATE and DELETE in the next chapter, but for now you'll concentrate on what you can do with the WHERE clause.

> **NOTE** *The different operators you'll look at here can be combined in an infinite number of combinations to provide constraints from the very simple that you've already seen to the hideously complex that look as though they go on forever. We can't provide an in-depth guide to everything here, but* The Programmer's Guide to SQL *(Apress, 2003) provides a good explanation.*

Using Comparison Operators

In both of the filtering examples you've seen, you've looked only at comparing two values to see if they're equal. These aren't the only operators available. Table 4-1 describes the standard comparison operators.

Table 4-1. The SQL Comparison Operators

Operator	Definition	Example
=	Equality	BookPublisherID = 1
<>	Inequality	BookPublisherID <> 1
<	Less than	BookPublisherID < 3
>	Greater than	BookPublisherID > 4
<=	Less than or equal to	BookPublisherID <= 3
>=	Greater than or equal to	BookPublisherID >= 4
IS NULL	Test for null values	BookPublisherID IS NULL

You should be familiar with all of the comparison operators; they work in the way that you'd expect.

The only one that you're likely to be unfamiliar with is the IS NULL operator. NULL values in the database can't be compared to any other value and won't appear in any comparison.

So, if you execute the following query, you'd expect to return every book that had a BookPublisherID of any value other than 1:

```
SELECT BookTitle
FROM Book
WHERE BookPublisherID <> 1
```

However, this isn't the case, and if NULL values are allowed for BookPublisherID, you'd have to test for this condition explicitly, like so:

```
SELECT BookTitle
FROM Book
WHERE BookPublisherID <> 1 OR BookPubliserID IS NULL
```

This will return the correct results—books that have a BookPublisherID that isn't equal to 1 and books that have a NULL value for BookPublisherID.

Using Logical Operators

You've already seen the OR logical operator in action when you used parameters to filter the query, and we sneaked it in again at the end of the discussion of comparison operators. This isn't the only logical operator that's available, as you can see in Table 4-2.

Table 4-2. The SQL Logical Operators

Operator	Definition	Usage
AND	Returns true if both conditions are true	a AND b
OR	Returns true if either condition is true	a OR b
NOT	Returns true if the condition is false	NOT a

As with the comparison operators, these operators function exactly as you'd expect them to function.

Using the IN and BETWEEN Operators

SQL also defines two other handy operators that you can use within the WHERE clause to make some of the clauses that you need to execute a little simpler.

The IN operator allows you to specify that you're looking within a series of noncontiguous values and is equivalent to using the OR operator to chain together several different equality comparisons.

If you wanted to return all the books that have a BookPublisherID of 1, 3, or 5, you could execute the following query:

```
SELECT BookTitle
FROM Book
WHERE BookPublisherID = 1 OR BookPublisherID = 3 OR BookPublisherID = 5
```

The IN operator allows you to do this more simply:

```
SELECT BookTitle
FROM Book
WHERE BookPublisherID IN (1,3,5)
```

Both queries will return the same results, as shown in Figure 4-16.

BookTitle	BookPublisherID
Beginning ASP.NET	1
Beginning ASP.NET 2.0 Preview	3
Beginning ASP.NET Databases	1
C# 2.0 Programmers Reference	3
Crypto .NET	5

Figure 4-16. Selecting from a series of values using the IN operator

Similarly, you can use the BETWEEN operator to specify that you're looking within a contiguous range of values. If you wanted to return all the books that have a BookPublisherID of 3, 4, or 5, you could use the AND, <=, and >= operators in conjunction to retrieve the correct books:

```
SELECT BookTitle
FROM Book
WHERE BookPublisherID >= 3 AND BookPublisherID <= 5
```

The BETWEEN operator allows you to simplify this, like so:

```
SELECT BookTitle
FROM Book
WHERE BookPublisherID BETWEEN 3 AND 5
```

Both of these queries will return the results shown in Figure 4-17.

BookTitle	BookPublisherID
Beginning ASP.NET 2.0 Preview	3
C# 2.0 Programmers Reference	3
Crypto .Net	5
Deep Down ASP.NET	4
Deep Down C#	4

Figure 4-17. Selecting from a range of values using the BETWEEN operator

One word of warning when using the BETWEEN operator: You'll notice that you use AND to specify the upper and lower values of the range. This isn't the same as using the AND operator as a logical comparison, so don't get the two confused.

Using the Execute Methods

Before .NET, the most common way of retrieving data from a database was to return an ADO Recordset and interrogate it to determine what you needed. Although this worked, sometimes this isn't appropriate—what if the SELECT query that you executed only ever returned one row containing a single column? Returning a complete Recordset and having to check that there was actually a Recordset before you looked at what the Recordset contained is very long winded.

ADO.NET improves on this by giving you three methods that you can use depending upon what your query needs to do, as shown in Table 4-3.

Table 4-3. The Command Object Execute Methods

Method	Description
`ExecuteNonQuery()`	Used when the SQL query doesn't return any data.
`ExecuteReader()` `ExecuteReader(behavior)`	Used when the SQL query is to return a series of rows from a SELECT query. The data is returned as the correct DataReader for the Command object.
`ExecuteScalar()`	Used when you only want to return the first column from the first row of the SELECT query.

> **NOTE** *There's also a fourth method,* `ExecuteXmlReader`, *which is specific to the* `SqlCommand` *object that you can use to return the results of a query as an* `XmlReader` *rather than a* `SqlDataReader`.

You've already looked at one of the ExecuteReader() methods, and you've seen that this returns a DataReader object that you can use. Unlike the other two ExecuteNonQuery() and ExecuteScalar() methods, the ExecuteReader() method requires an open connection to the database while it's in use, and this can cause you some connection problems. You'll look at this in a little more detail shortly and see why there are two versions of the ExecuteReader() method.

You use ExecuteNonQuery()when the query you're executing doesn't return any information at all from the database. If you're inserting, updating, or deleting data from the database or performing a Data Definition Language (DDL) query, there are no results to return, so you can use the ExecuteNonQuery() method. Although it doesn't return any records from the database, this method does return the count, if available, of the number of rows in the database you affected by the query.

The third method you have is ExecuteScalar(), which is used to return the first value in the first row of the set of records that would be returned. Although not immediately obvious why you'd want to return only this value, you'll see why you need it when you look at SQL scalar commands in Chapter 5.

Using ExecuteReader() and Closing Connections

As you know, the ExecuteReader() method returns a DataReader object that contains the results of the query you've executed against the database. You'll look at using the data that you've returned starting with Chapter 6, but for now you'll take a brief look at the two ways of calling ExecuteReader() and see how this impacts the connection to the database.

When you return a DataReader object from the database, you need to keep a connection to the database open for as long as you're using the DataReader. If the connection is closed, then any attempts to read data from the DataReader will result in an exception being thrown.

There are two overloaded ExecuteReader() methods that control how the connection to the database is handled:

- **ExecuteReader()**: This returns a DataReader and leaves it completely up to you to close the connection to the database.

- **ExecuteReader(behavior)**: This allows you to specify how you want the interaction with the database to take place. You can use several different behavior values, but for these purposes, you'll only ever use Command-Behavior.CloseConnection to close the connection to the database once the DataReader is closed or goes out of scope.

The default behavior for creating a DataReader is to leave the database connection open once the DataReader has been closed or gone out of scope. This is the method you've used throughout this chapter because the error handling you have in place ensures that the connection to the database is always closed.

Before we introduced error handling at the end of Chapter 3, the ExecuteReader() method was called with the CommandBehavior.CloseConnection specified, like so:

```
DataGrid1.DataSource = myCommand.ExecuteReader(CommandBehavior.CloseConnection);
DataGrid1.DataBind();
```

Although you don't explicitly close the connection using a behavior of CommandBehavior.CloseConnection, the connection to the database is automatically closed once the DataReader goes out of scope at the end of the Page_Load event handler.

It's up to you which version of this you want to use, but using the default behavior of leaving the connection open is perhaps the best one from a code readability point of view. There's an explicit Close() call on the connection, and after this point you know for definite that the connection to the database is closed. This is better coding practice because it forces you to think about what you're actually doing rather than relying on the .NET Framework to close objects for you.

Summary

This chapter covered quite a bit of ground. You've learned about the following:

- We've recapped the connection and command life cycle and discussed that the connection to the database should be open for as short a time as possible and the best order to perform the steps in the life cycle.

- You briefly looked at the four constructors for the Command object.

- We introduced SELECT by starting at a simple query from one table.

- You expanded your understanding of the SELECT query by looking at ordering results and by joining tables to retrieve information from both tables in the same query.

- You looked at filtering the results that you returned by modifying the query that you executed at runtime or using parameters to change the values within the query.

- We briefly discussed the WHERE clause and showed that this not only applies to the SELECT query but can also be used with the UPDATE and DELETE statements.

- You then briefly looked at the comparison and logical operators you can use with the WHERE clause and introduced the IN and BETWEEN operators you can use to simplify the constraints that you're adding to the queries.

- We closed the chapter by showing the three execute methods that are available on the Command object.

In this chapter, you've looked only at returning data from the database using the SELECT command and the `ExecuteReader()` method.

In Chapter 2, you saw that there are a lot more ways you can interact with the database, and we've also alluded to these throughout this chapter.

In the next chapter, you'll look at the INSERT, UPDATE, and DELETE queries and learn how you execute them against the database using the `ExecuteNonQuery()` method.

You'll also take a look at SQL scalar functions and how you can use the `ExecuteScalar()` method to return single values from the database rather than a complete DataReader.

CHAPTER 5

Commands and SQL Queries II

IN CHAPTER 4 we introduced the Command object and showed how to use the ExecuteReader() method to execute SELECT queries against the database to return the results. As you know from Chapter 2, the SELECT query isn't the only type of query you can execute. At the end of Chapter 4, you saw that you can use two further methods to execute these types of queries.

The two methods you'll explore further in this chapter are as follows:

- **ExecuteNonQuery()**: You can use this when the query you're executing doesn't return anything. These are the Data Definition Language (DDL) queries that modify the structure of the database and the INSERT, UPDATE, and DELETE queries you can use to modify the data in the database.

- **ExecuteScalar()**: You can use this when you're interested only in the first column in the first row of the result set. If you return any other data from the query, it's completely ignored.

You'll look at each of these methods in turn, along the way looking at the INSERT, UPDATE, and DELETE queries in a little more depth.

Scalar functions will also come under the microscope because they return a single value rather than a set of records and are ideally suited to being called using the ExecuteScalar() method.

At the end of the chapter, you'll spend a little while looking at how you can use Microsoft Access to build the majority of the queries you need.

Using the ExecuteNonQuery() Method

Although querying the database using SELECT queries will form the mainstay of your interactions with the database, sometimes you'll be executing queries that don't return any results. Before ADO.NET, you'd use the same syntax to execute a query that didn't return any data that you'd use to execute a query that returned a set of results as an ADO.Recordset.

The ExecuteNonQuery() method takes no parameters and executes the specified query against the database. The following two types of query are ideally suited to using this method of querying the database:

- **Data Definition Language (DDL)**: Any DDL queries you execute are used to modify the structure of the database and don't return a result set. We'll leave a discussion of DDL queries until Chapter 10.

- **INSERT, UPDATE, and DELETE queries**: Any queries that modify the data within the database won't return any results. You'll look at these three query types in this chapter.

Although not returning any records from the database, the ExecuteNonQuery() method does have a return value. If you're executing an INSERT, UPDATE, or DELETE query, the method returns the number of rows that were affected by the query. For DDL queries, the return value is -1, which indicates that the number of rows affected is unknown.

You'll begin your look at modifying the data in the database by inserting a new publisher. We'll then discuss how you can modify records in the database by changing the details for the publisher you've just entered and how you can delete records by deleting the publisher. At the end of the chapter, the INSERT, UPDATE, and DELETE query executed will leave the database as you found it.

> **NOTE** *We're providing an introduction to only the INSERT, UPDATE, and DELETE queries. You'll look at them in more detail in Chapter 6 onward. You'll also see that there's another way to execute these queries against the database that doesn't involve using the* ExecuteNonQuery() *method.*

Inserting Data

At the heart of the code to add new information to a database is the INSERT query. Although it may seem otherwise, sending an INSERT query to a database is the only way to do this, so you best get familiar with it.

Try It Out: Inserting Data

This example quickly introduces the INSERT query to add a new publisher to the database before showing the syntax in more detail. Follow these steps:

1. Start Web Matrix, and navigate to the `C:\BAND\Chapter05` folder.

2. Create a new `web.config` file, and replace the autogenerated code with the following:

   ```
   <configuration>
     <appSettings>
       <add key="MSDEConnectString" ⟰
         value="server=(local)\BAND;database=Books;uid=band;pwd=letmein" />
     </appSettings>
   </configuration>
   ```

3. Create a new simple data report page called `select.aspx`, and replace the two lines at the start of the `Page_Load` event handler with the following:

   ```
   string ConnectionString = ⟰
     ConfigurationSettings.AppSettings["MSDEConnectString"];
   string CommandText = "SELECT PublisherID, PublisherName, PublisherCity, ⟰
     PublisherWebsite FROM Publisher ORDER BY PublisherID";
   ```

4. Execute `select.aspx`, and you'll see a list of all of the publishers in the database, as shown in Figure 5-1.

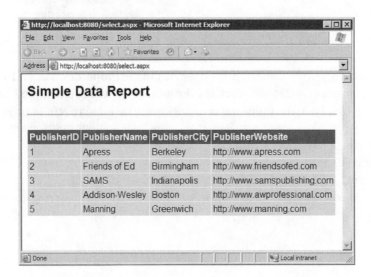

Figure 5-1. The publishers available before the addition

5. Leave the `select.aspx` page in Internet Explorer (you'll use it again shortly). Switch to Web Matrix, and create a new ASP.NET page called `insert.aspx`.

6. Switch to the All view of the page, and add the following imports after the page directive:

```
<%@ import Namespace="System.Data" %>
<%@ import Namespace="System.Data.SqlClient" %>
```

7. Switch to the Design view of the page, and add the **Records affected:** text at the start of the page and a label immediately following it. Change the ID of the label to lblRecords, and remove the default text. You should have a page design as shown in Figure 5-2.

Figure 5-2. You've added a label to show the number of records affected.

8. Select Page from the first drop-down list in the Properties box, and select the events icon. Double-click the drop-down list to the left of the Load event, and add the following code inside the `Page_Load` event handler:

```
// create the connection object you need
string ConnectionString =
  ConfigurationSettings.AppSettings["MSDEConnectString"];
SqlConnection myConnection = new SqlConnection(ConnectionString);
```

```
try{
  // create the Command object
  string CommandText = "INSERT Publisher (PublisherName, PublisherCity, ⤵
    PublisherContact_Email, PublisherWebsite) VALUES ('New Publisher', ⤵
    'Newcastle', 'bigcheese@newpublish.com', ⤵
    'http://www.newpublish.com')";
  SqlCommand myCommand = new SqlCommand(CommandText, myConnection);

  // execute the command and show the results
  lblRecords.Text = Convert.ToString(myCommand.ExecuteNonQuery());
}
catch (Exception ex)
{
  throw(ex);
}
finally
{
    // close the database connection
    myConnection.Close();
}
```

9. Execute the page by pressing F5 or clicking the start button on the toolbar. The INSERT query will be executed, and the number of rows affected will be returned, as shown in Figure 5-3.

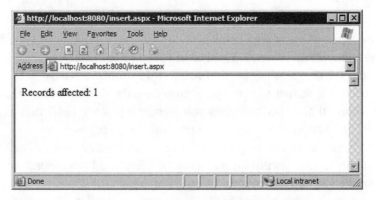

Figure 5-3. Confirmation that a publisher has been inserted

10. To verify that the data has been entered into the database, switch to `select.aspx` that you executed earlier and refresh the page. You should see that the new publisher has been added, as shown in Figure 5-4.

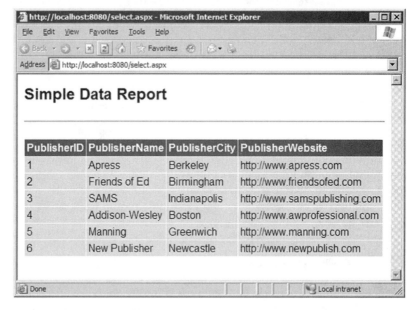

Figure 5-4. You can see that the publisher has been added.

How It Works

Before you start looking at adding the new publisher to the database, you need to set up the folder for this chapter. You'll create the now obligatory `web.config` file that contains the database connection string and a simple Web page, `select.aspx`, which you'll use to extract all of the publishers from the database. You've looked at this type of page before, and the query you execute is just a SELECT that returns the three columns from the database you're going to need.

In step 4, you looked at the publishers already in the database. As you can see, you've got only the five publishers you added in Chapter 2 because until now you didn't know how to add new records to the database.

The code for adding the new publisher is contained within a separate page. If you take a look at the code in the `Page_Load` event for `insert.aspx`, you'll see that it bears quite a resemblance to the code with which you're already familiar. The only differences are in the query that you send to the database and the way you execute the query.

If you look at the query you execute, you'll see that it's an INSERT query that inserts a new publisher into the Publisher table.

```
INSERT Publisher (PublisherName, PublisherCity, PublisherContact_Email, ↵
  PublisherWebsite) ↵
VALUES ('New Publisher', 'Newcastle', 'bigcheese@newpublish.com', ↵
  'http://www.newpublish.com')";
```

You'll look at the syntax of the INSERT query shortly, but for now just know that this will insert a new record into the Publisher table with the values specified.

The line that executes the query against the database has also changed. Instead of returning a SqlDataReader using the ExecuteReader() method, you use the ExecuteNonQuery() method to return the number of rows affected by the query. This is then displayed in the lblRows label, like so:

```
lblRows.Text = Convert.ToString(myCommand.ExecuteNonQuery());
```

You've inserted the first lot of data into the database, so there isn't a lot more you can do. Although this is a simple example intended to merely introduce INSERT before you look at its complete syntax, you'll see when you use the query in a real-life example in the next three chapters that you need to consider many things before you attempt to insert data into the database.

The INSERT Query

Compared to the complexities of SELECT, the INSERT query is quite simple.

```
INSERT [INTO] { table_name }
   { [(field_list)]
   { VALUES ( field_value_list ) }
}
```

It doesn't need to be split over three lines, but it does make it easier to see that there are six pieces to this statement.

- The keyword INSERT denoting the action to the database

- The optional keyword INTO to make the query more readable

- The `table_name` that determines the table to be added to

- The (comma-separated) `field_list` that names the fields in the new row you're giving values to

- The keyword VALUES that separates the `field_list` from the `field_value_list`

- The (comma-separated) `field_value_list` that contains a value for each of the fields in the `field_list` for the new row. Each value can be a literal, an expression saying how a value is to be determined from the values of other fields (firstname + surname, for example), the keyword DEFAULT indicating that the field should take its default value as defined in the database, or NULL.

- The number of the items in the `field_list` should equal the number of items in the `field_value_list` and be ordered in the same way. Thus, the first field named in the `field_list` will be filled with the first value in the `field_value_list`, the second with the second, and so on.

With this in mind, it shouldn't be too difficult to construct a simple INSERT query for any of the four tables in the sample database; in the last example you saw a query to insert a new publisher.

```
INSERT Publisher (PublisherName, PublisherCity, PublisherContact_Email,
   PublisherWebsite)
VALUES ('New Publisher', 'Newcastle', 'bigcheese@newpublish.com',
   'http://www.newpublish.com')
```

As you'll recall, there actually five columns in the Publisher table, and one of them you haven't specified. This isn't an error!

If a column is an identity field or has a default value, then you don't need to specify it when you're adding a new row; the database takes care of populating the column. So, even though you haven't specified the PublisherID field, the value has been entered automatically, as you can see in Figure 5-4, with a value of 6.

It's also possible to insert data into a database using the INSERT query without specifying the columns you want to insert the data into as long as you specify the data for all the columns (bar the identity fields) in the order they appear in the database. Even fields that have default values must be specified.

So, you could change the previous INSERT query to the following without any problems:

```
INSERT Publisher
VALUES ('New Publisher', 'Newcastle', 'bigcheese@newpublish.com',
  'http://www.newpublish.com')
```

Although inserting data without specifying a list of columns is perfectly valid, it makes more sense to actually specify the columns you want when inserting data. In the same way as you should always specify the columns in a SELECT query, you should always specify the columns you're trying to add data to during an INSERT. As with the SELECT query, it'll again be slightly quicker and makes it more apparent to which columns you're trying to add the data. With the INSERT query, there's also the additional problem that if a new column has been added to the table, you could end up putting data into the wrong column.

Updating Data

Although you've seen that you can insert new data into the database, sometimes you'll want to modify the data in the database. If a publisher changes its Web site address or moves location, you don't want to have to add a second publisher—the new publisher would be completely separate from the old publisher, and you've ran headlong into data integrity problems.

This is where the UPDATE query comes into play; like any other database operation, updating data is affected by sending a SQL query to a database—in this case, an UPDATE query.

Try It Out: Updating Data

You'll create a new page that allows you to modify the record you've added in the previous example. Follow these steps:

1. Start Web Matrix, and navigate to the C:\BAND\Chapter05 folder.

2. Open select.aspx page, and execute it. Find the new publisher in the results, and make a note of its PublisherID. In this case, as shown in Figure 5-4, you have a value of 6.

3. Open an Explorer window, and navigate to the C:\BAND\Chapter05 folder. Copy insert.aspx, and rename the copy to update.aspx.

4. Switch to the Code view of the page, and within the `Page_Load` event change the line that specifies the command text to the following, ensuring that the final value in the string (6 in this case) is the value noted in step 2:

```
string CommandText = "UPDATE Publisher ⤸
  SET PublisherName = 'Old Publisher', PublisherCity = 'Manchester' ⤸
  WHERE PublisherID = 6";
```

5. Start the page by pressing F5 or clicking the start icon on the toolbar. The query will be run against the database, and the record in the database will be updated. Again you'll see that the label shows that you've affected the first row in the database, as shown in Figure 5-5.

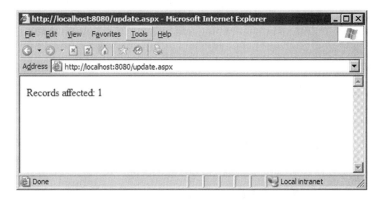

Figure 5-5. Confirmation that a publisher has been updated

6. If you again look at the list of publishers in `select.aspx`, you'll see that both the PublisherName and PublisherCity have been changed, as shown in Figure 5-6.

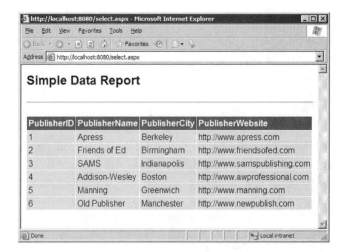

Figure 5-6. You can see that the publisher has been modified.

How It Works

The UPDATE query that you're using is about as simple as it can get.

```
UPDATE Publisher ⤶
SET PublisherName = 'Old Publisher', PublisherCity = 'Manchester' ⤶
WHERE PublisherID = 6
```

This UPDATE query tells the database to update the record in the Publisher table that has a PublisherID of 6. You want to change PublisherName and Publisher-Location, and you do this by specifying the columns what you want to change and the value that you want to change it to as a comma-separated list.

If you compare Figure 5-6 with Figure 5-4, you'll see that this is indeed the case, and the publisher that you added earlier has had its PublisherName and PublisherLocation columns changed while the PublisherWebsite column has remained the same. When executing an UPDATE query, only the columns that you explicitly specify are modified; any others remain unchanged.

The UPDATE Query

The UPDATE query allows you to modify tables in the database and change the values of data in the columns you specify. The basic syntax of the UPDATE query is as follows:

```
UPDATE { table_name }
{
  SET column1_name = expression1,
      column2_name = expression2,

          .
          .
          .

      columnM_name = expressionM
  [WHERE condition_list]
}
```

UPDATE has the following five basic components:

- The keyword UPDATE indicating the action to the database

- The table_name that identifies the table in which data will be updated

- The keyword SET to denote the start of the `set_list`

- A comma-separated list of assignments where individual fields are set to given values

- An optional list of conditions to identify the target rows preceded by the keyword WHERE

To update a record in a table, you specify the table you want to update and, after the SET keyword, specify a comma-separated list of columns and their new values. As you can see in the previous example, you're updating the Publisher-Name and PublisherCity columns, like so:

```
UPDATE Publisher ⤶
SET PublisherName = 'Old Publisher', PublisherCity = 'Manchester' ⤶
WHERE PublisherID = 6
```

The final part of the UPDATE query is the WHERE clause. In this example, you've used a simple WHERE clause that checks that PublisherID is equal to 6. As you saw in the previous chapter, the WHERE clause can be a lot more complex than this, and you're free to use any of the operators discussed. The WHERE clause follows the same rules irrespective of the type of query.

One word of warning regarding the WHERE clause: The WHERE clause, as with the SELECT query, is a completely optional constraint that you don't have to apply. Unless a WHERE clause is specified, the UPDATE query that you're executing will affect all the records in the table.

If you accidentally had forgotten to add the WHERE clause to the previous query and instead executed the following:

```
UPDATE Publisher ⤶
SET PublisherName = 'Old Publisher', PublisherCiry= 'Manchester'
```

then rather than updating the one record you wanted to update, all the publishers in the database would now have updated PublisherName and PublisherCity values. Be extremely careful that this is what you want to do before omitting the WHERE clause.

Deleting Data

The last piece in the jigsaw you need to consider is deleting data from the database. You've seen how you add data to the database using the INSERT query and how you can modify that data using the UPDATE query. Sometimes you want to delete data from the database; you accomplish this, not surprisingly, using the DELETE query.

Try It Out: Deleting Data

You're now going to delete the entry you've inserted and updated in the previous example. Follow these steps:

1. Open an Explorer window, and navigate to the C:\BAND\Chapter05 folder. Copy update.aspx, and rename the copy delete.aspx.

2. Switch to the Code view of the page, and within the Page_Load event change the line that specifies the command text to the following (making sure you're using the correct value for the publisher that you want to delete, in this case 6):

```
string CommandText = "DELETE Publisher WHERE PublisherID = 6";
```

3. Start the page by pressing F5 or clicking the start icon on the toolbar. The query will be run against the database and the results returned. Again you'll see that the label shows that you've had an affect on the first row in the database, as shown in Figure 5-7.

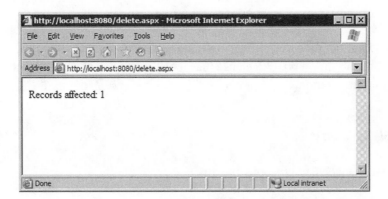

Figure 5-7. Confirmation that a publisher has been deleted

4. To verify that the data has been deleted, you can again use select.aspx, as shown in Figure 5-8.

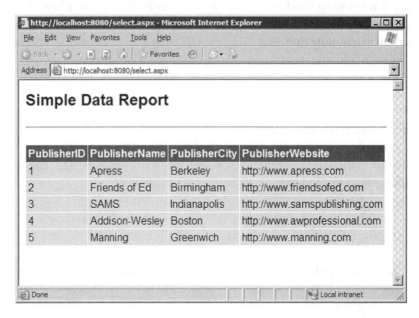

Figure 5-8. You can see that the publisher has been deleted.

How It Works

As with the previous two examples, you've simply changed one line in the Page_Load event. This time you're executing a delete query, like so:

```
DELETE Publisher WHERE PublisherID = 6
```

The DELETE query simply requires that you specify which table you want to delete from and then a WHERE clause that specifies the constraints you want to apply to the deletion.

The DELETE Query

The generic DELETE query looks like this:

```
DELETE [FROM]
{ table_name }
[WHERE condition_list]
```

It has the following four basic components:

- The keyword DELETE denoting the action to the database.

- The optional keyword FROM to make the statement more readable.

- The table_name that determines from which table the data will be deleted.

- An optional list of conditions to identify the target rows preceded by the keyword WHERE. If more than one condition is being used, each condition should either be combined using the AND or OR keywords.

So, as you saw in the previous example, you can delete a specific publisher by specifying the Publisher table and specifying a PublisherID value of 6:

```
DELETE Publisher WHERE PublisherID = 6
```

As with the UPDATE query, you must be careful when deleting data from the database because the WHERE clause is completely optional; if you omit it, you'll delete every single record in the table. If you accidentally execute the following query:

```
DELETE FROM Publisher
```

rather than deleting the one record that you require, you'd delete all the records in the table. Again, be careful—the database doesn't check that this is what you want to do!

> **NOTE** *A DELETE query works with whole rows only. You never delete single fields from a row; what you'd actually do in that case would be to change a field to an empty value or NULL if the database allowed it.*

Using the ExecuteScalar() Method

Although you've looked at the most common method that you have for returning data from a database (the ExecuteReader() method), sometimes you can avoid the overhead that goes with returning the results as a SqlDataReader().

If the query you're executing returns only a single value from the database, you can use the `ExecuteScalar()` method to return a single value rather than having to manipulate the `SqlDataReader` that's returned from the `ExecuteReader()` method.

> **NOTE** *You can perform the same task using the* `ExecuteReader()` *method and manipulating the* `SqlDataReader` *that's returned. However, this requires a lot more code and is slower than using the* `ExecuteScalar()` *method.*

Sometimes you want to return only one value from a query, and the most common is when you're using scalar functions to query a table within the database.

Scalar Functions

Scalar functions, or *aggregate functions* as Microsoft likes to call them, are mathematical functions defined within SQL that return a single value. Quite a few of these exist; Table 5-1 describes some of the more common ones.

Table 5-1. The Common Scalar Functions

Scalar Function	What It Does
`AVG(column)`	Returns the average value of the specified column
`COUNT(DISTINCT column)`	Counts the number of distinct values in the specified column
`COUNT(*)`	Gives the number of rows in the specified table
`MAX(column)`	Returns the maximum value in the specified column
`MIN(column)`	Returns the minimum value in the specified column
`SUM(column)`	Returns the total of all the values in the specified column

You can use scalar functions in several places in SQL, but by far the most common usage is returning them as columns from SELECT queries.

> **NOTE** *You can also use scalar functions as constraints in SELECT queries but only if you've grouped the columns in the query using the GROUP BY clause. In this case, you'd use the HAVING clause in place of the WHERE clause to apply the constraint. Both GROUP BY and HAVING are beyond the scope of this book.*

Try It Out: Using the ExecuteScalar() Method

In this example, you'll build upon one of the previous examples. We'll show how you can use the COUNT(*) scalar function and return the number of records that your query has matched. Follow these steps:

1. Open an Explorer window, and navigate to the C:\BAND\Chapter05 folder.

2. Copy select.aspx file, and rename the copied version to scalar.aspx.

3. On the Design view of the page and on a new line after the title of the page, enter **Publishers in the database:** and then add a label control. Change the ID of the label to lblTotal, and remove the control's default text. You should have a page that looks similar to that shown in Figure 5-9.

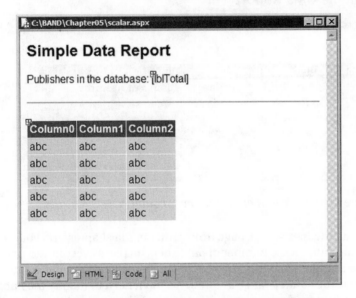

Figure 5-9. Adding a count of the number of publishers.

4. Switch to the Code view of the page, and add the following code immediately after opening the database in the Page_Load event handler (the additional code is bold):

```
myConnection.Open();

// COUNT THE BOOKS IN THE DATABSE
string CommandTextCount = "SELECT COUNT(*) FROM Publisher";
SqlCommand myCommandCount =
    new SqlCommand(CommandTextCount, myConnection);
```

```
// execute the command and show the results
lblTotal.Text = Convert.ToString(myCommandCount.ExecuteScalar());

DataGrid1.DataSource = ↵
    myCommand.ExecuteReader(CommandBehavior.CloseConnection);
```

5. Start the page by pressing F5 or clicking the start icon on the toolbar. The query will be run against the database, and the number of publishers in the database will also be displayed, as shown in Figure 5-10.

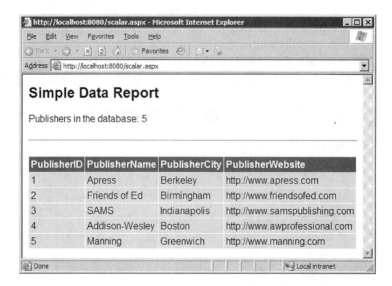

Figure 5-10. The count of the number of publishers is returned.

6. Execute the insert.aspx page from earlier in the chapter, and you should see the count of the number of publishers increase every time a new publisher is added. You'll also be able to execute update.aspx and delete.aspx and see the count change accordingly. You'll need to modify the PublisherID values for the new publishers that have been added to see the effect that update.aspx and delete.aspx make to the count of the publishers.

How It Works

You've used an earlier example as the basis for this example, and you've simply added a label to the page that you populate with the count of the number of publishers in the database. The count is returned by using the following COUNT(*) scalar function and returning this as the result from a SELECT query:

```
SELECT COUNT(*) FROM Publisher
```

This scalar function returns a count of the number of records in the database, and by specifying this as the only column, the query will return a single row containing a single column. This is how you use the `ExecuteScalar()` method.

The `ExecuteScalar()` method returns an object representing the value that has been returned from the query. In this case, you're returning an integer, and you need to convert this to a string before you can assign it to the `Text` property of the label, like so:

```
lblTotal.Text = Convert.ToString(myCommandCount.ExecuteScalar());
```

By executing the INSERT, UPDATE, and DELETE queries that you looked at in the previous examples, you can see that the count of the number of publishers is indeed increased and decreased as expected.

Using Microsoft Access to Build Queries

When you're creating a query, deciding what you want it to do is relatively easy whatever the type of query you want to execute. In other words, do you want to SELECT data from the database, INSERT a new row into a table, UPDATE the existing data, or DELETE data from the database? The hard part is writing the required SQL; writing correct SQL is tricky enough on a single table, but what when you have joins across two, three, or more tables?

You could learn every little nuance of SQL and write the query by hand every time, but writing queries is a time-consuming task, and it's easy to make mistakes. Thankfully, several tools are on the market that help you build SQL queries—just do a Google search for *SQL query builders* and see how many different products are available.

You'll now look at one tool that a lot of people have but may not have considered as an option for building queries—Microsoft Access. Although Microsoft Access has its own database format, it also has, since the release of Microsoft Office 2000, the ability to be used as the front end to the Microsoft SQL Server 2000 Desktop Engine (MSDE) and SQL Server databases.

In the examples that follow, you'll look at using Microsoft Access as the front end to MSDE, and you'll see how to generate a SELECT query and an INSERT query that you can use in your Web pages.

> **NOTE** *To use Microsoft Access to build queries against an MSDE database, you construct stored procedures because you can't simply create queries in the manner that you're expecting them. Unfortunately, we don't cover stored procedures until Chapter 9. However, Access is such a good tool to use when building queries that we'll explain how to use it anyway; all you're interested in is the SQL queries that are generated and not the details of what stored procedures are or how you use them.*

Try It Out: Constructing a SELECT Query in Microsoft Access

In this example, you'll generate queries in Microsoft Access by building the SELECT query you looked at in Chapter 4. You'll first build the simple query that returns all the results you require, and then you'll see that Microsoft Access makes it easy to add both constraints and ordering to the queries that you're building. Follow these steps:

1. Launch Microsoft access and select File ➤ New. From the dialog that is displayed select "Project using existing data" and specify a location and name to save the project on your machine.

2. In the Data Link Properties dialog box, shown in Figure 5-11, enter **(local)\BAND** as the server to connect to and specify the correct account to use—in this case, you want to use the sa account. From the database drop-down list, select the Books database.

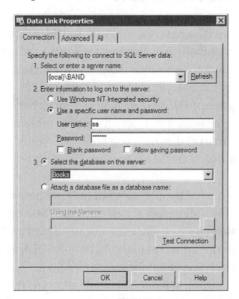

Figure 5-11. Specifying the database to connect to in Microsoft Access

3. Click Test Connection to ensure that the connection to the database can be made. If the connection to the database is successful, you'll see a confirmation dialog box, as shown in Figure 5-12.

Figure 5-12. Confirmation that the connection was successful

4. If a different dialog box is shown, such as the one in Figure 5-13, then the connection failed. You can find the actual error that has occurred at the end of the dialog message.

Figure 5-13. If the connection is unsuccessful, an error is displayed.

5. Click OK on the Data Link Properties dialog box. This will connect Access to the specified MSDE database and default to a view of the tables in the database.

6. Click the Queries link under the Objects sidebar to show the different queries that are in the database.

7. Double-click the Create Stored Procedure in Designer option to create a new stored procedure. This will open a window to create a new stored procedure and present you with the Add Table dialog box, as shown in Figure 5-14.

Figure 5-14. You can select the tables that you require.

8. You want only the Book and Publisher tables, and you can select them by holding the Ctrl key and clicking the names of the two tables. Click Add to add them to the query.

9. Clicking the Close button will hide the Add Table dialog box and allow you to see the two tables that have been added. As you can see in Figure 5-15, this also shows the relationships between the tables.

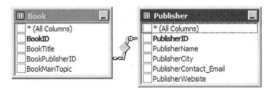

Figure 5-15. Microsoft Access shows the relationships between tables.

10. Select the BookID and BookTitle fields in the Book table by clicking in the checkbox to the left of the names. You also want the PublisherName from the Publisher table. As you select each column, the grid at the bottom of the window is populated. Once you've added all three columns, it will be as shown in Figure 5-16.

Column	Alias	Table	Output	Sort Type	Sort Order	Criteria	Or...	Or...	Or...
BookID		Book	✓						
BookTitle		Book	✓						
PublisherName		Publisher	✓						

Figure 5-16. Columns selected for the query

11. To test the query, you must first save the stored procedure by clicking the save icon in the toolbar. Call the stored procedure QueryExample1, and click OK.

12. Execute the query by clicking the red exclamation mark in the toolbar. This will run the stored procedure and return the results, as shown in Figure 5-17.

BookID	BookTitle	PublisherName
1	Starting Up C#	Friends of Ed
2	Beginning ASP.NET	Apress
3	Waking Up to .NET	SAMS
4	Starting Up VB. NET	Friends of Ed
5	Beginning ASP.NET Databases	Apress
6	Journeyman Webforms	Addison-Wesley
7	Journeyman Winforms	Addison-Wesley
8	Starting Up ADO.NET With C#	Friends of Ed

Record: 1 of 30

Figure 5-17. Results of executing the basic query

13. Switch back to the Design view for the query, click the Sort Type column for the BookTitle field, and select Ascending from the drop-down list. Add a new column to the query by selecting the BookPublisherID column from the Book table. Uncheck the checkbox in the output column and enter **@publisher** in the Criteria column. The Design pane at the bottom of the window should display, as shown in Figure 5-18.

Column	Alias	Table	Output	Sort Type	Sort Order	Criteria	Or...	Or...	Or...
BookID		Book	✓						
BookTitle		Book	✓	Ascending	1				
PublisherName		Publisher	✓						
BookPublisherID		Book				= @publisher			

Figure 5-18. Microsoft Access can also deal with ordering and filtering queries.

14. Execute the query again, and after prompting to save the query, you'll be required to enter a value for @publisher, as shown in Figure 5-19.

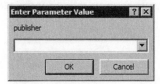

Figure 5-19. You must enter values for any criteria you've added to a query.

15. Enter a value of 1, and click OK. This will return all the books published by Apress, as shown in Figure 5-20.

BookID	BookTitle	PublisherName
2	Beginning ASP.NET	Apress
5	Beginning ASP.NET Databases	Apress
24	Delve Into Intermediate Language	Apress
11	Dive Into Databases With ASP.NET And VB. NET	Apress
19	MySQL in .NET	Apress
21	VB .NET Reflection Handbook	Apress

QueryExample1 : Stored Procedure

Record: 1 of 6

Figure 5-20. You can also filter and order results.

16. To view the query that has been executed, select View ➤ SQL View. This will return the entire stored procedure, including the SQL commands to create the procedure:

```
ALTER PROCEDURE dbo.QueryExample1
(@publisher int)
AS
SELECT dbo.Book.BookID, dbo.Book.BookTitle, dbo.Publisher.PublisherName
FROM dbo.Book INNER JOIN
    dbo.Publisher ON dbo.Book.BookPublisherID = dbo.Publisher.PublisherID
WHERE (dbo.Book.BookPublisherID = @publisher)
ORDER BY dbo.Book.BookTitle
```

17. Modify the WHERE clause of the query to read as follows:

```
WHERE (@publisher = 0 or dbo.Book.BookPublisherID = @publisher)
```

18. If you execute the query again, you'll see that you can now enter a value of 0 and return all the results while any other value will filter the results.

How It Works

Before you can start to use Microsoft Access, you must first create the project and set up the database connection details. The first four steps in this example create the Microsoft Access project.

As you've discovered, using Microsoft Access to create SELECT queries is simplicity itself. In steps 6 and 7, you selected which tables you wanted as part of the query, and in step 9 you selected what columns you wanted to display. Under the covers Microsoft Access takes care of the adding joins for the tables you've selected.

In the second part of the example, you expanded upon the basic query by adding filtering and ordering to the basic query.

To add constraints to a column, you simply add them to the criteria for that column. You can give a specific value as a constraint, or you can, as you have here, add a parameter that needs to be entered at runtime. If you have more than one criterion that you want to apply for a column, you can enter the extra criteria in the Or . . . columns.

You specify which columns you want to order by selecting Ascending or Descending in the Sort Type field for that column. You can even sort on hidden columns by unchecking the Output field; the column will be used to sort the results but won't actually be displayed in the results that are returned.

In the final step you saw how you can manually modify the SQL that's auto-generated in the SQL view of the query. Any changes you make are parsed by

Microsoft Access to check their validity, and any problems will generate an error that must be fixed before the query can be saved or executed.

The SQL view of the query also gives you access to the SQL that you need in order to execute the query within your pages. As mentioned earlier when creating queries, Microsoft Access is actually generating stored procedures in the database, and you can see this with the SQL at the start of the query.

```
ALTER PROCEDURE dbo.QueryExample1
(@publisher int)
AS
```

You'll see the syntax for creating and altering stored procedures in Chapter 9; for now you can safely ignore this part of the SQL query. The query that you actually require starts immediately after the AS keyword, and you can copy this for your own use.

Try It Out: Constructing an INSERT Query in Microsoft Access

In addition to SELECT queries, you can also use Microsoft Access to generate INSERT queries. Follow these steps:

1. If you've closed the Microsoft Access solution from the previous example, open it.

2. Switch to the Queries pane, and create a new stored procedure.

3. You're adding a new publisher, so select the Publisher table from the Add Table dialog box.

4. Select the Query Type option on the toolbar, and select the Append Values Query option, as shown in Figure 5-21.

Figure 5-21. Changing the query type

5. Select all the columns in the Publisher table except the PublisherID column. The selected columns will appear in the grid at the bottom. Give each of the columns a new value, as shown in Figure 5-22.

Column	New Value
PublisherName	@name
PublisherCity	@city
PublisherContact_Email	@email
PublisherWebsite	@website

Figure 5-22. Specifying values for an INSERT query

6. Save the query as QueryExample2, and then execute it. You'll be prompted for the four parameters in turn, and once all the parameters have been entered, the query will be executed.

7. This query returns no results, and you're presented with a dialog box informing you that the query execution was successful, as shown in Figure 5-23.

Microsoft Office Access ⊠

The stored procedure executed successfully but did not return records.

[OK]

Figure 5-23. Success confirmation dialog for an INSERT query

8. Switching to the SQL view of the query will show, if you ignore the stored procedure statements, that the following query has been created as you'd expect:

```
INSERT INTO dbo.Publisher
   (PublisherName, PublisherCity, PublisherContact_Email, PublisherWebsite)
VALUES (@name, @city, @email, @website)
```

How It Works

The process for creating an INSERT query isn't that much different from creating a SELECT query. After selecting the type of query you want, you select the table and the columns into which you want to insert data.

The grid at the bottom of the query window changes depending upon the query type; for an INSERT query, the only information you can enter is the new value for the column. As with constraints for SELECT queries, you're free to enter specific values or parameter names that must be entered at runtime.

Summary

In this chapter, we've concluded the introduction to the Command object. You learned about the following:

- You looked at the ExecuteNonQuery() method and how you can use this to execute queries that don't return any results.

- We introduced the INSERT, UPDATE, and DELETE queries and showed their syntax.

- You looked at scalar functions and saw how you can return values from these functions using the ExecuteScalar() method.

- The chapter closed by looking at Microsoft Access and how you can use this to generate SQL queries that you can use directly within your pages.

In this and the previous chapter, you saw the different types of query you can execute and the different methods the Command object exposes for executing these queries.

The examples you've seen so far have been simple pages that performed one task to give you a foundation to databases and the different queries you can perform. In the next three chapters, you'll build upon the techniques you've developed and look at how you build interactive pages. You'll also start to see the real power that's available to data-driven Web sites.

CHAPTER 6

DataReader and DataSet

IN CHAPTERS 4 AND 5, you saw in detail how you build and pass commands to a database, and you discovered the three types of result from a SQL statement: a confirmation, a scalar value, and a DataReader object. You also saw how to deal with scalars and confirmations. In this chapter, you'll continue your look at the third step in driving a page with data: handling the data correctly once it has been returned from the database. You have a large number of options for this, but they all boil down to whether you're going to work with the data directly from the database or save it on the server as *disconnected data*. You'll look at both options in this chapter, and you'll use the following techniques, which are all quite commonplace:

- Using the DataReader to work with the results of a query directly from the database

- Saving query results into a DataSet object on the server away from the database

- Creating a DataSet locally with your own data completely away from an external data source

Along the way, you'll look in some detail at both the DataReader and DataSet objects, their makeup, and their differences. At least one of these two objects will feature in every data-driven Web page you create, so it's good to be up to speed on how they work.

This chapter is only the first part of three in your journey through data handling. For now, we'll assume for the moment that the data you request doesn't need to be displayed on-screen. In Chapter 7, we'll assume that the data will be displayed on-screen but is read-only and won't need to be updated. Finally, in Chapter 8, you'll continue with building pages that allow you to create, modify, and delete data and reflect those changes back to the data source.

"Why not just look at DataReaders and DataSets as you go along?" we hear you cry. "Why put this interlude first?" These are good questions, but they have a simple answer, which we'll quite happily borrow from the world of Perl. For every data-related task you'll be looking at over the coming chapters, you can follow this motto: "There's More Than One Way To Do It." But they all stem from how DataReaders and DataSets work. If you don't look at these objects now and see the situations in which they're useful, you'll be less likely to choose the right option when building data-driven pages of your own.

The DataReader Object

The key to the whole topic of data handling is the DataReader object—or, if you prefer to be data provider–specific, the `SqlDataReader`, `OleDbDataReader`, and `OdbcDataReader` objects. True, they're optimized as appropriate for the technology they're based on, but their method calls and properties are, for all intensive purposes, identical, so we can just as easily refer to them all in one go. Rest assured that if we come to any incongruities, we'll make a note of them before continuing.

The DataReader is a strange little object. You may use it all the time, but it's intangible, representing only a pipeline in memory between the database and the Web page waiting for the data. In functional terms, it works much like a phone connection. While the phone connection is open, the page can speak queries to the database, which in turn can speak its results back to the page, but once the connection is closed, there's no trace of it or record of the data returned from the database except in the page itself. Only if you use another object, such as the DataSet, can you maintain an in-memory record of the results from the query. If you like, the additional object is the equivalent of an answering machine or phone-tapping mechanism.

The upshot of it only being a conduit in memory rather than a permanent place of storage is that when you access the data in a DataReader, the data is read-only. It also means you can access the results only one row at a time, and once you finish with a row and move onto the next one, you can't go back to it. You can go only forward. Of course, this means there are pros and cons to using only DataReaders in your page. On the plus side, you have the following:

- Using a DataReader is quick and efficient, as it doesn't need to worry about keeping track of every bit of data.

- A DataReader doesn't need to store data in memory, so it uses fewer resources in creating a page.

That's not to say there aren't any disadvantages.

- You can't do anything with the data such as sending changes back to the database. This would mean referring to data already passed through the reader, which isn't possible; DataReaders work only from database to client.

- DataReaders require exclusive access to a connection. Once open, nothing else can use a connection until the DataReader is closed.

A DataReader isn't picky about the amount of data passed through it. You could request a single item of information from a field or the entire contents of the database. As long as you understand how to access it, it won't complain.

A DataReader is the resulting object from a call to ExecuteReader() on a Command object.

```
SqlDataReader myReader = myCommand.ExecuteReader();
```

The general practice at this point is to assign (or *bind*) the values in a DataReader to controls on the Web form, and indeed that's what you've already done in the examples in Chapters 3 and 4. You've created a DataGrid control on the page, bound the data to it, and let ASP.NET take care of the display.

```
myGrid.DataSource = myReader;
myGrid.DataBind();
```

So far, all you've seen is the data displayed as a table thanks to that DataGrid, but you can bind information to several more data-aware Web form controls. For example, you can use a drop-down list, a set of radio buttons, or a calendar. We'll spend all of Chapter 7 on data binding, but there's another way to work with DataReaders that you'll look at here, and that's to iterate through them row by row.

Iterating Through a DataReader

It may seem a waste of time to work through the results of a query row by row and work with each when you can just bind it to a control and let the control take care of it all, but consider that data isn't always for display. You may be using a database table to store user information and site preferences. Rather than displaying it on the screen, information from these tables may be assigned straightaway to controls' properties or stored in a business object for use across the whole site. For example, you may create a Preferences object to store theme information for the whole site, store values from the database in its properties, and save it as a Session-level variable. Rather than accessing the database again, you just access the Session variable. If any preferences are changed during the session, they're saved to the Session variable and when the session is over, the changes are sent back to the database. This minimizes both potential connections to the database for this purpose and also the overhead of using many Session variables at a time. You just use one with lots of information rather than several containing individual pieces of information.

To iterate through the contents of a DataReader, you use its Read() method. If you haven't worked with Reader objects in general before, the idea is simple. A reader has a pointer that you use to keep track of where you are in the information coming through your reader. If you like, it's the same kind of thing that happens when someone uses their finger to keep their place on a page. Until they open the book and start to read, they can't see anything. The same thing applies in code. You can't access anything until you call Read() the first time, and each time you call Read() after that, the DataReader lets another row through for you to use. Read() will also return a boolean value each time you call it: true if there's another row for you to work with and false if you've reached the end of the query results, as shown in Figure 6-1.

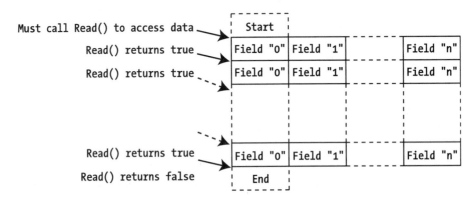

Figure 6-1. Working through rows in a DataReader using DataReader.Read()

Hence, you can use the call to Read() as the condition in a while loop. If your query returns no results, the first call to Read() ends the loop before you do anything. If not, the code will keep looping until there are no more results. In short, your page needs to have this skeleton code in it:

```
//Create the DataReader by calling ExecuteReader()
SqlDataReader myReader = myCommand.ExecuteReader();

//Iterate through the DataReader in a while loop
while (myReader.Read())
{
    .. processing instructions for each row in DataReader
}

//Close DataReader
myReader.Close();
```

Take care not to call Read() in the while statement and then again within the loop—say, in a method call—lest the code skip some of the results. It's easy to do but hard to track down later in the code.

Besides the actual data processing, it's important you close the DataReader using Close() after you've finished with it. Once a DataReader has been opened through a connection, nothing else can use that connection until the DataReader is closed. Even if an error occurs on that page, the connection is still isolated until the .NET garbage collector comes to dispose of the open DataReader. This is a needless waste of resources if all you have to do is make sure you close it. You also have a maximum number of connections that can be open at any one time, so under heavy loads, not closing your connections could actually generate errors, which is definitely not a good thing.

> **NOTE** *The examples in this chapter use the SqlClient data provider. You can find equivalent examples using the OLE DB and ODBC data providers in the code download for this book.*

Try It Out: Iterating Through a DataReader

In this example, you'll see that you can do more than just fill a DataGrid with the results of a database query by passing the results into the grid and calling DataBind(). This is what you've done in every example so far. Instead, you'll write a custom Publisher class, create an instance of it, and use a row of the Publisher table to populate it. In real life, you'd probably then use it in the business rules tier of your Web application, but as this is a straightforward example, you'll define a simple method on the Publisher object that neatly prints the values of its properties to the screen. Follow these steps:

1. In Web Matrix, create a new ASP.NET page called Iterating_Through_A_DataReader.aspx and save it to a new folder under BAND called Chapter06.

2. In Design view, drag a label control onto the blank page. You'll use this to demonstrate that your objects have been created. Make its Text property empty.

3. In All view, make sure the right data provider is included at the top of the page, like so:

```
<%@ Page Language="C#" %>
<%@ import Namespace="System.Data" %>
<%@ import Namespace="System.Data.SqlClient" %>
```

4. You have two distinct pieces of code to add to the page. The first is the class definition of the Publisher object. In Code view, add the following code:

```
public class Publisher
{
    public string Name;
    public string City;
    public string Email;
    public string Website;

    public Publisher()
    {}

    public string ToString()
    {
        string description = "";
        description = "Name : " + this.Name + "<br />";
        description += "City : " + this.City + "<br />";
        description += "Contact : <a href=mailto:" + this.Email + ">" + ⏎
            this.Email + "</a><br/>";
        description += "Homesite : <a href='" + this.Website + "'>" + ⏎
            this.Website + "</a><br/><br/>";

        return description;
    }
}
```

5. The second piece of code to add is the code for the Page_Load handler.

```
void Page_Load(object sender, EventArgs e)
{
    //set up connection string and SQL query
    string ConnectionString = Convert.ToString( ⏎
```

```
        ConfigurationSettings.AppSettings["MSDEConnectString"]);
    string CommandText = "SELECT PublisherName, PublisherCity, ↵
        PublisherContact_Email, PublisherWebsite FROM Publisher";

    //create SqlConnection and SqlCommand objects
    SqlConnection myConnection = new SqlConnection(ConnectionString);
    SqlCommand myCommand = new SqlCommand(CommandText, myConnection);

    try
    {
        //open connection to the database
        myConnection.Open();

        //run query
        SqlDataReader myReader = myCommand.ExecuteReader();

        while (myReader.Read())
        {
            Publisher p = new Publisher();
            p.Name = myReader.GetString(0);
            p.City = myReader.GetString(1);
            p.Email = myReader.GetString(2);
            p.Website = myReader.GetString(3);

            Label1.Text += p.ToString();
        }
        myReader.Close();
    }
    catch (Exception ex)
    {
        //If an exception occurs, handle it.
        throw (ex);
    }
    finally
    {
        //Whether you succeed or fail, close the database connection
        myConnection.Close();
    }
}
```

6. Now save this code, and then run it. When the page loads, you'll see that the label control contains details of all the publishers in the Publisher table written out, as in Figure 6-2, but not in tabular form. You have hyperlinks that work and an easier-to-read collection of data instead.

Figure 6-2. Iterating_Through_A_DataReader.aspx

How It Works

The aim of this page is to demonstrate that you can use a DataReader to source values for any objects you create, so you start by defining a new object class to use. In this case, it's a Publisher object whose properties cunningly mirror the information stored in the Publisher table.

```
public class Publisher
{
    public string Name;
    public string City;
    public string Email;
    public string Website;

    public Publisher()
    {}
```

To demonstrate that you've achieved this aim, you can add a label control to the page and a method that presents the information in a Publisher object neatly on the screen.

```
public string ToString()
{
    string description = "";
    description = "Name : " + this.Name + "<br />";
    description += "City : " + this.City + "<br />";
    description += "Contact : <a href=mailto:" + this.Email + ">" + ⤸
        this.Email + "</a><br/>";
    description += "Homesite : <a href='" + this.Website + "'>" + ⤸
        this.Website + "</a><br/><br/>";

    return description;
}
}
```

All that's left is Page_Load(), and apart from the following section, it's the same as all the previous examples. The key to this whole page is one small section of the code, as you saw earlier. Instead of plugging the results of myCommand.ExecuteReader() right into a DataGrid, you can access the DataReader directly, like so:

```
//run query
SqlDataReader myReader = myCommand.ExecuteReader();
```

The following is the while loop where you work through each row in turn. In this case, create a Publisher object, assign the current row of values from the Data-Reader to the new object's properties, and then echo them into the label control.

```
while (myReader.Read())
{
```

Inside the loop, you just create a new Publisher object and give each of its properties values from the corresponding fields in the DataReader. You're using the special accessor methods that are part of the DataReader object here, and you must select the right one for the type of object you want out of it. All the information in the Publisher table is strings, so you use GetString(). If you needed integers, you'd use GetInt32() or GetInt16(). There are 37 different Get----() methods for the SqlDataReader, and 25 for the OleDbDataReader and OdbcDataReader, so check the .NET documentation for which one will suit you.

All the Get----() methods take one argument—the index of the field you want in the current row supplied by the DataReader. So, if you look at the following query you sent to the database:

```
string CommandText = "SELECT PublisherName, PublisherCity,
    PublisherContact_Email, PublisherWebsite FROM Publisher";
```

you can see that PublisherName has index 0, PublisherCity has index 1, and so on. Figure 6-1 illustrates this, too. Why not just use the * wildcard to pull everything out of the table and then retrieve what you want? Well, you can, but it's just easier to work out the right index value from the query than from looking up the order of the fields in the database itself.

> **TIP** *In addition, it's good practice to query only for the information you require rather than for everything you may want and then pick and choose. Name the fields to be pulled from a table, and use a WHERE clause in a SELECT statement to make sure only the rows required are returned from the database.*

You can access fields in the current row from the DataReader in any order, and you don't have to access all the information in a particular row either. Just don't forget that you can't come back to it later. DataReaders are forward-only but only at row level.

```
Publisher p = new Publisher();
p.Name = myReader.GetString(0);
p.City = myReader.GetString(1);
p.Email = myReader.GetString(2);
p.Website = myReader.GetString(3);
```

As an alternative to using the Get----() methods, you can also access each field by name. For example:

```
Publisher p = new Publisher();
p.Name = myReader["PublisherName"].ToString();
p.City = myReader["PublisherCity"].ToString();
p.Email = myReader["PublisherContact_Email"].ToString();
p.Website = myReader["PublisherWebsite"].ToString();
```

The only problem here is that instead of returning a string, integer, or whatever you specify using a Get----() method, this approach always returns a generic System.Object object, which you must cast before you can use. Hence, the call to ToString() is appended to each line of code.

When you've finished creating the object, you display its details in the label control. If there's more information in the DataReader, the while loop will start creating another object. If not, the while loop finishes, and you close the DataReader by calling Close(), like so:

```
    Label1.Text += p.ToString();
}
myReader.Close();
```

On the same train of thought, DataReaders all rely on their connections to work, so make sure that the connection isn't closed before the DataReader is finished. The results won't be pretty.

DataReader Properties and Methods

The DataReader also provides some handy support properties and methods to help you process its contents with fewer errors and more intelligence. Table 6-1 describes the DataReader properties, and Table 6-2 describes the DataReader methods.

Table 6-1. DataReader Properties

Name	Type	Description
Depth	int	Returns the depth of the nesting in the DataReader for the current row. OdbcDataReader and OleDbDataReader only.
FieldCount	int	Returns the number of fields in the current row.
HasRows	boolean	Returns true if the DataReader contains any results (rows).
IsClosed	boolean	Returns true if the DataReader is closed.
RecordsAffected	int	Returns the number of rows.
Item	object	Returns the contents of a field in a row. Never use this by name. Instead, this is used in the background to access DataReader fields with myReader["fieldname"], for instance.

Table 6-2. DataReader Methods

Name	Return Type	Description
Close()	void	Closes the DataReader object
Read()	boolean	Moves to the next row in the DataReader. Returns true if a row exists. Returns false if at the end of the DataReader.
Get----(int)	-----	Returns and casts the contents of a field at index int in the row. You have to use the appropriate method for the type of object you want to retrieve.
IsDBNull(int)	boolean	Returns true if the field at index int contains a null value pulled from the database. Returns false otherwise.
NextResult()	boolean	Moves to the next table in the DataReader. Returns true if the next table exists. Returns false otherwise.

Note that the Depth and RecordsAffected properties are beyond the scope of this book, so we'll leave them for now. As for methods, we'll come to NextResult() at the end of Chapter 7. You use that when you send a group of Structured Query Language (SQL) statements to the database in one go and the resulting DataReader contains more than one table to scan.

You can use the remainder of these properties and methods to extend the previous example. You'll find the full code in the download for this chapter as Iterating_Through_A_DataReader_Extended.aspx. Let's start with HasRows. .NET 1.1 introduced this new property to the DataReader object in all data providers. This is a boolean value that's true if a DataReader does contain some information and false if it doesn't. Now, you can already detect this using while(DataReader.Read()), but HasRows allows you to be a bit neater and gives you an alternate check for a positive query if you aren't going to run straight through the while loop. You can add it to the earlier code, like so:

```
if (myReader.HasRows)
{
  while (myReader.Read())
  {
    ...
  }
}
else
{
  Label1.Text = "No rows returned.";
}
```

Once you know there's some information, you can make sure it's safe to retrieve it with the DataReader's Get----() methods using a combination of FieldCount and IsDBNull(). Before retrieving data from the row, you can scan it for any null fields, like so:

```
while (myReader.Read())
{
   for (int i=0; i<=(myReader.FieldCount-1); i++)
   {
      if (myReader.IsDBNull(i))
      {
         Label1.Text += "Warning: Field " + i + " is NULL.";
      }
   }
   //Process the Publisher objects
}
```

Finally, you can verify that the DataReader is closed when you finish with it by checking its IsClosed property, like so:

```
if (!(myReader.IsClosed))
{
  myReader.Close();
}
```

That about covers everything for DataReaders by themselves. You know how to iterate through them, and you'll learn how to bind data from them to controls on a Web form in the next chapter. You've even looked at the useful little properties such as HasRows and IsClosed that can make your life that much easier. What we haven't covered, however, is how to get past the fact that once you move past a row in a DataReader, you can't go back to it again because a DataReader is forward-only. The answer is simple. You must persist the data in a business object, as you've already seen, or more likely to a DataSet so you can continue to access it as tables, rows, and fields of data.

The DataSet Object

DataReaders are quick and fast, but they're much like pay-per-view television. The only way to watch a film again once you've finished watching it is to go back to the channel and request it again. DataSets, on the other hand, work like video recorders; you can record the film off the television and watch it as many times as you like, rewinding and fast-forwarding through it as much as you like. With DataSets then, you can store any data that may have come through a DataReader for use throughout the lifetime of a page—this idea of persisting data away from the database is known as *disconnected data*. In fact, it's even better than a video recorder because once you've got data inside a DataSet, you can alter that data, add to it, delete from it, and send all the changes made back to the database at the click of a button. This is handy—we wish we could do that with some Vin Diesel movies!

Of course, there's no reason why you can't use a DataSet just for displaying data in a page as well; once you've seen what makes a DataSet tick in this chapter, that's exactly what you'll do in Chapter 7—you'll use both a DataSet and a DataReader to supply read-only information to a page. It turns out that this won't be the only new object you can use as a data source, but we'll come back to that idea later.

> **CAUTION** *A DataSet may not rely on a connection to a database, but it still lasts only for the lifetime of the page. If the page posts back and must be reassembled, so too must the DataSet. Either that, or it must be persisted somehow for retrieval by the next page. As a result, take care only to query for the data that will be needed on the page. A DataSet is resident in memory, so the smaller it is, the fewer resources required to keep it there and the better the page performs and scales.*

How to Fill a DataSet

Your first goal is to get some basic code up and running that lets you use a DataSet as a data source. The basic code still follows the same three steps you saw way back in Chapter 1 but in a slightly different way than creating a DataReader.

First, you set up the Connection and Command objects as usual, like so:

```
void Page_Load(object sender, EventArgs e)
{
    //set up connection string and SQL query
    string ConnectionString = Convert.ToString( ⏎
        ConfigurationSettings.AppSettings["MSDEConnectString"]);
```

```
string CommandText = "SELECT * FROM Publisher";

//create SqlConnection and SqlCommand objects
SqlConnection myConnection = new SqlConnection(ConnectionString);
SqlCommand myCommand = new SqlCommand(CommandText, myConnection);
```

Now it's time for something new. You need to use a DataAdapter as the intermediary between the database and the DataSet itself, so you need to set this up before you create the DataSet itself, like so:

```
//create a new DataAdapter
SqlDataAdapter myAdapter = new SqlDataAdapter();

//Assign the command to the Adapter so it knows what command to
//send when Fill() is called
myAdapter.SelectCommand = myCommand;

//Create a DataSet object - any other constructors?
DataSet myDataSet = new DataSet();
```

Next, you open the connection and use the DataAdapter's Fill() method to transfer the query results from the database to the DataSet, like so:

```
try
{
    //now open connection to the database
    myConnection.Open();

    //Use the DataAdapter to fill the DataSet
    myAdapter.Fill(myDataSet);
}
catch (Exception ex)
{
    //If an exception occurs, handle it.
    throw (ex);
}
finally
{
    //Whether you succeed or fail, close the database connection
    myConnection.Close();
}
```

At this point, the DataSet is ready for work. You can iterate through it like you did with the DataReader earlier (and as we'll demonstrate later) or simply bind the information it contains to a DataGrid as you've done in pretty much every example preceding this chapter.

```
//The DataSet is now loaded.
//We need to bind it to a DataGrid and call DataBind() on it
myGrid.DataSource = myDataSet;
myGrid.DataBind();
}
```

> **NOTE** *You can find the example code in the Chapter06 directory of the code download for this book. It's called* `Simple_DataSet.aspx`.

This code is the simplest DataSet example possible, so you'll now add some more detail. Two new data-aware objects are here, and you need to learn more about them.

Understanding DataAdapter Objects

The eagle-eyed among you may have spotted what looks like an error in the previous code. It appears that we left out the following prefix for the DataSet object that identifies which data provider it is a part of:

```
DataSet myDataSet = new DataSet();
```

However, this isn't an error. The DataSet (and the family of objects it contains) are independent of any data provider. You can find their definitions in the `System.Data` namespace. In the grand scheme of things, this makes a lot of sense. Data providers are there to provide optimized access to a database and nothing more. The DataSet just stores data in memory and so should be optimized as best for .NET rather than for the database that it personally never contacts.

The key, as you may have guessed, is the DataAdapter object—or the `SqlDataAdapter`, `OleDbDataAdapter`, and `OdbcDataAdapter` objects, if you prefer. These are the objects that translate the data from the format associated with that particular data provider to the generic .NET format that the DataGrid uses. These *are* data-provider specific. However, their basic mechanisms are the same across the board. Their `Fill()` method causes data to be pulled from the database into a DataSet, and their `Update()` method pushes any changes made to the DataSet back to the database, as shown in Figure 6-3.

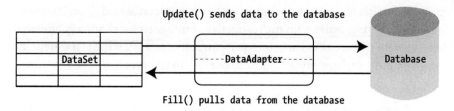

Figure 6-3. A DataAdapter object plays the middleman between DataSet and database.

Fill() and Update() are, unfortunately, not psychic, so you need to provide a DataAdapter with details of the Connection object it should use to access the database and the various SQL queries it should run when using Fill() and Update(). In PageLoad.aspx, you do all this in two easy lines of code. First, you create a SqlData-Adapter object; second, you assign the Command object you've already built (which holds a simple SELECT query to the Publisher table) to its SelectCommand property. The Command object is already associated with a Connection, so the DataAdapter is also by proxy.

```
SqlDataAdapter myAdapter = new SqlDataAdapter();
myAdapter.SelectCommand = myCommand;
```

Had you used the alternate constructor for the SqlDataAdapter, you could have written this in a single line, like so:

```
SqlDataAdapter myAdapter = new SqlDataAdapter(myCommand);
```

Indeed, two other versions of the SqlDataAdapter constructor (and of the OleDbDataAdapter and OdbcAdapter, too) lead toward providing the same information. The first takes two arguments, like so:

```
public SqlDataAdapter(string, SqlConnection);
```

In this case, the string is the SQL SELECT command written out in full, and the Connection object is as you'd expect. In the final variant, the SqlConnection object is replaced by another string parameter containing the connection string written out in full, like so:

```
public SqlDataAdapter(string, string);
```

The SQL query in these constructors is always the SELECT query that will be sent to the data source when Fill() is called. You can find it in the DataAdapter's

SelectCommand property. You'll also need to provide its UpdateCommand, InsertCommand, and DeleteCommand properties with the respective commands for changing, adding, and deleting data in the database before you can call Update() on the DataAdapter. You'll work with these three properties and Update() in Chapter 8.

> **NOTE** *Each of these four xxxCommand properties on a DataAdapter object contains a Command object and not just a string containing the relevant SQL query.*

Both Fill() and Update() can open a database connection if it's closed when they're called and will close it again once they're done. If it's already open, it'll remain open. If you want to close it, you must call Connection.Close() as you have in the code, or in Fill()'s case, you must use one of its many overloaded variations, which allows you to specify that it must close the connection after it has finished.

```
myAdapter.Fill(DataTable, myCommand, CommandBehavior.CloseConnection);
```

Of course, this particular variation of Fill() brings up another question. What's the first DataTable parameter? Well, it turns out there's a lot more to a DataSet than meets the eye.

DataSet Components

The DataSet is much more than a simple receptacle for query results. In fact, it can act as an almost complete relational database in its own right. A DataSet is, more technically, a container for one or more DataTable objects that are actually what contain the data you retrieve from the database.

- Each DataTable is referenced as DataSet.Tables["TableName"] or DataSet.Tables[index].

- Each DataTable contains a collection of DataColumn objects to represent the different pieces of information stored in the table. Each column can be referenced as DataSet.Tables["TableName"].Columns["FieldName"]. Properties such as AllowDBNull, Unique, and ReadOnly mimic those available in MSDE, mySQL, and Access.

- Each DataTable also contains a collection of DataRow objects to represent individual objects stored in the DataTable. Each row can be referenced as DataSet.Tables["TableName"].Rows[RowNumber].

- Individual fields in a DataTable object can be referenced as
  `DataSet.Tables["TableName"].Rows[RowNumber]["FieldName"]`.

- A DataSet also contains a collection of DataRelation objects that models the
  relationships between tables. Each DataRelation object contains the parent
  and child fields that are related. By default, a UniqueConstraint object is
  applied to the parent column, and a ForeignKeyConstraint object is applied
  to the child field. Thus, it mimics the way in which databases handle relationships. DataRelation objects can be referenced as
  `DataSet.Relations["RelationName"]`.

- Last but not least, the DataSet also lets you define custom views over the
  DataTables it contains. However, unlike the views offered by full relational
  databases, DataView objects offer only snapshots of the data when the
  DataView was created and aren't updated when the data is.

So, where was the DataTable in the previous example, `Simple_DataSet.aspx`?
Looking at the code, there was no mention of a DataTable anywhere when you
called the following:

```
myAdapter.Fill(myDataSet);
```

True, but by default the `Fill()` method will create a DataTable called `Table` if
one isn't specified and add the data to this. Also, when you set the DataGrid's `Data-
Source` property to just the DataSet, by default, this means it'll be bound to the first
table in the DataSet's Tables collection. Rather than leaving things to default, you
can name the DataTable to be filled and bound to in `PageLoad.aspx` with the following lines of code:

```
myAdapter.Fill(myDataSet, "Publisher");
myGrid.DataSource = myDataSet.Tables["Publisher"];
```

or with the following:

```
myGrid.DataSource = myDataSet.Tables[0];
```

depending on whether you prefer to use the table name or index position in the
DataSet's Tables collection. (Hint: Use the table name unless you're iterating
through the collection.)

For what seems a simple method, `Fill()` has many variations and rules that
are beyond the scope of this book. You could be here all day looking at this one
method. Indeed, you'll continue to discover more about it throughout this chapter, but if you prefer, the documentation that comes with the .NET software devel-

opment kit (SDK) (also available at `http://msdn.microsoft.com/library/en-us/` `cpref/html/frlrfSystemDataCommonDbDataAdapterClassFillTopic.asp`) on `Fill()` is complete and should be the first place to look for more information on it. For this book's part, you'll carry on with looking at the components of the DataSet and seeing how they fit together by re-creating the first example and iterating through a DataTable to create custom objects.

Try It Out: Iterating Through a DataSet

In this example, you'll take what you've learned about DataSets, DataTables, and the other objects in the group and replicate the previous example, "Iterating Through a DataReader." The aim is to gain a little more insight into how you access information inside a DataSet. Follow these steps:

1. In Web Matrix, open the previous example ASP.NET page `Iterating_Through_A_DataReader.aspx` and save it as `Iterating_Through_A_DataSet.aspx` in the Chapter06 directory.

2. In the Code view, change the code for the `Page_Load` handler as follows. First, add the code you've just seen to populate the DataSet with the contents of the Publisher table.

```
void Page_Load(object sender, EventArgs e)
{
    //set up connection string and SQL query
    string ConnectionString = Convert.ToString(↵
        ConfigurationSettings.AppSettings["MSDEConnectString"]);

    string CommandText = "SELECT PublisherName, PublisherCity, ↵
        PublisherContact_Email, PublisherWebsite FROM Publisher";

    //create SqlConnection and SqlCommand objects
    SqlConnection myConnection = new SqlConnection(ConnectionString);
    SqlCommand myCommand = new SqlCommand(CommandText, myConnection);

    //create a new DataAdapter
    SqlDataAdapter myAdapter = new SqlDataAdapter();

    //Assign the command to the Adapter
    myAdapter.SelectCommand = myCommand;

    //Create a DataSet object
    DataSet myDataSet = new DataSet();
```

```
//use try finally clauses around the time when the connection is open
try
{
    //now open connection to the database
    myConnection.Open();

    //Use the DataAdapter to fill the DataSet
    myAdapter.Fill(myDataSet, "Publisher");
}
catch (Exception ex)
{
    //If an exception occurs, handle it.
    throw (ex);
}
finally
{
    //Whether you succeed or fail, close the database connection
    myConnection.Close();
}
```

3. Now add the following code that iterates through the DataTable containing the data and populates the Publisher objects:

```
for (int i=0; i<=myDataSet.Tables["Publisher"].Rows.Count-1; i++)
{
    Publisher p = new Publisher();
    p.Name = myDataSet.Tables["Publisher"] ↵
        .Rows[i]["PublisherName"].ToString();
    p.City = myDataSet.Tables["Publisher"] ↵
        .Rows[i]["PublisherCity"].ToString();
    p.Email = myDataSet.Tables["Publisher"] ↵
        .Rows[i]["PublisherContact_Email"].ToString();
    p.Website = myDataSet.Tables["Publisher"] ↵
        .Rows[i]["PublisherWebsite"].ToString();

    Label1.Text += p.ToString();
}
}
```

4. Save this code, and run it. When the page loads, you'll see the same results as you got from the previous example, as shown earlier in Figure 6-2.

How It Works

You'll see a few more lines of code in this example than in the DataReader example, though not many. In fact, beyond the Page_Load handler, all the code is the same; you reviewed most of that code in the "How to Fill a DataSet" section as you discovered how to pull information from a database into a DataSet. Indeed, the only thing you've really changed in the first half of Page_Load is to name the DataTable in which the results of the query will be saved.

```
myAdapter.Fill(myDataSet, "Publisher");
```

Beyond that, the only new code in the example is for pulling individual fields into the respective properties of a Publisher object. For example, you use the following code to retrieve the name of the publisher:

```
p.Name = myDataSet.Tables["Publisher"].Rows[i]["PublisherName"].ToString();
```

You also saw this syntax earlier, but this section goes through it anyway. You start with the DataSet you created called myDataSet. You saved the contents of the Publisher table from the sample database into a DataTable object called Publisher, which you can reference as myDataSet.Tables["Publisher"]. A DataTable contains a DataRowCollection object, which you can query using its Count property to see how many rows you have to iterate through in code.

```
for (int i=0; i<=myDataSet.Tables["Publisher"].Rows.Count-1; i++)
```

You can access the rows inside the collection using their index number rather than their name, so you can reference each row as myDataSet.Tables["Publisher"].Rows[i]. You can then reference each field in a row either by name or by index, as in this code. If you aren't sure how many fields are in a row (users of wildcards take heed!), you can use the Count property of the row's DataColumnCollection and use another for loop to iterate through them again, like so:

```
for (int i=0; i<=myDataSet.Tables["Publisher"].Rows[i].Columns.Count-1; i++)
```

One awkward thing about using a DataSet and DataTables is the syntax, which can get quite long. However, you can make it easier to read by preempting the call to DataAdapter.Fill() and creating in advance the DataTable, DataRow, and Data-Column objects that it'd create on the fly. If you do this, you can reference those objects directly rather than through the DataSet. For example, if you created the DataTable object to store the query results in advance and added it to the DataSet manually, like so:

```
//Create a DataSet object
DataSet myDataSet = new DataSet();

//Create a DataTable Object
DataTable PublisherTable = new DataTable("Publisher");

//Add DataTable To DataSet
myDataSet.Tables.Add(PublisherTable);
```

then you can reference items of data in that table as follows:

```
p.Name = PublisherTable.Rows[i]["PublisherName"].ToString();
```

This is a bit more manageable. In the next section, you'll go one step further and build everything manually, even to the point of adding the data manually. This is a little extreme, but it demonstrates that the life of a DataSet isn't wholly dependent on a call to `DataAdapter.Fill()`.

Creating a DataSet from Scratch

Over the next few pages, you'll build a DataSet that mirrors the example database in terms of tables, strongly typed tables, and relationships. You're doing this for the following reasons:

- To get a feeling for the child objects and collections that a DataTable contains. Although you'll repeat the same tasks a few times, you'll try to look at several different ways of achieving them if you can.

- To understand a bit more about relationships between tables.

- To have this DataSet ready when you come to look at data binding, updating and adding data, and creating DataViews.

> **NOTE** *Strictly speaking, you should never need to model an entire database in a DataSet for the purposes of data binding, especially considering the resources it consumes. However, for demonstration purposes, you can live with it.*

You can find the complete example in the code download directory for Chapter 6. It's called `Building_A_DataSet.aspx`. The actual page generated is deliberately nothing fancy. It contains four DataGrids, one for each table in the Books database. They're there purely to demonstrate that the DataSet does indeed mimic the sample database.

```
<body>
    <form runat="server">
        <p>
            Name of the DataSet : <asp:Label id="DSName" runat="server" />
        </p>
        <p><asp:DataGrid id="PublisherGrid" runat="server" /></p>
        <p><asp:DataGrid id="AuthorGrid" runat="server" /></p>
        <p><asp:DataGrid id="BookGrid" runat="server" /></p>
        <p><asp:DataGrid id="WWWGrid" runat="server" /></p>
    </form>
</body>
```

As usual, the action takes place in the `Page_Load()` event handler. However, you'll see a fair amount of code, so rather than have it all in one place, it's split into several methods. Inside `Page_Load()` itself, it's pretty straightforward. You start by creating the Connection object, as follows:

```
void Page_Load(object sender, EventArgs e)
{
    //Get Connection String. Commands will come later
    string ConnectionString = Convert.ToString( ⏎
        ConfigurationSettings.AppSettings["MSDEConnectString"]);
    SqlConnection myConnection = new SqlConnection(ConnectionString);
```

Then you create a new DataSet object and build it to match the sample database, like so:

```
//create a new DataSet.
DataSet myDataSet = new DataSet("Books");

//Populate it with tables, relations, and data
GenerateBooksDataSet(myDataSet, myConnection);
```

Finally, you bind each table in the DataSet to its own DataGrid and call Data-Bind(), like so:

```
//Print out the name of the DataSet
DSName.Text = myDataSet.DataSetName;

//Bind each table to a Grid
PublisherGrid.DataSource = myDataSet.Tables["Publisher"];
AuthorGrid.DataSource = myDataSet.Tables["Author"];
BookGrid.DataSource = myDataSet.Tables["Book"];
WWWGrid.DataSource = myDataSet.Tables["WhoWroteWhat"];

//Data Bind The Page
Page.DataBind();
}
```

The key, of course, is the GenerateBooksDataSet() method, but again you're just marshaling your forces in this method. All you do here is call the methods that do the real work, like so:

```
void GenerateBooksDataSet(DataSet dset, SqlConnection conn)
{
    //Add four tables to the dataset;
    AddBookTable(dset);
    AddAuthorTable(dset);
    AddPublisherTable(dset);
    AddWhoWroteWhatTable(dset);

    //Add in the relationships between the tables;
    AddRelationships(dset);

    //Fill The Tables
    FillAuthorTable(dset, conn);
    FillPublisherTable(dset, conn);
    FillBookTable(dset, conn);
    FillWhoWroteWhatTable(dset, conn);

    return;
}
```

Adding DataTables to a DataSet

Adding a DataTable object to a DataSet object in code may seem new, but the methods you need to call and the properties you need to set mirror almost exactly the actions you took back in Chapter 2 when you built the sample database against an actual database server. Those actions are as follows:

- Creating the table

- Creating and naming the columns within the table

- Setting the column's data type and any other properties it should have

- Establishing the table's primary key

Variations exist in how you do this, but the aims are the same. You'll now look at the method `AddBookTable()` in the code for an example. You start by creating a new DataTable object that you'll name Book. You don't have to give a name to the DataTable constructor right away; you can set it later in the `TableName` property, but there's less code to work through this way.

```
void AddBookTable(DataSet dset)
{
    //Create a new DataTable called Book
    DataTable BookTable = new DataTable("Book");
```

Every DataTable has a Columns collection object, so to add a new DataColumn, you simply call the collection's `Add()` method. This will either add a DataColumn object that you've already defined to the table or create a new one, add it to the collection, and return it as its result for more work. This code uses the second option. As demonstrated, you can either set the new DataColumn to a variable for later reference or ignore the return value and just refer to the new DataColumn through the Columns collection, like so:

```
DataColumn BookID = BookTable.Columns.Add("BookID", typeof(Int32));
BookTable.Columns.Add("BookTitle", typeof(string));
```

`Add()` also takes up to three parameters: the name of the column, its data type, and, where applicable, the way to combine the contents of other columns in the same table to create its own contents. Note that you have to specify a .NET base type for a DataColumn's data type; thus, `Varchar(255)` has no meaning here and would create an error.

For a list of data types, refer to `ms-help://MS.NETFramework-SDKv1.1/cpref/html/frlrfSystemDataDataColumnClassDataTypeTopic.htm`.

```
BookTable.Columns.Add("BookPublisherID", typeof(Int32));
BookTable.Columns.Add("BookMainTopic", typeof(string));
```

With the columns in the table established, you can attend to their behavior. Should their contents be unique in each field? Can they be null, and so on? Each DataColumn object has a set of properties that match those you saw in Chapter 2. By default, you set the most common properties as follows: `AllowDBNull` is true, `Unique` is false, and `ReadOnly` is false. Also, for text, `MaxLength` equals -1 by default, which implies there's no maximum string length for a field in this column. For a database column containing an autonumber, you must also set the `AutoIncrement` property to true, along with the `AutoIncrementSeed` property for a start value, such as 1. This latter property doesn't have a default value, but the `AutoIncrementStep` property does: 1.

You need to make the following adjustments:

```
BookTable.Columns["BookTitle"].MaxLength = 100;
BookTable.Columns["BookTitle"].AllowDBNull = false;
BookTable.Columns["BookMainTopic"].MaxLength = 25;
BookTable.Columns["BookMainTopic"].AllowDBNull = false;
```

Finally, you need to set BookID to be the table's primary key. This will automatically set its `AllowDBNull` property to false, and its `Unique` property will be true. Note that a DataTable's `PrimaryKey` property actually requires an array of DataColumn objects in case the table's primary key is a composite one and contains more than one field. You'll see this at work when you build the WhoWroteWhat table.

```
BookTable.PrimaryKey = new DataColumn[] {BookID};
BookTable.Columns["BookID"].AutoIncrement = true;
BookTable.Columns["BookID"].AutoIncrementSeed = 1;
```

Last, but not least, you add the whole DataTable to the DataSet's Tables collection, like so:

```
  dset.Tables.Add(BookTable);
}
```

So, as long as you stick to the same methodical way of adding fields to a table in a database, adding DataColumns to a DataTable will remain a straightforward process in code. You'll now look at a couple of variations in the other `AddxxxTable()` methods.

AddAuthorTable() neatly shows that you needn't add a DataTable to a DataSet once it has been fully defined. Like the Add() method for a DataTable's Columns collection, the Add() method for a DataSet's Tables collection allows you to create and add a blank DataTable with a given name as well as add an already established one. Thus, you can make the following call and use the DataTable returned by Add() to define the table:

```
void AddAuthorTable(DataSet dset)
{
    DataTable AuthorTable = dset.Tables.Add("Author");

    ...
}
```

AddWhoWroteWhatTable() also demonstrates how you deal with composite primary keys. You simply add all the DataColumn objects in the primary key to the DataTable's PrimaryKey array, like so:

```
void AddWhoWroteWhatTable(DataSet dset)
{
    DataTable WWWTable = new DataTable("WhoWroteWhat");
    WWWTable.Columns.Add("WWWBookID", typeof(Int32));
    WWWTable.Columns.Add("WWWAuthorID", typeof(Int32));
    WWWTable.PrimaryKey = new DataColumn[] ⤶
       {WWWTable.Columns["WWWBookID"], WWWTable.Columns["WWWAuthorID"]};

    dset.Tables.Add(WWWTable);
}
```

Note that if more than one DataColumn is added to the PrimaryKey array, only their AllowDBNull properties will be changed from their default to true. Their Unique property remains false, in contrast to the situation where the primary key is only one field when Unique is set to true.

Setting Up Relationships in a DataSet

In Chapter 2, you learned how a relationship between two columns was first established and then clarified by a constraint: A unique constraint would ensure that the parent column contained unique values in each field and a foreign key constraint would cover what happened to all the entries in a child table when the corresponding entry in the parent table was altered somehow. The same is true of relationships between DataTables in a DataSet, as you'll see in this section.

If you recall, the sample database has three relationships between tables, as shown in Figure 6-4. Each is backed by a foreign key constraint that says that a change in the parent table will cascade down into the child tables unless the parent entry has been deleted, in which case the child entry will become null.

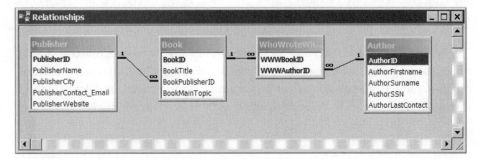

Figure 6-4. Three relationships to create

All three relationships are built in the same way in AddRelationships(), so you'll look at just one—the relationship between the Book and Publisher tables. The first step to take in the code is to establish which two columns are related to each other and which is the parent and which the child. This you'll do by identifying the DataColumn object that represents them explicitly, like so:

```
void AddRelationships(DataSet dset)
{
    DataColumn parentColumn = dset.Tables["Publisher"].Columns["PublisherID"];
    DataColumn childColumn = dset.Tables["Book"].Columns["BookPublisherID"];
```

Once you've done this, you can establish the DataRelation object, give the relation a name (BookToPublisher), and use Add() to add it to the DataSet's Relations collection. Note that unlike all the Add() functions you've seen in this section, this Add() won't create a blank DataRelation for you to use. You *have* to provide the related columns for the DataRelation to be created.

```
DataRelation newRelation = ⤸
    new DataRelation("BookToPublisher", parentColumn, childColumn);
dset.Relations.Add(newRelation);
```

With the relation established, you can set constraints on a parent or child column by assigning one to the DataRelation's ParentKeyConstraint or ChildKey-Constraint property, respectively. In this case, you need to establish a foreign key constraint on the child column, like so:

```
ForeignKeyConstraint newFK = newRelation.ChildKeyConstraint;
newFK.DeleteRule = Rule.SetNull;
newFK.UpdateRule = Rule.Cascade;
newFK.AcceptRejectRule = AcceptRejectRule.Cascade;
```

And that's it. The rest of AddRelationships() essentially repeats this code to put the other two relationships in place. All that remains is to flip the switch that turns on these rules. Once you do that, any data now entered, altered, or deleted in the DataSet will be subject to these rules and may be rejected accordingly.

```
    dset.EnforceConstraints = true;
}
```

Creating DataRows

With each DataTable and the relationships between them established, all that's left is to add some data to the tables. You've already seen how to use Fill() to fill tables, but that's not the only way to add information to a DataTable. You can also create and populate DataRows, adding them individually to the corresponding DataTable. The FillPublisherTable() method demonstrates this.

The first option to work with a DataRow (and the recommended one) is to create an empty DataRow object by calling NewRow() on the DataTable object for which you want to create the row.

```
void FillPublisherTable(DataSet dset, SqlConnection conn)
{
    DataRow NewRow = dset.Tables["Publisher"].NewRow();
```

The advantage with this method is that the DataRow object will know what each field is called and the type of value it should contain, having ascertained it from the DataTable object to which the row is being added. It will therefore generate an exception if you try to add values that go against the rules on the table. When you have added values as appropriate, you use Add() to add it to the Rows collection for that DataTable, like so:

```
NewRow["PublisherID"] = 1;
NewRow["PublisherName"] = "APress";
NewRow["PublisherCity"] = "Berkeley";
NewRow["PublisherContact_Email"] = "someguy@apress.com";
NewRow["PublisherWebsite"] = "http://www.apress.com";
dset.Tables["Publisher"].Rows.Add(NewRow);
```

The second option to add data to a DataTable is to create not a DataRow object but an array of generic objects that matches the fields in the table. The obvious disadvantage here is that you can create an illegal value for a field that will be picked up only when you try and Add() it to the DataTable's Rows collection.

```
Object[] NewRowFields = new Object[5];
NewRowFields[0] = 2;
NewRowFields[1] = "Friends Of Ed";
NewRowFields[2] = "Birmingham";
NewRowFields[3] = "aneditor@friendsofed.com";
NewRowFields[4] = "http://www.friendsofed.com";
dset.Tables["Publisher"].Rows.Add(NewRowFields);
```

Several of the examples in the .NET SDK build up rows of data using loops to generate values, which is handy for examples, but in general, you'll probably end up using a DataAdapter to fill a DataTable once you've created it. The following is a word or two of warning about using Fill() in this situation:

- If you call Fill() on a blank DataTable, as you did in the earlier "Iterating Through a DataSet" section, the DataTable will assign each column in the DataTable a name and data type as best it can from the fields in the query results it's storing. However, properties such as AllowDBNull and ReadOnly will remain at their defaults, and the PrimaryKey for the table won't be set.

- In contrast, if you call Fill() on a DataTable whose details you've defined as you have in this example, the DataAdapter will try to match DataColumn names with field names in the query results and fill in the values accordingly. If it can't match a field name with a DataColumn, it will create a new DataColumn with the same name as the field and use that instead, so be careful that either column and field names match up or that you use aliases in your SQL statement.

That said, one version of Fill() you didn't try earlier allows you to specify a subsection of the results from a query to add to a DataTable. This fits in nicely with the problem you now have with the DataTable copy of the Publisher table in `FillPublisherTable()`. Using code to create the first two rows manually means that the versions of `Fill()` you've used so far would try and duplicate those two rows if you called them now. Moreover, this would cause an error because values in the Primary key field would be duplicated, which isn't allowed. This new version of `Fill()` allows you to say which row in the results you start filling from and how many rows you want to add to the DataTable.

```
SqlDataAdapter PublisherAdapter = new SqlDataAdapter();
SqlCommand PublisherCommand = ⤸
    new SqlCommand("SELECT * FROM Publisher", conn);
PublisherAdapter.SelectCommand = PublisherCommand;

conn.Open();
```

The first parameter identifies the DataSet you're working with, the second is the index number of the row in the results of the `SelectCommand` to start filling with, and the third is the number of rows to add to the DataTable, which is identified by the fourth parameter.

```
    PublisherAdapter.Fill(dset, 2, 3, "Publisher");
    conn.Close();

    return;
}
```

Note that the `SelectCommand` still retrieves all the rows from the Publisher table even though you use only three of them. If you wanted to retrieve only the three rows required, you'd need to alter the SELECT query rather than use this variant of `Fill()`.

DataSet vs. DataReader

Now that you've got a rough idea of how a DataSet works, it's time to take a look at how it compares with a DataReader. The two have some obvious differences. Before you start using them as sources of on-screen data, it's time for a recap before you move onto the next chapter. Table 6-3 lists the differences you've seen so far and a few related ones.

Table 6-3. Comparing DataReaders and DataSets

DataReader	DataSet
A DataReader is specific to a data provider (for example, `SqlDataReader`, `OdbcDataReader`, and `OleDbDataReader`).	The DataSet class isn't a part of any data provider. It's specific to .NET only. However, the DataAdapter used to fill the DataSet with `Fill()` is specific to a data provider.
The data retrieved through a DataReader is read-only.	The data retrieved through a DataSet is read-write.
The data retrieved through a DataReader is forward-only. Once the data has been cycled through, the DataReader must be closed and re-created in order to reaccess the data.	You can work with data in a DataSet in any order you choose as many times as you like.
A DataReader presents data through a direct connection to the data source. Only one row of data is stored in Internet Information Services (IIS) memory at any one time.	A DataSet stores all the data from the data source in IIS memory at once.
A DataReader is fast.	A DataSet is slower than a DataReader.
A DataReader takes up few IIS and memory resources but annexes the database connection until it's closed.	A DataSet takes up a lot more memory/IIS resources to store all the data, but it doesn't hold up a database connection until it's closed. The connection needs to be open only when `Fill()` is called.
A DataReader lasts as long as the connection to the database is open. It can't be persisted in a cookie or a session variable.	A DataSet lasts only until the page is reloaded (posted back) unless it's somehow persisted (for example, in a session variable).
Fields in a DataReader are referenced by index number or name.	You can reference fields in a DataSet by name, but you must also name the DataTable and identify the row (index) that contains the field.
A DataReader has no concept of primary keys, constraints, views, or any other relational database management system (RDBMS) concept except row and field.	A DataSet contains DataTables. A primary key may be set for each DataTable, and relationships and constraints may be established between them. DataViews may be created over the DataSet.
You can't update a data source through a DataReader.	You can make changes to data in a DataSet and then upload those changes back to the data source.
A DataReader connects to only one data source.	A DataSet can be filled with `Fill()` from multiple data sources.

You'll also compare DataSet and DataReader at the end of Chapter 7 with respect to the theory and techniques you learn there. The intention is that by the end of that chapter, you'll be able to make a sound judgment on which object should be used as the source of data for any ASP.NET pages you're writing. You can't use DataReaders to send changes back to the database, so you won't do this in Chapter 8. However, using DataSets isn't the only way to update a database, as you'll see.

Good Practices

The next chapter looms, but before you start putting data on the screen, we'll quickly recap some useful coding tips covered in this chapter.

- Query only for the information you want to use. For example, don't query for three fields per row if you're using only two. Likewise, use a WHERE clause in a SELECT statement to retrieve only the rows of information that are required rather than every row in the database.

- If you're using a DataReader, make sure you close it with `Close()` as soon as you can. Similarly, make sure you use `Close()` for your Connection as well.

- Use the DataReader's `HasRows` and `IsDBNull` properties to avoid any unwanted error messages when working with data.

- If you're using a DataSet, be aware exactly of how calling `Fill()` will work with the DataSet you're using. Will it create new columns in a DataTable or use the other ones there? Make sure the fields you're querying for in the database match those in the DataTable you're targeting.

- Don't forget that primary keys and relationships in a DataSet won't be copied over from a database. You must create them in code.

- Even though `Fill()` may close a Connection object automatically, it won't do any harm to call `Connection.Close()` explicitly in case it doesn't.

Summary

In this chapter, you looked in detail at the DataReader and DataSet objects. These are the two objects most commonly used as the receptacle for query results by data-driven pages.

You learned that the DataReader is a read-only, forward-only, data provider-specific window on the results of the query sent by a page and that you can iterate through those results a row at a time using the DataReader's Read() method. Individual pieces of information can be identified in the current row in a DataReader by name and by index number and can be vetted before being used with the DataReader's HasRows and IsDBNull properties.

In contrast, you saw that the DataSet is data-provider independent. It's a container for a group of objects that can describe with some accuracy the table structure and relationships in a database, and because it's all in memory, the query results stored in a DataSet are read-write and can be accessed in any order. You can either build a complete data structure in code from scratch or Fill() it using a DataAdapter object.

In the next chapter, you'll discover the three ways to bind information that's available through the two objects to any control on an ASP.NET page.

CHAPTER 7

Displaying Data on a Page

IN CHAPTER 6, you spent your time looking at the two most important objects in ADO.NET: the DataReader and the DataSet. You saw how they differed from each other; specifically, the DataReader is a transient object and provides forward-only, read-only access to the results of any query you send to the database, and the DataSet is a read-write, random-access representation of any database that stays in memory even when the connection to the data source closes. You saw how they could be populated with data from a data source and how you could pull that data into something more useful for your site, such as a business object.

In this chapter, you'll continue your work with these two objects and discover the various ways of retrieving and displaying read-only data on a page. You'll learn that *data binding* information to controls has three variations depending on which of the following you're attempting:

- Binding individual fields to specific properties of the controls on a page

- Binding a column of fields into a data-aware control such as a RadioButtonList or a DropDownList

- Binding a large amount of data into a DataGrid and customizing the DataGrid accordingly

You'll also see that the trade-off between the speed of the DataReader and the availability of the DataSet often makes a difference in the way you build even simple pages.

Now, the phrase *read-only* may sound limiting to you, but Web sites send you a lot more read-only data than data you can alter. Take, for example, search engine results, product details on an e-commerce site, news reports from the innumerable feeds on the Web, auction pages, and so on. They're all read-only unless you have the administrative privileges to change them. Regardless, you may be itching to get straight onto editable data, and you'll look at how to handle that and the associated extra coding baggage in Chapter 8.

For the less impetuous, you'll see that working with read-only data isn't a yoke to bear, but on the other hand, it isn't a bag of feathers. You have less to do when you don't have to accommodate creating, updating, and deleting data, but you still have plenty of ways to screw it up.

Data Binding

In Chapter 1, we described how a data-aware ASP.NET page is basically a static template into which data is added dynamically from a data source. This "plugging in" of data to a page is more commonly known as *data binding*. Even though there are various techniques to this discipline based on how much data you want to bind and what Web form controls you want to bind them to, the basic steps you take are always the same.

1. Add a data-aware control to the ASP.NET page.

2. Associate a source of data with the control or the properties of the control.

3. Call DataBind() on the control or on the page.

All the examples in Chapters 3 and 4, for instance, followed these three steps with the barest minimum of code, binding the query results to a DataGrid object.

```
SqlDataReader myReader = myCommand.ExecuteReader();
myGrid.DataSource = myReader;
myGrid.DataBind();
```

You'll spend the rest of this chapter looking at how you expand upon these few lines of code to produce more than an HTML table in its default colors that displays the data, one field per table cell. As mentioned, lots of variations exist, but they all fall into one of the following three categories:

- Binding single fields to the properties or value of a control. This is often known as *inline binding*.

- Binding a list of values (one column in a table) to a control. For convenience, we'll call this *list binding*.

- Binding a table of values to a control. For convenience, we'll call this *table binding*.

Before you get to any code, you should see how the four steps differ based on which of the three tasks you're attempting. You'll also keep an eye on good practice. As a site grows, it's your responsibility to make sure it continues to perform well, so you'll need to preserve resources most of all and database resources in particular.

Data-Aware Web Form Controls

All three data binding methods apply *only* to ASP.NET Web form controls because the whole process takes place on the server before the page is sent to the client. So then, you can use only those controls whose tags begin <asp:...> and contain the attribute runat="server" for data binding. Technically speaking, every Web form control must understand how to bind data to at least its properties because it inherits the DataBind() method as something it must implement from its parent Control class. At the least, this means that every ASP.NET Web form control understands inline binding and can set its properties to values from a database, and for some it means that they know how to bind lists and tables of data into their structure. Table 7-1 shows which groups of controls support which type of binding.

Table 7-1. Web Form Controls and the Data They Support

Control Type	Control Names	Binding Supported
Text based	Label, Literal, Hyperlink, Xml	Inline binding
Form items	TextBox, CheckBox, RadioButton, Button, LinkButton, ImageButton	Inline binding
Images and spaces	Image, AdRotator, Panel, PlaceHolder	Inline binding
Tabular	Table, Calendar	Inline binding
Validation	RequiredFieldValidator, CompareValidator, RegularExpressionValidator, RangeValidator, CustomValidator, ValidationSummary	Inline binding
Form lists	CheckBoxList, RadioButtonList, DropDownList, ListBox	Inline binding, list binding
Data-aware controls	DataGrid, DataList, Repeater	Inline binding, list binding, table binding
Web Matrix specific	mxDataGrid	Inline binding, list binding, table binding

It may seem that only a few controls support list and table binding, but they're pretty powerful—you'd be surprised!!

Associating Data to Control

The following sections contain three questions to ponder. How much data do you need to pull from your data source, which object do you stream it into, and how do you associate it to a control?

How Much Data Do You Need?

Starting from the top, you've already learned that you can use the SELECT statement to query for as much or as little data as is required for binding to the controls on your page. It makes sense then to query only for what you need. This is a theme broached in Chapter 6.

For example, inline binding requires you to identify individual fields to take values from, so why take a whole table's worth? Depending on the .NET object you're sourcing the data from (see the next section), it may not matter if it contains several rows of data, because you can specify which row and field to use. As you know, however, the DataReader presents only a row at a time, so you may want to query only for a specific row of data with a statement such as the following:

```
SELECT UserCategory, PreferredColorScheme, ConnectionSpeed
FROM UserPreference
WHERE UserName = 'Dan Maharry'
```

In a similar vein, if you're looking to list bind a control, you need to present the control with a set of rows, each containing *two* fields—one that represents the text for items in the list and one that provides the values for items that will be passed on when selected by a user. So, for example, if you wanted a drop-down list containing the list of publishers in the database, you could use the following statement to query the database, using the PublisherName field to display in the list and the PublisherID to make a note of the selections:

```
SELECT PublisherID, PublisherName
FROM Publisher
```

In the case of table binding, you can query whatever you need, but try to restrict your query to just what you need. It's possible to hide columns in a DataGrid or a Repeater, but why bother if you didn't need the column in the first place?

Don't forget that there's no reason a DataGrid or similar can't be bound to a query whose result is only one or two fields large.

Data Source Objects

Although we're restricting you to just the DataReader and DataSet objects in this chapter, it's worth noting that you can use many other objects as the source of the data to which you're binding a control.

For list and table binding, you can use any of the following:

- ArrayList objects

- Collections

- DataReader objects

- DataView objects

- DataRow objects

- DataTable objects in datasets

- Any other object that .NET can iterate through because it implements the IEnumerable interface

- Any function whose return value is one of the previous objects

And, if you don't mind installing Web Matrix on your server, you can also use its DataSource, SqlDataSourceControl, and AccessDataSourceControl objects, too.

If you're inline binding a single value to a control property, you can use practically any other single value from any other object available to you, as long as you know the syntax to get the value from the object.

> **TIP** *Whatever object you use for the data source, make sure the control doing the binding can see it. This usually means declaring it (the DataReader, DataSet, and so on) as a global variable within the <script> block of the page.*

Creating the Association

This step comes before calling DataBind() and as such means that a control or control property can't be bound to data based on the values bound into some other control—not unless you're using PostBack in the page to react to choices made by the user anyway. (We'll come back to PostBack in a minute.)

Inline binding is quite different from list or table binding at this stage, because you must associate the control property with the data field that will fill it in the HTML section of the page rather than the code section. For those of you who worked with classic ASP, inline binding is reminiscent of the way you inserted ASP code into pages. Let's say you wanted to bind a label's text control. You'd use the following in the page:

```
<asp:Label id="Label1" runat="server" text='<%# expression %>'>
```

The expression in the text has to identify the source for the value you want bound to the label's Text property and must be surrounded by <%# ... %> tags. You'll look more closely at how expressions work in this situation in a minute.

In contrast, list and table binding can be set up in both the code and the HTML part of the page. Both need you to set the DataSource property for the control you're binding to the DataReader/DataSet you're using. If you're binding to a list control, you also need to set its DataValueField and DataTextField properties to the fields in your queried data.

Calling DataBind()

This shouldn't be too difficult. You just call DataBind(), don't you? Well, yes, but on what object? Every Web form control implements this interface because it has to as a derivative of its parent class, System.Web.UI.Control, and one of its intricacies is that a call to DataBind() on a control will also call DataBind() on any controls contained within it. So, you could call it on a Label control, and just that particular binding would occur. On the other hand, you could call Page.DataBind(), and the command would also filter down to every control on the page.

You need to also consider a second issue here. Should a page rebind to a data source each time a page posts back? Consider a page containing lots of form controls populated by binding RadioButtonLists, DataGrids, and other elements to a data source with the eventual aim to update the user's answers to the form back to the database. You have no need to bind the controls to the data source more than once because its purpose is purely to set up the form, not to record the answers given to it. It would be a huge waste of resources to rebind the data every time the user set a new control and caused the form to post back, especially if the form was complex. It would also lose the values the user had entered onto the form if it was posted back because the rebinding would write over them. Not good.

Inline Binding

It may be more common to inline bind data from a DataSet or a DataView object, as you'll do in a minute, but the technique is no less valid against a DataReader. Doing so also raises a few points, noted previously, that may be missed if you used an object that keeps the data in memory before you use it.

Try It Out: Inline Binding from a DataReader

In this example, you'll mimic the results from the "Try it Out: Iterating Through a DataReader" section in the previous chapter and print the details of a publisher in your sample database. Rather than use a single control to present the results, you'll use two Label and two Hyperlink controls to echo the results.

1. In Web Matrix, create a new ASP.NET page called
   `Inline_Binding_DataReader.aspx` and save it to the Chapter07 folder. You may need to create this directory.

2. In Design view, drag two Label controls to the page. Name the first
   lblName and the second lblCity. Now drag two Hyperlink controls to the page. Name them hypEmail and hypWebsite. Finally, add one more Label control called lblError to house any error messages should something untoward happen (oh, the horror!). Now clear the Text properties for all five controls. With a bit of added plain text, your page should look something Figure 7-1.

Figure 7-1. Basic layout for `Inline_Binding_DataReader.aspx`

3. In All view, make sure you've included the right data provider at the top of the page.

```
<%@ Page Language="C#" %>
<%@ import Namespace="System.Data" %>
<%@ import Namespace="System.Data.SqlClient" %>
```

4. Switch to Code view. You need to set up the DataReader to query for publisher details and add your standard code for database access.

```
//must declare the DataReader globally else the page can't see it.
SqlDataReader myReader;

void Page_Load(object sender, EventArgs e)
{
    //set up connection string and SQL query
    string ConnectionString = Convert.ToString ⤸
        (ConfigurationSettings.AppSettings["MSDEConnectString"]);
    string CommandText = "SELECT PublisherName, PublisherCity, ⤸
        PublisherContact_Email, PublisherWebsite FROM Publisher ⤸
        WHERE PublisherID = '1'";

    //create SqlConnection and SqlCommand objects
    SqlConnection myConnection = new SqlConnection(ConnectionString);
    SqlCommand myCommand = new SqlCommand(CommandText, myConnection);

    //use try finally clauses when the connection is open.
    try
    {
        //open connection to the database
        myConnection.Open();

        //run query
        myReader = myCommand.ExecuteReader();

        if (myReader.Read())
        {
            // Process results here.
        }
        else
        {
            lblError.Text="No results to databind to.";
        }
        myReader.Close();

    }
```

```
      catch (Exception ex)
      {
          //If an exception occurs, handle it.
          throw (ex);
      }
      finally
      {
          //Whether you succeed or fail, close the database connection
          myConnection.Close();
      }
  }
```

5. Now you need to set which data should be bound and to what. Switch over to HTML view, and add the following:

```
<body>
    <form runat="server">
    <p>
        <asp:Label id="lblName" runat="server">
            Name: <%# DataBinder.Eval (myReader, "[0]") %>
        </asp:Label>
        <br />

        City:
        <asp:Label id="lblCity" runat="server"
            Text='<%# DataBinder.Eval (myReader, "[1]") %>' />
        <br />

        Contact:
        <asp:HyperLink id="hypEmail" runat="server"
            NavigateUrl='mailto: <%# DataBinder.Eval (myReader, "[2]") %>'
            Text='<%# DataBinder.Eval (myReader, "[2]") %>' />
        <br />

        Homesite:
        <asp:HyperLink id="hypWebsite" runat="server"
            NavigateUrl='<%# DataBinder.Eval (myReader, "[3]") %>'>
            <%# DataBinder.Eval (myReader, "[3]") %>
        </asp:HyperLink>
    </p>
    <p>
        <asp:Label id="lblError" runat="server"></asp:Label>
    </p>
    </form>
</body>
```

6. You've added the data-aware controls to the page and associated them with the required data retrieved from the database. All that's left to do is call DataBind(). Switch to Code view, and add the following:

```
if (myReader.Read())
{
    Page.DataBind();
}
else
{
    lblError.Text="No results to databind to.";
}
myReader.Close();
```

7. Now save the code, and view the page in a browser. When the page loads, all appears to be well, but is it? Move your cursor over the e-mail link, as shown in Figure 7-2, and you'll see that the link isn't to mailto: someguy@apress.com. You'll have to change it.

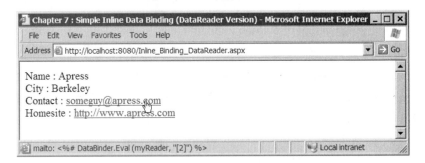

Figure 7-2. All is not well with this link.

8. To fix the problem, you could revert to using the DataReader's GetString() method you saw in Chapter 6 and fix it in Page_Load() with a line of code such as this:

```
hypEmail.NavigateUrl = "mailto:" + myReader.GetString(2);
```

9. However, a much more elegant solution exists. A second version of the call to DataBinder.Eval() takes a format string as its third parameter, so you can alter hypEmail's NavigateUrl property to be as follows:

```
navigateurl='<%# DataBinder.Eval (myReader, "[2]", "mailto:{0}") %>'
```

10. Problem solved. Save, and test the code again. Sure enough—the link now works.

How It Works

Let's compare what you've done to the checklist for data binding you saw in the previous section. The aim of the page is to display a publisher's details on the page, just as you did in the first example of this chapter. However, you'll limit your results to just a single publisher. Displaying a list of publishers would imply list binding, which we'll cover in the next section. Instead, you pull just a single publisher's details from the database and work with that.

```
SELECT PublisherName, PublisherCity, PublisherContact_Email, PublisherWebsite ⤶
    FROM Publisher WHERE PublisherID = '1'
```

> **TIP** *Microsoft DataBase (MDB) file users may come unstuck here, as these files don't play nicely with quotes around a value in a WHERE clause. Simply remove them for the example to work.*

First on the checklist is to add some controls to the Web page, so you add a control for each detail in the database. That way, you can experiment a bit with combinations of text and bound data to see what works and what doesn't.

The second step is to associate the fields of data to the controls. For the first Label control, you've mixed the binding expression with the text value of the control's tag. In the expression itself, you call DataBinder.Eval(), which is a static method and thus always available.

```
<asp:Label id="lblName" runat="server"> Name:
    <%# DataBinder.Eval (myReader, "[0]") %>
</asp:Label>
```

This requires two arguments: the name of the data source object (myReader) and a string stating from which field to take the value. Because you're using a DataReader, you can reference the field using its index value in the row, much as you did with the Get---() methods. As demonstrated in Chapter 6, you can equally use the text name of the field to reference it, like so:

```
<asp:Label id="lblName" runat="server"> Name
            : <%# DataBinder.Eval (myReader, "[PublisherName]") %> </asp:Label>
```

In the second control, you're binding a value to the Text property of the Label control. Of course, this amounts to the same thing, but it does show that you can bind to both property and value.

```
City : <asp:Label id="lblCity" runat="server"
    text='<%# DataBinder.Eval (myReader, "[1]") %>'> </asp:Label>
```

> **NOTE** *You have to use double quotes around the second parameter of Eval and therefore single quotes around the binding expression as a whole because .NET associates single quotes with single character values, not strings, and will throw an error when it tries to parse [1] as a single character. HTML, on the other hand, isn't as picky about quotes as long as they're paired correctly.*

In the third control, you've attempted to bind to two control properties, Text and NavigateUrl. However, you encountered the problem that hyperlinks require e-mail addresses to be prefixed with mailto: for them to be recognized as e-mail addresses rather than Web addresses by the browser. Thus, you tried to concatenate text and binding expression inside the control's attribute, like so:

```
Contact: <asp:HyperLink id="hypEmail" runat="server"
    NavigateUrl='mailto: <%# DataBinder.Eval (myReader, "[2]") %>'
    Text='<%# DataBinder.Eval (myReader, "[2]") %>' />
```

This doesn't work because you can't mix the two inside the property of a control. As soon as you do, ASP.NET regards the binding expression as literal text instead of the placeholder for data that it is. Also, *you have no way to alter the value of the field in the DataReader*. But it *is* possible to format the value of the field as it's being bound to the control using the alternate version of DataBinder.Eval(). You just pass it the format string mailto:{0} as its third parameter, and Eval() will retrieve the field from the DataReader, substitute it for the placeholder {0}, and assign the newly formatted string to the property:

```
<asp:HyperLink id="hypEmail" runat="server" ⏎
    NavigateUrl='<%# DataBinder.Eval (myReader, "[2]", "mailto:{0}") %>' ⏎
    Text='<%# DataBinder.Eval (myReader, "[2]") %>' > </asp:HyperLink>
```

Finally, the fourth Web control on the page demonstrates that you can bind to both the properties and the text value of a control at the same time.

```
Website : <asp:HyperLink id="hypWebsite" runat="server"
            NavigateUrl='<%# DataBinder.Eval (myReader, "[3]") %>'>
            <%# DataBinder.Eval (myReader, "[3]") %>
        </asp:HyperLink>
```

With all the placeholders for the data set up, it's just a matter of creating the DataReader, accessing the first row (you still have to call Read() or else there's nothing to bind to), and calling DataBind().

```
//run query
myReader = myCommand.ExecuteReader();

if (myReader.Read())
{
    Page.DataBind();
}
else
{
    lblError.Text="No results to databind to.";
}
myReader.Close();
```

Note that you've called DataBind() on the whole page rather than the individual controls. If you comment out this call, nothing will get set at all. As a slight extension of this example, try experimenting with binding individual controls just to prove that binding to one label won't affect the others unless they too are explicitly bound. Perhaps create a Panel object that contains some of the controls and call DataBind() on that to prove that it's not just the DataBind() method in the Page object that filters down to its children.

Try It Out: Inline Binding to a DataSet

Inline binding to values stored in a DataSet works in much the same way as the previous example with a DataReader. The main difference is that the binding expression is slightly different to accommodate the syntax used to identify fields, rows, and tables inside a DataSet. To see it in action, you'll adapt the previous exercise to do the same job but use a DataSet instead of a DataReader. Before wrapping up, we'll also demonstrate that a DataSet isn't a forward-only data source like the DataReader.

1. In Web Matrix, open `Inline_Binding_DataReader.aspx` and resave it to the Chapter07 folder as `Inline_Binding_DataSet.aspx`.

2. Switch to Code view. Rather than a DataReader, you need to alter `Page_Load()` to use a DataSet. You'll use the same basic code you saw in Chapter 6 to build it, as follows:

```
DataSet myDataSet = new DataSet();

void Page_Load(object sender, EventArgs e)
{
   string ConnectionString = Convert.ToString( ↵
      ConfigurationSettings.AppSettings["MSDEConnectString"]);
   string CommandText = "SELECT * FROM Publisher";

   //create SqlConnection and SqlCommand objects
   SqlConnection myConnection = new SqlConnection(ConnectionString);
   SqlCommand myCommand = new SqlCommand(CommandText, myConnection);

   //create a new DataAdapter - any other constructors?
   SqlDataAdapter myAdapter = new SqlDataAdapter();
   myAdapter.SelectCommand = myCommand;

   //use try finally clauses when the connection is open.
   try
   {
      //now open connection to the database
      myConnection.Open();

      //Use the DataAdapter to fill the DataSet
      myAdapter.Fill(myDataSet, "Publisher");
   }
   catch (Exception ex)
   {
      //If an exception occurs, handle it.
      throw (ex);
   }
```

```
    finally
    {
        //Whether you succeed or fail, close the database connection
        myConnection.Close();
    }
    Page.DataBind();
}
```

3. Now you set which property is bound to which field in the DataTable. Switch to HTML view, and add the following:

```
<p>
    <asp:Label id="lblName1" runat="server"> Name:
        <%# DataBinder.Eval (myDataSet.Tables["Publisher"].Rows[0], ↵
          "[PublisherName]") %>
        </asp:Label>
    <br />
    City:
    <asp:Label id="lblCity1" runat="server" ↵
        text='<%# DataBinder.Eval ↵
        (myDataSet.Tables["Publisher"].Rows[0], ↵
        "[PublisherCity]") %>'></asp:Label>
    <br />
    Contact:
    <asp:Hyperlink id="hypContact1" runat="server" ↵
        text='<%# DataBinder.Eval ↵
        (myDataSet.Tables["Publisher"].Rows[0], ↵
        "[PublisherContact_Email]") %>' ↵
        navigateurl='<%# DataBinder.Eval ↵
        (myDataSet.Tables["Publisher"].Rows[0], ↵
        "[PublisherContact_Email]", "mailto:{0}") %>'></asp:Hyperlink>
    <br />
    Homesite:
    <asp:Hyperlink id="hypHomesite1" runat="server" ↵
        navigateurl='<%# DataBinder.Eval ↵
        (myDataSet.Tables["Publisher"].Rows[0], ↵
        "[PublisherWebsite]") %>'>
        <%# DataBinder.Eval (myDataSet.Tables["Publisher"].Rows[0], ↵
            "[PublisherWebsite]") %>
    </asp:Hyperlink>
```

4. Now save the code, and view the page in a browser (see Figure 7-3). The results are the same as for binding to a DataReader.

Figure 7-3. Inline binding to a DataSet

5. Go back to the HTML view, and duplicate the controls and binding expressions on the page. Now change the binding expressions so that they bind to fields from various rows, both ahead and behind from the previous expression. For example:

```
<asp:Label id="lblName2" runat="server">
    Name: <%# DataBinder.Eval (myDataSet.Tables["Publisher"].Rows[4], ⟲
    "[PublisherName]") %> </asp:Label>
<br />
    City: <asp:Label id="lblCity2" runat="server" ⟲
    text='<%# DataBinder.Eval (myDataSet.Tables["Publisher"].Rows[2], ⟲
    "[PublisherCity]") %>'></asp:Label>
```

6. Save the page, and view it again (see Figure 7-4). You'll see that the DataTable has no problem. The DataReader would of course choke on this. Try it, and have a go. The only way to work at random with a table with a DataReader is to keep rebuilding it.

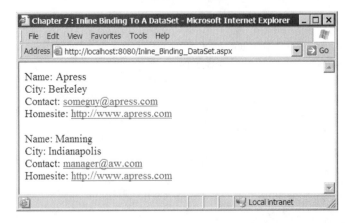

Figure 7-4. The DataSet gives you random access through a table.

How It Works

You'll see only two major differences between this and the previous example. The first is that you're using a DataSet containing a DataTable called Publisher to provide the data to bind to, and the second is the syntax you use in the binding expressions. Everything else is the same, demonstrating that there's no limit to inline binding text and control properties at the same time.

This example may seem to contradict the previous note that urges you to query only for what you'll use in a page. You queried for everything in the Publisher table, like so:

```
string CommandText = "SELECT * FROM Publisher";
```

However, we did this deliberately to demonstrate that, unlike a DataReader, you can work backward in the DataSet as well as forward.

Inside the binding expressions, you should recognize the slightly unwieldy syntax by now. Each expression identifies a field in a DataSet unambiguously. The second parameter of a call to DataBinder.Eval names the specific field, and the first identifies the specific row that contains the field. If you recall from the previous example, the call when binding to a field in DataReader looked like this:

```
Name: <%# DataBinder.Eval (myReader, "[0]") %>
```

because a DataReader only ever contains one row at a time. It's therefore enough to identify the reader and then the index position of the field in that row. If you start with a DataSet, you need to use a call like this:

```
Name: <%# DataBinder.Eval (myDataSet.Tables["Publisher"].Rows[0], ↵
"[PublisherName]") %>
```

because you must first identify the DataSet, then the DataTable within it, and the specific row within that in one go so that the second parameter can name the field in that row. You still have no way to alter the actual value of the field because it's bound to the control, but if you need to format the value of the field, you just add the format string as the third parameter of the call to Eval().

```
navigateurl='<%# DataBinder.Eval (myDataSet.Tables["Publisher"].Rows[0], ↵
"[PublisherContact_Email]", "mailto:{0}") %>'
```

You could alter the data in the DataSet before calling DataBind() rather than using the alternate version of Eval(), but what purpose would that serve?

List Binding

In comparison to inline binding, list and table binding are somewhat less complex processes to pass data into a data-bound control with, but usually they require more work beyond the call to DataBind() to finesse your control into a useful piece of the page for the user. If you consider the four Web form controls you can list bind to—the CheckBoxList, the RadioButtonList, the DropDownList, and the ListBox—you can see straight away that their purpose is to elicit a response from the user for information to be used elsewhere in the page. In this section then, you'll look first at how to bind data to these four controls and then see the choices a user has made from these lists.

As you know from using these controls before and even from working with HTML option lists, the key to finding out what the user has chosen is to establish a unique value for each option that can be retrieved from the form once the choice has been made. And, of course, you also need some text to display against each choice. In HTML, that means something like this:

```
<select name="ListBox1" size="5" id="ListBox1">
    <option value="1">Apress</option>
    <option value="2">Friends Of Ed</option>
    <option value="3">SAMS</option>
    <option value="4">Addison-Wesley</option>
    <option value="5">Manning</option>
</select>
```

On the screen, it looks something like Figure 7-5.

A ListBox

Figure 7-5. You can build a simple check box by list binding.

Apress, Friends Of Ed, and so on, are displayed in the browser, and the choice registers in the form as 1, 2, 3, and so on. When you're binding to a list control then, you need to establish a DataSource containing two fields per row—one for the text to be displayed and the other to identify the choice the user has made. For example:

```
SELECT PublisherID, PublisherName FROM Publisher
```

With the DataSource established, you have to tell the control which field does what. You do this by setting the control's `DataTextField` and `DataValueField` properties as appropriate, either in HTML or in code.

```
<asp:RadioButtonList id="RadioButtonList2" runat="server"
    DataSource="<%# myReader %>"
    DataTextField="PublisherName"
    DataValueField="PublisherID" />
```

> **NOTE** *If you do set it in code, make sure you set the DataSource before the other two properties, or you'll get an error.*

The four list controls have the following two relevant properties:

- `DataMember` is for use with DataSets, as you'll see in a coming example.

- `DataTextFormatString` lets you set the format for the text displayed in the list and comes in handy when you're dealing with currency, dates, and numbers. See `ms-help://MS.NETFrameworkSDKv1.1/cpref/html/frlrfsystemwebuiwebcontrolslistcontrolclassdatatextformatstringtopic.htm` for examples.

All that's left to do then is call `DataBind()` on the list control. The implementation of the `DataBind()` method includes a call to `Read()` if the data source is a DataReader object, so the core code for the whole three-stage binding process could be as simple as the following:

```
myConnection.Open();
myReader = myCommand.ExecuteReader();
RadioButtonList1.DataBind();
myReader.Close();
myConnection.Close();
```

This is true of all four list controls, and you can see this illustrated in `List_Binding_DataReader.aspx` in the Chapter07 directory of the code download for this book. Another thing you'll soon discover is that you can use only a DataReader as a list control's data source on a one-to-one basis. Unlike inline binding where you can bind many properties to the same field in a DataReader, you can't bind many list controls to the same fields in a DataReader. Actually, you can't bind more than one list control to the same DataReader. Once `DataBind()` has been called on one of the list controls, it works through all the rows in a DataReader, which of course is forward-only, so you can't go back to the beginning and bind the same information. The only way to bind all three controls from the same source is to use something other than a DataReader—a DataSet, for example—as the data source. You can see this in `List_Binding_DataSet.aspx`, also in the Chapter07 directory of the code download.

To sum up, if you're using a DataReader as your data source for a page, either use several in the page or make sure you've inline bound what you need to before binding the rest of the query results to a list or table. This will bind all the remaining data in the DataReader to itself and not share data with any other lists, table controls, or individual properties. Failing that, use a DataSet as your data source. Remember that you can bind any number of controls to it, even several tables and lists.

That said, you'll now look at a common application of data-bound lists: using the selection from a list to look up data from another table.

Try It Out: Single-Value Lookup Lists with a DataReader

In this example, you'll build a page with two stages. In the first stage, you'll populate a list control with information from the Publisher table. Specifically, you'll make the name of all the publishers in the database appear on the screen and use their respective PublisherIDs to track which publisher has been clicked. In the second stage, you'll use the PublisherID value to search in the Book table for all the books associated with that publisher and then display that in a DataGrid, as shown in Figure 7-6.

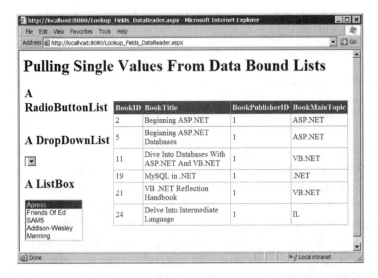

Figure 7-6. Using a simple lookup list

We've covered how to bind data to lists and to a DataGrid, so the key bit is picking up the choice from the list and is the reason why this exercise is only part one of two. In this part, you'll look at the case where you can select only one item at a time from a list. In the second, you'll see how to accommodate multiple selections.

1. In Web Matrix, create a new ASP.NET page called Lookup_Fields_DataReader.aspx and save it to the Chapter07 folder you've previously created.

2. In Design view, drag a RadioButtonList, a DropDownList, and a ListBox control onto the page. These three list controls can all enforce the selection of just one option from the choices they'll contain. Finally, add a DataGrid to the page. This will show you the details of the books by the publisher selected from the list. In the download, you've used an HTML table to lay it out nicely, as shown in Figure 7-7.

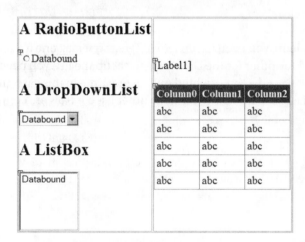

Figure 7-7. Laying out the list controls

3. For each of the list controls, set DataSource to myReader, DataTextField to PublisherName, and DataValueField to PublisherID. Finally, set Auto-PostBack to True. Last but not least, make sure the ListBox's SelectionMode property is set to single.

4. In All view, make sure you've included the right data provider at the top of the page, like so:

```
<%@ Page Language="C#" %>
<%@ import Namespace="System.Data" %>
<%@ import Namespace="System.Data.SqlClient" %>
```

5. In Code view, you need to declare the DataReader as a global variable and then write the Page_Load() event handler. All the code in the page is in this handler. It begins by setting up the Connection and Command objects, like so:

```
SqlDataReader myReader;

void Page_Load(object sender, EventArgs e)
{
    string ConnectionString = Convert.ToString( ⤶
        ConfigurationSettings.AppSettings["MSDEConnectString"]);
    SqlConnection myConnection = new SqlConnection(ConnectionString);
    SqlCommand myCommand = new SqlCommand();
    myCommand.Connection = myConnection;

    try
    {
        myConnection.Open();
```

6. Inside the try loop, you need to run two different queries: one for setting up the list and the other for the DataGrid. To set up the list, you need to add the following code. You can bind only to one list—in this case, the RadioButtonList—so the calls to bind the other list controls are commented out.

```
if (!(Page.IsPostBack))
// If this page is posted back get the selected value and display
// books released by publisher. you don't need to rebind the value
// for the lists either. They are stored in the viewstate.
    {

//set up SQL query for Publisher table
myCommand.CommandText = ⤶
    "SELECT PublisherID, PublisherName FROM Publisher";

    //run query
    myReader = myCommand.ExecuteReader();

    RadioButtonList1.DataBind();
    //DropDownList1.DataBind();
    //ListBox1.DataBind();

    myReader.Close();
}
```

7. To set up the DataGrid, you need the following code. Again, you're using only the RadioButtonList, so the calls against the other list controls are commented out.

```
else
// If this page isn't posted back you need to set up one of the list boxes
{

    //set up SQL query for Book table
    myCommand.CommandText = ⏎
        "SELECT * FROM Book WHERE BookPublisherID=" + ⏎
        RadioButtonList1.SelectedItem.Value;
    //myCommand.CommandText = ⏎
    //    "SELECT * FROM Book WHERE BookPublisherID=" + ⏎
    //    DropDownList1.SelectedItem.Value;
    //myCommand.CommandText =
    //    "SELECT * FROM Book WHERE BookPublisherID=" + ⏎
    //    ListBox1.SelectedItem.Value;

    myReader = myCommand.ExecuteReader();
    DataGrid1.DataSource = myReader;
    DataGrid1.DataBind();

    myReader.Close();
}
```

8. And last but not least, you need to tidy things up, like so:

```
    }
    catch (Exception ex)
    {
        //If an exception occurs, handle it.
        throw (ex);
    }
    finally
    {

        //Whether you succeed or fail, close the database connection
        myConnection.Close();
    }
}
```

9. Now save the page, and run it in a browser. Select one of the publisher's names from the list. The page will post back to the server and—hey, presto—return with the details for the books released by that publisher.

How It Works

We've discussed a great deal of this code already, but it makes a lot of difference to see it in action; seeing how DataTextField and DataValueField translate inside a data-bound list, for example, is helpful. The page as a whole is subject to the small problem of being able to bind only one of the three lists at a time, but it turns out that there are only two lines of code you need to change to use the list control of your choice—everything else is generic. The alternate lines for using the Drop-DownList and ListBox are commented out in the previous code.

You've set up the data source for the list in the Design view, so all you need to worry about is when to call the appropriate code. In this case, it's straightforward. When the page is first loaded, you need to populate the list from the database. However, this list will never change as you use the page, so you need not repopulate it each time you click the values it contains. Consequently, you set up a simple test to check whether the page has posted back. If it hasn't, you'll populate the list.

```
if (!(Page.IsPostBack))
{
```

Although the DataTextField and DataValueField properties specify what will populate the list, there's still no need to query the database for any more than those fields. You're using a DataReader, so you can't access any extra information from it anyway once you DataBind() it to the list.

```
myCommand.CommandText = "SELECT PublisherID, PublisherName FROM Publisher";

//run query
myReader = myCommand.ExecuteReader();

RadioButtonList1.DataBind();
//DropDownList1.DataBind();
//ListBox1.DataBind();

myReader.Close();
}
```

You set the list controls' AutoPostBack properties to True so any time you select an option from the list, the page posts back and you can update the DataGrid accordingly.

```
else
{
```

All three list controls expose the currently selected item in the list through their SelectedItem property. You can use its Text and Value properties to retrieve the exact details. In this case, you need the PublisherID for the book search, so you use SelectedItem.Value because you set PublisherID to DataValueField in the list control.

```
//set up SQL query for Book table
myCommand.CommandText = "SELECT * FROM Book WHERE BookPublisherID=" + ⤸
    RadioButtonList1.SelectedItem.Value;
//myCommand.CommandText = ⤸
//   "SELECT * FROM Book WHERE BookPublisherID=" + ⤸
//   DropDownList1.SelectedItem.Value;
//myCommand.CommandText = ⤸
//   "SELECT * FROM Book WHERE BookPublisherID=" + ⤸
//   ListBox1.SelectedItem.Value;
myReader = myCommand.ExecuteReader();
DataGrid1.DataSource = myReader;
DataGrid1.DataBind();

    myReader.Close();
}
```

An alternate way to go here would be to use the list control's SelectedValue and SelectedText properties. This produces the same results in this scenario where you can select only one item from the list. As you'll see in the next example, however, this isn't the case for multiselect lists. Nor can you use the SelectedItem property to find all the list items selected in a group. You must choose another tack.

Try It Out: Multiple-Value Lookup Lists with a DataReader

In this example, you'll see what alternative methods you can employ to deal with list controls that allow multiple selections. You can't rely on using the SelectedItem property because this will return only the first item selected in the list. Instead, you must iterate through the list each time and build up a SQL statement accordingly. Follow these steps:

1. In Web Matrix, create a new ASP.NET page called Multiple_Lookup_Fields_ DataReader.aspx and save to the Chapter07 folder you've previously created.

2. In Design view, drag a CheckBoxList and a ListBox control onto the page. Both of these support multiple selections. Now add a Label control and a DataGrid. You'll use the Label control to make sure the SQL statements you generate are correct. The example in the download uses a table like Figure 7-7 demonstrates.

3. For each of the list controls, set their DataSource property to myReader, DataTextField to PublisherName, and DataValueField to PublisherID. Now set their AutoPostBack property to True. Last but not least, make sure that the ListBox's SelectionMode property is set to Multiple.

4. The code for this example begins much the same as the previous one. You need to include the right data provider for the database and declare the Connection and Command objects. The difference begins inside the Page_Load event handler, when binding the right list controls and setting the Label control's Text property. Again, because the DataReader can bind only one of the two list controls, the other is commented out.

```
if (!(Page.IsPostBack))
{
    myCommand.CommandText = ↵
        "SELECT PublisherID, PublisherName FROM Publisher";
    myReader = myCommand.ExecuteReader();

    ListBox1.DataBind();
    //CheckBoxList1.DataBind();
    Label1.Text = "Select a publisher";

    myReader.Close();
}
```

5. To determine which items are selected in the list control, you must iterate through the control and build up the query from the results. The equivalent code for the list control you're not using is commented out.

```
else
// If this page isn't posted back, set up one of the list boxes
{

    //set up SQL query for Book table
    string Query = "SELECT * FROM Book WHERE BookPublisherID IN (";
    bool gotResult = false;
```

```
//for (int i=0; i<CheckBoxList1.Items.Count; i++)
for (int i=0; i<ListBox1.Items.Count; i++)
{
    //if (CheckBoxList1.Items[i].Selected)
    if (ListBox1.Items[i].Selected)
    {
      Query += "'" + CheckBoxList1.Items[i].Value + "',";
      gotResult = true;
    }
}
```

6. Now you find out if any items were checked. If so, you run the query you built. If not, you run a different query that will produce no results and so clear the grid.

```
if (gotResult)
{
    Query = Query.Remove((Query.Length - 1), 1);
    Query += ")";
    Label1.Text = Query;
    myCommand.CommandText = Query;
}
else
{
    Label1.Text="Select a publisher";
    myCommand.CommandText = ↵
        "SELECT * FROM Book WHERE BookPublisherID = 0";
}

    myReader = myCommand.ExecuteReader();
    DataGrid1.DataSource = myReader;
    DataGrid1.DataBind();
    myReader.Close();
}
```

7. And again, matching the last example, you wrap up the code by closing the connection. Save the page, and run it in your browser. You'll see the ListBox containing the by-now-familiar list of publishers. To select more than one item from here, hold down the Ctrl key as you select them. The grid will adjust to include book information from all the publishers selected. Figure 7-8 shows the same results but from using the Check-BoxList.

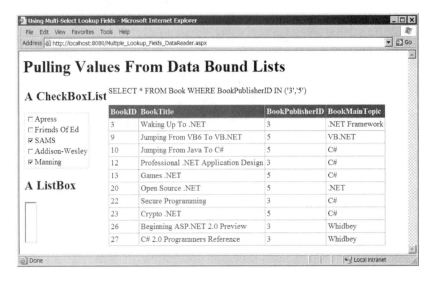

Figure 7-8. Pulling multiple values from a CheckBoxList

How It Works

Much of the code is the same as the previous example, so we won't go over it here. The major change is to the code to generate a query for book information for the DataGrid, and that means the code executed when the page has been reloaded.

The SQL SELECT statement uses the IN keyword to let you search for fields with one of a given set of values, so you'll use that to form your query. Your queries then will take the following shape:

```
SELECT * FROM Book WHERE BookPublisherID IN ('1','2')
```

You'll need code that inserts the ID number for each one selected into the query, like so:

```
{

    //set up SQL query for Book table
    string Query = "SELECT * FROM Book WHERE BookPublisherID IN (";
    bool gotResult = false;
```

The strategy here is to iterate through each item in the list and see if it has been selected. Fortunately, each ListItem object has a Selected property, which is true if it has been selected and false otherwise. If it has been selected, you pull its Value into the query.

```
//for (int i=0; i<CheckBoxList1.Items.Count; i++)
for (int i=0; i<ListBox1.Items.Count; i++)
{
    //if (CheckBoxList1.Items[i].Selected)
    if (ListBox1.Items[i].Selected)
    {
      Query += "'" + CheckBoxList1.Items[i].Value + "',";
      gotResult = true;
    }
}
```

> **TIP** *Again, MDB file users should remove the extra quotes from the values added to the IN statement for this example to work.*

We've included the boolean gotResult to keep track of whether anything has been selected. If it has, you close the SQL query and set it to the Command object. If the user has unselected all the items in the list, you send it a query that you know will return no results. This will ensure the DataGrid doesn't continue to show a list of books for a publisher that isn't selected.

```
if (gotResult)
{
    Query = Query.Remove((Query.Length - 1), 1);
    Query += ")";

    Label1.Text = Query;
    myCommand.CommandText = Query;
}
else
{
    Label1.Text="Select a publisher";
    myCommand.CommandText = ⏎
       "SELECT * FROM Book WHERE BookPublisherID = 0";
}
```

You have, of course, lots of ways to extend this example. One aspect you haven't investigated, for instance, is using event handlers rather than the postback mechanism to react to choices made and unmade from your lists. For example, you could write a handler for a CheckBoxList's CheckedChanged event to run a revised SQL query on the data in memory rather than requery from the database, but of course you couldn't do that with a DataReader. You'd need a data source that you could reuse. Cue the DataSet.

Try It Out: Look Up Fields Using DataSets and Events

In this exercise, you'll see how the code for list binding a DataTable in a DataSet to a control is almost identical to list binding to a DataReader, but it can have a completely different result. You'll also see an alternate way to handle a list containing lookup fields as a trigger for doing something else on the page. In the DataReader version of this exercise, you handled the user selection in the Page_Load() method. This time around, you'll use event handlers.

The two stages of the page remain the same. In the first stage, a list displays of all the publishers stored in the database. When someone selects a publisher—a single publisher only (you'll deal with multiple selections in a minute)—the page will post back and run the event handler that displays a DataGrid showing all the books associated with that publisher. The second stage then discerns the ID of the publisher selected from the list, saves that publisher's books in a DataTable called Book, and presents them in a DataGrid on the page. Follow these steps:

1. In Web Matrix, open Lookup_Fields_DataReader.aspx and save it to the Chapter07 folder as Lookup_Fields_DataSet.aspx.

2. For each list controls, change the DataSource property to myDataSet.Tables["Publisher"]. All their other properties can stay the same.

3. In Code view, you need to swap the word *DataSet* for *DataReader* and change Page_Load() accordingly. To make it easier to read, you put the routine that populates a DataTable in the DataSet into its own method called BuildDataSetTable(). This will get called several ways, so it's easier to see what's going on if you do this.

```
DataSet myDataSet = new DataSet();

    void BuildDataSetTable(string commandText, string tableName)
    {
        //set up connection string and SQL query
        string ConnectionString = Convert.ToString( ⏎
           ConfigurationSettings.AppSettings["MSDEConnectString"]);

        //create SqlConnection and SqlCommand objects
        SqlConnection myConnection = new SqlConnection(ConnectionString);
        SqlCommand myCommand = new SqlCommand(commandText, myConnection);
```

```
        //Create the SqlDataAdapter
        SqlDataAdapter myAdapter = new SqlDataAdapter(myCommand);

        //Open connection and fill table in DataSet
        try
        {
            myConnection.Open();
            myAdapter.Fill(myDataSet, tableName);
        }
        catch (Exception ex)
        {
            throw(ex);
        }
        finally
        {
            myConnection.Close();
        }
    }
```

4. Now you define `Page_Load()`. You need deal only with populating the list controls here when the page first loads, so the code needs to be run only when the page hasn't been posted back.

```
void Page_Load(object sender, EventArgs e)
{
    if (!(Page.IsPostBack))
    //Page is new, so fill the lists from Publisher table
    {
        string SelectPublisher = ⤸
            "SELECT PublisherID, PublisherName From Publisher";
        BuildDataSetTable(SelectPublisher, "Publisher");

        Label1.Text = "Select a Publisher";

        //You bind individual controls rather than the page as the
        //DataGrid will have nothing to bind to at the moment
        DropDownList1.DataBind();
        RadioButtonList1.DataBind();
        ListBox1.DataBind();
    }
}
```

5. Now you'll implement the second stage of the page using event handlers. All list controls have an event called SelectedIndexChanged, which fires when a user changes the option selected in a list. It's this event you need to handle for each list control on the page. In the HTML view, add the following attribute to the RadioButtonList control. Repeat this for the DropDownList and ListBox controls, changing the name of the handler in the attribute as appropriate.

```
OnSelectedIndexChanged="RadioButtonList1_SelectedIndexChanged"
```

6. In Code view, add the actual handler routines, like so:

```
void RadioButtonList1_SelectedIndexChanged(object sender, EventArgs e) {
    string SelectBook = ⤸
        "SELECT * FROM Book WHERE BookPublisherID=" + ⤸
        RadioButtonList1.SelectedItem.Value;
    BuildDataSetTable(SelectBook, "Book");
    DataGrid1.DataBind();
}

void DropDownList1_SelectedIndexChanged(object sender, EventArgs e) {
    string SelectBook = ⤸
        "SELECT * FROM Book WHERE BookPublisherID=" + ⤸
        DropDownList1.SelectedItem.Value;
    BuildDataSetTable(SelectBook, "Book");
    DataGrid1.DataBind();
}

void ListBox1_SelectedIndexChanged(object sender, EventArgs e) {
    string SelectBook = ⤸
        "SELECT * FROM Book WHERE BookPublisherID=" + ⤸
        ListBox1.SelectedItem.Value;
    BuildDataSetTable(SelectBook, "Book");
    DataGrid1.DataBind();
}
```

7. Now save the page, and run it in a browser. Select one of the publisher's names from the list. The page will post back to the server, run the appropriate event handler, and return with the details for the books released by that publisher (see Figure 7-9).

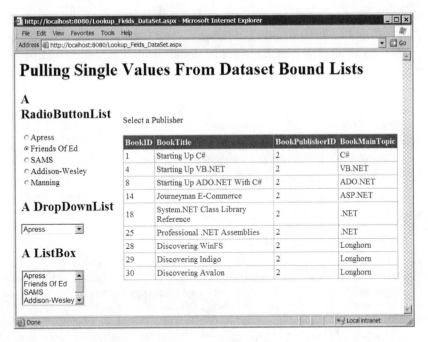

Figure 7-9. Backing lookup lists with a DataSet

How It Works

The most immediate difference between this example and its DataReader equivalent is that all three list controls have been populated in this page. Because of its forward-only nature, you can bind only one list control to a DataReader at a time. In contrast, you can reuse the contents of a DataTable as many times as you like, so you can use all three controls on the same page.

Beyond this fairly large functional difference, however, the code seems to be more or less the same. You still identify a DataKeyField and a DataValueField for each list control, and they work as usual, as does the control's DataSource property, but there's a slight variation you could use here that applies to list and table binding. For either type of binding to work, you have to identify the specific DataTable for the control to bind to. In the example, you've done this directly by identifying it in the controls' DataSource properties.

```
DataSource='<%# myDataSet.Tables["Publisher"] %> '
```

Alternately, you could just set the `DataSource` to the DataSet and identify the table name with the control's `DataMember` property. The purpose of the `DataMember` property is to identify specific tables in a multiresult data source, so this solution works fine as well and is perhaps more flexible if your page is working with large DataSets.

```
DataSource='<%# myDataSet %>' DataMember="Publisher"
```

The event handlers are all straightforward. Because each handler is associated with a specific list control, you know which one to check for the newly selected publisher ID. With that, you can derive the correct SQL query and populate the waiting DataGrid from the DataTable storing the results of the query.

> **NOTE** *This isn't the tidiest example in the book, but it does illustrate the concepts we needed to get across. If you'd like a small challenge, try to write one method that handles all three events and determines which control fired the event in the first place. Once you've done that, generate the right SQL statement and populate the DataGrid as before, but clear the selections from the other two list controls so there's no confusion as to where the selection was made.*

One other thing you don't do with this example is store (persist) the DataSet between stages for use when the page is regenerated. In this case, there's no point because the data required for display changes with each postback. Compare this with when you're sorting and paging DataGrids later in the "Try It Out: Sorting and Paging With a DataSet" section of this chapter. In that case, the data bound to the grid remains the same, but your view of it changes. Thus, it makes more sense to persist the DataGrid for this task, which you'll do in the next example.

The same differences between using a DataSet and a DataReader are evident if you rewrite the earlier example that uses multiselect list controls instead of the three used in this example. Both ListBox and CheckBoxList controls are populated instead of one or the other, and you could use the `DataMember` property again to specify a DataTable in a DataSet if you so wanted. The only changed piece of code, which you can find in `Multiple_Lookup_Dataset_Fields.aspx` in the Chapter07 folder of the download for the book, handles determining which publishers are selected across both lists (see Figure 7-10).

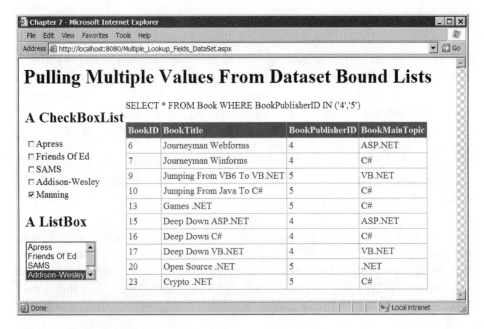

Figure 7-10. Multiple value lookup lists

Table Binding

You've come to the last of the three binding varieties in ASP.NET. For simplicity's sake, we'll call it *table binding*. With this, you can bind any number of fields per row from a data source to a Web form control that supports it. You've already seen this in action a number of times when you used a DataGrid on your pages, but you have many more options than the one standard you've seen so far. In the following sections then, you'll look at the following:

- The different controls that support table binding

- How to customize those controls to present their information more clearly

- How to enable the automatic sorting of data by the controls

- How to enable data paging

In Chapter 8, we'll expand further on these themes by enabling these controls to add, edit, and delete data from the database rather than just view it, but we're getting ahead of ourselves.

Working the Controls

Three controls support table binding—the Repeater, the DataList, and the Data-Grid—but each has its quirks and is more applicable to one task than another. You've already seen how to associate and bind data to a DataGrid. At its simplest, the whole operation needs only the following four lines of code:

```
myReader = myCommand.ExecuteReader();
DataGrid1.DataSource = myReader;
DataGrid1.DataBind();
myReader.Close();
```

The same is true on the coding side for the DataList and Repeater as well, but as you can see from `Table_Binding_DataReader.aspx`, there's more to them than just that. Both rely on you *defining row templates* that they'll use to display each row in the data source. This may sound complex, but it isn't really. Figure 7-11 shows the basic example of `Table_Binding_DataReader.aspx`.

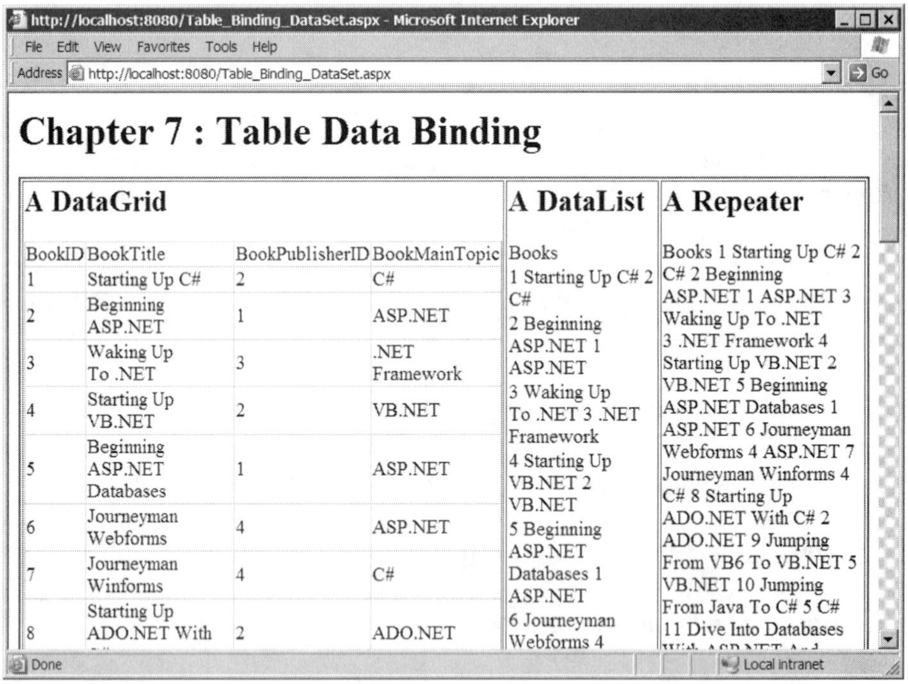

Figure 7-11. DataGrid, DataList, and Repeater controls

On this page, you're binding and displaying the whole of the Book table to each control. The DataGrid takes care of itself; it already understands what rows and fields are and that each field in a table should be placed in its own table cell. In contrast, a DataList only knows what a row is. When you bind a database table to it, a DataList still works row by row, but it doesn't create individual table cells for each field in a row. You have to write an <ItemTemplate> to describe how you want this done. A Repeater goes one further and simply spouts out everything bound to it in one paragraph, distinguishing neither field nor row. Like a DataList then, you need to create a template for the row for a Repeater. The following is an example:

```
<asp:DataList id="DataList1" runat="server">
   <ItemTemplate>
      <asp:Label id="Label1" runat="server"
         text='<%# DataBinder.Eval(Container, "DataItem.BookID") %>' />
      <asp:Label id="Label2" runat="server"
         text='<%# DataBinder.Eval(Container, "DataItem.BookTitle")%>' />
      <asp:Label id="Label3" runat="server"
         text='<%# DataBinder.Eval(Container, "DataItem.BookPublisherID")%>' />
      <asp:Label id="Label4" runat="server"
         text='<%# DataBinder.Eval(Container, "DataItem.BookMainTopic") %>' />
   </ItemTemplate>
</asp:DataList>
```

You can define several kinds of row template for DataLists and Repeaters, and we'll get to them in a minute. The basic one, however, is the ItemTemplate. Like its counterparts, you can think of each template as a mini-page where you can place any combination of text, HTML, more Web form controls, and, most important, instructions on how and where to bind the fields in the data source in that row. When the call to DataBind() is made, the mini-page template is repeated for each row in the data.

The template in the example is necessarily simple. We've declared that each row in the DataList will contain four Label controls, one for each field in the Book table. To associate the fields in the data with the Labels, you inline bind them. The binding expression may look strange, but it's easily understood.

```
<%# DataBinder.Eval(Container, "DataItem.BookTitle")%>
```

You've come across the static DataBinder.Eval method before. The first parameter locates the data source, and the second locates the field that will be bound. Container in this case means that the data source is the container control for this template—or, rather, the DataList. You can use this nomenclature in any template.

As you may have noticed, a row corresponds to an item here, and you can refer to the field you want by name through the DataItem object beholden to the DataList.

And that's the template. In `Table_Binding_DataReader.aspx` (and `Table_Bind-ing_DataSet.aspx`, which works in the same way), we've added this template to both DataList and Repeater. Figure 7-11 shows the results and demonstrates neatly how the three controls differ.

You can find a complete list of differences between the three controls in the .NET documentation at `http://msdn.microsoft.com/library/en-us/vbcon/html/vbcondisplayinglistsusingwebcontrols.asp`. The following summarizes the differences:

- A DataGrid displays your data as a neatly formed grid by default. You can customize the display grid extensively through various properties, as you'll see shortly. You can even switch it off in favor of the template approach used by DataLists and Repeaters. In this case, however, the templates are for columns, not rows. With a little extra code, DataGrids can easily support sorting, paging, editing, adding, and deleting data from the data source.

- A DataList displays your data, one item per line (or per column), according to a template you must provide. It won't separate individual pieces of information unless told to do so in the template. You can customize the display of the DataList extensively through various properties to match up with the templates you define. DataLists support the editing, adding, and deleting of data but not sorting or paging. It supports templates to define the header of the list, to define the footer of the list, to highlight alternating rows in the list, and to highlight the row either currently selected or currently being edited.

- A Repeater is completely dependent on the template you provide for displaying data. For example, unless you include line breaks in the template, it will display incoming data on one line (as it did in Figure 7-11). You must do any customization through the templates. The Repeater supports templates for alternate rows, headers, footer, and row separators. However, the data is read-only and can't readily support paging or sorting.

For the rest of this chapter, you'll focus on the DataGrid because it's the most versatile control of the three and the most powerful. Most of the customizations you can add to a DataGrid, you can also add to a DataList, so read on if you want to use those. If you're interested in the Repeater, refer to `http://www.sitepoint.com/article/1014` and `http://www.dotnetjohn.com/articles/articleid58.aspx` for more details. It really is truly useful. You can find many more links, of course, via Google. Just search for *ASP.NET Repeater* or *ASP.NET DataList*.

Customizing the DataGrid

Don't worry—you won't see those four lines of code that bind data to a DataGrid again. We've covered that enough already. What you'll look at in this section are the ways to make the DataGrid more presentable and easier for the browser to manage. Consider the case where you're querying for more than 50 rows from a database. No one really wants to look at a page containing such a large table. It's bad enough looking at one with 30 rows as you have in `Customizing_DataReader_DataGrids_1.aspx`. In this section then, you'll look at the following four ways to improve this dreary black-and-white table:

- Changing the column headings and making the data itself more readable.

- Adding some color to the table by defining styles.

- Enabling the grid to sort the data by the contents of a field.

- Enabling the grid to page the data presenting it as several pages of data with fewer rows of data that can be navigated through, rather than all in one. This technique is known as *paging*.

You'll also stick to using the DataReader as the data source, which will demonstrate neatly one or two problems you could encounter as you build your pages. Nothing is perfect, after all, not even the DataReader. You'll find parallel code in the download folder for this chapter using the DataSet. Later, in the "Paging and Sorting with a DataSet" section, you'll learn how the DataSet solves quite a few of the problems you'll see here.

Customizing the Data

The first task is to make the data itself more presentable. When data is bound to a DataGrid, the field name used in the database table is presented as the column header. That's fine when you're designing databases, but BookPublisherID just doesn't cut it when read by a user—neither does reading the actual Publisher ID from the Book table rather than the name of the Publisher itself.

Now, you could customize the DataGrid by setting its `AutoGenerateColumns` property to false and working in the same fashion as DataLists and Repeaters. In this case, you define how the grid renders each particular field with BoundColumn objects rather than templates for each row, but the principles are the same. You won't look at this approach now, but you'll look at it in Chapter 8. Instead, leave AutoGenerateColumns as the default (True) and use the SQL query to make the change.

You saw in Chapter 4 how to use an INNER JOIN in a SQL statement to retrieve data from one table based on values from another. You'll use that technique here to return the publisher's name for each book rather than the PublisherID number. Instead of the following:

```
SELECT * FROM Book
```

you now have this:

```
SELECT Book.BookID, Book.BookTitle, Publisher.PublisherName,
       Book.BookMainTopic FROM Book
       INNER JOIN Publisher ON Book.BookPublisherID = Publisher.PublisherID
```

That sorts the grid contents, but how do you influence the column names? Easy. You alter the SQL query again and use *aliases* as needed for each field. SQL defines the AS keyword in SELECT statements that tells a database to return an alternate name for a field in its results for a query. If you wanted to "rename" the BookMainTopic field in the Book table to Topic in the results of a query, then you could use SELECT Book.BookMainTopic AS Topic, which would do the trick. Bearing this in mind then, you can add aliases to the query and complete the first of the four tasks.

```
SELECT Book.BookID, Book.BookTitle AS Title,
       Publisher.PublisherName AS Publisher,
       Book.BookMainTopic AS Topic FROM Book
       INNER JOIN Publisher ON Book.BookPublisherID = Publisher.PublisherID
```

You can see the results in Customizing_DataReader_DataGrids_2.aspx and in Figure 7-12.

You could argue that you don't really need to show the BookID column, but it's useful to demonstrate paging and sorting later, so we'll leave it in.

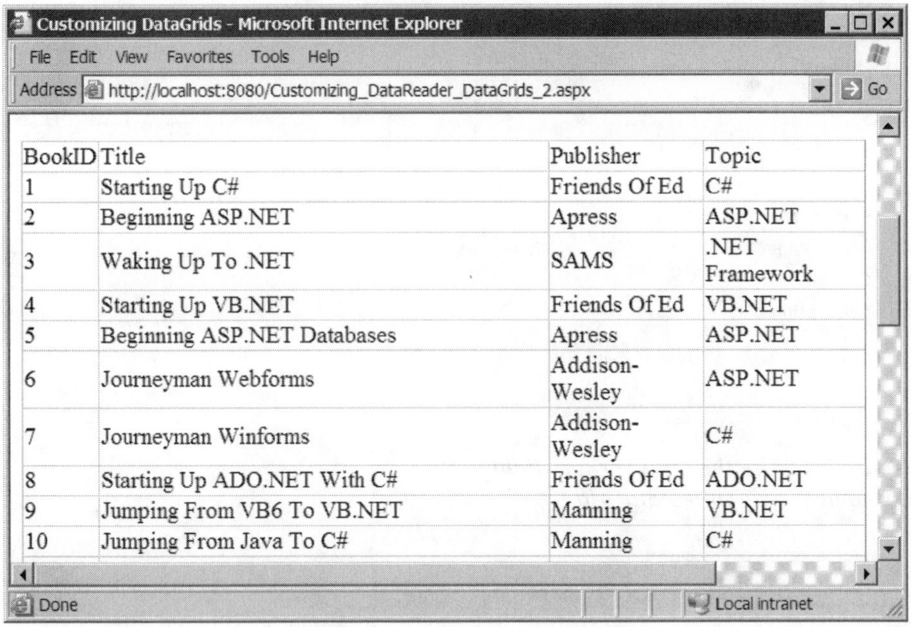

BookID	Title	Publisher	Topic
1	Starting Up C#	Friends Of Ed	C#
2	Beginning ASP.NET	Apress	ASP.NET
3	Waking Up To .NET	SAMS	.NET Framework
4	Starting Up VB.NET	Friends Of Ed	VB.NET
5	Beginning ASP.NET Databases	Apress	ASP.NET
6	Journeyman Webforms	Addison-Wesley	ASP.NET
7	Journeyman Winforms	Addison-Wesley	C#
8	Starting Up ADO.NET With C#	Friends Of Ed	ADO.NET
9	Jumping From VB6 To VB.NET	Manning	VB.NET
10	Jumping From Java To C#	Manning	C#

Figure 7-12. Field aliases appear as column headers.

Adding Styles

The contents of the grid are now a bit more readable, so you'll now focus on the grid itself. It's a bit drab in black and white, so let's add some color. To do this, you can define style templates for rows in the grid. The whole process is similar to the ItemTemplates that work with DataLists and Repeaters, but as the DataGrid automatically generates a grid for a row, all you're left with to decide is how each row will be presented—colors, fonts, text alignment, cell padding, cell width, and so on.

The whole process is actually made easier by Web Matrix, which contains several predefined color schemes to apply straight onto the DataGrid. Simply select your DataGrid in Design view and then hit the Auto Format link in the Properties panel (see Figure 7-13). A dialog box will appear, allowing you to select a color scheme on the left and preview it on the right (see Figure 7-14).

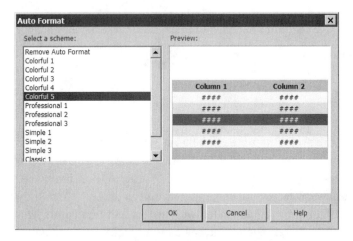

Figure 7-13. Use the Auto Format dialog
box to help style your DataGrid.

Figure 7-14. The Auto Format dialog box lets you choose
several predefined styles for a DataGrid.

In Customizing_DataReader_DataGrids_3.aspx, go ahead and choose to use the
Colorful 5 scheme for no other reason than it uses most of the row styles available
to you and lets you see how they're used. The resulting code looks like this:

```
<asp:DataGrid id="DataGrid1" runat="server" BorderWidth="1px" BorderColor="Tan"
            BackColor="LightGoldenrodYellow" CellPadding="2"
            GridLines="None" ForeColor="Black">
    <FooterStyle backcolor="Tan"></FooterStyle>
    <HeaderStyle font-bold="True" backcolor="Tan"></HeaderStyle>
```

```
<PagerStyle horizontalalign="Center" forecolor="DarkSlateBlue"
            backcolor="PaleGoldenrod"></PagerStyle>
<SelectedItemStyle forecolor="GhostWhite"
                   backcolor="DarkSlateBlue"></SelectedItemStyle>
<AlternatingItemStyle backcolor="PaleGoldenrod"></AlternatingItemStyle>
</asp:DataGrid>
```

The style information in the `<asp:DataGrid>` tag itself sets the defaults for
the whole of the grid, and the various `<xxxStyle>` tags define deviations from that
default, much like the way that CSS works. In fact, you can work with the following
seven different styles:

- ItemStyle sets up the default style for a row in the grid.

- AlternatingItemStyle defines a style for every other row in the grid, making it
  easier for the reader to follow a line across the grid.

- HeaderStyle defines the style for the column header row.

- FooterStyle looks after the style for the footer of the grid.

- SelectedItemStyle is applied to a row when it's selected.

- EditItemStyle is applied to a row when it's being edited.

- PagerStyle is applied to the footer when it displays page navigation links.

Don't be afraid to try different styles and to create your own. Feel free to use
the examples, say in Chapter 3, as your base.

An Interactive Grid

Now that you've made the DataGrid more presentable and the information it contains more readable, you have one other card to play: to help the grid present the
information interactively. At the moment, it just displays all the information that
results from a query in one go in the order it was entered into the database. However, you can add the following two common features that come in handy:

- **Sorting:** You can set up the grid so that clicking a column header sorts the
  information it contains by the entries in that column.

- **Paging**: You can set up the grid so that it displays only a small number of rows "per page," making it easier to read, with links to move through further pages of data until it has all been shown.

You can add both features with little code, but paging in particular brings up some interesting points to consider, especially if you're using a DataReader.

A Grid That Sorts

A grid that sorts can come in handy for users when they're checking data. In these examples so far, it'd be a lot easier to see which publisher is associated with which books if you could sort the data in the grid by the contents of the Publisher column. On eBay, for example, it's a lot more helpful if you can sort which auctions are finishing last than having the information sorted by description.

To enable your grids to sort, you follow these steps:

1. Set the Grid's AllowSorting property to true. You can do this either in code or as part of the <asp:DataGrid> tag. This turns the column headers into hyperlinks that fire the grid's SortCommand event when clicked.

2. Create an event handler for the DataGrid's OnSortCommand event. ASP.NET relies on you to provide the routine that will re-sort the data for it by the given column. In the following code, you hook it to a function named Sort_Grid:

   ```
   <asp:DataGrid ... AllowSorting="True" OnSortCommand="Sort_Grid">
   ...
   </asp:DataGrid>
   ```

3. In the event handler, requery for data ordered by the requested column. SQL provides the keywords ORDER BY, ASC, and DESC to specify that data returned from a query is sorted by a given column in either ascending or descending order. The syntax is as follows:

   ```
   SELECT ... FROM ... ORDER BY column_name (ASC or DESC)
   ```

4. All you need to do then is establish which column header was clicked and append ORDER BY column_name to the original query for the grid. By default, the data is in ascending order if you don't specify ASC or DESC. Then you just rebind the data to the grid. Fortunately, the sortexpression property generated as part of the SortCommand event contains the name of the field the data needs to be sorted by.

```
void Sort_Grid(object sender, DataGridSortCommandEventArgs e)
{
    string sortQuery = originalQuery + " ORDER BY ";
    sortQuery += e.SortExpression.ToString();
    BindGrid(sortQuery);
}
```

> **TIP** *The* sortexpression *property actually returns the alias of the field if one is used in the query that generated the DataGrid as you did here. MSDE and MySQL have no problem with this, but MDB files will mistake an alias for a parameter and throw an error in this example as a result. You must add extra code to work around this.*

Note that this means you aren't specifying the data already attached to the DataGrid. It doesn't work that way. When users click the column header, the page posts back and runs the event handler. This queries the database for the same data but ordered as required. Then it rebinds it to the Data-Grid. You can't avoid a new query to the database.

5. Make sure that the initial call to DataBind() in Page_Load() occurs only when the page hasn't posted back. That is, make sure the original query is called only when the page is first loaded like so:

```
void Page_Load(object sender, EventArgs e)
{
    if (!(Page.IsPostBack))
    {
        BindGrid(BasicQuery);
    }
}
```

If this check isn't made, each time the page reloads, the data is queried twice—once in Page_Load and then again in the SortCommand event handler, which is run after Page_Load().

Customizing_DataReader_Datagrids_4.aspx follows these rules and has sorting enabled without a hitch (see Figure 7-15). Just click a column header to sort the data. You may want to extend this functionality by sorting a grid in normal order if a column header is clicked an odd number of times and in reverse order if it's clicked an even number of times.

One thing that's worth pointing out in this example is that if a DataGrid is backed by a DataReader, then the sorting itself is executed by a SQL statement. Thus, once you enable sorting, you have to take that into account whenever you rebuild the DataReader. This can make things complicated, as you'll see when you add paging in the next section. Compare this to the situation where you use a DataSet instead of a DataReader. The DataSet will actually sort the data it contains internally, which means the complications are taken away. You'll learn more about this after you look at paging with DataReaders.

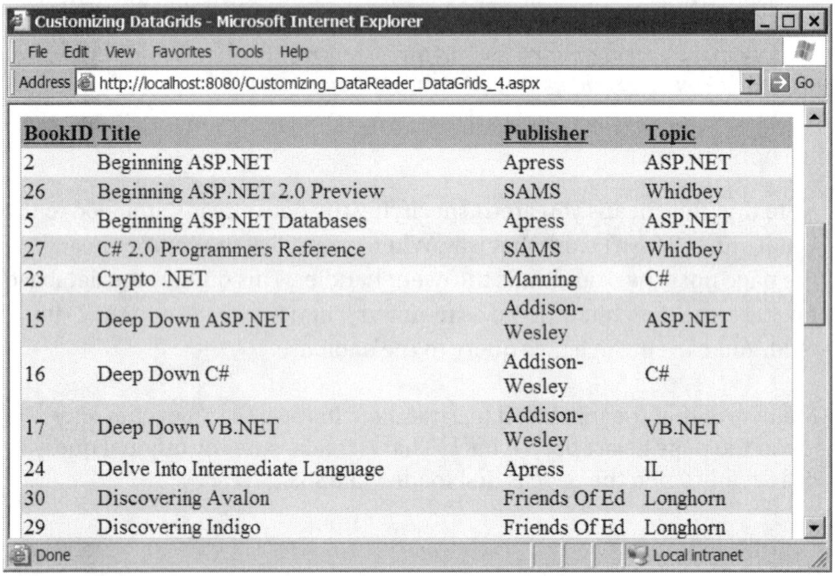

Figure 7-15. Sorting the Book table by book title

A Grid That (Custom) Pages

Unless you're incredibly specific in searching the Web, chances are that search engines return thousands of results. It'd be impractical to display all those on one page, so they're divided into pages of 10 (or 25 or whatever you've set the default to) results so you can move through them more effectively. This technique is known as *paging*.

.NET defines two types of paging, depending on the source of data that the DataGrid is using. If the data source is located in memory and implements ICollection, then you can get .NET to do most of the work. This is the case for such things as DataSets and DataViews, but not so for DataReaders that neither implement the required interface nor are resident in memory. In this case, you must implement your own custom paging solution; at its simplest, the technique is similar to adding sort functionality to the grid. You have to include the paging in the SQL statement.

To add paging to the Grid, you need to follow these steps:

1. Set the Grid's AllowPaging property to true. You can do this either in code or as part of the `<asp:DataGrid>` tag. This adds a row at the bottom of the grid containing links to move through the pages. Exactly what the links look like is governed by the `<PagerStyle>` style you saw earlier. When one of these links is clicked, it raises a `PageIndexChanged` event. To set up a custom paging solution, set the grid's AllowCustomPaging property to true.

   ```
   <asp:DataGrid ... AllowPaging="True" AllowCustomPaging="True">
   ```

2. In a non-custom paging situation, .NET keeps track of how many items are in the query results and what page the user is on so the navigation controls make sense. However, using a DataReader requires a custom solution, so you need to set this up specifically. First, you must set `VirtualItemCount` to the total number of rows returned for the query when not paged. You can do this by running a `COUNT()` query on the database, like so:

   ```
   void Set_VirtualItemCount()
   {
       string countQuery = "SELECT COUNT(BookID) FROM Book";
   ...
       DataGrid1.VirtualItemCount = (int)myCommand.ExecuteScalar();
   ...
   }
   ```

   You also need to set the DataGrid's `PageSize` property to the number of records you want to show at a time. The default is 10.

3. Create an event handler for the DataGrid's PageIndexChanged event. In this custom case, you need to provide the code that will hand the grid a page of data at a time rather than the whole set of results. In the noncustom case, the paging is done for you. You need only to requery all the data and pass the grid its new page number. In the following code, we've named the event handler `Change_Page()`:

   ```
   <asp:DataGrid AllowPaging="True" OnPageIndexChanged="Change_Page"
                 AllowCustomPaging="True" ... />
   ```

4. In the event handler, query the database for the specific page of data requested by the user. SQL has no concept of pages per se, so you have to translate it for the database. You can use the BookID field to key on here. For example, if you assume that every page will contain ten records, the first one contains the books with ID 1 to 10, the second page contains books with ID 11 to 20, and so on. You can use the DataGrid's PageSize property and the page number to figure out which records you need and use SQL's BETWEEN keyword to convey that range for the database. For example, to retrieve the second page's data, you'd use the following SQL query:

```
SELECT ... FROM Book WHERE BookID BETWEEN '11' and '20'
```

You can retrieve the current page index (0 for first page, 1 for second, and so on) from the NewPageIndex property generated by the PageIndexChanged event, like so:

```
void Change_Page(object sender, DataGridPageChangedEventArgs e)
{
  //Calculate the start and end indexes of the search
  DataGrid1.CurrentPageIndex = e.NewPageIndex;

  //Indexes are zero-based but autonumbers are not.
  int startIndex = ⏎
     (DataGrid1.CurrentPageIndex * DataGrid1.PageSize) + 1;
  int endIndex = ⏎
     (DataGrid1.CurrentPageIndex + 1) * DataGrid1.PageSize;

  //Now create the right SQL query string.
  string pageQuery = BasicQuery + " WHERE BookID BETWEEN '";
  pageQuery += startIndex.ToString();
  pageQuery += "' AND '";
  pageQuery += endIndex.ToString();
  pageQuery += "'";

  BindGrid(pageQuery);
}
```

5. A repeat warning: Make sure that the initial call to DataBind() in Page_Load() occurs only when the page hasn't posted back. That is, make sure the original query is called only when the page is first loaded, like so:

```
void Page_Load(object sender, EventArgs e)
    {
        if (!(Page.IsPostBack))
        {
            BindGrid(BasicQuery);
        }
    }
```

If this check isn't made, each time the page reloads, the data is queried twice—once in Page_Load() and then again in the PageIndexChanged event handler, which is run after Page_Load().

Now this code works nicely and is implemented in Customizing_DataReader_Datagrids_5.aspx (see Figure 7-16) without a problem, but it has several issues. Just open the page and click a few links; the major problem should become apparent. The sort and page routines work *independently* of each other. So if you sort the grid by Topic and then move to the next page, the next page shows the next ten rows of the grid as sorted by BookID, not Topic. Likewise, if you move to the second page of the results and then sort, you get the first page of results but on the second page. Contrast this problem in the custom paging solution with .NET's (noncustom) paging solution in the next section, which takes care of this.

The other problem is that this paging solution assumes that the values for BookID are consecutive and have no gaps. What happens if you delete book 18 and continue using the same code? You have a page containing nine entries, not ten. What happens if BookID contains globally unique identifiers (GUIDs) rather than integers? Can you use a range then?

This conversation gets pretty complex pretty quickly, so we'll leave the issue unresolved here except to say that it's quite easy to stream the contents of a DataReader into a DataSet and have .NET do all the hard work for you. As hinted earlier, the answer lies in using a DataSet rather than a DataReader.

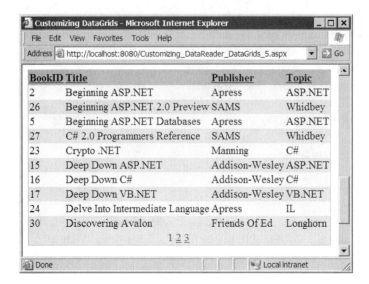

Figure 7-16. A DataGrid with paging switched on

Try It Out: Paging and Sorting with a DataSet

In this example, you'll enable sorting and paging on a DataGrid that uses a DataSet as its data source. Tweaking the SQL query to improve the data and adding color to the DataGrid work in the same way as you did in the previous example, so you'll now focus on sorting and paging. Follow these steps:

1. In Web Matrix, create a new ASP.NET page called
   `Customising_Dataset_DataGrids.aspx` and save it to the Chapter07 directory
   in your code folder.

2. In Design view, drag a DataGrid onto the page and call it myGrid. Select
   it on the page, and click the Auto Format hyperlink from the Properties
   window to open the color scheme chooser. Pick one—it doesn't matter
   which—and select OK.

3. In Code view, add the code that generates the DataSet and binds it to
   myGrid. You know that this generation will occur only the first time the
   page is called, so you test to see whether the page has posted back before
   this code executes.

```
void Page_Load(object sender, EventArgs e)
{
    if(!(Page.IsPostBack))
    {
```

```csharp
//set up connection string and SQL query
string ConnectionString = Convert.ToString( ⤶
    ConfigurationSettings.AppSettings["MSDEConnectString"]);
string CommandText = "SELECT Book.BookID, Book.BookTitle AS Title, ⤶
    Publisher.PublisherName AS Publisher, ⤶
    Book.BookMainTopic AS Topic FROM Book INNER JOIN Publisher ON ⤶
    Book.BookPublisherID = Publisher.PublisherID";

//create SqlConnection and SqlCommand objects
SqlConnection myConnection = new SqlConnection(ConnectionString);
SqlCommand myCommand = new SqlCommand(CommandText, myConnection);

//create a new DataAdapter
SqlDataAdapter myAdapter = new SqlDataAdapter();

//Assign the command to the Adapter so it knows
//what command to send when Fill() is called
myAdapter.SelectCommand = myCommand;

//Create a DataSet object - any other constructors?
DataSet myDataSet = new DataSet();


//use try finally clauses when the connection is open.
try
{
    //now open connection to the database
    myConnection.Open();

    myAdapter.Fill(myDataSet, "Book");
}
catch (Exception ex)
{
    //If an exception occurs, handle it.
    throw (ex);
}
finally
{
    //Whether you succeed or fail, close the database connection
    myConnection.Close();
}

//The DataSet is now loaded. Now bind it to a DataGrid and
//call DataBind() on it
```

```
myGrid.DataSource = myDataSet.Tables["Book"];
myGrid.DataBind();

Session["BookList"] = myDataSet;
    }
}
```

At this point, you have a colored DataGrid with well-presented information but that neither pages nor sorts. Save it, and run it to see how it looks so far. You can also find the code thus far as Customizing_DataSet_Data-Grids_3.aspx from the Chapter07 folder in your code download.

4. To add sorting, you need to set the DataGrid's AllowSorting property to true and handle its SortCommand event. In HTML view then, change the DataGrid's definition as follows:

```
<asp:DataGrid ... AllowSorting="True" OnSortCommand="Sort_Grid">
...
</asp:DataGrid>
```

and add the following code in Code view:

```
void Sort_Grid(object sender, DataGridSortCommandEventArgs e)
{
    DataSet BookDataSet = (DataSet)Session["BookList"];
    DataView SortedView = new DataView(BookDataSet.Tables["Book"]);

    SortedView.Sort = e.SortExpression;
    myGrid.DataSource = SortedView;
    myGrid.DataBind();
}
```

5. To add paging, you need to set the DataGrid's AllowPaging property to true and handle its PageIndexChanged event. In HTML view, add the following two attributes to the DataGrid tag:

```
<asp:DataGrid ... AllowPaging="True" OnPageIndexChanged="Page_Grid">
...
</asp:DataGrid>
```

and add the following code in Code view:

```
void Page_Grid(object sender, DataGridPageChangedEventArgs e)
{
```

```
DataSet BookDataSet = (DataSet)Session["BookList"];

myGrid.CurrentPageIndex = e.NewPageIndex;
myGrid.DataSource = BookDataSet;
myGrid.DataBind();
}
```

6. Save the page, and open it in a browser. The DataGrid does indeed now support sorting and paging, but the two still don't work together, as demonstrated in Figure 7-17. You can find it as `Customizing_DataSet_DataGrids_5.aspx` in the code download.

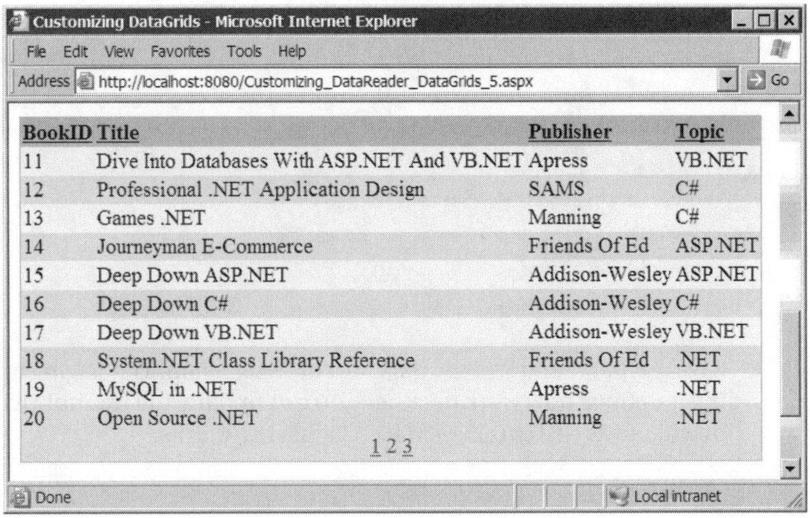

BookID	Title	Publisher	Topic
11	Dive Into Databases With ASP.NET And VB.NET	Apress	VB.NET
12	Professional .NET Application Design	SAMS	C#
13	Games .NET	Manning	C#
14	Journeyman E-Commerce	Friends Of Ed	ASP.NET
15	Deep Down ASP.NET	Addison-Wesley	ASP.NET
16	Deep Down C#	Addison-Wesley	C#
17	Deep Down VB.NET	Addison-Wesley	VB.NET
18	System.NET Class Library Reference	Friends Of Ed	.NET
19	MySQL in .NET	Apress	.NET
20	Open Source .NET	Manning	.NET

1 2 3

Figure 7-17. Changing pages resets the sort order so far.

Sorting works fine within a page, but as soon as you change the page number, the DataGrid re-sorts the DataTable by BookID. Happily, you can sort this out. You just need to keep a track of what column the grid is currently sorted by.

> **NOTE** *Compare this example with the DataReader example thus far. All the sorting and paging was being controlled by the SQL statement that filled the DataReader. With a DataSet, you haven't changed the SQL statement at all. In fact, you call a SQL statement only once when you initially build the DataSet, and all paging and sorting is done internally by the DataSet. This means also that the problem you saw with Access and the ORDER BY clause is negated because the DataSet does the sorting for you.*

7. In Code view, change the end of the `Sort_Grid()` event handler to add the following line:

```
myGrid.DataSource = SortedView;
myGrid.DataBind();
Session["SortExpression"] = e.SortExpression;
}
```

8. Finally, you need to rewrite the `Page_Grid()` event handler a bit, like so:

```
void Page_Grid(object sender, DataGridPageChangedEventArgs e)
{
    DataSet BookDataSet = (DataSet)Session["BookList"];

    DataView SortedView = new DataView(BookDataSet.Tables["Book"]);
    SortedView.Sort = (string)Session["SortExpression"];

    myGrid.DataSource = SortedView;
    myGrid.CurrentPageIndex = e.NewPageIndex;
    myGrid.DataBind();
}
```

9. Save the page, and run the page in a browser again. The paging and sorting functions now work together. You can find the full example in the code download as `Customizing_DataSet_DataGrids_6.aspx`.

How It Works

The earlier solution in Chapter 5 to enable sorting and paging on a DataGrid was limited by the fact that you were using a DataReader as a source of data. As a DataReader is just a direct channel to the results of a query coming straight from the database, the only way to sort the data in the grid or divide it into pages is as the result of a SQL SELECT statement customized according to the action requested. This means you have to build these SELECT statements yourself.

The situation is different when you provide a DataSet as the data source for a DataGrid to which you want to add paging and sorting. In this case, because the DataSet is resident in memory, .NET can be hands-on with the data and work with it internally before binding it to the DataGrid. All it requires from you in general are a couple of hints.

Let's start with sorting. As discussed in the previous "Try It Out: Paging and Sorting with a DataSet" section, because the actual data attached to the DataGrid never changes and isn't particularly large, you can save it in a session variable between postbacks rather than requery the database each time the page is regenerated. Obviously, this isn't such a good idea with large amounts of data because it will quickly eat up server resources, but for these purposes, it works fine and demonstrates another useful technique.

As a result, the actual sort routine isn't particularly long. First, you retrieve the DataSet from the session variable where you left it.

```
void Sort_Grid(object sender, DataGridSortCommandEventArgs e)
{
    DataSet BookDataSet = (DataSet)Session["BookList"];
```

The key to this routine is that because you're using a DataSet, you can define a DataView object based on the DataTable containing the data for the grid and work with that.

```
DataView SortedView = new DataView(BookDataSet.Tables["Book"]);
```

If you recall from Chapter 6, a DataView is a snapshot of the information in a DataTable, which you can filter and shape as you want. Once you're happy with the view, you can then bind a DataGrid, list control, control property, and so on, to the View rather than the raw DataTable underneath it.

In this case, a DataView has a property called Sort, which carries the name of the columns by which the data in the view is sorted and the order (ascending or descending) in which the data is sorted. You know from the earlier sorting example that you can determine the name of this column from the SortExpression passed to the method as part of the EventArgs parameter. All you do is introduce them. With that done, you just bind the DataGrid to the DataView and call DataBind(), like so:

```
    SortedView.Sort = e.SortExpression;
    myGrid.DataSource = SortedView;
    myGrid.DataBind();
}
```

You've already made sure that the DataGrid is initialized only when the page is first loaded by surrounding that code in an if(!(Page.IsPostback)) clause, so you're done.

Adding paging is even easier when you're working a DataSet. You had to implement your own custom paging solution when using a DataReader because the data wasn't actually located in memory. Thus, you had to create your own custom SQL queries that paged the data for you and use VirtualItemCount to help .NET figure out exactly how many pages would cover the data in total. This wasn't foolproof and didn't work with the sort routine either. In contrast, a DataSet *is* resident in memory, and .NET takes care of pretty much everything for you. All you actually need do is update the DataGrid with the number of the page the user wants to see and rebind the DataSet to the DataGrid. Easy.

```
void Page_Grid(object sender, DataGridPageChangedEventArgs e)
{
    DataSet BookDataSet = (DataSet)Session["BookList"];
    myGrid.CurrentPageIndex = e.NewPageIndex;
    myGrid.DataSource = BookDataSet;
    myGrid.DataBind();
}
```

Or is it? The one thing this hands-on example showed was that this code didn't actually cater to much cooperation between the sorting and paging routines. You could sort any page of data by any column without a problem, but once you switched pages the data displayed was automatically re-sorted by BookID. But why?

The answer lies in Page_Grid(). When a new page is called for by the user, Page_Grid() rebinds the DataGrid to the DataSet itself, not the sorted DataView of it.

```
myGrid.DataSource = BookDataSet;
```

Part of the solution then is to re-create the DataView in this routine as well and bind to that.

```
void Page_Grid(object sender, DataGridPageChangedEventArgs e)
{
    DataSet BookDataSet = (DataSet)Session["BookList"];

    DataView SortedView = new DataView(BookDataSet.Tables["Book"]);
```

The other part is keeping track of which column the data is currently being sorted by. This you can do with another session variable, which you set each time Sort_Grid is fired. When Page_Grid is fired, you just retrieve that session variable and apply it to the DataView before you DataBind() the DataSet to the grid.

```
    SortedView.Sort = (string)Session["SortExpression"];

    myGrid.DataSource = SortedView;
    myGrid.CurrentPageIndex = e.NewPageIndex;
    myGrid.DataBind();
}
```

So then, it's a much smoother ride all around when you use a DataSet as the data source for a DataGrid, and, as you'll see later, you can alter the contents of the DataSet via the grid and update those changes to the database itself.

Handling Multiple Queries

In the following sections, you'll look at one more data handling technique: handling multiple query results in one go. You know from Chapter 2 that when you send a database a command, it doesn't necessarily have to contain one SELECT statement, one UPDATE request, or one INSERT command, for example. It could contain several, each separated by a semicolon. So what happens when you send multiple SELECT queries to a database within the same command? Well, it depends whether you're using a DataReader or a DataSet.

A DataReader will contain individual results for each of the queries sent. Scalar results are treated as one-row results containing one field with the scalar in that field. All you need to do is navigate between the results (they come in the order the queries were made) in the DataReader using the NextResult() method mentioned in Chapter 6 and bind them to controls in the usual way.

When a DataAdapter object's SelectCommand contains more than one SELECT statement and Fill() is called on that DataAdapter, one of two things happen.

If the call to Fill() contains the name of a table to send the results to—for example, myAdapter.Fill(myDataSet, "Author");—the results of the first SELECT query are stored in a DataTable with that name, Author. The results of the second SELECT query are stored in another DataTable called Author1, those for the third query are stored in a DataTable called Author2, and so on. The DataAdapter just keeps creating new DataTables based on the name given to Fill() with a new number tacked onto the end to distinguish it.

If the call to Fill() doesn't hold the name of the DataTable to send the results to—for example, myAdapter.Fill(myDataSet);—the DataAdapter will create DataTables called Table, Table1, Table2, and so on, until all the individual query results have been assigned a DataTable.

If any of the SELECT queries returns a scalar value rather than a row of data from the database, the DataTable holding it will contain one DataRow with one field in it called Column1. The scalar value will be stored in that field.

> **NOTE** *Neither MySQL nor MDB files support the use of batch queries, so this example works only against MSDE.*

Try It Out: Handling a Batch Of Results

In this example, you'll execute one command at the database but instead of that command containing just one SQL query as usual, it will contain three.

```
SELECT * FROM Publisher;
SELECT * FROM Author;
SELECT COUNT(*) FROM Book
```

The aim will be to discover how to go between different results in a DataReader and if there are any difficulties when some of those queries result in scalar values instead of tables of data. Follow these steps:

1. In Web Matrix, create a new ASP.NET page called
    Handling_Multiple_Queries_DataReader.aspx and save it to the Chapter07 folder you previously created.

2. In Design view, drag two DataGrids and a Label control onto the page. Call these myGrid, myOtherGrid, and myLabel.

3. In All view, make sure you've included the right data provider at the top of the page.

    ```
    <%@ Page Language="C#" %>
    <%@ import Namespace="System.Data" %>
    <%@ import Namespace="System.Data.SqlClient" %>
    ```

4. You don't have to worry about prettifying the results in this example as you did in the previous section, so the code you need to write consists of just the Page_Load() routine and declaring the DataReader as a global variable so you can inline bind to it. In Code view then, add the following code:

    ```
    SqlDataReader myReader;

    void Page_Load(object sender, EventArgs e)
    {
        //set up connection string and SQL query
        string ConnectionString = Convert.ToString( ↵
            ConfigurationSettings.AppSettings["MSDEConnectString"]);
        string CommandText = "SELECT * FROM Publisher; ↵
            SELECT * FROM Author; SELECT COUNT(*) FROM Book";
    ```

```
//create SqlConnection and SqlCommand objects
SqlConnection myConnection = new SqlConnection(ConnectionString);
SqlCommand myCommand = new SqlCommand(CommandText, myConnection);

//use try finally clauses when the connection is open.
try
{
    //open connection to the database
    myConnection.Open();

    //run query
    myReader = myCommand.ExecuteReader();

    //myReader now contains two tables - one for Publisher,
    //one for Book. Calling DataBind() works to the end of
    //a table. In this case, publisher
    myGrid.DataSource = myReader;
    myGrid.DataBind();

    //To switch to the Book table, call NextResult.
    myReader.NextResult();

    //Calling DataBind() now applies to the book table.
    myOtherGrid.DataSource = myReader;
    myOtherGrid.DataBind();

    //Despite it being a scalar result,
    //the Book Count is stored in its own 'table'.
    //Inline bind it in the normal way, but don't forget to
    //call Read() first to move the cursor to the row
    //containing the data.

    myReader.NextResult();
    myReader.Read();
    Label2.DataBind();

    myReader.Close();

}
catch (Exception ex)
{
    //If an exception occurs, handle it.
    throw (ex);
```

```
        }
        finally
        {
            //Whether you succeed or fail, close the database connection
            myConnection.Close();
        }
    }
```

5. Save the code, and run it in a browser. You'll see that each control correctly displays one of the three results from the batch query (see Figure 7-18).

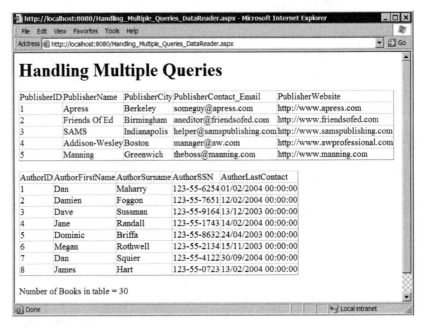

Figure 7-18. Handling multiple results is no problem for DataReader or DataSet.

How It Works

You won't see anything remarkable in the controls you've used to display the data; all the interesting stuff is in the Page_Load() handler. It begins just like the many other Page_Load() handlers you've used in this chapter. The only difference is the batch query you set to the CommandText variable.

```
void Page_Load(object sender, EventArgs e)
{
    //set up connection string and SQL query
    string ConnectionString = Convert.ToString( ↵
        ConfigurationSettings.AppSettings["MSDEConnectString"]);
    string CommandText = "SELECT * FROM Publisher; ↵
        SELECT * FROM Author; SELECT COUNT(*) FROM Book";

    //create SqlConnection and SqlCommand objects
    SqlConnection myConnection = new SqlConnection(ConnectionString);
    SqlCommand myCommand = new SqlCommand(CommandText, myConnection);

    //use try finally clauses when the connection is open.
    try
    {
        //open connection to the database
        myConnection.Open();
        //run query
        myReader = myCommand.ExecuteReader();
```

Once you've called ExecuteReader(), the DataReader returned to the page contains three separate query results available in the order the queries were made. The first one then is the contents of the Publisher table, and you can bind this to a grid in the same fashion as before.

```
myGrid.DataSource = myReader;
myGrid.DataBind();
```

The key point here is that DataBind() binds only the contents of the first result to the grid and not the contents of all three results as you may assume. This means you have control over what controls bind to which table without the fear that calling DataBind() on a control will spin you through all the results without stopping.

To access the next query result, you need to call NextResult() on the DataReader. In the context of this example, this makes available the contents of the Author table.

```
myReader.NextResult();
```

NextResult() works much like Read() in that it returns a boolean value. It returns true if it finds another set of query results to work with and false if it doesn't. Thus, you can build a check into your code to make sure the results you think you've got are actually there.

You could even use it in a loop as you do Read(), but the following is a word of caution if you do: Calling DataBind() on a DataGrid, NextResult(), and then calling the DataBind() on the same DataGrid will not result in the one grid containing the results of two queries. Instead, the second call to DataBind() will wipe the grid and then add the new data. This isn't convenient. You have to call DataBind() on two different grids to display both sets of results on the page. The same goes for any list or inline binding you want to do. Be careful not to call DataBind() on the same object twice!

```
//Calling DataBind() now applies to the author table.
myOtherGrid.DataSource = myReader;
myOtherGrid.DataBind();
myReader.NextResult();
```

The last query in the batch may be a bit confusing. Surely you need to call ExecuteScalar to retrieve the count of the items in the Book table? Actually, no. The DataReader's third result is exactly that scalar value and no more. It can't be list bound or table bound to a control, but it can be inline bound to a control's property or text value using the same code you saw earlier.

Remembering to call Read() on the DataReader before you try to access the value, you can tie the scalar result to a control as if it were the first field of a row.

```
<asp:Label id="Label2" runat="server">
  <%# DataBinder.Eval (myReader, "[0]") %>
</asp:Label>

...

      myReader.Read();
      Label2.DataBind();
      myReader.Close();

  }
```

Memory concerns aside for the minute, you can add as many queries to one batch command as you want. The only requirement when you're using a DataReader to work through all the results from the database is that you have to deal with them in the order the original queries were laid out in CommandText. It doesn't matter if those queries return confirmations, scalar values, or rows of data. As long as you handle them correctly, and you close the DataReader at the end of processing, it doesn't matter what order the queries are made.

In contrast, working with multiple results stored in a DataSet is pretty much the same as working with a single result. As long as you remember the name of the table each result will be stored in, you can access anything in the DataSet directly without needing to cycle through them as you do with a DataReader. You can find an example of this in the code download as Handling_Multiple_Queries_DataSet.aspx.

DataSet vs. DataReader

Before you finish this chapter, you'll quickly look at how the DataSet and DataReader compare across the techniques demonstrated in this chapter. You've learned how to bind various amounts of data to different controls, and in general the code you've used has changed almost entirely as a result of using either a DataReader or a DataSet. So before you learn how to update a data source, you'll take stock and compare DataReader and DataSet. Each has its own advantages and disadvantages, so it's pretty key to make the right choice for each page. Table 7-2 outlines the main differences.

Table 7-2. DataSet vs. DataReader for Displaying Read-Only Data

DataReader	DataSet
The data retrieved through a DataReader is forward-only and must be cycled through by calling Read(). Once the data has been cycled through, the DataReader must be closed and re-created to reaccess the data.	You can work with data in a DataSet in any order you choose as many times as you like.
Binding expressions can use either the index number of the field in the DataReader or the field name itself. Thus, they're quite simple to write and use.	Fields in a DataSet can be referenced by name, but you must also name the DataTable and identify the row (index) that contains the field. This means more complex binding expressions.
Data retrieved through a DataReader must be requeried for after a postback.	A DataSet may be stored in a session variable during postbacks if it isn't too great a drain on resources.
A DataReader connects to only one data source.	A DataSet can be filled using Fill() from multiple data sources
Most suited for quickly binding data to Web form controls.	Most suited for working with complex data and data that needs to be updated on a page.
You can bind only one list or table control to a DataReader. It must be re-created if you want to use another such control on the same page.	You can bind as many list or table controls to a single DataSet as are needed on the page.

continued

Table 7-2. DataSet vs. DataReader for Displaying Read-Only Data (continued)

DataReader	DataSet
Using a DataReader behind a DataGrid forces you to generate SQL statements that page and sort data for you. This leads you to difficulties when you need to combine these.	Using a DataSet behind a DataGrid means you can rely on .NET to do the sorting and paging for you.
Multiple results stored in a DataReader must be cycled through (by calling NextResult) and used in the order the queries were made originally.	Multiple results are stored in separate tables in a DataSet and may be used in any order by referencing the right table.

Summary

You don't have to surf far on the Web to see parallels between the examples you've seen in this chapter and, for example, the pages of an e-commerce or a business site where individual pieces of information are placed all around the page as well as in an orderly list or grid. Dealing with read-only data is a big subject even before you start altering it. This chapter could have contained plenty more if we had decided to go beyond the basics.

You've discovered the following three techniques to bind read-only data to a page:

- Inline bind a piece of information from the current row in the DataReader or from a DataSet to the property or the text value of a control on the page.

- Bind the query results to a list control such as a RadioButtonList or a Drop-DownList. This requires you to nominate a field for the text of each list item and another field to act as the value for each list item.

- Bind the query results to a table-based control such as a DataGrid, DataList, or Repeater. Unless you tell it otherwise, the DataGrid will present the results in a preformatted grid, one field per table cell; the DataList and Repeater, on the other hand, must be given a template for each row of information to be displayed.

You learned that you can customize the DataGrid quite heavily even when it autogenerates a grid to display query results. You can use SQL to make the data more readable, use styles to make it more attractive to the eye, and implement simple sort and paging functions to improve the way that users can view the results.

Lastly, you saw that you can work just as well with multiple results stored in a DataReader or a DataSet. It's just a case of knowing how to navigate to the result you want.

In the next chapter, you'll finish your look at handling the data from a query by exposing it as read-write data. You'll also learn how to send the changes made to that data back to the database.

CHAPTER 8

Writing Data from a Page

PREVIOUSLY, IN CHAPTERS 6 AND 7, you contented yourself with pulling some data from a database without altering it. In this chapter about handling data, you'll discover how to write a page that allows a user to add, alter, and delete the contents of a database. At the core of these three operations are three SQL statements, but the process of building up those statements is something new.

In this chapter then, we'll cover the following:

- Using single-value and list controls to build up a statement sent directly to the database with a call to ExecuteNonQuery()

- Validating those controls to make sure no invalid changes are made

- Using a DataSet to store any changes made to the data on the server until a call is made to update the database with those changes

- Building a DataGrid that allows you to edit and delete data within a single control

In an effort to keep this chapter reasonably short, you'll double up some of these techniques. Thus, you'll use a DataSet as the data source for an editable DataGrid and use other (validated) form controls to build up a query to be run with ExecuteNonQuery(). This works out rather nicely because the DataGrid can't easily be set up to add new information to a database, and the technique for using form controls is the same regardless of whether you're adding, editing, or deleting data.

Note that we haven't mentioned the DataReader so far, and it's with good reason. A DataReader works only one way: bringing query results from a data source to a page. It can't be used in the other direction to send alterations to a data source. When the examples in this chapter use a DataReader object, it's purely to reflect the changes made to the data on the screen.

> **TIP** *In the interest of keeping the code in the chapter concise, we've used batch queries to populate Web form controls. Of course, this means the examples as given in the text work against only Microsoft SQL Server 2000 Desktop Engine (MSDE). You can find working examples for MySQL and Access in the code download for the book. The techniques used are the same, but you have to run each SQL query individually rather than all in one go. This means the code is a bit more complex.*

Making Changes to a Database

It has taken you a while to get here, but it's good to know that adding something to a database is just as easy as taking something from it. Indeed, those three basic steps you first discovered back in Chapter 1—creating the connection, sending the command, and handling the results—still hold true. The only difference is that you'll need to use a new set of commands depending on what you want to do, and the results will generally be a scalar value indicating the number of rows in the database that have changed as the result of the command. It's your choice whether you use this result.

We've mentioned these new commands already in Chapters 2 and 5, but in this chapter, we'll cover the following more closely:

- The SQL INSERT statement to add new rows to a table in a database

- The SQL UPDATE statement to change rows already in a database

- The SQL DELETE statement to remove rows from a database

Unlike the SELECT statement, which just retrieves data, these three all have rules to obey—rules you created as you built up the database and created relationships between tables, and rules you'll need to bear in mind as you create those SQL statements so they work as you intend and don't return an error. What was the data type for this field? What was its maximum length? Was it a key? Can it be null? The onus is on you to make sure that the data you try to add to a table obeys its rules.

You also need to decide how you fire these commands and when. Do you call ExecuteNonQuery() on a Command object or call Update() on a DataSet? Do you handle the result that's returned? How do you handle errors? If you're using a DataSet, do you update the database every time a field is changed or wait until the user clicks a button to go ahead? Like dealing with data for display, the basics are straightforward, but you need a little more brainpower to make the page user-friendly (and idiot-proof).

Adding New Data to the Database

You'll always have information to change and new knowledge to collect, so providing a way to add new information to your databases is pretty crucial. Some sites may hide this functionality away in the administration section of their site, but it depends on what the database models and who is logged on. For instance, Amazon hides the functionality to add new product information away from you, the public, but it does let you add new feedback, secondhand listings, and user information to its database, provided you're logged in. Similarly, eBay allows anyone to add a new auction to its database, but only the auctioneer to change those details. Security, then, is an important issue but one to consider only after a few other things are in place.

INSERT Statements

At the heart of the code to add new information to a database is the SQL INSERT statement. Although it may seem otherwise, sending an INSERT command to a database is the only way to do this, so you best get familiar with it. Compared to SELECT, it's quite simple. You saw its syntax back in Chapter 5, but as a quick reminder, it looks like this:

```
INSERT [INTO] { table_name }
    { [(field_list)]
    { VALUES ( field_value_list ) }
}
```

With this in mind, it shouldn't be too difficult to construct a simple INSERT statement for any of the four tables in the sample database. For example, if you wanted to add a new publisher to the Publisher table, you'd use the following command:

```
INSERT INTO publisher (PublisherID, PublisherName, PublisherCity, ⤷
    PublisherContact_Email, PublisherWebsite)
VALUES (6, 'OUP', 'Oxford', 'him@oup.com', 'http://www.oup.com')
```

When the database executes this, a new row will be created in the Publisher table, and the values 6, OUP, and so on will be added into their respective fields, as shown in Table 8-1.

Table 8-1. Values in the New Publisher Table Row

PublisherID	PublisherName	PublisherCity	PublisherContact_Email	PublisherWebsite
6	OUP	Oxford	him@oup.com	http://www.oup.com

Another point to remember about INSERT is that it works only with a single table at a time. If, then, you're working with complex data that would be sourced from two or more tables in a database, you'll have to write a batch command containing an INSERT command for each table to be updated. For example, to add details for a new book to the sample database, you'd have to write an INSERT command for both the Book and WhoWroteWhat tables at the least. If the new book was written by an author not in the database, you'd have to create an INSERT for the Author database as well.

The database regenerator scripts in the code download illustrate this point really well. Both contain INSERT statements for each row in each table, with each table populated in the correct order so that no data entry breaks any of the constraints you've laid on the database. Oh, yes, the INSERT statement may be simpler than SELECT, but it needs just as much consideration.

Working to the Database's Rules

Unlike playground rules, database rules aren't made to be broken, and you need to keep the following in mind when you're inserting new data into a table using INSERT:

Primary keys: You have to provide a unique value for the field(s) in a table's primary key. If you don't, the database will return an error. Thus, you need to ensure that when you insert a new row into a table using INSERT, it contains a valid and unique value for the primary key.

Things are a bit simpler if the primary key you use in the table is an autoincremented integer field, such as the PublisherID field in the Publisher table, the AuthorID field in the Author table, or the BookID field in the Book table. By establishing such a primary key, you can omit this field from the INSERT's field_list because the database itself will automatically generate the value for you as you add the new row.

Foreign keys: If one of the fields in a table is a foreign key, you must ensure that any value you try to add to that field already exists as a value for the primary key in the corresponding table. In this example then, you have to add new publishers and new authors before you can add new books.

Mandatory fields: If a table doesn't allow a field to be NULL, you must give it a value when you add a new row. Either the user provides a value, you give it a default value when the user doesn't, or you keep nudging the user for a value until he does.

Field data types: Each field must be given a value of the appropriate type.

Each of these rules complicates things. Can you ensure that values are unique? What Web form controls best suit the entering of data for each field? How do you enter a default value and make sure a field is given a certain value? There can be no better answer than by example.

Try It Out: Inserting a New Book with INSERT

In this example, you'll write a page that allows you to add details of a new book to the sample database, including its authors and publishers. This example won't cover the addition of new authors or publishers, however—that's left to you as an exercise.

This particular page will have two stages to it. On loading, the page displays a form with which the user can provide the details of the new book. You'll see how the database's rules mentioned previously inform how to build the form and what validation controls to use to ensure that each field has at least some sort of value. Once the user clicks a button to add the new book data, the page validates the data. If it's OK, it uploads the new book to the database and puts two DataGrids on the screen to display the new book information to show that it has been success-fully added to the database and the various SQL INSERT statements used in the page. Figure 8-1 shows the page after adding a new book to the database.

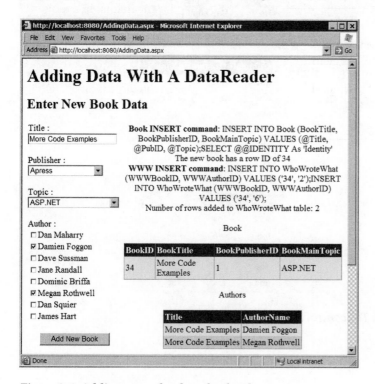

Figure 8-1. Adding a new book to the database

> **NOTE** *This database has a lot going on; besides the finished page, the code download for this chapter also contains three "work-in-progress" pages that coincide with code up to a certain stage. You'll find this code as* AddingData_1.aspx, AddingData_2.aspx, *and* AddingData_3.aspx.

Follow these steps:

1. In Web Matrix, create a new ASP.NET page called AddingData.aspx and save it to a new Chapter08 directory in your code folder.

2. You'll focus on the first stage of the page first—building the form to add books. You'll need a button control to kick off the second stage, a textbox for the user to add the Book's title, DropDownLists for Publisher and Topic, and a CheckBoxList control to choose the book's authors. You'll call these SubmitButton, BookTitle, BookPublisherList, BookTopicList, and Book-AuthorList, respectively. You can see how they're laid out in Figure 8-2. Note that this also shows the DataGrid controls for the second stage, which you'll come to later in step 5.

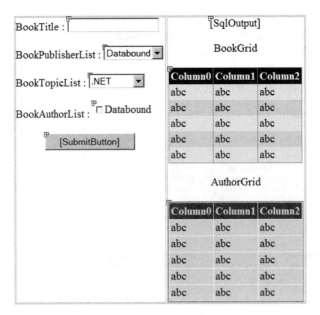

Figure 8-2. The control layout for AddingData.aspx

3. In Code view, add a declaration for the DataReader object that you'll be binding the controls to in a moment and the connection string. You'll use that in several different functions across the page. You'll also add the code to bind the contents of the DataReader to the controls.

```
SqlDataReader SetupDataReader;
string ConnectionString = Convert.ToString( ↵
   ConfigurationSettings.AppSettings["MSDEConnectString"]);

void Page_Load(object sender, EventArgs e)
{
  if (!(Page.IsPostBack))
  {
    string SelectCommand = ↵
      "SELECT PublisherID, PublisherName from Publisher; ↵
      SELECT AuthorID, ↵
      (AuthorFirstName + ' ' + AuthorSurname) AS AuthorName ↵
      FROM Author";

    //create SqlConnection and SqlCommand objects
    SqlConnection myConnection = new SqlConnection(ConnectionString);
    SqlCommand myCommand = new SqlCommand(SelectCommand, myConnection);

    try
    {
      myConnection.Open();
      SetupDataReader = myCommand.ExecuteReader();

      //Setup Publisher DropDownList
      ddlBookPublisher.DataBind();

      //Move to Author results
      SetupDataReader.NextResult();

      //Setup Author CheckBoxList
      chkBookAuthors.DataBind();
    }
    catch (Exception ex)
    {
      throw ex;
    }
    finally
    {
```

```
            if (myConnection.State == ConnectionState.Open)
            {
              myConnection.Close();
            }
          }
        } // end if !Postback
      }
```

4. Now you can add the data binding information to the four form controls.
   In HTML view, they look like this:

```
<p>
    Title :   <asp:TextBox id="BookTitle" runat="server"></asp:TextBox>
</p>
<p>
    Publisher :
    <asp:DropDownList id="BookPublisherList" runat="server"
        DataTextField="PublisherName" DataSource="<%# SetupDataReader %>"
        DataValueField="PublisherID"> </asp:DropDownList>
</p>
<p>
    Topic :
    <asp:DropDownList id="BookTopicList" runat="server">
        <asp:ListItem Value=".NET">.NET</asp:ListItem>
        <asp:ListItem Value="ADO.NET">ADO.NET</asp:ListItem>
        <asp:ListItem Value="ASP.NET">ASP.NET</asp:ListItem>
        <asp:ListItem Value="C#">C#</asp:ListItem>
        <asp:ListItem Value="IL">IL</asp:ListItem>
        <asp:ListItem Value="Longhorn">Longhorn</asp:ListItem>
        <asp:ListItem Value="VB.NET">VB.NET</asp:ListItem>
        <asp:ListItem Value="Whidbey">Whidbey</asp:ListItem>
    </asp:DropDownList>
</p>
<p>
    Author :
    <asp:CheckBoxList id="BookAuthorList" DataValueField="AuthorID"
        DataTextField="AuthorName" DataSource="<%# SetupDataReader %>"
        runat="server"></asp:CheckBoxList>
</p>
<p align="center">
    <asp:Button id="SubmitButton" onclick="SubmitButton_Click"
        runat="server" Text="Add New Book"></asp:Button>
</p>
```

5. With the entry form sorted out, you need to implement the second stage—
    what happens when a user clicks the submit button. Add the following
    event handler to the code in the page:

```
void btnSubmit_Click(object sender, EventArgs e)
{
    SqlConnection myConnection = new SqlConnection(ConnectionString);

    //Insert new Book into table and store new BookID number
    string newBookID = InsertNewBook(myConnection);

    //Add Book to Author rows in WhoWroteWhat table
    InsertWWWEntries(newBookID, myConnection);

    //Bind Book Table To DataGrid
    DisplayBookAndAuthors(newBookID, myConnection);
}
```

6. All three functions in the button click handler write something to the
    screen, so you need to set up the controls they'll write to before you write
    the functions. In Design view again, add a Label control called SqlOutput
    and two DataGrid controls called BookGrid and AuthorGrid to the page,
    as shown in Figure 8-2. Add some color to the DataGrids using the Auto-
    format wizard.

7. The first job in the second stage of the page is to add the new book details
    to the database. You do this inside a function called InsertNewBook that
    returns the BookID value for the new entry.

```
string InsertNewBook(SqlConnection conn)
{
    string NewBookID = "0";

    //Need to start with the appropriate INSERT method for the Book table.
    string InsertBookCommand = ⤸
        "INSERT INTO Book (BookTitle, BookPublisherID, BookMainTopic) ⤸
        VALUES (@Title, @PubID, @Topic);SELECT @@IDENTITY As 'Identity' ";

    //Create and add Parameter value for BookTitle
    //Specify the length to catch overly long titles.
    //This counts as secondary validation
    SqlParameter TitleParam = ⤸
        new SqlParameter("@Title", SqlDbType.VarChar, 100);
    TitleParam.Value = BookTitle.Text;
```

```
//Create and add Parameter value for PublisherID
SqlParameter PubIDParam = new SqlParameter("@PubID", SqlDbType.Int);
PubIDParam.Value = BookPublisherList.SelectedItem.Value;

//Create and add Parameter value for BookTopic
//Of course, this should be an enum so length wouldn't be an issue.
//As it is you include the length
SqlParameter TopicParam = ↵
    new SqlParameter("@Topic", SqlDbType.VarChar, 25);
TopicParam.Value = BookTopicList.SelectedItem.Value;

//Check SQL INSERT statement is correct
SqlOutput.Text = "<b>Book INSERT command</b>: " + ↵
    InsertBookCommand + "<br/>";

//Create Command object
SqlCommand InsertCommand = new SqlCommand (InsertBookCommand, conn);

// add all parameters to the Command object
InsertCommand.Parameters.Add (TitleParam);
InsertCommand.Parameters.Add (PubIDParam);
InsertCommand.Parameters.Add (TopicParam);

try
{
    conn.Open();

    NewBookID = InsertCommand.ExecuteScalar().ToString();
}
catch (Exception ex)
{
    throw ex;
}
finally
{
    if (conn.State == ConnectionState.Open)
    {
        conn.Close();
    }
}

//Make a note of the new BookID
SqlOutput.Text += "The new book has a row ID of " + ↵
```

```
        NewBookID + "<br/>";

    return NewBookID;
}
```

8. With the new book in the database, you need to associate this new book
   with its authors, so you need to add some new entries to the WhoWrote-
   What table. You do this inside the InsertWWWEntries function.

```
void InsertWWWEntries(string BookID, SqlConnection conn)
{
    //No need to add parameters here because we're not adding
    //stuff in from the Web page
    string Stub ="INSERT INTO WhoWroteWhat (WWWBookID, WWWAuthorID) ⏎
        VALUES ('" + BookID + "', '";
    string InsertWWWCommand = "";
    int RowsEntered = 0;

    //need to assume that at least one value has been selected.
    //validation must do that.
    for (int i=0; i<BookAuthorList.Items.Count; i++)
    {
        if (BookAuthorList.Items[i].Selected)
        {
            InsertWWWCommand += ⏎
                Stub + BookAuthorList.Items[i].Value + "');";
        }
    }

    //Check SQL INSERT statement is correct
    SqlOutput.Text += "<b>WWW INSERT command</b>: " + ⏎
        InsertWWWCommand + "<br/>";

    //Create Command object
    SqlCommand InsertCommand = new SqlCommand (InsertWWWCommand, conn);

    try
    {
        conn.Open();
        RowsEntered = InsertCommand.ExecuteNonQuery();
    }
    catch (Exception ex)
    {
```

```
        throw ex;
    }
    finally
    {
        if (conn.State == ConnectionState.Open)
        {
            conn.Close();
        }
    }

    SqlOutput.Text += "Number of rows added to WhoWroteWhat table: " + ⏎
        RowsEntered.ToString();
}
```

9. Finally, you need to prove that all the data was entered correctly, so you select and bind the new data in the two tables to the DataGrids and display them on the screen.

```
void DisplayBookAndAuthors(string NewBookID, SqlConnection conn)
{
    //No need for params here because we're not including user input.
    //Strictly speaking, you could add them in, though.
    string myCommand = "SELECT * from Book Where Book.BookID = '" + ⏎
        NewBookID + "';";
    myCommand += "SELECT Book.BookTitle AS Title, ⏎
        (Author.AuthorFirstName + ' ' + Author.AuthorSurname) AS AuthorName ⏎
        FROM WhoWroteWhat ⏎
        INNER JOIN Book ON Book.BookID = WhoWroteWhat.WWWBookID ⏎
        INNER JOIN Author ON Author.AuthorID = WhoWroteWhat.WWWAuthorID ⏎
        WHERE WhoWroteWhat.WWWBookID = '" + NewBookID + "';";

    SqlCommand SelectBookCommand = new SqlCommand(myCommand, conn);

    try
    {
        conn.Open();
        SqlDataReader BooksDataReader = SelectBookCommand.ExecuteReader();
        BookGrid.DataSource = BooksDataReader;
        BookGrid.DataBind();

        BooksDataReader.NextResult();

        AuthorGrid.DataSource = BooksDataReader;
        AuthorGrid.DataBind();
    }
```

```
catch (Exception ex)
{
    throw ex;
}
finally
{
    if (conn.State == ConnectionState.Open)
    {
        conn.Close();
    }
}
}
```

10. Save the page, and open it in your browser. If you prefer not to type all this code, try running AddingData_2.aspx from the code download—this contains all the code thus far. All will run as intended, but errors will occur if you leave out values for one or more of the fields. You need to make sure that the user gives each form control a valid value. To do this, you need to add some validation controls to the page.

11. In Design view, add three RequiredFieldValidator controls and a Custom-Validator control to the page. Name them CheckTitle, CheckPublisher, CheckTopic, and CheckAuthor, respectively, as shown in Figure 8-3.

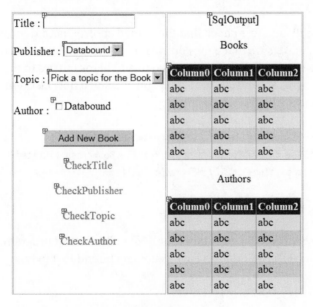

Figure 8-3. Adding validation controls

In HTML, their complete declarations look like this:

```
<p align="center">
  <asp:RequiredFieldValidator id="CheckTitle" runat="server"
    ErrorMessage="Please add the title for the book"
    ControlToValidate="BookTitle"></asp:RequiredFieldValidator>
</p>
<p align="center">
  <asp:RequiredFieldValidator id="CheckPublisher" runat="server"
    ErrorMessage="Please identify the book's publisher"
    ControlToValidate="BookPublisherList"></asp:RequiredFieldValidator>
</p>
<p align="center">
  <asp:RequiredFieldValidator id="CheckTopic" runat="server"
    ErrorMessage="Please pick a topic for the book."
    ControlToValidate="BookTopicList"></asp:RequiredFieldValidator>
</p>
<p align="center">
  <asp:CustomValidator id="CheckAuthor" runat="server"
    ErrorMessage="You must select at least one author for the book"
    OnServerValidate="CheckAuthor_ServerValidate"
    ClientValidationFunction="CheckAuthors"></asp:CustomValidator>
</p>
```

12. RequiredFieldValidators check that the named control has a value, so you need to make sure that each control doesn't have a value already. BookTitle is blank anyway, but you need to add blank entries to the two DropDownList controls. In HTML, you can add a new ListItem to BookTopicList by hand.

```
<asp:DropDownList id="BookTopicList" runat="server">
    <asp:ListItem Value="">Pick a topic for the Book</asp:ListItem>
    <asp:ListItem Value=".NET">.NET</asp:ListItem>
    ...
</asp:DropDownList>
```

13. You also have to add the extra entry for BookPublisherList programmatically after the Publisher names have been data bound to it in Page_Load().

```
//Setup Publisher DropDownList
BookPublisherList.DataBind();
ListItem blank = new ListItem("Choose a Publisher", "");
BookPublisherList.Items.Add(blank);
blank.Selected = true;
```

14. Finally, you need to implement the server-side and client-side validation routines for the CustomValidator that checks whether any authors have been selected. In HTML view, add the following script to the <head> of the page:

```
<head>
    <script language="javascript">
    <!--
        function CheckAuthors(source, args) {
            var count = false;
            var CtrlColl = document.forms[0].elements;

            for (var i=0; i < CtrlColl.length; i++)
            {

              if (CtrlColl[i].name.substring(0, 14) == 'BookAuthorList')
              {
                if (CtrlColl[i].checked)
                {
                  count = true;
                  break;
                }
              }
            }
            args.IsValid = (count == true);
        } //-->
    </script>
</head>
```

15. Finally, in Code view, add the server-side validation routine.

```
void CheckAuthor_ServerValidate(object sender, ServerValidateEventArgs e)
{
    bool isValid = false;
    for (int i=0; i<BookAuthorList.Items.Count; i++)
    {
        if (BookAuthorList.Items[i].Selected)
        {
            isValid = true;
        }
    }
    e.IsValid = isValid;
}
```

Save, and run the page again. The page now checks the form for valid data before it's added to the database.

How It Works

The first stage of this page needs to take the rules of the sample database into consideration. You'll add a new row to the Book table, so the first task is to figure out which control suits adding the value for each field.

BookID: This is the primary key for the Book table, but it's also an autonumber, so you don't need to insert a value for this field. It will be added for you automatically.

BookTitle: A book's title is just text, so a TextBox is just fine.

BookPublisherID: This is a foreign key from the Publisher table so it can hold only values already in the Publisher table. It makes sense to give the user a choice of publishers from a list, so you'll use a DropDownList and bind the publisher names to the DataTextField of the list and the publisher ID to its DataValueField. You could use any data-aware list control, but DropDownList will do fine.

BookTopic: It's at this point it becomes obvious that the sample database design is (deliberately) flawed and that book topics should really be in their own table. This would mean you could bind the topics to a list control and keep control of the topics to be assigned a new book. However, they're not, so you have to write the list in full. This is a good example of one of the repercussions of bad database design.

Authors: The Book and Author tables have a many-to-many relationship with each other, so you need to offer the user a way to select multiple authors for the book. A CheckBoxList seems the way to go. The author's name will be bound to the DataTextField, and the ID will be bound to the DataValueField.

To populate the list controls, you've used a DataReader to query the publishers and authors from the database. You've also filled the book topic list manually; it's certainly not the best way to do it, but it does mean you can see how to validate these lists a bit more clearly. Note how you've used the expression (`AuthorFirstName + ' ' + AuthorSurname`) to present the full names of the authors in the CheckBox list rather than just their surnames.

```
string SelectCommand = "SELECT PublisherID, PublisherName from Publisher; ⏎
    SELECT AuthorID, (AuthorFirstName + ' ' + AuthorSurname) AS AuthorName ⏎
    FROM Author";
```

The remainder of the code for the first stage—the validation controls—is purely to make the form more idiot-proof. Because the database was defined such that no column allows nulls, every field must have a value when you try to add a new row. Your strategy then must be to set every control on the form to the no value to force the user to add or choose one. The TextBox for the book title is set to empty by default, as is the CheckBoxList, but you have to add a ListItem to the two Drop-DownLists with an empty value, which will be selected by default. BookTopicList has been written out by hand, so you can add the blank item by hand, as well.

```
<asp:ListItem Value="">Pick a topic for the Book</asp:ListItem>
```

By adding it to the top of the list, it's selected by default as required. For the other DropDownList, you have to add the blank item programmatically once the other items have been added from the DataReader. Remember, any items already in a list control are removed when DataBind() is called on the control. You simply add a new ListItem to the control and make sure it's selected.

```
BookPublisherList.DataBind();
ListItem blank = new ListItem("Choose a Publisher", "");
BookPublisherList.Items.Add(blank);
blank.Selected = true;
```

Now, the CheckBoxList control is unusual when it comes to working against validation controls in that they can't be the target of a validation control's Control-ToValidate property. Doing so will cause an error, so the only way to check that at least one of the authors has been selected is to use a CustomValidator with which you can give both client-side and server-side functions. In this case, both functions simply run through each check box in the list and check to see if any of them are checked. If any are, the validator reports that it's valid.

```
function CheckAuthors(source, args)
{
   var count = false;
   var CtrlColl = document.forms[0].elements;

   for (var i=0; i < CtrlColl.length; i++)
   {
      if (CtrlColl[i].name.substring(0, 14) == 'BookAuthorList')
      {
         if (CtrlColl[i].checked)
         {
            count = true;
```

```
            break;
        }
      }
    }
    args.IsValid = (count == true);
}
void CheckAuthor_ServerValidate(object sender, ServerValidateEventArgs e)
{
    bool isValid = false;
    for (int i=0; i<BookAuthorList.Items.Count; i++)
    {
        if (BookAuthorList.Items[i].Selected)
        {
            isValid = true;
        }
    }
    e.IsValid = isValid;
}
```

With the first stage complete, you need to determine how the book data in the form is inserted into the two tables in the database. You'll need to create one INSERT for the book itself and then one per author for the WhoWroteWhat table. You'll encounter one snag, though. The WhoWroteWhat table uses the BookID of a book to link to an author in the WhoWroteWhat table. Once you've added the new book to the table, how do you discover the new ID it has (automatically) been given? Fortunately, you have two ways around it. The following example uses a macro called @@IDENTITY for the job, which does the job of returning the new ID assigned to the book by the database:

```
INSERT INTO Book (BookTitle, BookPublisherID, BookMainTopic) ⮠
    VALUES (@Title, @PubID, @Topic);SELECT @@IDENTITY As 'Identity'
```

Thus, when you execute this batch command, you do so by calling Execute-Scalar() rather than ExecuteNonQuery() so you can capture the new BookID and incorporate it into the INSERTs to WhoWroteWhat. ExecuteScalar() returns a generic object rather than a string or an integer, so you call ToString() on it to make it easier to handle.

```
string InsertNewBook(SqlConnection conn)
{
    string NewBookID = "0";
    string InsertBookCommand = ⮠
        "INSERT INTO Book (BookTitle, BookPublisherID, BookMainTopic) ⮠
            VALUES (@Title, @PubID, @Topic);SELECT @@IDENTITY";
```

. . .

```
  //Create Command object
  SqlCommand InsertCommand = new SqlCommand (InsertBookCommand, conn);
```
. . .
```
  try
  {
    conn.Open();

    NewBookID = InsertCommand.ExecuteScalar().ToString();
  }
```
. . .
```
  }
```

One other thing to note is that you're using parameters in the INSERT statements in the interest of security. You could just build up the statement with string concatenation, but as you learned in Chapter 4, parameters prevent users from trying to harm your database by sending malevolent SQL instructions through the TextBox control. You should also recall from Chapter 4 that OLE DB users use question marks to signify parameters rather than @Name. Hence, you should use the following INSERT statement:

```
INSERT INTO Book (BookTitle, BookPublisherID, BookMainTopic) ⤸
   VALUES (?, ?, ?);SELECT @@IDENTITY";
```

These question marks are assigned in strict order, so you'll have to create the BookTitle parameter first, then create the PublisherID, and then create the topic. Switch them around, and you'll get errors, because .NET tries to assign a BookTitle to a PublisherID field, for instance.

> **NOTE** *@@IDENTITY works fine in this example, but it can run into trouble working with DataSets when many people are using the page at the same time. In this case, and especially when working with stored procedures, use* scope_identity() *instead.*

With the BookID in hand, you can now add the appropriate entries to the WhoWroteWhat table by iterating through the CheckBoxList and creating an INSERT statement for every check box that has been selected, like so:

```
INSERT INTO WhoWroteWhat (BookID, AuthorID) VALUES ('56', '6');
```

You're not using parameters here for two reasons. First, there's no danger of SQL insertion attacks via a check box, and second, string concatenation lends itself much more cleanly to iterating through the check box and then opening a connection afterward to execute the INSERTs. In using parameters, the code to execute the statement must be contained within the loop because you're calling one INSERT statement many times rather than creating lots of statements and executing them all in one go.

```
void InsertWWWEntries(string BookID, SqlConnection conn)
{
    //No need to add parameters here.
    //We're not adding stuff in from the web page
    string Stub ="INSERT INTO WhoWroteWhat (WWWBookID, WWWAuthorID)
        VALUES ('" + BookID + "', '";
    string InsertWWWCommand = "";
    int RowsEntered = 0;

    //need to assume that at least one value has been selected.
    //validation must do that.
    for (int i=0; i<BookAuthorList.Items.Count; i++)
    {
        if (BookAuthorList.Items[i].Selected)
        {
            InsertWWWCommand += Stub + BookAuthorList.Items[i].Value + "');";
        }
    }

    //Check SQL INSERT statement is correct
    SqlOutput.Text += "<b>WWW INSERT command</b>: " + InsertWWWCommand + "<br/>";

    //Create Command object
    SqlCommand InsertCommand = new SqlCommand (InsertWWWCommand, conn);

    try
    {
        conn.Open();
        RowsEntered = InsertCommand.ExecuteNonQuery();
    }
    ...
}
```

Finally, you query for the new data and bind it to a couple of DataGrids on the page. You've seen how to do this many times before, but it's worth noting the second select statement you use to display author names against book titles.

```
SELECT Book.BookTitle AS Title,
       (Author.AuthorFirstName + ' ' + Author.AuthorSurname) AS AuthorName
       FROM WhoWroteWhat
   INNER JOIN Book ON Book.BookID = WhoWroteWhat.WWWBookID
   INNER JOIN Author ON Author.AuthorID = WhoWroteWhat.WWWAuthorID
   WHERE WhoWroteWhat.WWWBookID = '" + NewBookID + "'";
```

You haven't come across it before, but SQL SELECT statements aren't limited to one JOIN and can stretch across many tables in one go as long as each field and table are identified unambiguously. This particular statement pulls out the rows from the WhoWroteWhat table that contains the BookID for the new book and then (via the first join) the name of the new book and (via the second join) the author names that correspond to the AuthorIDs in each row with the book.

Deleting Data from the Database

By the time we finished writing that previous example, we had 30 extra junk book titles in the database to remove. The same will probably be true when you start working with your own databases. It makes sense therefore for the next task to be deleting data from tables in a database. You're still under the same rules laid out by the database, but this time you have to consider how a database deals with deleting data.

- Unlike Windows, databases don't have a Recycle Bin. Once a user says delete some data, it's gone; the only way to get it back is to reinsert it.

- The foreign key constraints you lay on your tables may cause the database to delete additional data from related tables depending on how the constraint is set.

The moral of these tales is to make users absolutely sure that they want to delete information before they actually do, and warn them if any other data will be removed. In fact, you could even take it out of their hands and not give them the opportunity to delete data in the first place. Databases allow any kind of user—administrative or not—to delete data from a table, so you may want to add code that allows only specific users to do this. For the rest, perhaps you could pretend to delete the data by adding an extra boolean column to the tables called Visible; if it's true, the row is available to the user, and if the user has "deleted" it, Visible is false and not available. That said, this is more of a personalization feature of a site than a data-access one, so you won't touch on this any further, but it's a key point to consider when you design your site.

SQL DELETE Statements

Like any other database operation, you delete data by sending a SQL statement to a database—in this case, a DELETE statement. It doesn't matter how it's sent— perhaps by calling ExecuteNonQuery() on a Command object or Update() on a DataAdapter object—but this is the only way to do it.

You saw the following generic DELETE statement back in Chapter 5:

```
DELETE [FROM]
{ table_name }
[WHERE condition_list]
```

Like the INSERT statement, DELETE can work on only one table at a time, which is probably a good thing. A rogue statement such as DELETE * could wipe all the data out at once if it was a valid statement, a bit like del *.* would do in a DOS prompt. Indeed, DELETE works with whole rows only. You never delete single fields from a row; what you'd actually do in that case would be to change a field to an empty value or NULL if the database allowed it.

> **CAUTION** *We've said it already, but be careful when you're using DELETE state-ments. A lot of work can easily get flushed away if you aren't.*

Sympathy for the User: DataGrid ButtonColumns

In the INSERT example, you used a collection of individual form elements to let the user specify the field values for a new book and then displayed it in a DataGrid as confirmation. You could carry on using simple form elements in this exercise— perhaps binding book names to a DropDownList and deleting the one selected in the list when a button is clicked—but you can easily code a more elegant solution, which you'll look at here.

The DataGrid object can display much more than just the results of a data query as you've used it to do so far and have again in Editing_Deleting_Data_1.aspx. In fact, to make it more interactive, you can add columns of buttons and links to it, allowing you to work with a row of data in the grid given the button that was clicked. In this special case, you'll use a button to indicate that its row should be deleted from the database. Depending on the purpose of your page, the button could signify that the row should be added to a shopping cart, copied to another location, or selected to have an e-mail sent to it.

The object that enables you to do all this is the `<asp:ButtonColumn>` object, which you add to the DataGrid's Columns collection, like so:

```
<asp:DataGrid id="DataGrid1" runat="server">
   <Columns>
      <asp:ButtonColumn Text="Delete"
         ButtonType="PushButton" CommandName="Delete" />
   </Columns>
</asp:DataGrid>
```

When you `DataBind()` to the DataGrid, any autogenerated columns will appear as usual, but there will now also be a column of form buttons to the left displaying the value of the ButtonColumn's `Text` property, as shown in Figure 8-4 and demonstrated in `Editing_Deleting_Data_2.aspx`.

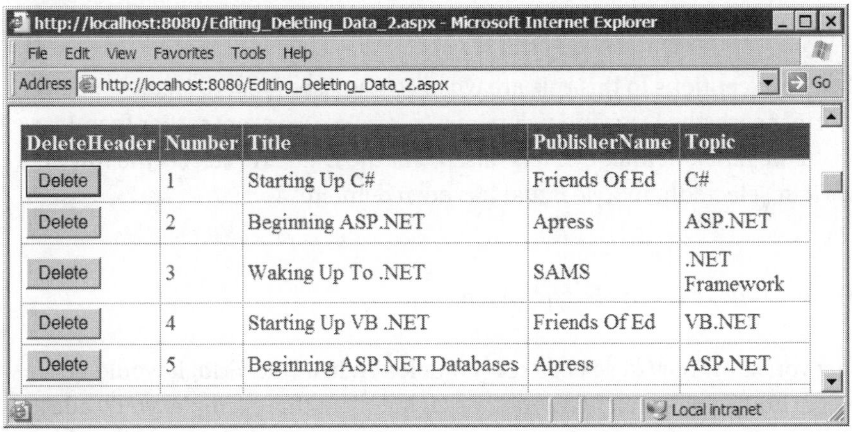

Figure 8-4. The ButtonColumn as rendered in a DataGrid

The `<asp:ButtonColumn>` has two other key properties that should be given values: `ButtonType` and `CommandName`. `ButtonType` lets you specify whether the new column contains form buttons or hyperlink-like buttons. `CommandName` identifies the action associated with the button and ties into the event handler called when the button is clicked.

By default, when a button in a `ButtonColumn` is pressed, the DataGrid raises an event called `ItemCommand`. If the DataGrid contains only one ButtonColumn, you can just write an event handler accordingly for that action. If it contains more than one, you can identify which action to take from the `CommandName`, like so:

```
void ItemsGrid_Command(Object sender, DataGridCommandEventArgs e)
{
    switch(((PushButton)e.CommandSource).CommandName)
    {
        case "AddToCart":
            AddToCart(e);
            break;

        case "SomethingElse":
            SomethingElse(e);
            break;

        default:
            // Do nothing.
            break;
    }
}
```

The two exceptions to this rule are when `CommandName` is set to Delete or Select. In the former case, the DataGrid will raise a `DeleteCommand` event rather than `Item-Command`. In the latter, neither event is raised, but the DataGrid selects the row and displays it in SelectedItemStyle if that has been defined.

Try It Out: Delete with the DataGrid

Now that you know how to select a row for deletion in a DataGrid, it would be rude not to build a page that demonstrates it in full. In this example, you'll add a DeleteColumn to a DataGrid bound to the Book table. You'll find the basic DataGrid in `Editing_Deleting_Data_1.aspx`. You can find the results in `Editing_Deleting_Data_2.aspx`.

There are three simple steps to adding a functional Delete column to a Data-Grid. If you want to type the code yourself, open Editing_Deleting_Data_1.aspx and add the code yourself.

1. Add a <asp:ButtonColumn> to the DataGrid.

```
<asp:DataGrid id="DataGrid1" runat="server">
   <Columns>
      <asp:ButtonColumn Text="Delete" ButtonType="PushButton"
         HeaderText="DeleteHeader" FooterText="DeleteFooter"
         CommandName="Delete"></asp:ButtonColumn>
   </Columns>
</asp:DataGrid>
```

2. Add and implement an event handler for the DataGrid's onDeleteCommand event.

```
<asp:DataGrid id="DataGrid1" runat="server"
             onDeleteCommand="DataGrid1_DeleteCommand">
...
void DataGrid1_DeleteCommand(object sender, DataGridCommandEventArgs e)
{
    string DelCommand = "DELETE FROM WhoWroteWhat WHERE BookID = '"+ ⏎
        e.Item.Cells[1].Text +"';";
    DelCommand += "DELETE FROM Book WHERE BookID = '"+ ⏎
        e.Item.Cells[1].Text +"'";

    Status.Text += "<b>DELETE command used:</b> " + DelCommand;

    //create SqlConnection and SqlCommand objects
    SqlConnection myConnection = new SqlConnection(ConnectionString);
    SqlCommand myCommand = new SqlCommand(DelCommand, myConnection);

    //use try finally clauses when the connection is open.
    try
    {
        //open connection to the database
        myConnection.Open();

        //run query & bind to DataGrid
        myCommand.ExecuteNonQuery();
    }
    catch (Exception ex)
```

```
        {
            throw (ex);
        }
        finally
        {
            if (myConnection.State == ConnectionState.Open)
            {
                myConnection.Close();
            }
        }

        BindGrid();
        return;
    }
```

3. Make sure that Page_Load() binds data to the DataGrid only the first time the page is loaded.

```
void Page_Load(object sender, EventArgs e)
{
    if (!(Page.IsPostBack))
    {
        BindGrid();
    }
}
```

4. Save, and run the code. Delete a few rows from the DataGrid and then check in your database administrator program that those rows have indeed been deleted.

How It Works

Adding a Delete column to a DataGrid isn't especially tricky, as you've seen, but you should be aware of a couple of potential gotchas when you implement the event handler for the DataGrid's DeleteCommand event.

In this example, you're deleting only a row at a time, so the onus is on you to identify the row that has been selected for deletion using the primary key of the table and to relay that to the DELETE statement. By using the primary key, you can ensure that only one row is deleted at a time. So you discover the BookID for the row to be deleted and work with that. The DELETE statement will then look like this:

```
DELETE FROM Book WHERE BookID = 'Selected_BookID'
```

All the information you need is in the `DataGridCommandEventArgs` object parameter for the event handler.

```
void DataGrid1_DeleteCommand(object sender, DataGridCommandEventArgs e)
{
    ...
}
```

You can access the entire row selected for deletion as `e.Item`, a DataGridItem object, so you can retrieve the BookID from there. A DataGridItem object contains a collection of TableCell objects called Cells, so provided you know the order of the fields in the DataGrid, as shown in Figure 8-5, you can identify the one containing the BookID and retrieve it.

DeleteHeader	Number	Title	PublisherName	Topic
Delete	1	Starting Up C#	Friends Of Ed	C#

Figure 8-5. A row in a DataGrid is modeled by a DataGridItem, which contains a collection of TableCell objects.

Like all collections, Cells is zero-based, so the TableCell containing the BookID is index 1, and you can retrieve the BookID for the row to be deleted as `e.Item.Cells[1].Text`. Indeed, you can retrieve any value from the row using this syntax:

```
DelCommand += "DELETE FROM Book WHERE BookID = '"+ e.Item.Cells[1].Text +"'";
```

Now if you just ran this DELETE statement by itself, you'd get an error back from the database saying that you can't delete the Book row because there are rows in the WhoWroteWhat table that depend on this one, and it violates the relationship you set between the two when you built the database. The key then is to delete these dependent rows from the WhoWroteWhat table *before* you delete the row from the Book table. Fortunately, all you need to do for this is use the BookID again as the WWWBookID field, so you can create the DELETE FROM WhoWrote-What statement and then tack on the DELETE FROM Book statement at the end.

```
string DelCommand = "DELETE FROM WhoWroteWhat WHERE WWWBookID = '"+ ↵
    e.Item.Cells[1].Text +"';";
DelCommand += "DELETE FROM Book WHERE BookID = '"+ ↵
    e.Item.Cells[1].Text +"'";
```

There's no point deleting from Book and then WhoWroteWhat. The same error would occur.

The rest of the code is straightforward. You create a Connection object and a Command object containing the DELETE statement and call ExecuteNonQuery() on the Command object.

```
//create SqlConnection and SqlCommand objects
SqlConnection myConnection = new SqlConnection(ConnectionString);
SqlCommand myCommand = new SqlCommand(DelCommand, myConnection);

//use try finally clauses around the time when the connection is open.

{
    //open connection to the database
    myConnection.Open();

    //run query & bind to DataGrid
    myCommand.ExecuteNonQuery();
}
catch (Exception ex)
{
    throw (ex);
}
finally
{
    if (myConnection.State == ConnectionState.Open)
    {
        myConnection.Close();
    }
}
```

Deleting data is the simplest thing you have to do in this chapter, but it's also the most final. It's worth saying again then that you need to take care when implementing it.

Editing Data

The last task in this chapter is to allow users to edit data already in the database. You've designed the database to reduce the number of errors you may make, but that won't stop users from making them, so you'll need to provide some way to correct them. Even if there aren't errors in your data, you still may need to update data anyway. For example, an inventory system needs to keep updating the number of items in stock at any one time or the number of items sold, personalization systems need to update data when users update their preferences, and so on.

The process of editing data is much like adding it, with the slight change that you're starting the process with values that already exist. You still have to work with the rules of the database—the keys, the constraints, and so on. And like you did earlier, you must try to use the best Web form control for each field when users come to edit it, lest they provide invalid values and the SQL UPDATE statement (which you'll come to in a minute) returns an error. So then, you may prefer to use a list control against foreign key values or a check box for boolean values rather than a TextBox.

The UPDATE Statement

As usual, the whole operation of editing data comes down to generating and running a SQL statement. In this case, it's an UPDATE statement, which has the following syntax (see Chapter 5 for an explanation):

```
UPDATE { table_name }
{
  SET column1_name = expression1,
      column2_name = expression2,

          .

          .

          .

      columnM_name = expressionM
  [WHERE condition_list]
}
```

Now UPDATE isn't limited to working with one table at a time, but it's probably easier to do so to start. As with DELETE, you can execute UPDATE statements by calling either ExecuteNonQuery() on a Command object or Update() on a DataAdapter, depending on whether you're using a DataReader or a DataSet in your code. It's safe to say that erroneous values may also creep into these statements and users are only human, so you may want to validate potential new values for the database before you update it in the same fashion as you did for adding a completely new row earlier.

Building an Editable DataGrid

As with the previous example, there's no reason why you can't use individual form
controls to edit a row from the database and send the changes back, but you'll
continue working with a DataGrid here because it's neat on-screen, and it allows
you to look at several more DataGrid features we haven't touched on before.

Design Mode vs. Edit Mode

In a superhero kind of way, the DataGrid has been hiding a second life from you.
Thus far, you've been working with it only in design mode where all the data it displays is read-only. In edit mode, the DataGrid allows any fields in a selected row to
be altered as long as they aren't defined as read-only. Figure 8-6 shows the two
modes in action.

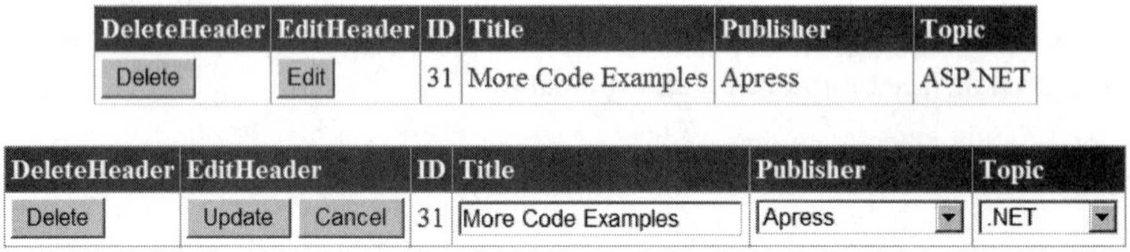

DeleteHeader	EditHeader	ID	Title	Publisher	Topic
Delete	Edit	31	More Code Examples	Apress	ASP.NET

DeleteHeader	EditHeader		ID	Title	Publisher		Topic	
Delete	Update	Cancel	31	More Code Examples	Apress	▼	.NET	▼

Figure 8-6. DataGrid in design mode (top) and edit mode (bottom)

When in edit mode, the simple literal control that displays the data in a table
cell is replaced with a TextBox containing the data value by default, but as Figure
8-6 shows, this can be changed for a more appropriate control given the type of
data being altered.

To switch between the two modes, you use another new column type for a
DataGrid, the `<asp:EditCommandColumn>` type, which can be added to the DataGrid's
Columns collection like so:

```
<asp:DataGrid id="DataGrid1" runat="server" >
   <Columns>
      <asp:EditCommandColumn ButtonType="PushButton" UpdateText="Update"
         CancelText="Cancel" EditText="Edit"></asp:EditCommandColumn>
   </Columns>
</asp:DataGrid>
```

Whilst in design mode, the EditCommandColumn displays one button: the edit button. The DataGrid raises the EditCommand event when this is clicked. You need to handle this event to switch the grid over into edit mode. When the DataGrid is in edit mode, this column shows two buttons: the update button and the cancel button. The DataGrid raises the UpdateCommand and CancelCommand events, respectively, when these buttons are clicked. The CancelCommand event handler should just switch the DataGrid back to design mode, and the UpdateCommand event handler should update the database with any changes made to the selected row in the DataGrid before switching to design mode.

> **TIP** *For the three buttons to display, you must give values for each of the Edit-CommandColumn's* EditText, CancelText, *and* UpdateText *properties.*

The actual switch from design to edit mode is made by setting the DataGrid's EditItemIndex property to the index number of the row in the DataGrid to be edited. Inside the EditCommand handler, this is simple enough. Note that you must rebind the DataGrid to show the DataGrid in edit mode.

```
void DataGrid1_EditCommand(object sender, DataGridCommandEventArgs e)
{
    //Selects the row and switches it into edit mode
    DataGrid1.EditItemIndex = e.Item.ItemIndex;

    //Rebind the grid to see the changes
    BindGrid();
    return;
}
```

When you want to switch from edit to design mode, you set EditItemIndex to -1 and rebind the DataGrid again.

```
void DataGrid1_CancelCommand(object sender, DataGridCommandEventArgs e)
{
    //Deselects the row and switches it out of edit mode into design mode
    DataGrid1.EditItemIndex = -1;

    //Rebind the grid to see the changes
    BindGrid();
    return;
}
```

The only problem you have is that autogenerated columns such as those you've been using so far are always read-only, so switching between design and edit modes doesn't do a great deal. You can't actually edit anything in a column that's autogenerated.

BoundColumns

The solution then is to set the DataGrid's `AutoGenerateColumns` property to false and define each data column in the grid as either a BoundColumn or a TemplateColumn. In Chapter 7, we noted that you don't have to make a DataGrid more readable by complicating the SQL SELECT statement that generates the results to which it binds. This is the alternative. BoundColumns are the simplest, so you'll start with them.

Like a ButtonColumn or an EditCommandColumn, an `<asp:BoundColumn>` corresponds to a single column in a DataGrid object, but it contains data bound from the data source attached to the DataGrid it's a part of. Inheriting the data source to be bound to from the DataGrid then, you need to attach the specific field it's bound to, and you do this with the `DataField` property. You can also give the column a header other than the name of the data field it's bound to with the `HeaderText` property, and you can state whether the field it contains becomes editable when the DataGrid is in edit mode by setting its `ReadOnly` property to false or true. If it helps, you can think of an autogenerated column in a DataGrid as a BoundColumn whose `HeaderText` is set to the name of the data field it's bound to and whose `ReadOnly` property is set to true.

Thus, you can redefine a read-only DataGrid containing the contents of the Book table from this:

```
<asp:DataGrid id="DataGrid1" runat="server"
    DataSource="<%# myReader %>" AutoGenerateColumns="True">
</asp:DataGrid>
```

into a read-write DataGrid for the Book table, with the only noneditable field being the BookID that a user doesn't need to alter.

```
<asp:DataGrid id="DataGrid1" runat="server"
    DataSource="<%# myReader %>" AutoGenerateColumns="False">
    <Columns>
        <asp:ButtonColumn Text="Delete" ButtonType="PushButton"
            CommandName="Delete" />
        <asp:EditCommandColumn ButtonType="PushButton" UpdateText="Update"
            CancelText="Cancel" EditText="Edit" />
```

```
      <asp:BoundColumn DataField="BookID" HeaderText="ID" ReadOnly="True"/>
      <asp:BoundColumn DataField="BookTitle" HeaderText="Title" />
      <asp:BoundColumn DataField="BookPublisherID" HeaderText="Publisher" />
      <asp:BoundColumn DataField="BookMainTopic" HeaderText="Topic" />
    </Columns>
</asp:DataGrid>
```

When a user now clicks the edit button, the row selected will present all the BoundColumns whose ReadOnly property is set to false (this is the default value) as editable strings in a TextBox control (see Figure 8-7).

Figure 8-7. Fields in writable BoundColumns become TextBoxes in edit mode.

This is great—you're making progress here, but there's still a question. You've learned during your efforts to add new rows to a database that some Web form controls make more sense than others when it comes to choosing a new value for them, and the same holds true here. By leaving the user to edit the name of a book's publisher, you're leaving it to chance that the user will correctly spell the publisher according to its entry in the Publisher table. If they misspell it or attempt to change it to a publisher not yet in the Publisher table, the database will return an error because it can't link a book to a publisher that doesn't exist in the Publisher table. It'd be much wiser to replace the TextBox control with a list control of some description such as a DropDownList so that they don't have the option of spelling something wrong. If the user wants to add a new publisher, then they should do so elsewhere.

Unfortunately, the BoundColumn is quite limited and will produce only TextBox controls in a field when a DataGrid is in edit mode. If you want a DropDownList or some other control to take its place in edit mode, you'll have to replace the Bound-Column with a TemplateColumn.

TemplateColumns

TemplateColumns work much like the DataList and Repeater controls you saw back in Chapter 7, but whereas those controls work specifically with rows of data, a TemplateColumn works with a column. Adding one to a DataGrid is a matter of adding a <asp:TemplateColumn> element to the DataGrid's Columns collection, but there's a little more to do to get it running as required than setting a few properties. Inside the element you can include up to four other child elements, as follows:

```
<asp:DataGrid id="DataGrid1" runat="server"
   DataSource="<%# myReader %>" AutoGenerateColumns="False">
   <Columns>
      <asp:TemplateColumn HeaderText="Publisher">
         <HeaderTemplate>Publisher</HeaderTemplate>
         <ItemTemplate>
            <asp:Label>...</asp:Label>
         </ItemTemplate>
         <EditItemTemplate>
            <asp:DropDownList>...</asp:DropDownList>
         </EditItemTemplate>
         <FooterTemplate></FooterTemplate>
      </asp:TemplateColumn>
   </Columns>
</asp:DataGrid>
```

The FooterTemplate and HeaderTemplate elements define how the footer and header for that column should look. The ItemTemplate defines how the column will appear when the DataGrid is in design mode, and the EditItemTemplate covers how it will appear when the DataGrid is in edit mode. All four elements can contain any other tags, HTML, or ASP.NET. It's most likely though that at the least the ItemTemplate and the EditItemTemplate elements will contain a Web form control that binds to one or more fields of data, as implied in the previous code.

The key to working with TemplateColumns is to remember that nothing is done for you. If you don't specify an EditItemTemplate, nothing will appear in that column when the DataGrid is in edit mode. If you don't specify an ItemTemplate, nothing will appear in that column when the DataGrid is in design mode, and so on.

With that said, we've established how to go about making the Book table editable through a DataGrid. Let's put it into code.

Try It Out: Update with the DataGrid

In this example, you'll take the DataGrid with the Delete button column you created in the previous example and make it a read-write grid using all the different column types we've discussed. You can find the final result in Editing_Deleting_Data_3.aspx (see Figure 8-8).

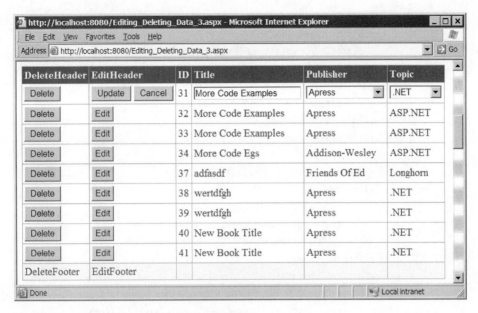

Figure 8-8. Template columns in edit mode

Follow these five steps to add edit functionality to a DataGrid:

1. Redefine the HTML definition of the DataGrid in terms of BoundColumns and TemplateColumns. Don't forget to include an EditCommandColumn or set the DataGrid's AutoGenerateColumns property to false.

```
<asp:DataGrid id="DataGrid1" runat="server"
    DataSource="<%# myReader %>" AutoGenerateColumns="False">
    <Columns>
        <asp:ButtonColumn Text="Delete" ButtonType="PushButton"
            HeaderText="DeleteHeader" FooterText="DeleteFooter"
            CommandName="Delete" />
        <asp:EditCommandColumn ButtonType="PushButton"
            UpdateText="Update" CancelText="Cancel" EditText="Edit" />
        <asp:BoundColumn DataField="Number"
            ReadOnly="True" HeaderText="ID" />
        <asp:BoundColumn DataField="Title" HeaderText="Title" />

        <asp:TemplateColumn HeaderText="Publisher">
            <ItemTemplate>
                <asp:Label runat="server"
                    text='<%# DataBinder.Eval(Container, ⤸
                        "DataItem.Publisher") %>' />
```

```
        </ItemTemplate>
        <EditItemTemplate>
            <asp:DropDownList id="PublisherSelect" runat="server"
                DataTextField="PublisherName"
                DataValueField="PublisherID"
                DataSource='<%#myPublishers()%>' />
        </EditItemTemplate>
    </asp:TemplateColumn>

    <asp:TemplateColumn HeaderText="Topic">
        <ItemTemplate>
            <asp:Label runat="server"
                text='<%# DataBinder.Eval(Container, ⏎
                    "DataItem.Topic") %>' />
        </ItemTemplate>
        <EditItemTemplate>
            <asp:DropDownList id="BookTopicSelect" runat="server">
                <asp:ListItem Value=".NET">.NET</asp:ListItem>
                <asp:ListItem Value="ADO.NET">ADO.NET</asp:ListItem>
                <asp:ListItem Value="ASP.NET">ASP.NET</asp:ListItem>
                <asp:ListItem Value="C#">C#</asp:ListItem>
                <asp:ListItem Value="IL">IL</asp:ListItem>
                <asp:ListItem Value="Longhorn">Longhorn</asp:ListItem>
                <asp:ListItem Value="VB.NET">VB.NET</asp:ListItem>
                <asp:ListItem Value="Whidbey">Whidbey</asp:ListItem>
            </asp:DropDownList>
        </EditItemTemplate>
    </asp:TemplateColumn>
  </Columns>
</asp:DataGrid>
```

2. Write an event handler for the DataGrid's `EditCommand` event that switches the DataGrid into edit mode.

```
<asp:DataGrid id="DataGrid1" runat="server"
    OnEditCommand="DataGrid1_EditCommand"
    DataSource="<%# myReader %>" AutoGenerateColumns="False">
...
void DataGrid1_EditCommand(object sender, DataGridCommandEventArgs e)
{
    //Selects the row and switches it into edit mode
    DataGrid1.EditItemIndex = e.Item.ItemIndex;
```

```
    //Rebind the grid to see the changes
    BindGrid();
    return;
}
```

3. Write an event handler for the DataGrid's CancelCommand event that switches the DataGrid to design mode.

```
<asp:DataGrid id="DataGrid1" runat="server"
    OnEditCommand="DataGrid1_EditCommand"
    OncacelCommand="DataGrid1_CancelCommand"
    DataSource="<%# myReader %>" AutoGenerateColumns="False">
...
void DataGrid1_CancelCommand(object sender, DataGridCommandEventArgs e)
{
    //Switches DataGrid into design mode
    DataGrid1.EditItemIndex = -1;

    //Rebind the grid to see the changes
    BindGrid();
    return;
}
```

4. Write an event handler for the DataGrid's UpdateCommand event that pulls the updated data from the DataGrid, sends them to the database, and then switches the database back to design mode.

```
void DataGrid1_UpdateCommand(object sender, DataGridCommandEventArgs e)
{
    // Need to retrieve the contents of each cell in the edited row.
    string BookID = e.Item.Cells[2].Text;
    string BookTitle = ((TextBox)e.Item.Cells[3].Controls[0]).Text;
    string BookPublisherID = ((DropDownList)e.Item.↵
        FindControl("PublisherSelect")).SelectedItem.Value;
    string BookTopic = ((DropDownList)e.Item.↵
        FindControl("BookTopicSelect")).SelectedItem.Value;

    //Now build up the INSERT command. We'll use parameters again.
    string UpdateCommand = "UPDATE Book SET BookTitle = @Title, ↵
        BookPublisherID = @PubID, BookMainTopic = @Topic ↵
        WHERE BookID = @BookId";

    //Create and add Parameter value for BookID
```

```
SqlParameter BookIDParam = ⏎
   new SqlParameter("@BookID", SqlDbType.Int);
BookIDParam.Value = BookID;

//Create and add Parameter value for BookTitle
SqlParameter TitleParam = ⏎
   new SqlParameter("@Title", SqlDbType.VarChar, 100);
TitleParam.Value = BookTitle;

//Create and add Parameter value for PublisherID
SqlParameter PubIDParam = new SqlParameter("@PubID", SqlDbType.Int);
PubIDParam.Value = BookPublisherID;

//Create and add Parameter value for BookTopic
SqlParameter TopicParam = ⏎
   new SqlParameter("@Topic", SqlDbType.VarChar, 25);
TopicParam.Value = BookTopic;

//create SqlConnection and SqlCommand objects
SqlConnection myConnection = new SqlConnection(ConnectionString);
SqlCommand myCommand = new SqlCommand(UpdateCommand, myConnection);

myCommand.Parameters.Add(BookIDParam);
myCommand.Parameters.Add(TitleParam);
myCommand.Parameters.Add(PubIDParam);
myCommand.Parameters.Add(TopicParam);

// execute the command
try
{
   myConnection.Open();
   myCommand.ExecuteNonQuery();
}
catch (Exception ex)
{
   throw ex;
}
finally
{
   myConnection.Close();
}

//Deselects the row and switches it back into design mode
DataGrid1.EditItemIndex = -1;
```

```
        //Rebind the grid to see the changes
        BindGrid();
        return;
    }
```

5. Make sure that `Page_Load()` binds data to the DataGrid only the first time the page is loaded.

```
void Page_Load(object sender, EventArgs e)
{
    if (!(Page.IsPostBack))
    {
        BindGrid();
    }
}
```

6. Save, and run the code. Edit a few rows of data in the DataGrid, and then check in your database administrator program that those rows have actually been altered.

How It Works

We've already covered the majority of the code in this example with the exception of the `UpdateCommand` event handler, so let's look at that. Your first task is to retrieve the new values for the fields in the edited row of the DataGrid. Retrieving the BookID is fine. You use the same code as you did to retrieve it for the `DeleteCommand` handler. But what's going on with the other three fields?

```
void DataGrid1_UpdateCommand(object sender, DataGridCommandEventArgs e)
{
    // Need to retrieve the contents of each cell in the edited row.
    string BookID = e.Item.Cells[2].Text;
    string BookTitle = ((TextBox)e.Item.Cells[3].Controls[0]).Text;
    string BookPublisherID = ((DropDownList)e.Item. ↵
        FindControl("PublisherSelect")).SelectedItem.Value;
    string BookTopic = ((DropDownList)e.Item. ↵
        FindControl("BookTopicSelect")).SelectedItem.Value;
```

When a DataGrid row is being edited, the fields that aren't read-only are made editable in other Web form controls, so you have to consider this. The value of the cell is no longer inside just the cell; it's inside a control inside a cell.

BoundColumns are uniform in the way they behave when in edit mode. The edited value is rendered in a TextBox, which is the only control in the cell, so you know how to locate it. It's the first control in the Controls collection of the Cell. When you retrieve it from the collection, you have to cast it from a generic Control object back into a TextBox and retrieve the edited value from its Text property. This technique will work against any BoundColumn.

```
string BookTitle = ((TextBox)e.Item.Cells[3].Controls[0]).Text;
```

TemplateColumns are a little trickier because the controls you use in their ItemTemplates and EditItemTemplates are *dynamic* controls and are only available at the actual point they've been rendered on the screen. This means that you can't take a leaf out of the BoundColumn trick book and retrieve a value with a line of code like this:

```
string PubID = ((DropDownList)e.Item.Cells[4].Controls[0]).SelectedItem.Value;
```

By the time the UpdateCommand handler is running, the DropDownList doesn't exist in the cell anymore, so all this line will get you is an error from the server saying that this cast doesn't work. The solution is to use the FindControl() method on the edited grid row and get ASP.NET to search for it by name. This will return a generic Control object that you cast back to a DropDownList and then work with as normal.

```
string BookPublisherID = ((DropDownList)e.Item.↵
    FindControl("PublisherSelect")).SelectedItem.Value;
```

Once you've retrieved the four values, you use them as parameters—remember, there's user input here, so you take no chances; you could use validation controls here too if you wanted—and use ExecuteNonQuery to send the UPDATE statement to the database.

```
UPDATE Book
SET BookTitle = @Title,
    BookPublisherID = @PubID,
    BookMainTopic = @Topic
WHERE BookID = @BookId
```

You're editing only one row at a time, so you identify the row in the database using its primary key, BookID, and update all the other rows, whether or not they've been changed. Finally, you switch the DataGrid back to design mode and rebind to it so you can see the updates, like so:

```
//Deselects the row and switches it out of edit mode into design mode
DataGrid1.EditItemIndex = -1;

//Rebind the grid to see the changes
BindGrid();
```

The dynamic nature of the two DropDownLists in the TemplateColumns also causes you a bit of hassle when it comes to binding data to them. Because they're dynamic, they become "available" only once the DataGrid has been generated— in other words, you can't just bind the data into the same data source as Bound-Columns; you have to provide a second one. In this case, you've used another new technique and set the DataSource for publisher DropDownlList to a function that returns a SqlDataReader. This is perfectly valid.

```
<asp:TemplateColumn HeaderText="Publisher">
    ...
    <EditItemTemplate>
        <asp:DropDownList DataSource='<%#myPublishers()%>'
            id="ddlPublisherSelect" runat="server" DataTextField="PublisherName"
            DataValueField="PublisherID" ></asp:DropDownList>
    </EditItemTemplate>
</asp:TemplateColumn>
```

You have one proviso if you want to return a DataReader object from a function: to make sure that the connection closes when it's closed. To do this, you can tell the Command object to close it when it's done by passing a CommandBehavior value as a parameter to ExecuteReader.

```
SqlDataReader myPublishers()
{
    //Fill DropDownList
    string SelectText = "SELECT PublisherID, PublisherName FROM Publisher";

    //create SqlConnection and SqlCommand objects
    SqlConnection myConnection = new SqlConnection(ConnectionString);
    SqlCommand myCommand = new SqlCommand(SelectText, myConnection);

    //can't use try close because function needs to return the DataReader
    myConnection.Open();

    //run query and bind to DropDownList
    return myCommand.ExecuteReader(CommandBehavior.CloseConnection);
}
```

Summary

If there's one thing to learn above all else in these past three chapters, it's that while a SQL statement is at the center of every data operation, there are many ways to get that SQL statement defined and executed and its results examined. You can use DataReaders and DataSets interchangeably as the exchange media between the page and the database. You can use DataGrids almost exclusively for all data operations, a much looser set of form elements, or a mix of the two. You can do almost anything you like as long as you form the SQL correctly and obey the rules of the database you've defined.

You shouldn't regard these chapters as the dogmatic way to do any one particular task. Their purpose is to present various techniques that you may or may not choose to use in your own pages. Whether you use any one block of code is up to you, but you do at least now know where some code works and where other code doesn't work as well.

CHAPTER 9

Stored Procedures

WHEN YOU EXECUTED Structured Query Language (SQL) queries against the database in previous chapters, the one commonality is that the query is contained within the page where the execution will apply. Although you saw that this works effectively with simple SELECT, INSERT, UPDATE, and DELETE queries, you'll soon see that formulating a query this way isn't always a suitable solution.

SQL provides you with a better solution for executing queries against a database that's beneficial for both runtime performance and design-time development—stored procedures. Put simply, a *stored procedure* is a construct to store queries on the server, so the same query is available for any application that wants to use it.

The queries you've looked at so far have always been *single* queries that performed only one action; for example, you've performed SELECT queries that return one set of results and INSERT queries that insert data into a single table. When you step into more complex data (and a need for more complex results), you'll find this way of working constrictive.

Stored procedures can contain just single SQL queries, and when they do so, they're naturally direct replacements for *single* queries. However, stored procedures are a powerful tool that can deliver much more than this. As you'll shortly see, they can increase the performance of your queries and make maintaining Web sites a whole lot easier. They may contain multiple queries and exploit the power of SQL itself, which has more facility than you'd think, as it's a mature language in its own right.

> **NOTE** *We won't present all the intricacies of SQL and all the different commands that are supported. You can find an introduction to SQL in Appendix B.*

In this chapter, you'll look at the following:

- Why you need stored procedures

- How to create stored procedures and give users access to them

- How to execute stored procedures through a Command object

- How you can alter and delete stored procedures you've already created

- How to make stored procedures more flexible using input parameters

- How to return information from stored procedures using output parameters

Currently, MySQL doesn't support stored procedures (although it's planned for future versions), and Microsoft DataBase (MDB) files have their own form of stored procedures, which are called, confusingly, *queries*. Therefore, this chapter focuses exclusively on using stored procedures within a Microsoft SQL Server 2000 Desktop Engine (MSDE) database.

Why Stored Procedures?

In a nutshell, using stored procedures gives you the following benefits:

Maintenance: Hard-coded queries on individual pages mean a string of SQL on each and every one of those pages. If you use the same query on several pages and need to change the query, you have to make the changes in every page. Stored procedures make maintaining the site easier by having only one copy of the query.

Security: Allowing direct access to the tables within the database to applications, as you've already seen in Chapter 2, forces you to grant "too much" access to the database. By using stored procedures, you only allow the user access to the tables through stored procedures, and you can apply suitable controls.

Speed: If you pass a query string to the server, you have to compile it before it can be executed. If you pass the same query three times, the database has to compile the query three times. Stored procedures are compiled when they're created, which is the end of it—all subsequent usage is with a speedy, precompiled piece of code. In addition, the database also optimizes the stored procedure, by using information related to the structure of the database.

Flow control: SQL defines several flow-control structures that you're familiar with from C# (such as the IF statement and WHILE and FOR loops), and these aren't available if you pass the SQL query directly from the page. With stored procedures, you can perform all the flow control you need within the database, thus removing the data processing burden from within the page. A database is designed to process data—so you should take advantage of the database's natural talent.

Reduced network traffic: Stored procedures allow you to process the results at the database and return only the required results to the page.

Creating Stored Procedures

To create a stored procedure, you must use a Data Definition Language (DDL) query. You'll look at DDL queries in more detail in Chapter 10 and see several different DDL queries, but for now all you need to know is that DDL queries allow you to change the structure of the database.

The DDL query to create stored procedures is CREATE PROCEDURE, which, in its simplest form, is as follows:

```
CREATE PROCEDURE <name>
AS
<queries>
```

You give the stored procedure a name, and you can include whatever SQL queries you want after the AS command.

Try It Out: Creating a Stored Procedure

This introduction to stored procedures will start with using SQL Web Data Administrator to create a stored procedure that returns all the publishers from the database. You'll see here that the tools you have at your disposal make it quite easy to create stored procedures. Follow these steps:

1. Open SQL Web Data Administrator, and log into the (local)\BAND server using the sa account.

2. Select the Books database, and then select the Stored Procedures option in the left menu. This will give a list of all the stored procedures in the database, currently none, as shown in Figure 9-1.

3. Click the Create New Stored Procedure option, and enter **stpGetPublishers** as the name of the stored procedure.

4. Click the Create button to proceed to the page that allows you to enter the stored procedure (see Figure 9-2).

5. Enter the following after the precompleted stored procedure declaration:

```
SELECT PublisherName
FROM Publisher
ORDER BY PublisherName
```

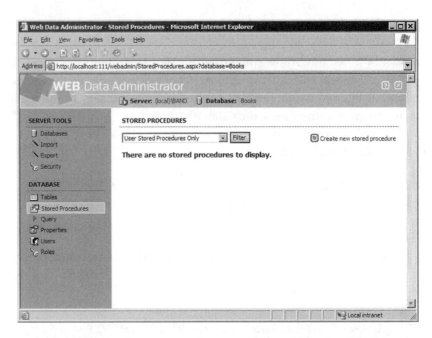

Figure 9-1. Stored procedure management in SQL Web Data Administrator

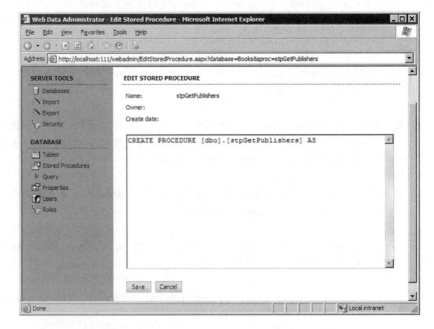

Figure 9-2. Creating a stored procedure

6. Click Save to save the stored procedure. This will return you to the list of stored procedures in the database, and you'll see the one you've just created, as shown in Figure 9-3.

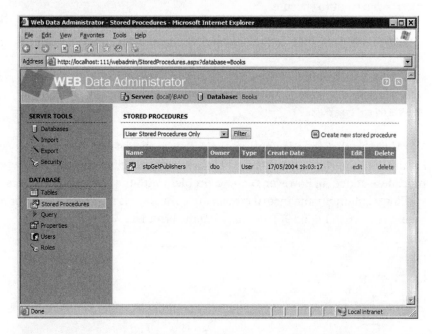

Figure 9-3. The new stored procedure has been saved to the database.

7. Select the Query option in the left menu, and enter the following query into the text area:

```
GRANT EXEC ON stpGetPublishers TO BAND
```

8. Click Execute to execute the GRANT query against the database. If this query executes correctly, the page should reload and no message is returned.

How It Works

In this example, you've created your first stored procedure in the Books database. Granted, it's a simple stored procedure that doesn't do a lot of work, but it does give you a gradual introduction to the basic concept.

The first thing to look at is the account you use to access SQL Web Data Administrator. To execute DDL queries, you must use an account with administrator privileges within the database. In this case, you must use the sa account because the band account has permissions only on certain objects and doesn't have any administrator privileges.

Creating a stored procedure using SQL Web Data Administrator, as you can see in step 4, does some of the work for you and automatically adds the CREATE PROCEDURE [dbo].[stpGetPublishers] AS code for you. All you have to do is add the queries you want to execute.

In this case, you use the following simple query, which returns the PublisherName field for all the publishers in the database, ordered by the PublisherName field:

```
SELECT PublisherName
FROM Publisher
ORDER BY PublisherName
```

After you click the Save button, the database checks that the stored procedure is valid. If it's valid, you return to the list of stored procedures with your new stored procedure added. If, however, there's a problem with the stored procedure, such as spelling a column name incorrectly, an error message is returned. The error message, as shown in Figure 9-4, details what the error is.

Figure 9-4. Errors are returned if you try to save an invalid stored procedure.

Once any errors are corrected, the stored procedure will be saved, and you then need to turn your attention to allowing users access to the stored procedure.

By default, this stored procedure won't be available for use with any of the accounts in the database other than the account that created the stored procedure—in this case, the sa account. As you've already seen, running applications using this account isn't recommended. We've created a login called band that we're using to access the database from our Web pages. You can give an account permission to execute the stored procedure by granting it the EXEC permission using a GRANT similar to the ones you saw in Chapter 2, like so:

```
GRANT EXEC ON stpGetPublishers TO band
```

Unfortunately, SQL Web Data Administrator suffers from quite a major problem. For queries that don't return any results—that is, any query except SELECT—you don't have any results to display. You have to simply assume that, unless you have an error when you execute the GRANT query, the permissions have been applied correctly.

Security and Stored Procedures

As you know, you must explicitly grant permissions for users to access the objects in the database. In Chapter 2, you saw that to enable a SELECT query to be executed against a table, you needed to give the user specific permissions to SELECT information from the table. So to give the band account SELECT permissions on the Publisher table, you'd execute the following:

```
GRANT SELECT ON Publisher TO band
```

You'd have to also give similar permission if you wanted to grant the band account INSERT, UPDATE, or DELETE permissions on the table.

Stored procedures also have to have permissions applied in order for an account to be able to execute them. Stored procedures don't have SELECT, INSERT, UPDATE, or DELETE permissions but instead have a single permission, EXEC.

The syntax to grant the EXEC permission for a stored procedure is the same as granting any other permission. Use the following:

```
GRANT EXEC ON stpGetPublishers TO band
```

And similarly, if you want to remove an existing EXEC permission, you can use the REVOKE query to remove the permission, like so:

```
REVOKE EXEC on stpGetPublishers TO band
```

You can also explicitly deny using the EXEC permission on a stored procedure with the following DENY query:

```
DENY EXEC on stpGetPublishers TO band
```

NOTE *Once a user has been granted the EXEC permission on a stored procedure, no other permissions are required for that user to execute the stored procedure. The user executing the stored procedure doesn't need any permissions on the tables that the stored procedure accesses—the database assumes that the stored procedure is correct and allows it access to all the tables within the database.*

Calling Stored Procedures

You've now got a stored procedure in the database that will return all the publishers in the database. Next you need to look at how you call the stored procedure for execution instead of passing a query. Thankfully, there isn't an awful lot that changes between passing queries and calling a stored procedure.

Whenever you've executed queries against the database, you've always just passed the query into the Command object and used the correct execute method. For example:

```
SqlCommand myCommand = new SqlCommand("SELECT BookTitle FROM Book", ⤸
   myConnection);
SqlDataReader myReader = myCommand.ExecuteReader();
```

To use a stored procedure in place of a query, you need to tell the Command object that you're using a stored procedure rather than a query. You do this by setting the CommandType property of the Command object.

When executing a SQL query, you use the default CommandType of CommandType.Text. Executing a query is the default, so you don't need to set the CommandType property, which is why you haven't seen this property before now.

So, to call a stored procedure, you simply pass the name of the procedure instead of a SQL query and tell the SqlCommand object you're passing the name of a stored procedure by setting the CommandType property to CommandType.Stored-Procedure.

Try It Out: Calling a Stored Procedure

Now that you have a stored procedure in the database and have set its permissions correctly, you can use that stored procedure in place of a SQL query within a page. We'll quickly show how to do this and use the Simple Data Report template in Web Matrix to cut down on the amount of code you need to write. Follow these steps:

1. Open Web Matrix, and navigate to the C:\BAND\ folder. Create a new folder called Chapter09.

2. In the Chapter09 folder, create a new web.config file and replace its contents with the following:

```
<configuration>
  <appSettings>
    <add key="MSDEConnectString" ⤶
      value="server=(local)\BAND;database=Books;uid=BAND;pwd=letmein" />
  </appSettings>
</configuration>
```

3. Create a new simple data report called simple.aspx.

4. Switch to the Code view in Web Matrix, and change the Page_Load event to
    the following:

```
void Page_Load(object sender, EventArgs e) {
  SqlConnection myConnection = new SqlConnection();

  try
  {
    string ConnectionString = ⤶
      ConfigurationSettings.AppSettings["MSDEConnectString"];
    string CommandText = "stpGetPublishers";

    myConnection.ConnectionString = ConnectionString;
    SqlCommand myCommand = new SqlCommand(CommandText, myConnection);
    myCommand.CommandType = CommandType.StoredProcedure;

    myConnection.Open();

    DataGrid1.DataSource = myCommand.ExecuteReader();
    DataGrid1.DataBind();
  }
  catch (Exception ex)
  {
    throw(ex);
  }
  finally
  {
    myConnection.Close();
  }
}
```

5. Execute the page, and you'll see that the stored procedure you've created is executed and that the results are returned as expected (see Figure 9-5).

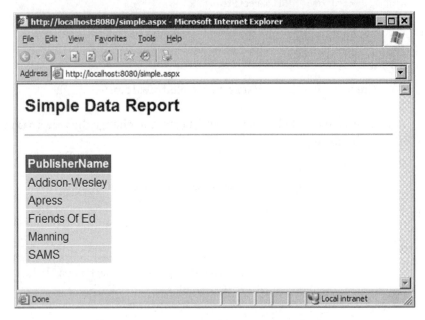

Figure 9-5. Results from executing the stpGetPublishers *stored procedure*

How It Works

The code for the Page_Load event is almost identical to the code you looked at in Chapter 4 for passing a SQL query to the database. The three lines of code that are of particular interest to you are as follows:

```
string CommandText = "stpGetPublishers";
SqlCommand myCommand = new SqlCommand(CommandText, myConnection);
myCommand.CommandType = CommandType.StoredProcedure;
```

Instead of a SQL query, you give the name of the stored procedure as the CommandText to the constructor for the SqlCommand object. You then tell the SqlCommand object that what you're passing in is the name of a stored procedure and not a SQL query by setting the CommandType property to CommandType.Stored-Procedure.

> **NOTE** *If you don't set the* CommandType *correctly for the stored procedure, the stored procedure will still execute because the database makes an intelligent guess. That is, an invalid query is probably a stored procedure name. However, if you explicitly instruct the database that you're passing in a stored procedure name, it not only makes your code more readable, but it also makes it slightly quicker because you're removing the weight of forcing the database to choose a "best fit" from the instruction it receives.*

Which Execute Method?

As you learned in the earlier chapters, you can use three execute methods to execute a query against the database. Which one you use depends upon what the query that you're executing is doing. To recap, the three methods that you can use are as follows:

- **ExecuteNonQuery()**: You use this when the query doesn't return any results from the database.

- **ExecuteReader()**: You use this when you want to return a result set from a SELECT query.

- **ExecuteScalar()**: You use this when you want to return only the first field from the first row of the returned result set.

You also have the same choice when you use stored procedures, and you should choose the method that matches what the stored procedure does.

Altering and Deleting Stored Procedures

Being able to add stored procedures to your database is all well and good, but you also need some way of modifying or deleting them. You can accomplish both of these tasks using two other DDL commands.

To modify a stored procedure, you use the ALTER PROCEDURE query, specifying the name of the stored procedure you want to modify as well as the complete new contents of the stored procedure, like so:

```
ALTER PROCEDURE <name>
AS
<new queries>
```

To delete a stored procedure from the database, you simply use the DROP PROCEDURE query, like so:

```
DROP PROCEDURE <name>
```

SQL Web Data Administrator shields you from having to remember the syntax of these commands by providing options to complete both of these tasks from the user interface; if you look at Figure 9-3, you'll see that along with the name, owner, and type of stored procedure, you have options to both edit and delete the stored procedure.

You'll take a quick look at modifying stored procedures, but we'll skip a discussion of how to delete stored procedures using SQL Web Data Administrator, as there's not a lot to say. Clicking Delete gives a Yes/No prompt, and if you click Yes, you'll delete the stored procedure.

Try It Out: Modifying a Stored Procedure

Sometimes it'll become necessary to change the stored procedures you've already created. SQL Web Data Administrator makes this task easy. Follow these steps:

1. Open SQL Web Data Administrator, and log into the (local)\BAND server using the sa account.

2. Select the Books database, and then select the Stored Procedures option in the left menu. This will give the list of stored procedures in the database, as shown in Figure 9-3 earlier.

3. Click the Edit link to modify the stpGetPublishers stored procedure. Figure 9-6 shows the current stored procedure.

4. Change the stored procedure to the following:

```
ALTER PROCEDURE [dbo].[stpGetPublishers] AS
SELECT PublisherID, PublisherName
FROM Publisher
ORDER BY PublisherName
```

5. Click the Save button to save the stored procedure.

6. Open Web Matrix, and execute the simple.aspx page you created in the previous example. As shown in Figure 9-7, this will return the results from the stored procedure, with the addition of the PublisherID field.

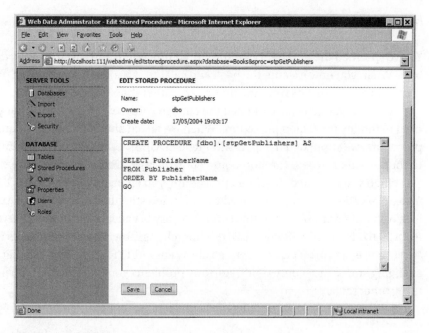

Figure 9-6. Modifying an existing stored procedure

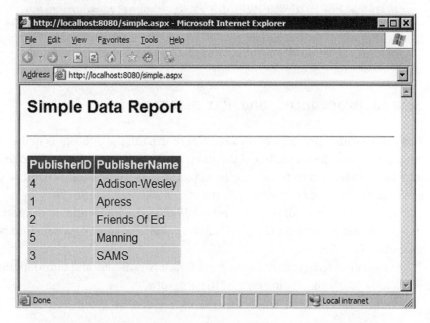

Figure 9-7. Results from executing the modified stored procedure

How It Works

You've specified the new query for the stored procedure and saved it to the database. When you now execute the page and call the `stpGetPublishers` stored procedure, you get the results from the new query rather than the old one.

However, you may have noticed the change you made in the query that you used to modify the stored procedure. When we talked about changing the stored procedure, we stipulated using ALTER PROCEDURE, yet SQL Web Data Administrator presents you with the stored procedure using CREATE PROCEDURE.

When you modified the stored procedure, you changed this to use ALTER instead of CREATE before you saved the modified stored procedure. When using SQL Web Data Administrator, this isn't necessary because you can use CREATE PROCEDURE and ALTER PROCEDURE interchangeably. However, it makes more sense to use the correct DDL query, so always use ALTER PROCEDURE when changing stored procedures—it'll stop any problems you may encounter when using other tools.

> **CAUTION** *Although CREATE PROCEDURE and ALTER PROCEDURE are interchangeable within SQL Web Data Administrator, they aren't the same thing. If you try to use CREATE PROCEDURE to modify a stored procedure that already exists in another tool, such as* osql.exe, *an error will be generated because the stored procedure already exists.*

Stored Procedures and Parameters

The simple stored procedure you looked at returns all the publishers in the database. This is just the beginning of the story. By responding dynamically to users and their interaction with your pages, as you've seen in the earlier chapters, you can impart real power to your applications.

In Chapter 4 you looked at two methods of modifying queries. We mentioned that one of these methods, using parameters, was how you'd pass data into stored procedures.

SQL defines two types of parameters (input parameters and output parameters), and you'll look at using each of these in turn.

Making Flexible Stored Procedures with Input Parameters

You saw that parameters can pass data into the SqlCommand object to modify the query you want to execute. The way you pass parameters into stored procedures is the same.

Using input parameters with stored procedures is a two-stage process:

1. Define the parameters in the stored procedure declaration.

2. Add the parameters to the SqlCommand object before the call is made to execute the stored procedure.

Creating a Stored Procedure with Input Parameters

Creating a stored procedure that requires parameters to be supplied isn't more complex than creating a stored procedure that doesn't accept parameters. You need to modify the stored procedure declaration slightly to list the parameters that are required, as follows:

```
CREATE PROCEDURE <name>
<parameters>
AS
<queries>
```

The parameters list is simply a list giving the name of the parameter, its type, and any default value it may have. If there's more than one parameter, you separate them with commas, like so:

```
@name1 type = default,
@name2 type = default
```

All parameters that you include in the stored procedure declaration must be passed to the stored procedure by the calling application—if they aren't, an error is thrown. If you're sure you don't want to pass the parameter, you can override this behavior by giving the parameter a default value. This will be used if the parameter isn't supplied a value by the calling application. If you always want a value to be passed to the stored procedure, then you don't specify a default value.

You'll now look at creating a stored procedure using SQL Web Data Administrator that accepts a parameter that modifies the results that are returned as part of the query. This stored procedure will also introduce you to the idea of flow control and in particular the IF statement to control what actions the stored procedure takes.

Try It Out: Create the Stored Procedure with Input Parameters

You'll create a new stored procedure that accepts a PublisherID and returns a list of published books or, if a PublisherID isn't specified, returns all the books in the database. Follow these steps:

1. Open SQL Web Data Administrator, and log into the (local)\BAND server using the sa account. Open the Books database, select the Stored Procedures option in the left menu, and then click the Create New Stored Procedure link at the top of the page.

2. Enter a stored procedure name of **stpGetBooksByPublisher**.

3. In the dialog box for entering the stored procedure, add the following:

```
CREATE PROCEDURE [dbo].[stpGetBooksByPublisher]
@publisher int = null
AS

IF (@publisher IS NULL) BEGIN
  SELECT Book.BookID, Book.BookTitle, Book.BookMainTopic,
    Publisher.PublisherName
  FROM Book
    INNER JOIN Publisher on Book.BookPublisherID = Publisher.PublisherID
  ORDER BY Book.BookTitle
END ELSE BEGIN
  SELECT BookID, BookTitle, BookMainTopic
  FROM Book
  WHERE BookPublisherID = @publisher
  ORDER BY Book.BookTitle
END
```

4. Click Save to save the stored procedure to the database.

5. Select the Query option in the left menu, and enter the following query into the text area:

```
GRANT EXEC ON stpGetBooksByPublisher TO BAND
```

6. Click Execute to execute the query against the database.

How It Works

The way you've created this new stored procedure is the same way you created the stpGetPublishers stored procedure, and, unsurprisingly, you'll create every stored procedure this way. It's the structure of the stored procedure in which you should be interested.

SQL Web Data Administrator creates the basics of the stored procedure for you, and the first thing you must do is add the parameters you want to the definition. You do this between the stored procedure name and the AS statement, like so:

```
CREATE PROCEDURE [dbo].[stpGetBooksByPublisher]
@publisher int = null
AS
```

You've only got one parameter in this particular query, and it's called @publisher. The name must be prefixed by the @ symbol to indicate that it's a user variable (as opposed to a system variable that will have @@ at the front), and, as you'll see when you call the stored procedure in the next example, this is the name you'll need to use when adding the parameter to the SqlCommand object.

> **NOTE** As you saw in Chapter 4, the naming of the parameters is important if you're using the SqlCommand object but is less so if you're using the OleDbCommand object. The SqlCommand object uses the names of the parameters to match what you're passing to the stored procedure with what the stored procedure expects. Conversely, the OleDbCommand object uses the order in which you pass the parameters to the stored procedure, ignoring the names completely.

After the name of the parameter, you have the parameter's type. For types that require a size as well (such as the varchar type), you also have to include the size you're expecting.

The final detail you specify for the parameter is any default value you want the parameter to take. The default value you specify can be any value that's valid for the parameter's type, or, as shown here, you can specify that it has a value of null. As you'll see, you want to trap the condition whereby the parameter isn't supplied. Using null provides the simplest way of doing this—if you use a valid parameter value as the default, there's always a chance that the default value you've chosen is a value that may be passed into the stored procedure.

> **CAUTION** *One caveat exists for using null as the default value for parameters. Using the* SqlCommand *object to pass an empty string (in other words, one that contains nothing at all) to a stored procedure results in the pass action failing— the empty string is not passed to the stored procedure. In this case, using null may not be appropriate, and you should stipulate an empty string explicitly using two single quotes.*

Now that you've added the parameter to the stored procedure, you must then use it. You're obviously going to use it to modify what's returned from the SELECT query, but you'll go a little further and use the parameter to determine which of two SELECT queries you want to execute.

Deciding the Execution Path

If you don't want to filter the books that are returned as part of the query, you can assume that you won't pass a value into the stored procedure and that it'll take the default value of null. You can use the following to determine the route through the stored procedure by using the IF statement and in particular whether it's equal to the default value of null:

```
IF (@publisher IS NULL) BEGIN
    ...
END ELSE BEGIN
    ...
END
```

Using the IF statement, as in C#, you can control what's executed within the stored procedure. As the condition of the IF statement, you can use any valid SQL that returns a true or false value—you can do simple comparisons as you have here (all the usual operators are here), or you can use scalar functions (such as EXISTS) to control execution.

Depending upon whether the condition evaluates to true or false, you take a different path. If true, you follow the path before the ELSE statement, and if false, you follow the path after the ELSE statement.

NOTE *The BEGIN and END statements in SQL are equivalent to the opening and closing braces in C#. As with C#, you don't need them if you have only one statement as part of the conditional path, but it makes the SQL code a lot easier to read if they're present.*

If you have a null value for @publisher, you know that you don't want to filter the query and execute a SELECT query that returns the BookID, BookTitle, BookMainTopic, and PublisherName for all the books in the database.

```
SELECT Book.BookID, Book.BookTitle, Book.BookMainTopic,
   Publisher.PublisherName
FROM Book
   INNER JOIN Publisher on Book.BookPublisherID = Publisher.PublisherID
ORDER BY Book.BookTitle
```

If, however, you have a non-null value for @publisher, indicating that one has been passed into the stored procedure, you use this to constrain the SELECT query and return a slightly different list of columns, like so:

```
SELECT BookID, BookTitle, BookMainTopic
FROM Book
WHERE BookPublisherID = @publisher
ORDER BY Book.BookTitle
```

Passing Parameters to Stored Procedures

You've already seen in Chapter 4 how to pass parameters to a query, and the method of passing them to a stored procedure is no different.

You need to create a SqlParameter object and set the name, type, and value before adding it to the Parameters collection of the SqlCommand object.

Try It Out: Passing Parameters to a Stored Procedure

You'll now build a slightly more complex example that displays the books in the database and uses the stpGetBooksByPublisher stored procedure to filter for which publisher you're returning the books. You'll populate the list of publishers by using the stpGetPublishers stored procedure you saw earlier. Follow these steps:

1. Open Web Matrix, navigate to the C:\BAND\Chapter09 folder, and create a new filtered data report called input.aspx.

2. Enter **Select a Publisher:** next to the drop-down list.

3. Switch to the Code view in Web Matrix, and change the Page_Load event to the following:

```
void Page_Load(object sender, EventArgs e) {
  if (!Page.IsPostBack) {
    SqlConnection myConnection = new SqlConnection();

    try
    {
      string ConnectionString = ↵
        ConfigurationSettings.AppSettings["MSDEConnectString"];
      string CommandText = "stpGetPublishers";

      myConnection.ConnectionString = ConnectionString;
      SqlCommand myCommand = new SqlCommand(CommandText, myConnection);
      myCommand.CommandType = CommandType.StoredProcedure;

      myConnection.Open();

      // execute the command and bind to the DropDownList
      DropDownList1.DataSource = myCommand.ExecuteReader();
      DropDownList1.DataTextField = "PublisherName";
      DropDownList1.DataValueField = "PublisherID";
      DropDownList1.DataBind();

      // insert an "All" item at the beginning of the list
      DropDownList1.Items.Insert(0, ↵
        new ListItem("-- All Publishers --", "0"));
    }
    catch (Exception ex)
    {
      throw(ex);
    }
    finally
    {
```

```
      myConnection.Close();
    }
  }
}
```

4. Change the `ApplyFilter_Click` event to the following:

```
void ApplyFilter_Click(Object sender, EventArgs e) {
  SqlConnection myConnection = new SqlConnection();

  try
  {
    // create the connection and open it
    string ConnectionString = ↵
      ConfigurationSettings.AppSettings["MSDEConnectString"];
    string CommandText = "stpGetBooksByPublisher";

    myConnection.ConnectionString = ConnectionString;
    SqlCommand myCommand = new SqlCommand(CommandText, myConnection);
    myCommand.CommandType = CommandType.StoredProcedure;

    // do we need to add the @publisher parameter
    if (DropDownList1.SelectedValue != "0"){
      // create the parameter and add it to the Parameters Collection
      SqlParameter myParameter1 = new SqlParameter();
      myParameter1.ParameterName = "@publisher";
      myParameter1.SqlDbType = SqlDbType.Int;
      myParameter1.Value = DropDownList1.SelectedValue;
      myCommand.Parameters.Add (myParameter1);
    }

    myConnection.Open();

    // execute the command and bind to the DataGrid
    DataGrid1.DataSource = myCommand.ExecuteReader();
    DataGrid1.DataBind();
  }
  catch (Exception ex)
  {
    throw(ex);
  }
  finally
  {
    myConnection.Close();
  }
}
```

5. Execute the page, and you'll see that the drop-down list is populated with the list of publishers. Make sure the -- All Publishers -- option is selected, and click the Show Titles button. This will execute the stored procedure and return all the books in the database, as shown in Figure 9-8.

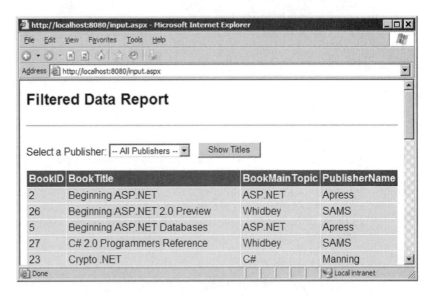

Figure 9-8. Results showing all the books in the database

6. Select the Apress option in the drop-down list, and click the Show Titles button. This will execute the stored procedure, passing in the publisher details that you require and returning the results as shown in Figure 9-9.

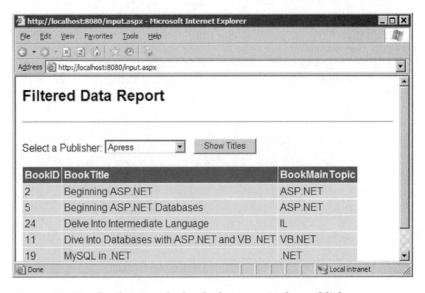

Figure 9-9. Results showing the books for a particular publisher

How It Works

This example is the same example as you saw in Chapter 4 when you looked at passing parameters to queries—all you've changed is the use of stored procedures rather than a direct SQL query.

This example has the following two parts:

- Populating the drop-down list when the page first loads in the Page_Load event handler

- Applying the ApplyFilter_Click event handler that's fired when clicking the Show Titles button

Populating the drop-down list in the Page_Load event handler happens by calling the stpGetPublishers stored procedure you created and then modified in the earlier examples. You use the ExecuteReader() method to return a SqlDataReader containing the PublisherID and PublisherName for all the publishers in the database, and you bind this to the drop-down list. You then add the -- All Publishers -- entry that has a value of 0.

The ApplyFilter_Click Event Handler

The part you're most interested in for this example is the code within the Apply-Filter_Click event handler.

You'll call the stpGetBooksByPublisher stored procedure and create the Command object, passing in the name of the stored procedure and the connection you want to use. You then set the CommandType property to CommandType.StoredProcedure.

A check is then made of the selection from the drop-down list to determine if you need to add the parameter; as you'll recall, you don't have to add this if you don't need to do so. You added an -- All Publishers -- entry to the drop-down list with a value of 0, so you can simply check that the SelectedValue of the drop-down list is equal to 0. If it is, you don't want to add the parameter, and if it isn't, you want to add the parameter with the correct value.

You've already looked at adding parameters to a SqlCommand object; there's nothing here you haven't seen before.

The first thing you have to do is create a SqlParameter object and give it the correct name. Because you're using the SqlCommand object, you need to use the name that the stored procedure expects, so you use @publisher, like so:

```
// create the parameter
SqlParameter myParameter1 = new SqlParameter();
myParameter1.ParameterName = "@publisher";
```

You then specify the type of the parameter from the SqlDbType enumeration and set the value of the parameter to the value selected in the drop-down list, like so:

```
myParameter1.SqlDbType = SqlDbType.Int;
myParameter1.Value = DropDownList1.SelectedValue;
```

Once the parameter has been created and correctly populated, you can add it to the Parameters collection of the SqlCommand object, like so:

```
// add it to the command object
myCommand.Parameters.Add (myParameter1);
```

You then use the ExecuteReader() method of the SqlCommand object to return a SqlDataReader object and bind this to the data grid.

When the stored procedure is executed, the route that's taken depends upon whether you've added the parameter to the SqlCommand object or not, as we discussed when you created the stored procedure in the previous example.

Returning Data Using Output Parameters

Although you've now seen how you can pass parameters to a stored procedure, this isn't the end of parameters. You can also use them to return values from a stored procedure.

You've already looked at two ways of returning data from the database in the ExecuteReader() and ExecuteScalar() methods, which are used to return information from a SELECT query. Sometimes, however, you want to execute a query that doesn't return any results directly but returns information detailing what you've just done. If you're inserting information into the database, you may want to return a key for what you've just inserted. Output parameters are the key to this.

You can modify the values of user variables within stored procedures, and if they're parameters, the changed value may be returned to the calling application. If the parameter is an input parameter, the value isn't returned, but for output parameters the changed value is returned.

> **NOTE** *The name* output parameter *is perhaps a bit misleading because an output parameter is more accurately an input/output parameter. You can pass a value into a stored procedure using an output parameter, and any changes to the parameter will be reflected in the parameter once control has returned from the stored procedure.*

To use output parameters instead of input parameters, you don't actually have to do a lot of work. You can accomplish it in the following two stages:

1. Tell the stored procedure that the parameter is an output parameter.

2. Tell the `SqlCommand` object that the stored procedure is an output parameter and then retrieve the changed value from the Parameters collection after the stored procedure has executed.

You'll now look at both of these in turn.

Creating a Stored Procedure with Output Parameters

To use output parameters within the stored procedure, you use the OUTPUT statement with the definition of the parameter, like so:

```
@name type = default OUTPUT
```

You're free to mix input and output stored procedures however you want in the stored procedure declaration.

As with input parameters, you can also give output parameters default values that will be used if the parameter isn't passed to the stored procedure by the calling application. You may be wondering why you'd create an output parameter that you may not use, but as you'll see in the example, they can come in quite handy.

Try It Out: Create the Stored Procedure with Output Parameters

You'll now look at building upon the stored procedure in the previous example to include an output parameter that returns the number of books for the selected publisher. Follow these steps:

1. Open SQL Web Data Administrator, and log into the (local)\BAND server using the sa account. Open the Books database, and select the Stored Procedures option in the left menu.

2. Select the Edit option for the `stpGetBooksByPublisher` stored procedure.

3. Modify the stored procedure to the following:

```
CREATE PROCEDURE [dbo].[stpGetBooksByPublisher]
   @publisher int = null,
   @rows int = 0 OUTPUT
AS
```

```
IF (@publisher IS NULL) BEGIN
  SELECT Book.BookID, Book.BookTitle, Book.BookMainTopic,
    Publisher.PublisherName
  FROM Book
    INNER JOIN Publisher on Book.BookPublisherID = Publisher.PublisherID
  ORDER BY Book.BookTitle

  SET @rows = @@ROWCOUNT
END ELSE BEGIN
  SELECT BookID, BookTitle, BookMainTopic
  FROM Book
  WHERE BookPublisherID = @publisher
  ORDER BY Book.BookTitle

  SET @rows = @@ROWCOUNT
END
```

4. Click Save to save the modified stored procedure to the database.

How It Works

As you can see from the stored procedure declaration, you've added the following output parameter of type int called @rows:

```
@rows int = 0 OUTPUT
```

You'll use this to return the count of the number of rows that are returned for the publisher you've selected.

You've given @rows a default value, as you're now going to be using the stored procedure in at least two places. If you open the input.aspx page from the previous example, you'll see it still performs the same way even though the stored procedure that's being called has an output parameter that you don't specify. If you didn't have a default value for @rows, an error would be generated if you tried to call the stored procedure without adding the parameter.

You use the SET statement to assign values to variables, and you can set @rows to the number of rows returned using the @@ROWCOUNT system variable, like so:

```
SET @rows = @@ROWCOUNT
```

@@ROWCOUNT returns the number of rows that the previous SQL query returned or affected and is valid not only for SELECT but also for DELETE, INSERT, and UPDATE.

Returning Parameters from Stored Procedures

You've already seen how you add input parameters to the SqlCommand object; adding output parameters is no more difficult. The only thing you have to change is the direction of the parameter.

Parameters by default are defined as input parameters. In the previous examples, you haven't had to specify a direction for the parameter, as you've been using only input parameters. For output parameters, you need to specify the direction.

You specify the direction for a parameter using the Direction property and setting it to one of the values in the System.Data.ParameterDirection enumeration.

The default value for the Direction property is ParameterDirection.Input. If you wanted to specify it for an input parameter, you'd specify it as follows:

```
myParameter.Direction = ParameterDirection.Input
```

For output parameters, you have the following two possible values:

- **ParameterDirection.Output**: This will return the value from the stored procedure, but any value you attempt to send to the stored procedure is ignored.

- **ParameterDirection.InputOutput**: InputOutput allows values to be passed into the stored procedure by the parameter and will return the parameter value from the stored procedure.

Although you'd be forgiven for thinking that you need only one possible option for output parameters, ADO.NET provides two. Although MSDE allows all OUTPUT parameters to accept an input value, ADO.NET makes a distinction between the two.

If you declare a parameter as solely an output parameter, as follows:

```
myParameter.Direction = ParameterDirection.Output
```

then even if you give it a value before calling the stored procedure, the value will not be passed to the stored procedure. The output value will be set correctly, but any input value is completely ignored.

On the other hand, if you define the parameter as an InputOutput parameter:

```
myParameter.Direction = Parameter.Direction.InputOutput
```

then any value you give it will also be passed to the stored procedure.

Try It Out: Returning Parameters from a Stored Procedure

You'll build on the last example and return the number of rows from the stpGet-BooksByPublisher stored procedure using an output parameter. Follow these steps:

1. Copy input.aspx from the previous example, and rename it to output.aspx.

2. Switch to the HTML view of the page, and add the following bold code to the contents of the <form> tag:

```
<p>
  Select a Publisher:
  <asp:DropDownList id="DropDownList1" runat="server">
    </asp:DropDownList>
   
  <asp:Button id="Button1" onclick="ApplyFilter_Click" runat="server"
    Text="Show Titles"></asp:Button>
</p>
<p>
  Returned <asp:Label id="Label1" runat="server">0</asp:Label> books.
</p>
<asp:datagrid id="DataGrid1" runat="server" EnableViewState="False"
  ForeColor="Black" BackColor="White" CellPadding="3" GridLines="None"
  CellSpacing="1">
  <HeaderStyle font-bold="True" forecolor="white"
    backcolor="#4A3C8C"></HeaderStyle>
  <ItemStyle backcolor="#DEDFDE"></ItemStyle>
</asp:datagrid>
```

3. Switch to the Code view for the page, and modify the code in the Apply-Filter_Click event handler to add the second parameter and retrieve the output parameter after the stored procedure has executed, like so:

```
    myCommand.Parameters.Add (myParameter1);
}


// add the @rows parameter
SqlParameter myParameter2 = new SqlParameter();
myParameter2.ParameterName = "@rows";
myParameter2.SqlDbType = SqlDbType.Int;
myParameter2.Direction = ParameterDirection.InputOutput;
myCommand.Parameters.Add (myParameter2);
```

```
myConnection.Open();

// execute the command and bind to the DataGrid
SqlDataReader myReader = myCommand.ExecuteReader();
DataGrid1.DataSource = myReader;
DataGrid1.DataBind();
myReader.Close();

// now get the output parameter
Label1.Text = Convert.ToString(myCommand.Parameters["@rows"].Value);
}
catch (Exception ex)
```

4. Execute the page, select the -- All Publishers -- option in the drop-down list, and click the Show Titles button. This will execute the stored procedure, return all the books in the database, and update the count of the number of books returned, as shown in Figure 9-10.

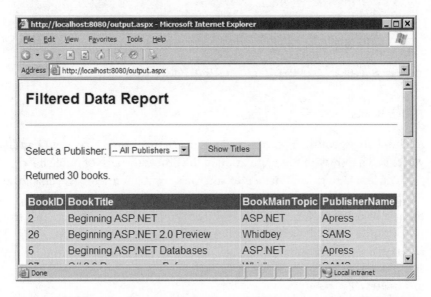

Figure 9-10. Results showing the books and the book count for all the books

5. Select the Apress option in the drop-down list, and click the Show Titles button. This will execute the stored procedure returning only the books for Apress and the count of the number of books that have been returned, as shown in Figure 9-11.

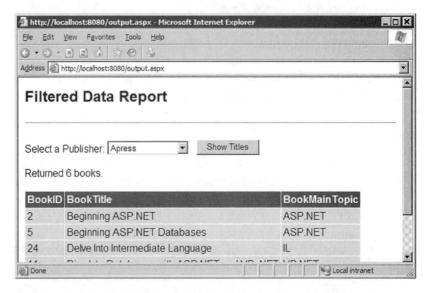

Figure 9-11. Books and their count for a particular publisher

How It Works

All the changes you've made are again to the `ApplyFilter_Click` event handler, as you're still happy with the population of the drop-down list of publishers.

The first change you make is to add the output parameter. As you can see, you declare the parameter as you have all the other parameters you've used. The only thing you've done differently is to specify the direction of the parameter, like so:

```
// add the @rows parameter
SqlParameter myParameter2 = new SqlParameter();
myParameter2.ParameterName = "@rows";
myParameter2.SqlDbType = SqlDbType.Int;
myParameter2.Direction = ParameterDirection.Output;
myCommand.Parameters.Add (myParameter2);
```

The one change you've had to make to the code is the way you retrieve the results and bind them to the data grid, like so:

```
// execute the command and bind to the DataGrid
SqlDataReader myReader = myCommand.ExecuteReader();
DataGrid1.DataSource = myReader;
DataGrid1.DataBind();
myReader.Close();
```

You have to deal with the ExecuteReader() method and the SqlDataReader that it returns in this manner because of the way that the data is returned from the database when you're retrieving a SqlDataReader. The SqlDataReader must be closed before the output parameters are populated, and to do that you must create a local instance of the reader, bind it to the data grid, and then manually close the reader. Only at this point are you able to use the output parameters from the stored procedure.

> **NOTE** *If you were using* ExecuteScalar() *or* ExecuteNonQuery() *to execute a stored procedure that has output parameters, you wouldn't have any problems and wouldn't need to worry about closing things before you can access the output parameters. This isn't strictly a "problem" with the implementation of the* ExecuteReader() *method, but it's a big enough issue to warrant its own Microsoft Knowledge Base article (*http://support.microsoft.com/default.aspx?scid=kb;en-us;Q308621*).*

Once the SqlDataReader has been closed, you can retrieve the values of the output parameters simply by using the name of the parameter as the indexer to the Parameters collection of the Command object, like so:

```
// now get the output parameter
Label1.Text = Convert.ToString(myCommand.Parameters["@rows"].Value);
```

You're after the value of the parameter, so you use the Value property. This property returns an object that you can then cast to whatever type you want. In this case, you want to set the Text property of a label control, so you convert the value to a string.

Summary

You started this chapter by looking at stored procedures and why you'd use them. The chapter covered the following reasons for using stored procedures:

- Simplified maintenance

- Increased security

- Increased performance

- Reduced network traffic

After looking at why you'd use stored procedures over direct SQL queries, you then took a step back from the relative complexities of the previous chapters. You created several stored procedures that utilized the following options you have for passing and returning data to and from stored procedures:

- Returning data using SELECT and `ExecuteReader()`

- Passing parameters using input parameters

- Returning data using output parameters

You also saw that there's very little difference between calling a stored procedure and executing a SQL command; you pass the stored procedure name as the query to execute and tell the `SqlCommand` object you're executing a stored procedure by specifying `CommandType.StoredProcedure`.

In the next chapter, you'll look at the DDL subset of SQL and see what it can do. You can perform all the actions graphically in the book until this point using SQL itself. You've seen this in action with the CREATE PROCEDURE and ALTER PROCEDURE queries used in this chapter. But as you'll soon see, you can use SQL to create the entire database without ever going near a graphical tool.

CHAPTER 10

Modifying the Database Structure

In the previous nine chapters, you've learned everything you need to know to start building dynamic data-driven Web sites. In the next three chapters, you'll apply some real-world understanding to the process and look at building a complete application. Before then, though, you still have one topic to look at—the SQL Data Definition Language (DDL).

In Chapter 2 you saw that you can execute the following two types of SQL queries:

- Data Manipulation Language (DML) queries for querying data. These are the SELECT, INSERT, UPDATE, and DELETE statements we've already covered.

- DDL queries for modifying the structure of the database.

In Chapter 2 you looked at using SQL Web Data Administrator and MySQL Control Center to create the database and tables you need. The graphical clients allow you to manipulate databases, and this shields you from the majority of the DDL queries that exist. Under the covers, however, both graphical clients use DDL queries to accomplish the task you specified graphically.

Chapter 2 also briefly covered some of the DDL queries that are available when you need to add functionality to the database that isn't supported by the graphical clients. Further, you added both indexes and relationships to your sample databases using DDL queries.

In the intervening chapters, you concentrated extensively on DML queries and built several examples that interacted with the database. You briefly reacquainted yourself with DDL in Chapter 9 when you looked at CREATE PROCEDURE; in this chapter, you'll turn your attention to DDL queries and learn what you can do with them.

To look at the DDL queries, you need to use a tool that allows you to enter queries and execute them directly against the database. As you've already seen, both SQL Web Data Administrator and MySQL Control Center allow you to do this. For most of the examples in this chapter, you'll use the graphical clients.

Sometimes, however, you can't use a graphical tool to query the database; in these cases, you need to dive into the murky world of command-line tools. Both MSDE and MySQL have command-line clients that are installed by default; you'll briefly look at these before you begin examining the various DDL queries.

After briefly presenting the command-line tools, we'll discuss the following DDL tasks for both MSDE and MySQL:

- Creating databases

- Creating tables

- Adding, modifying, and removing table columns

- Creating and deleting indexes

- Creating and deleting table relationships

- Deleting tables

- Deleting databases

You won't look at the DDL queries for creating stored procedures in this chapter. Chapter 9 provided a complete discussion of the CREATE PROCEDURE, ALTER PROCEDURE, and DROP PROCEDURE syntax, so instead of repeating the information here, we refer you to that chapter.

> **NOTE** *This chapter is intended as a brief introduction to DDL, not a complete reference work. Entire books have been written about the subject, so we skim the surface of what's possible. If we attempted to provide a complete reference at this stage in your database career, you'd be likely to run away and swear off databases forever! If you don't believe us, compare the examples that you'll see against the scripts we've provided in the download. From looking at the scripts, you'll see that we don't cover a lot of advanced topics; you'll probably agree that you don't want that much detail at this stage.*

Command-Line Tools

Both MSDE/SQL Server and MySQL install a command-line tool that can connect to both local and remote databases and allow SQL queries to be executed against the database.

Although the tools are similar, they have differences; the following sections show each of these in turn.

> **NOTE** *You have a lot more options for both* osql.exe *and* mysql.exe *than what you'll see here. You can find more details of* osql.exe *at* http://msdn.microsoft
> .com/library/en-us/coprompt/cp_osql_1wxl.asp; *for* mysql.exe, *refer to*
> http://www.mysql.com/doc/en/mysql.html.

osql.exe

osql.exe is installed as part of the MSDE install, and if the default installation folder has been accepted, it'll be in the c:\program files\microsoft sql server\ 80\tools\bin folder.

To use osql.exe, you must specify the server to connect to and the security credentials you want to use for the connection.

To specify the server, you use the -S parameter followed by the server to which you want to connect.

> **NOTE** *If you fail to specify which server you want to connect to,* osql.exe *will assume you want to connect to the default instance of MSDE on the local machine.*

The security credentials you specify depend upon whether you're using Windows Authentication. If you want to use Windows Authentication, you specify this with the -E parameter. If, however, you want to use SQL Authentication, you must specify the username and password by using the -U and -P parameters, respectively.

So, to connect to the (local)\BAND server using Windows Authentication, you'd use the following command line:

```
osql -E -S (local)\BAND
```

To connect to the same server using SQL Authentication and the band account, you'd need to specify the username and password you want to use, as follows:

```
osql -U band -P letmein -S (local)\BAND
```

If you're being security conscious, then typing a password in plain text is a big problem. You can force osql.exe to ask you for the password rather than specifying it on the command line by simply omitting the -P parameter, and you'll be prompted for the password before the connection is made.

```
osql -U band -S (local)\BAND
```

Although you can now connect to the server using the correct credentials, you still may not be connected to the correct database—if no database is specified, the database that's used will be the default database for the user (in most cases, this will be the master database). You can specify the database to use once a connection has been made using the USE SQL statement, but it's equally valid to specify this on the command line using the -d parameter followed by the database name.

So, to connect to the Books database on the (local)\BAND server using the band account, you'd using the following command:

```
osql -U band -S (local)\BAND -d Books
```

If for some reason the connection to the database is refused, the error message that's returned by osql.exe is quite helpful. If for some reason you've specified the incorrect login details, you'd get a "Login failed for user" message; if you've specified an invalid database, you'd get a "Cannot open database requested in login" message. You can use this error message to fix the error and try to connect to the database again.

Try It Out: Querying an MSDE Database via the Command Line

You'll begin your introduction to DDL using the osql.exe command-line tool. You'll use this to execute a simple query against the Books database. Follow these steps:

1. Open a command prompt, enter the following command, and then press Return:

    ```
    osql -U band -S (local)\BAND -d Books
    ```

2. At the prompt, enter **letmein** as the password. This will open the osql.exe command-line tool, as shown in Figure 10-1.

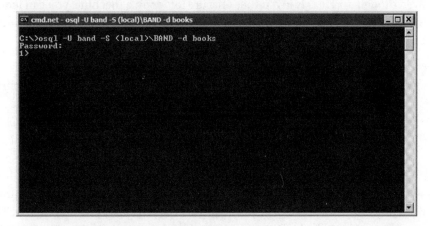

Figure 10-1. osql.exe *ready to accept commands*

3. Enter the following at the 1> prompt, and press Return:

```
SELECT * FROM Publisher ORDER BY PublisherName
```

4. At the 2> prompt, enter **GO** and press Return. This will execute the command and return the results, as shown in Figure 10-2.

Figure 10-2. Query results from osql.exe

5. Close osql.exe by entering **EXIT** or **QUIT** and pressing Return.

How It Works

Even though `osql.exe` is in a rather obscure folder on a machine, you can launch it from anywhere because the folder that it's in has been added to the command-line execution path.

> **NOTE** *The command-line execution path in Windows allows command-line tools to be executed irrespective of the directory that contains the executable and the current directory. The MSDE installer adds the correct path for `osql.exe` to the path variable, so you don't need to worry about its location.*

On the command line, you specify the server, database, and user account you want to use and force `osql.exe` to ask you for the password you want to use. This stops anyone from looking over your shoulder and seeing the passwords you're using. This isn't a massive security headache, but you should be doing all you can to ensure that your database password remains secret.

Once you've connected to the database, you execute a simple SELECT query against the Publisher table and return all the entries in the table, as shown previously in Figure 10-2.

One thing to be careful with is using the GO command. Using `osql.exe` you can enter several queries separated by semicolons or spread one query across several different lines (which is quite valuable if you have complex queries). Only when `osql.exe` sees a GO command does it execute the query or queries you've entered.

You close the connection to the database and `osql.exe` by using either the QUIT or EXIT command; you can use these commands interchangeably.

mysql.exe

The MySQL command-line tool is installed in the bin folder of the MySQL installation; if the defaults have been accepted, it'll be in the `c:\mysql\bin` folder.

Specifying the server, database, and security credentials for `mysql.exe` is similar to `osql.exe`.

To specify the server you want to connect to, you use the -h parameter followed by the name of the server to which you want to connect.

> **NOTE** *If the server isn't specified, an attempt will be made to connect to MySQL on the local machine.*

You specify the security credentials you want to use with the -u and -p parameters, as with osql.exe, except that with mysql.exe the switches themselves must be lowercase. If you want mysql.exe to prompt for the password, specify the -p parameter without a value.

You can specify the database you want to connect to by using the -D parameter or by simply adding the database name as the last thing on the command line. If you don't specify a database, you'll connect to the server but won't connect to a database; therefore, you must change to the database you want to access with the USE statement.

So, to connect to the Books database on the local machine using the band account, you'd use the following command line:

```
mysql -u band -p Books
```

Try It Out: Querying a MySQL Database via the Command Line

In this example, you'll use mysql.exe to connect to the Books database and execute a simple query to return all the publishers in the database. Follow these steps:

1. Open a command prompt, and navigate to the c:\mysql\bin folder.

2. Enter the following, and press Return:

   ```
   mysql -u band -p Books
   ```

3. At the prompt, enter **letmein** as the password. This will open the mysql.exe command-line tool, as shown in Figure 10-3.

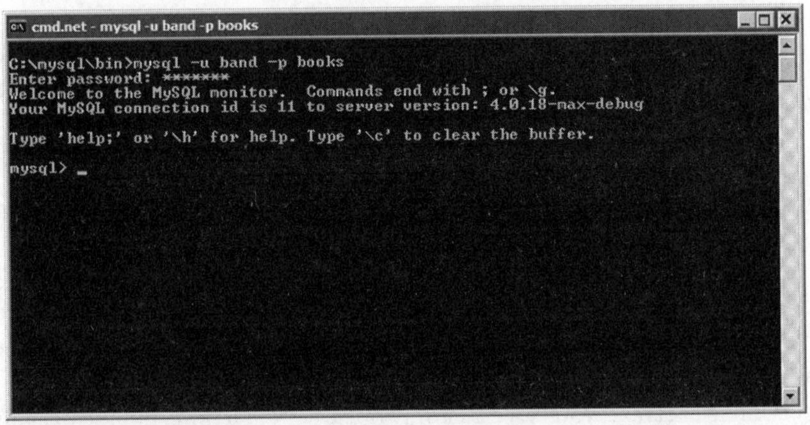

Figure 10-3. mysql.exe *ready to accept commands*

4. Enter the following query, and press Return:

```
SELECT * FROM Publisher ORDER BY PublisherName;
```

5. This will execute the query and return the results, as shown in Figure 10-4.

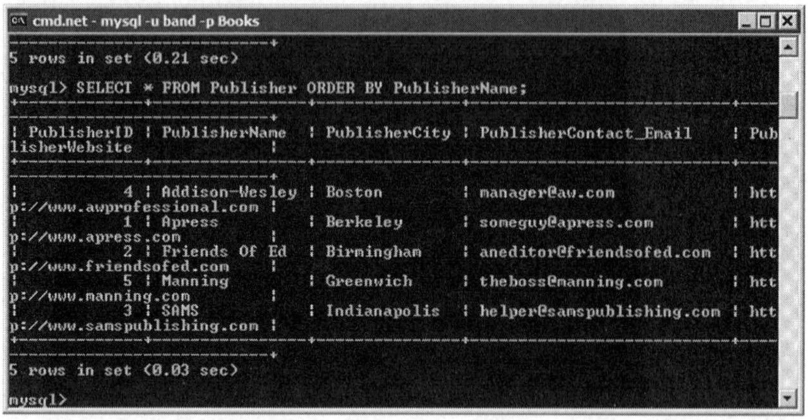

Figure 10-4. Query results from mysql.exe

6. Close osql.exe by entering **EXIT** or **QUIT** and pressing Return.

How It Works

Unlike osql.exe, the path to the mysql.exe executable isn't added to the path as standard; you must navigate to the correct folder before you can execute it. You could, of course, use the full path for the executable if you require.

> **NOTE** *If you're going to use* mysql.exe *a lot, it's a lot easier to add the path to the executable in the Windows path. You can do this by adding* C:\mysql\bin *to the end of the path in Windows—in the* autoexec.bat *file or, on Windows 2000 onward, by modifying the* PATH *environment variable.*

Once you've entered the password and connected to the database, you enter the queries you want to execute; they're executed, and the results are returned in a tabular format.

Unlike osql.exe, you can enter only one query at a time, but it can again be across multiple lines. Instead of the GO command that osql.exe uses, mysql.exe uses the semicolon to specify that a query is complete and should be executed.

As with `osql.exe`, you can also use QUIT or EXIT to close the connection to the database and exit osql.exe.

Creating Databases

The first DDL query you need to look at is the query to create a database. When we first introduced DDL in Chapter 2, you briefly learned about CREATE TABLE. In Chapter 9, you looked at CREATE PROCEDURE, so it'll perhaps come as no surprise that there's a corresponding CREATE query for creating databases.

Try It Out: Creating a Database

The first DDL query you'll look at is CREATE TABLE. You'll use this to build a database that you query in later examples without destroying the database you've been using in the previous chapters. Follow these steps:

1. Open the command-line client for the database you want to use.

1a. To open the MSDE Administrator, open a command prompt, type the following, and press Return:

```
osql -U sa -S (local)\BAND
```

1b. To open the MySQL Control Center, open a command prompt and navigate to the `C:\mysql\bin` folder before executing the following command:

```
mysql -u root -p
```

2. At the password prompt, enter the correct password, which in this case is secpas for both MSDE and MySQL.

3. At the command prompt, enter the query to create the database.

3a. For MSDE, enter the following on two separate lines:

```
CREATE DATABASE BooksTemp
GO
```

3b. For MySQL, enter the following command:

```
CREATE DATABASE BooksTemp;
```

4. The database will be created, and a confirmation message will be returned.

4a. For MSDE, the database will be created, and the details of the data and log files will be given, as shown in Figure 10-5.

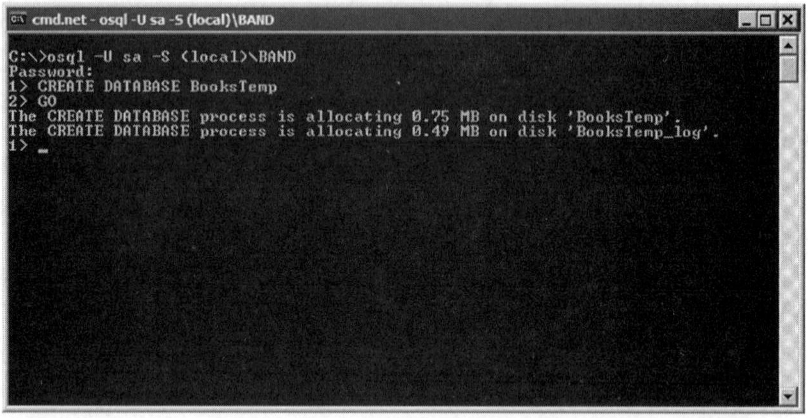

Figure 10-5. Database created successfully using osql.exe

4b. For MySQL, you simply get a message saying that the query you've executed is correct, as shown in Figure 10-6.

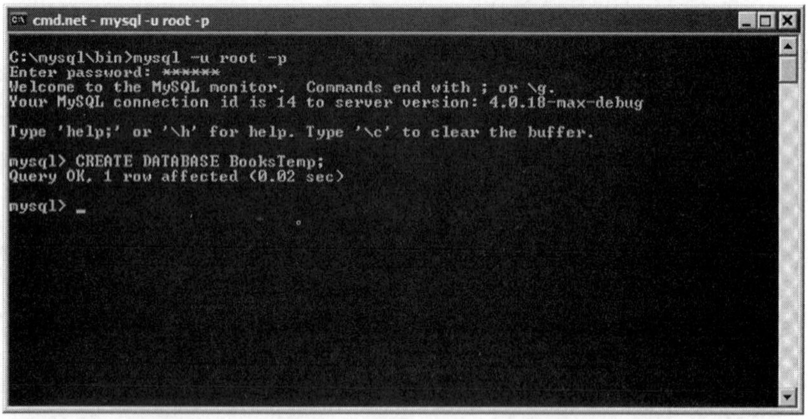

Figure 10-6. Database created successfully using mysql.exe

5. Exit the command-line tool by typing either **EXIT** or **QUIT** and hitting Return.

6. To verify that the databases have been created correctly, fire up the graphical tool you've been using, and you'll see the database has been created.

6a. Open SQL Web Data Administrator, and you'll immediately see that the BooksTemp database you've just created is visible alongside the real database you've been using, as shown in Figure 10-7.

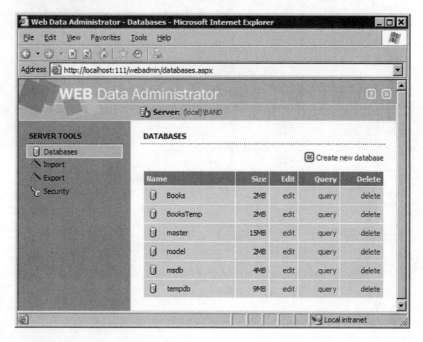

Figure 10-7. SQL Web Data Administrator showing that the database has been created

6b. Open the MySQL Control Center, and you'll immediately see that the BooksTemp database you've just created is visible alongside the real database you've been using, as shown in Figure 10-8.

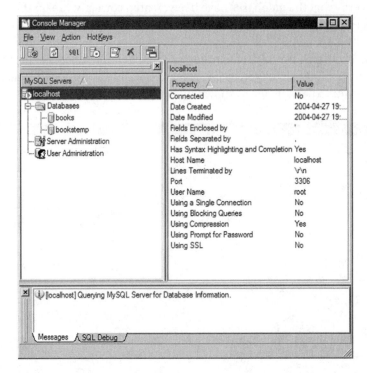

Figure 10-8. MySQL Control Center showing that the database has been created

7. Close both graphical clients.

How It Works

The syntax for the query to create a database is the same whether you're using MSDE or MySQL. You're fortunate that this is the case, and as you'll shortly see, this is one of the few instances where you can use the same query with both MSDE and MySQL.

The thing to notice before you execute the query is that you're logged into the server as the administrator account (the sa account for MSDE and the root account for MySQL) rather than the band account you've been using to execute DML queries. As you saw in Chapter 2, you should only ever use an account that has the privileges you need, and the ability to execute DDL queries should be the most jealously guarded privilege. You use the administrator account because this is the only account in the system that has permission to execute the DDL queries you need.

To create a database, you use the CREATE query, specifying that you want to create a database and then follow this with the name of the database you want to create, as follows:

```
CREATE DATABASE BooksTemp
```

So, with this one line of SQL, you're constructing a BooksTemp database. When you execute this query, the database structure is created before control is returned.

Although this version of CREATE DATABASE is the simplest you can get, you can apply a plethora of options to the query to modify how the database is constructed, and these options are different for MSDE and MySQL.

All these other options are way beyond the scope of this book; you can find further details for MSDE and MySQL, respectively, at the following locations:

- http://msdn.microsoft.com/library/en-us/tsqlref/ts_create_1up1.asp

- http://dev.mysql.com/doc/mysql/en/CREATE_DATABASE.html

Now that you've created the database, you can create the tables that make up the database.

Creating Tables

You briefly saw in Chapter 2 that CREATE TABLE is the DDL query for creating tables. For those of you who've been waiting for a fuller discussion, your prayers will now be answered!

The basic structure of the CREATE TABLE command is as follows:

```
CREATE TABLE <table-name>
(
   <column1-name column1-type column1-options>,
   <column2-name column2-type column2-options>,
...
   <columnN-name columnN-type columnN-options>,
   <table-options>
)
```

That is, you specify the name of the table and then specify each of the columns that make up the table by giving the name of the column, the type of the column, and any other options you need for the column.

Most of the options you can supply for columns are beyond what we want to show here. You can find these details (as well as a lot more database-specific options for creating tables) for MSDE and MySQL, respectively, at the following locations:

- `http://msdn.microsoft.com/library/en-us/tsqlref/ts_create2_8g9x.asp`

- `http://dev.mysql.com/doc/mysql/en/CREATE_TABLE.html`

You'll look at how you create the four tables of the Books database in both MSDE and MySQL using the graphical client you have available. As you'll soon see, the queries to create the tables are similar for the two databases, but they're different enough to warrant their own examples.

Try It Out: Creating Tables in MSDE

In this example, you'll switch from using the command-line to using SQL Web Data Administrator. You'll use this graphical client to execute four CREATE TABLE queries to create the four tables that make up the BooksTemp database. Follow these steps:

1. Open SQL Web Data Administrator, and select the query option for the BooksTemp database.

2. In the query text area, enter the following:

    ```
    CREATE TABLE Publisher (
        PublisherID int IDENTITY NOT NULL PRIMARY KEY,
        PublisherName varchar (50) NOT NULL,
        PublisherCity varchar (50) NOT NULL,
        PublisherContact_Email varchar (100) NOT NULL,
        PublisherWebsite varchar (100) NOT NULL
    )
    ```

3. Click the Execute button. This will execute the query, and the only sign that the query hasn't failed is the lack of an error message.

4. To verify that the Publisher table has been created, click the Tables option in the left menu. You'll see that the table has indeed been created, as shown in Figure 10-9.

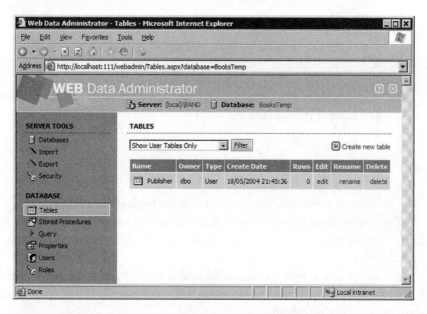

Figure 10-9. Despite the lack of feedback, the table has been created.

5. Create the Author table by executing the following query:

```
CREATE TABLE Author (
  AuthorID int IDENTITY NOT NULL PRIMARY KEY,
  AuthorFirstName varchar (50) NOT NULL,
  AuthorSurname varchar (50) NOT NULL,
  AuthorLastContact smalldatetime
)
```

6. Create the Book table by executing the following query:

```
CREATE TABLE Book (
  BookID int IDENTITY NOT NULL PRIMARY KEY,
  BookTitle varchar (100) NOT NULL ,
  BookPublisherID int NOT NULL ,
  BookMainTopic varchar (25) NOT NULL
)
```

7. Create the final table, the WhoWroteWhat table, by executing the following query:

```
CREATE TABLE WhoWroteWhat (
    WWWBookID int NOT NULL,
    WWWAuthorID int NOT NULL,
    PRIMARY KEY (WWWBookID, WWWAuthorID)
)
```

8. You can verify that all four tables have been created correctly by clicking the Tables option in the left menu.

How It Works

The queries you've just used have created all the tables you need.

The table names are fairly obvious and don't really need any explanation. It's the column definitions and column options that are the important things for you to understand.

The first thing to notice is that a column definition contains, as we've already briefly mentioned, the name of the column, its data type, and any options you want to apply to that column.

So, if you take the Publisher table as the example, you'll see that you're creating the following five columns:

```
PublisherID int IDENTITY NOT NULL PRIMARY KEY,
PublisherName varchar (50) NOT NULL,
PublisherCity varchar (50) NOT NULL,
PublisherContact_Email varchar (100) NOT NULL,
PublisherWebsite varchar (100) NOT NULL
```

The column name and data type are fairly self-explanatory, and it's the column options that are the details you need to understand.

The first that you see is the IDENTITY option, which specifies that the column is an identity field (in other words, one that automatically updates when you insert an entry into the table).

You can also specify whether the column you're adding doesn't allow null values. You accomplish this by using the NOT NULL option. By default, a column will accept null values, and if you don't want this behavior, you don't have to specify this option. You can see this if you look at the AuthorLastContact column in the Author table.

```
AuthorLastContact smalldatetime
```

Of course, if you want to be explicit in your definition of whether a column will accept a null value, you can also specify this using the NULL option. The following line is functionally equivalent to the previous version:

```
AuthorLastContact smalldatetime NULL
```

The one column option you haven't looked at is PRIMARY KEY. This allows you to specify that the column in question is, not surprisingly, the primary key for the table. If you've got a single column making up the primary key, then you can use this terminology for specifying the key as you do in the Publisher, Book, and Author tables. However, if the primary key is a composite key and contains more than one column, you must use an alternative syntax, as in the WhoWroteWhat table, to specify the primary key, like so:

```
PRIMARY KEY (WWWBookID, WWWAuthorID)
```

You specify the columns that make up the key as a comma-separated list within the brackets of the PRIMARY KEY table option.

Try It Out: Creating Tables in MySQL

In this example, you'll see that the SQL queries to create tables in MySQL are similar to those that you'd use when creating the tables in MSDE. However, as you'll see, there are differences. Follow these steps:

1. Open MySQL Control Center, and select the SQL option from the toolbar.

2. In the query text area, switch to the correct database.

    ```
    USE BooksTemp;
    ```

3. Hitting the execute icon on the toolbar will cause the query to execute and the current database to change to BooksTemp.

4. Replace the text in the query text area with the following:

    ```
    CREATE TABLE Publisher (
      PublisherID int NOT NULL AUTO_INCREMENT PRIMARY KEY,
      PublisherName varchar(50) NOT NULL,
      PublisherCity varchar(50) NOT NULL,
      PublisherContact_Email varchar(100) NOT NULL,
      PublisherWebsite varchar(100) NOT NULL
    ) TYPE=InnoDB;
    ```

5. Hitting the execute icon on the toolbar will cause the query to execute and a success message to be returned, as shown in Figure 10-10.

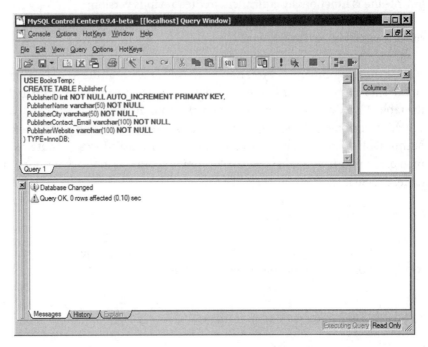

Figure 10-10. MySQL Control Center provides a little more feedback.

6. Create the Author table by executing the following query:

```
CREATE TABLE Author (
    AuthorID int NOT NULL AUTO_INCREMENT PRIMARY KEY,
    AuthorFirstName varchar(50) NOT NULL,
    AuthorSurname varchar(50) NOT NULL,
    AuthorLastContact datetime
) TYPE=InnoDB;
```

7. Create the Book table by executing the following query:

```
CREATE TABLE Book (
    BookID int NOT NULL AUTO_INCREMENT PRIMARY KEY,
    BookTitle varchar(100) NOT NULL,
    BookPublisherID int(11) NOT NULL,
    BookMainTopic varchar(25) NOT NULL
) TYPE=InnoDB;
```

8. Create the final table, the WhoWroteWhat table, by executing the following query:

```
CREATE TABLE WhoWroteWhat (
   WWWBookID int NOT NULL,
   WWWAuthorID int NOT NULL,
   PRIMARY KEY  (WWWBookID, WWWAuthorID)
) TYPE=InnoDB;
```

9. You can verify that all four tables have been created correctly by closing the SQL editor and selecting the BooksTemp database and then the Tables option.

How It Works

Before you start executing queries against the database, you first must specify which database you want to use. When you use SQL Web Data Administrator for accessing the MSDE database, you select a database to execute the queries against. Unfortunately, this option isn't available within MySQL Control Center, so you must specify the database manually using the USE statement followed by the database name.

Once you've selected which database you want to use, you can execute the queries that you use to create the tables within the database. You'll see that these are similar to the corresponding commands in MSDE.

One of the things you need to watch out for in SQL is the different names that the different databases have for the data types they allow. While most of the data types will be the same, sometimes the data types have different names or have to be specified slightly differently. The only instance of this in the queries you've seen is the AuthorLastContact field in the Author table—for MSDE you have to have a data type of smalldatetime, but for MySQL you have a data type of datetime.

> **NOTE** *In Appendix B you'll see a comparison between the MSDE and MySQL data types and the corresponding type in the* SqlDbType *enumeration.*

The options you can specify are also pretty similar—you have the NOT NULL, NULL, and PRIMARY KEY notation for columns that operate in the same way for MySQL as they do for MSDE, and you can also specify a composite key using the same terminology.

The one column option that's different between MSDE and MySQL is the IDENTITY option in MSDE—in MySQL you must specify this type of column using the AUTO_INCREMENT option.

Adding, Modifying, and Removing Columns

You've now seen how to create tables in both MSDE and MySQL. This is fine as long as you've created the table correctly in the first place and as long as the requirements for the data that the table will hold don't actually change. If they do change, then you'll need some method of modifying the table.

The basic query to modify a table in the database is ALTER TABLE. Depending upon what you actually want to do, the other details you must supply will change.

If you want to add a column to a table, you must use the ADD syntax of the query, specifying the new column you want to add, like so:

```
ALTER TABLE <table-name> ADD <column-name column-type column-options>
```

You specify the new column in the same way as you'd specify the column when creating the table. Further, all the options you have available when creating the table are also available here.

To delete a column, you use the DROP COLUMN syntax and specify the column you want to delete, like so:

```
ALTER TABLE <table-name> DROP COLUMN <column-name>
```

Sometimes, you'll also need the ability to change the definition of a column; you accomplish this slightly differently in MSDE and MySQL.

For MSDE, you use the ALTER COLUMN syntax and specify the old column name and the new definition for the column, like so:

```
ALTER TABLE <table-name> ALTER COLUMN <column-name> <column-type column-options>
```

MySQL allows you to do the same thing but uses the CHANGE COLUMN syntax for this. You must specify the old name of the column as well as the complete definition, including the column name, for the modified column, like so:

```
ALTER TABLE <table-name> CHANGE COLUMN <column-name>
  <column-name column-type column-options>
```

Be careful when modifying columns because it's easy to lose data if you don't think things through fully—whether this is from a data type conversion that was unintended or because a column's length has been reduced. Neither MSDE nor MySQL will warn that this is about to occur; both will just assume you know what you're doing.

> **NOTE** *The differences between the MSDE and MySQL syntax for modifying columns is because this functionality isn't defined in the SQL specification. Most databases allow this functionality, but their implementations are all slightly different.*

Although you've seen perhaps the three most important uses of the ALTER TABLE query, you can do a lot more using ALTER TABLE. If you want more information, refer to the documentation, for MSDE and MySQL, respectively, at the following locations:

- `http://msdn.microsoft.com/library/en-us/tsqlref/ts_aa-az_3ied.asp`

- `http://dev.mysql.com/doc/mysql/en/ALTER_TABLE.html`

Try It Out: Changing a Table Definition

In this example, you'll modify the Author table by adding two columns. You'll then modify one of the columns to increase the amount of information that can be stored within the field. Follow these steps:

1. Open either SQL Web Data Administrator or MySQL Control Center.

1a. For SQL Web Data Administrator, select the query option on the BooksTemp database.

1b. For MySQL Control Center, select the SQL option from the toolbar and switch to the BooksTemp database by executing the following statement:

```
USE BooksTemp;
```

2. Create two new columns on the Author table by executing two queries.

2a. For MSDE, execute the following three queries:

```
ALTER TABLE Author ADD AuthorSSN char(11) NULL
ALTER TABLE Author ALTER COLUMN AuthorSSN char(11) NOT NULL
ALTER TABLE Author ADD AuthorWebsite varchar(50) NULL
```

2b. For MySQL, execute the following two queries:

```
ALTER TABLE Author ADD AuthorSSN char(11) NOT NULL;
ALTER TABLE Author ADD AuthorWebsite varchar(50) NULL;
```

3. Verify that the new columns have been added to the table.

3a. For MSDE, select the Tables option and then select the Author table. You'll see that the new columns have been added and the details match those that you've given, as shown in Figure 10-11.

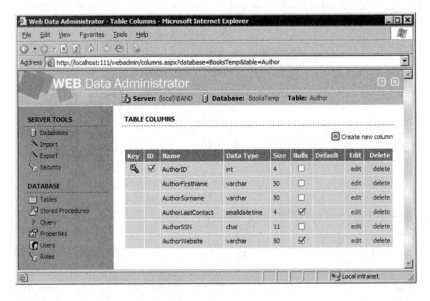

Figure 10-11. Verifying that the new columns have been added to the table

3b. For MySQL, close the SQL editor and expand the Tables option of the BooksTemp database. Clicking the Author table will show the definition for the table, and, as shown in Figure 10-12, the new columns have indeed been added.

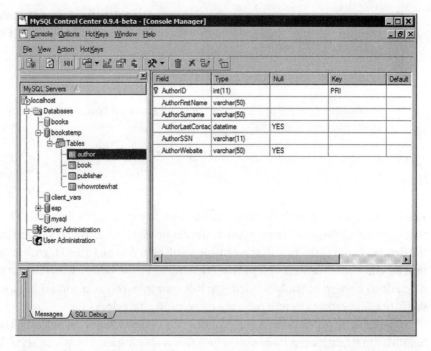

Figure 10-12. Verifying that the new columns have been added to the table

4. Switch back to the editor, and execute the queries to modify the columns you've just added.

4a. For MSDE, execute the following query:

```
ALTER TABLE Author ALTER COLUMN AuthorWebsite varchar(100)
```

4b. For MySQL, execute the following:

```
USE BooksTemp;
ALTER TABLE Author CHANGE COLUMN ↵
   AuthorWebsite AuthorWebsite varchar(100);
```

5. Go back and verify that the length of the AuthorWebsite column has indeed changed from 50 characters to 100 characters.

6. Again in the editor, execute the command to delete the AuthorWebsite column you've just added and modified. The command in this case is the same for both MSDE and MySQL.

```
ALTER TABLE Author DROP COLUMN AuthorWebsite
```

7. Verify that the column has been deleted and that you're left with only one new column, AuthorSSN, in the Author table.

How It Works

The first thing you do in the example is add two columns to the database. One of these, for the eagle-eyed among you, is the AuthorSSN column that's in the original database and is the one that we purposefully left off the CREATE TABLE definition for the Author table in the previous example. The database won't be the same if you don't have it, so you've added it in this example. You also add an Author-Website column that contains a string of up to 50 characters.

One thing to note here is a slight difference in the way that MSDE and MySQL handle columns that can have null values when altering a table. While MySQL will allow new columns to be added that can't have a null value, MSDE won't allow the column to be created. As you can see, you've created the AuthorSSN column to allow null values in MSDE, like so:

```
ALTER TABLE Author ADD AuthorSSN char(11) NULL
```

However, for MySQL, you can create this column and specify that you won't allow null values, like so:

```
ALTER TABLE Author ADD AuthorSSN char(11) NOT NULL;
```

Although you've created the two columns differently, you can execute, an ALTER COLUMN query in MSDE to force the column to always have a value, like so:

```
ALTER TABLE Author ALTER COLUMN AuthorSSN char(11) NOT NULL
```

You can't do a lot about this. MSDE and MySQL handle this slightly differently, and you've just got to be aware that these slight differences occur. You've accomplished the same column definition, but it has taken two queries in MSDE and only one in MySQL.

You're also altering the AuthorWebsite column for both databases. Fifty characters isn't really enough to hold a Web site address, so you double the size. Again, the two databases have slightly different functionality to do this, but they both accomplish the same thing.

For MSDE, you use the following ALTER COLUMN syntax:

```
ALTER TABLE Author ALTER COLUMN AuthorWebsite varchar(100)
```

For MySQL, you use the following CHANGE COLUMN syntax:

```
ALTER TABLE Author CHANGE COLUMN AuthorWebsite AuthorWebsite varchar(100);
```

Because you're increasing the sizes of the columns, you don't run the risk of losing any data—you're getting bigger not smaller. If you had made the change the other way and reduced the size of the column from 100 characters to 50 characters, anything that was contained in the final 50 characters would be permanently lost, so be careful. Once you've lost the information, you have no way to get it back.

So now that you've added the two columns that the customer requires and fixed the problem that you've given yourself with having a column that's too short, the customer decides that they want another change (customers *always* want changes at the last minute). No longer do they want to store the author's Web site, so you can delete the column from the table using the following query:

```
ALTER TABLE Author DROP COLUMN AuthorWebsite
```

You simply specify the column you want to delete and execute the query. You don't get a confirmation, so make sure you're deleting the correct column before executing!

Creating and Deleting Indexes

Once you've created the necessary tables in the database, it's possible to create indexes on the tables. You've already looked at the DDL to create indexes for MSDE, CREATE INDEX, in Chapter 2 because SQL Web Data Administrator doesn't provide the ability to add indexes. You used MySQL Control Center to perform the same task in MySQL. However, the SQL syntax for creating indexes is the same for both MSDE and MySQL.

You can also programmatically delete indexes using DROP INDEX .

Creating Indexes

You add indexes to the database using the following CREATE INDEX query:

```
CREATE INDEX <index-name> ON <table-name> ( <column-name> )
```

When creating an index, the first thing you need to specify is a name for the index. MSDE defaults to using a name of the form *IX_column* where *column* is the column that's being indexed. It's best to stick to a consistent naming scheme—one that's easily understood if you need to come back to the database in the future. The MSDE naming scheme is as good as any.

You then specify the table you're adding the index to and the column you want to index.

You can find more information on the CREATE INDEX command for MSDE and MySQL, respectively, at the following locations:

- http://msdn.microsoft.com/library/en-us/tsqlref/ts_create_64l4.asp

- http://dev.mysql.com/doc/mysql/en/CREATE_INDEX.html

> **NOTE** *To add relationships to the database in MySQL, you must define indexes on all the foreign keys in the relationships. If an index isn't defined, an error will be generated when creating the relationship. MSDE doesn't have this restriction, and you can create relationships without the indexes.*

Try It Out: Creating Indexes

You'll now add indexes to the four tables you created in the previous example. You'll add indexes for four different columns—three of these you need when you look at relationships shortly, but you'll add the fourth index only so that you can delete it in the next example. Follow these steps:

1. Open either SQL Web Data Administrator or MySQL Control Center.

1a. For SQL Web Data Administrator, select the query option on the Books-Temp database.

1b. For MySQL Control Center, select the SQL option from the toolbar and switch to the BooksTemp database by executing the following statement:

```
USE BooksTemp;
```

2. Execute the four queries to create the indexes.

2a. For MSDE, execute the following:

```
CREATE INDEX IX_WWWAuthorID ON WhoWroteWhat (WWWAuthorID)
CREATE INDEX IX_WWWBookID ON WhoWroteWhat (WWWBookID)
CREATE INDEX IX_BookPublisherID ON Book (BookPublisherID)
CREATE INDEX IX_BookMainTopic ON Book (BookMainTopic)
```

2b. For MySQL, execute the following:

```
CREATE INDEX IX_WWWAuthorID ON WhoWroteWhat (WWWAuthorID);
CREATE INDEX IX_WWWBookID ON WhoWroteWhat (WWWBookID);
CREATE INDEX IX_BookPublisherID ON Book (BookPublisherID);
CREATE INDEX IX_BookMainTopic ON Book (BookMainTopic);
```

3. You can check that the indexes have been created by attempting to create the index again. Try to create the following index again with this command:

```
CREATE INDEX IX_BookMainTopic ON Book (BookMainTopic)
```

4. For MSDE, you'll receive an error message explaining that the index already exists, as shown in Figure 10-13. Figure 10-14 shows the error message for MySQL.

The following error occured while executing the query:
Server: Msg 1913, Level 16, State 1, Line 1
There is already an index on table 'Book' named 'IX_BookMainTopic'.

Figure 10-13. Duplicate index error message in MSDE

Figure 10-14. Duplicate index error message in MySQL

How It Works

As you can see, the four CREATE INDEX queries are the same for both MSDE and MySQL. The only difference in the SQL that's executed to create the indexes stems from the way that graphical tools handle multiple statements. With MSDE, you can have queries on separate lines, but for MySQL, you need queries separated by semicolons.

Deleting Indexes

To delete an index, you use DROP INDEX. For MSDE, the syntax is as follows:

```
DROP INDEX <table-name>.<index-name>
```

For MySQL, the syntax is slightly different.

```
DROP INDEX <index-name> ON <table-name>
```

Whichever version of the syntax you require, you must specify both the name of the index and the table for the index. This will drop the index from the specified table without any warning, and you can't recover an index that has been deleted.

You can find more information on the DROP INDEX command for MSDE and MySQL, respectively, at the following locations:

- http://msdn.microsoft.com/library/en-us /tsqlref/ts_de-dz_5j5k.asp

- http://dev.mysql.com/doc/mysql/en/DROP_INDEX.html

Try It Out: Deleting Indexes

To show how to use DROP INDEX, you'll now delete one of the indexes you created in the previous example. Follow these steps:

1. Open either SQL Web Data Administrator or MySQL Control Center.

1a. For SQL Web Data Administrator, select the query option on the Books-Temp database.

1b. For MySQL Control Center, select the SQL option from the toolbar and switch to the BooksTemp database by executing the following statement:

```
USE BooksTemp;
```

2. Execute the query to drop the index.

2a. For MSDE, execute this:
```
DROP INDEX Book.IX_BookMainTopic
```

2b. For MySQL, execute this:
```
DROP INDEX IX_BookMainTopic ON Book
```

3. To verify that the index has been deleted, execute the DROP INDEX query again.

4. For MSDE, you'll receive an error message explaining that the index doesn't exist, as shown in Figure 10-15. Figure 10-16 shows the error message for MySQL.

The following error occured while executing the query:
Server: Msg 3701, Level 11, State 7, Line 1
Cannot drop the index 'Book.IX_BookMainTopic', because it does not exist in the system catalog.

Figure 10-15. Unknown index error message in MSDE

[localhost] ERROR 1091: Can't DROP 'IX_BookMainTopic'. Check that column/key exists

Figure 10-16. Unknown index error message in MySQL

How It Works

As you can see, deleting indexes is easy. Unfortunately, no warning is given that you're about to delete an index and that you should be careful with what you're doing.

However, in this case, the lack of warning isn't really a problem because you can simply re-create the index without any loss of data. When you look at deleting tables and databases shortly, you'll see that the lack of warning can be a problem, though.

Creating and Deleting Relationships

In Chapter 2, you looked at the relationships between tables; we also discussed how it's these relationships that give a database its real power. After all, they wouldn't be called *relational databases* unless there was a relation in there somewhere.

Relationships aren't the be-all and end-all of databases, however. You can run a perfectly acceptable database solution without implementing any relationships in the database, instead relying on the SQL queries you write. While this is perfectly acceptable and a lot of databases have no relationships explicitly defined, you should always use relationships if the database you're using implements them.

Creating Relationships

As you saw in Chapter 2, a relationship will exist between two columns. For the Book database, for example, you have a relationship between a book and a publisher—the BookPublisherID column in the Book table and the PublisherID column in the Publisher table.

You need a SQL query that can model this relationship; in this case, you can use the ADD CONSTRAINT syntax of the ALTER TABLE query.

> **NOTE** *The ADD CONSTRAINT version of the ALTER TABLE query allows you to do more than simply add relationships to the table. You can add primary keys to tables using this method, and you can also specify indexes and keys that contain multiple columns using this command. This is all beyond the scope of what we can cover in a beginner's book, so if you want to find out more, refer to the ALTER TABLE syntax at* `http://msdn.microsoft.com/library/en-us/tsqlref/ts_aa-az_3ied.asp` *for MSDE and* `http://dev.mysql.com/doc/mysql/en/ALTER_TABLE.html` *for MySQL.*

The syntax of the ADD CONSTRAINT version of the ALTER TABLE query is as follows:

```
ALTER TABLE <table-name> ADD CONSTRAINT <relationship-name>
  FOREIGN KEY ( <column-name> )
  REFERENCES <table-name> ( <column-name> )
```

This is a little more involved than the other DDL queries you've seen so far in this chapter, but it isn't that complex. Honest! You'll start by looking at the query line by line.

The first thing you need to specify is the table to which the relationship is being applied. You always apply a constraint to the foreign key side of the relationship, so for the Publisher to Book relationship, you'd add the constraint to the Book table—you have multiple books and only one publisher.

You must then specify a name for the relationship—if you don't have a name, you can't ever refer to it, and in the database *everything* must have a name. MSDE defaults to using a name of the form *FK_table1_table2* where *table1* is the table containing the foreign key and *table2* is the table containing the primary key, but you're free to use whatever you want as the name of the relationship (limited by the SQL naming conventions, of course). It's probably best to stick to a consistent naming scheme and one that's easily understood if you need to come back to the database in the future—the MSDE naming scheme is as good as any.

You then tell the database that you're creating a foreign key (using the fairly obvious FOREIGN KEY syntax) and specify, in brackets, which column you want as the foreign key.

Finally, you must let the database know with which table and column you're creating the relationship. You do this after the REFERENCES clause, and you specify the table name followed by the column name in brackets.

That's it. You now know how to add a relationship between two tables. Theory is one thing, but now you'll actually do it.

> **NOTE** *As we pointed out when looking at indexes earlier, you can add an index to a table in MySQL only if the foreign key of the relationship is contained within an index. If the foreign key isn't in an index, a rather cryptic* errno:150 *error is thrown, and you must add the index before you can add the relationship to the database.*

Try It Out: Creating Relationships

In this example, you'll add the relationships that exist in the database using the ADD CONSTRAINT version of the ALTER TABLE query. Follow these steps:

1. Open either SQL Web Data Administrator or MySQL Control Center.

1a. For SQL Web Data Administrator, select the query option on the Books-Temp database.

1b. For MySQL Control Center, select the SQL option from the toolbar and switch to the BooksTemp database by executing the following statement:

```
USE BooksTemp;
```

2. Add the relationship between the Book and Publisher table by executing the following query:

```
ALTER TABLE Book ADD CONSTRAINT FK_Book_Publisher
FOREIGN KEY (BookPublisherID)
REFERENCES Publisher (PublisherID)
```

2a. In MSDE, a successful creation will be indicated by no error message being returned.

2b. In MySQL, you can see that the relationship has been created by the message returned, as shown in Figure 10-17.

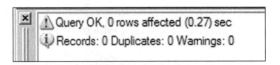

Figure 10-17. MySQL Control Center reports on relationship creation.

3. Add the relationships for the WhoWroteWhat table by executing the following two queries.

3a. For MSDE, execute the following:

```
ALTER TABLE WhoWroteWhat ADD CONSTRAINT FK_WhoWroteWhat_Author
FOREIGN KEY (WWWAuthorID)
REFERENCES Author (AuthorID)

ALTER TABLE WhoWroteWhat ADD CONSTRAINT FK_WhoWroteWhat_Book
FOREIGN KEY (WWWBookID)
REFERENCES Book (BookID)
```

3b. For MySQL, execute the following:

```
ALTER TABLE WhoWroteWhat ADD CONSTRAINT FK_WhoWroteWhat_Author
FOREIGN KEY (WWWAuthorID)
REFERENCES Author (AuthorID);

ALTER TABLE WhoWroteWhat ADD CONSTRAINT FK_WhoWroteWhat_Book
FOREIGN KEY (WWWBookID)
REFERENCES Book (BookID);
```

How It Works

In this example, you've added the three relationships you require to the database using three separate ALTER TABLE queries.

The first query adds the relationship between books and publishers, like so:

```
ALTER TABLE Book ADD CONSTRAINT FK_Book_Publisher
FOREIGN KEY (BookPublisherID)
REFERENCES Publisher (PublisherID)
```

You're creating a relationship between the BookPublisherID column in the Book table and the PublisherID column in the Publisher table. The way you've structured the relationship ensures that you'll have one publisher that can be related to several books since the BookPublisherID column is the foreign key and the PublisherID column is a primary key in the Publisher in the Book table.

The other two relationships that you create follow a similar pattern.

```
ALTER TABLE WhoWroteWhat ADD CONSTRAINT FK_WhoWroteWhat_Author
FOREIGN KEY (WWWAuthorID)
REFERENCES Author (AuthorID)

ALTER TABLE WhoWroteWhat ADD CONSTRAINT FK_WhoWroteWhat_Book
FOREIGN KEY (WWWBookID)
REFERENCES Book (BookID)
```

Here you're creating the two relationships that the WhoWroteWhat table has with the Author and Book tables, respectively. The relationships are both created on the WhoWroteWhat table because a book can have several authors and an author can have written several books.

One problem that you have with using SQL Web Data Administrator to enter DDL queries is that you don't get any feedback on a query that doesn't return any results—this applies to all the DDL queries, not just the ALTER TABLE query you're seeing here.

SQL Web Data Administrator also doesn't give you any means of checking what relationships have been added to a database, so you're forced into using other means to check whether a relationship exists. You can't check what the relationship does—only that it exists. In other words, you have no way of checking that it does what you expect.

Deleting Relationships

Once you've created relationships in the database, you may need to modify those relationships at some point in the future. Unlike modifying table columns, there's no concept of modifying a relationship in the database—if you need to change a relationship, you must delete the old one and then create the new one.

Deleting a relationship is slightly different depending upon whether you're using MSDE or MySQL because they refer to a relationship as different things and use different queries to delete relationships.

In MSDE, a relationship is called a *constraint*, and you use the DROP CONSTRAINT version of the ALTER TABLE query, like so:

```
ALTER TABLE <table-name> DROP CONSTRAINT <relationship-name>
```

MySQL calls it a foreign key and uses the DROP FOREIGN KEY version, like so:

```
ALTER TABLE <table-name> DROP FOREIGN KEY <relationship-name>
```

You can simply drop a relationship by specifying the table that the relationship was created on and specifying the name of the constraint you want to delete.

> **NOTE** *If you try to delete a relationship from the wrong table—in other words, from the primary key side of the relationship—an error will be thrown as the relationship isn't defined on that table. Remember what we mentioned previously about using a consistent naming scheme that was easy to decipher—if you have a consistent and meaningful naming scheme, you can avoid a lot of these errors.*

Try It Out: Deleting Relationships

In this example, you'll start the process of dismantling the database you've built through the previous examples. You'll first look at deleting the relationships in the database and then look at deleting tables and ultimately the database itself. Follow these steps in the following examples:

1. Open either SQL Web Data Administrator or MySQL Control Center.

1a. For SQL Web Data Administrator, select the query option on the BooksTemp database.

1b. For MySQL Control Center, select the SQL option from the toolbar and switch to the BooksTemp database by executing the following statement:

```
USE BooksTemp;
```

2. Drop the relationship between the Book and Publisher table.

2a. For MSDE, execute the following query:.

```
ALTER TABLE Book DROP CONSTRAINT FK_Book_Publisher
```

In MSDE, a successful deletion will be indicated by no error message being returned.

2b. For MySQL, execute the following query:

```
ALTER TABLE Book DROP FOREIGN KEY FK_Book_Publisher
```

In MySQL, you can see that the relationship has been deleted by the message returned, as shown in Figure 10-18.

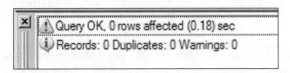

Figure 10-18. MySQL Control Center reports on relationship deletion.

How It Works

As in most cases, destroying something is much easier than creating it. To delete relationships, you simply specify the name of the relationship you want to delete as well as the table to which the relationship belongs. The only wrinkle is that you need to specify the relationship as a CONSTRAINT in MSDE and a FOREIGN KEY in MySQL.

As with creating relationships, you have no way of checking that a relationship has been deleted using SQL Web Data Administrator. If you attempt to delete the relationship again, you'll get a message telling you that the relationship doesn't exist.

Deleting Tables

As you've just seen, deleting relationships is a lot easier than creating them. This is the same for deleting tables and, as you'll see shortly, for deleting databases.

To delete a table from the database, you use the DROP TABLE query, like so:

```
DROP TABLE <table-name>
```

Executing this query will delete the table without any warning, so be extremely careful that you're deleting the correct table and that deleting the table is indeed what you want to do.

Try It Out: Deleting Database Tables

In the previous example, you saw how to delete relationships from tables within the database. This example will use DROP TABLE to delete entire tables from the database. You'll delete only three of the four tables that are in the database, as you'll require at least one table for the next example. Follow these steps:

1. Open either SQL Web Data Administrator or MySQL Control Center.

1a. For SQL Web Data Administrator, select the query option on the Books-Temp database.

1b. For MySQL Control Center, select the SQL option from the toolbar and switch to the BooksTemp database by executing the following statement:

```
USE BooksTemp;
```

2. Execute the following query to drop the Publisher table:

```
DROP TABLE Publisher
```

3. Now try to execute the following query to drop the Author table:

```
DROP TABLE Author
```

4. Executing this query will result in an error being thrown.

4a. For MSDE, the error is a *FOREIGN KEY constraint* error, as shown in Figure 10-19.

The following error occured while executing the query:
Server: Msg 3726, Level 16, State 1, Line 1
Could not drop object 'Author' because it is referenced by a FOREIGN KEY constraint.

Figure 10-19. MSDE error if attempting to delete a table in a relationship

4b. For MySQL, the error is a *foreign key constraint fails* error, as shown in Figure 10-20.

Figure 10-20. MySQL error if attempting to delete a table in a relationship

5. You can't delete the Author table because it's contained in a relationship with the WhoWroteWhat table. The WhoWroteWhat table is the owner of the relationship, so you can delete that table like so:

```
DROP TABLE WhoWroteWhat
```

6. This will delete the relationships owned by the WhoWroteWhat table, so you can now delete the Author table by executing the same delete query, as raised the error in step 4:

```
DROP TABLE Author
```

7. To verify that the three tables have been deleted, you can use the graphical tool to see what tables are left in the database. You should have only one table left.

7a. For MSDE, click the Tables option in the left menu. As you'll see in Figure 10-21, you still have one table left, Book, in the database.

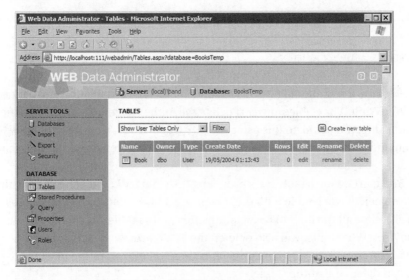

Figure 10-21. Verifying that the tables have been deleted from the database in MSDE

7b. For MySQL, close the SQL command window and select the Tables option of the BooksTemp database. As you'll see in Figure 10-22, you have only the Book table remaining.

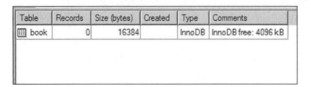

Table	Records	Size (bytes)	Created	Type	Comments
▦ book	0	16384		InnoDB	InnoDB free: 4096 kB

Figure 10-22. Verifying that the tables have been deleted from the database in MySQL

How It Works

As you can see, deleting tables is simple and therefore dangerous! Be sure you're deleting the correct table!

The first table you've deleted from the database is the Publisher table.

```
DROP TABLE Publisher
```

Executing the query simply deletes the table from the database. When you try to delete the Author table, however, you run into problems.

The Author table provides a primary key for a relationship within the database, so it can't simply be deleted. As you'll recall, you created a relationship between the WhoWroteWhat and Author table, like so:

```
ALTER TABLE WhoWroteWhat ADD CONSTRAINT FK_WhoWroteWhat_Author
FOREIGN KEY (WWWAuthorID)
REFERENCES Author (AuthorID)
```

Because the Author table provides the primary key in a relationship defined for the WhoWroteWhat table, you can't delete the Author table without first deleting the relationship. You could do this using a DROP CONSTRAINT or DROP FOREIGN KEY command similar to those you've already looked at, but you use a different solution here.

You can't delete a table if it's providing the primary key in the relationship, but you can delete a table if it's the foreign key in the relationship, and doing so will delete all the foreign key relationships for the table. So, in deleting the WhoWroteWhat table, you also deleted the FK_WhoWroteWhat_Author and FK_WhoWroteWhat_Book relationships. Once these relationships are deleted, you can delete the Author table.

You'll notice that you haven't had any problems deleting tables that have indexes on them. As you'll recall, you specified indexes on the WhoWroteWhat table, yet the table was deleted without any problems. Unlike relationships, an index deals with only one table, and deleting the table automatically deletes any indexes for the table.

Deleting Databases

If you thought deleting a table was easy and a good way to lose data, then deleting a database is just as easy—just with a lot more scope to delete a lot of data you didn't want deleted.

The query to drop a database is as follows:

```
DROP DATABASE <name>
```

This will delete the entire database along with any tables, relationships, and data that still exists in the database. SQL provides no safeguards against deleting entire databases, and this emphasizes why you need to restrict access to the database, and in particular any administration privileges. If someone has the password for the administrator account, they can delete everything on the server easily. Keep your administrator password secure, and don't give any other account any administrator privileges.

We already said be careful when deleting tables, but you should be even more careful that you're doing exactly what you want to do when deleting databases.

Try It Out: Deleting a Database

To delete the database, you'll now switch back to using the command-line tools to execute a DROP DATABASE query. Follow these steps:

1. Open the command-line client for the database you want to use.

1a. To open the MSDE command-line tool, open a command prompt, type the following, and press Return:

```
osql -U sa -S (local)\BAND
```

1b. To open the MySQL command-line tool, open a command prompt and navigate to the C:\mysql\bin folder before executing the following command:

```
mysql -u root -p
```

2. Enter a password of secpas when prompted.

3. At the command prompt, enter the query to delete the database.

3a. For MSDE, enter the following on two lines:

```
DROP DATABASE BooksTemp
GO
```

3b. For MySQL, enter the following query:

```
DROP DATABASE BooksTemp;
```

4. The database will be deleted, and a confirmation message will be returned. For MSDE, the confirmation message is as shown in Figure 10-23. For MySQL, a brief message is returned, as shown in Figure 10-24.

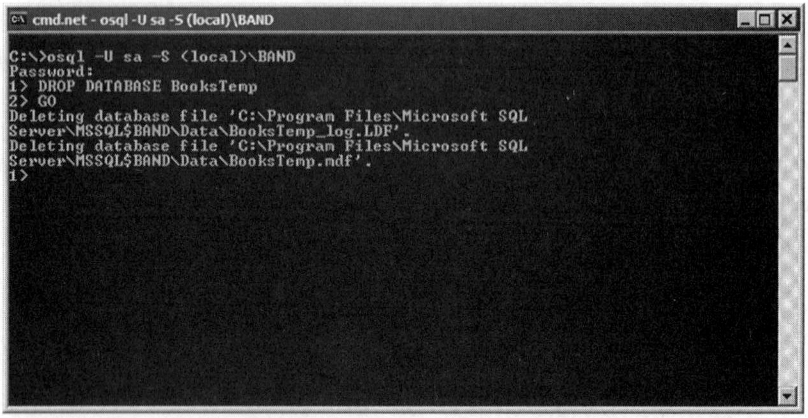

Figure 10-23. Database successfully deleted in MSDE

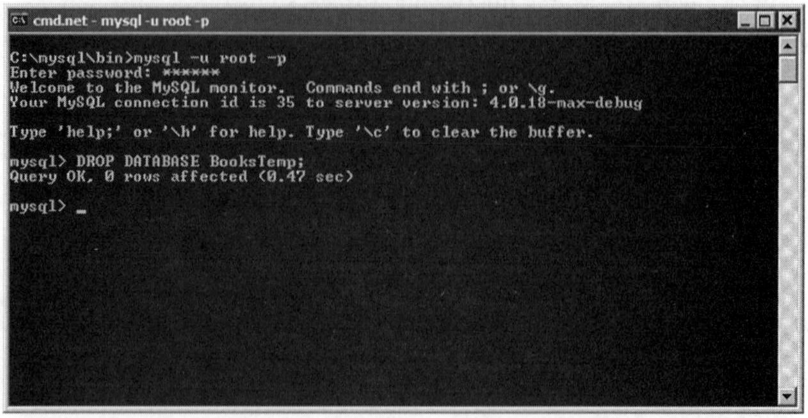

Figure 10-24. Database successfully deleted in MySQL

How It Works

There isn't an awful lot to say except be careful! The DROP DATABASE query deletes databases with no warning.

Summary

In this chapter you've taken a whirlwind tour through the DDL "subset" of SQL, yet you've hardly scratched the surface. If you look at the scripts provided in the code download, you'll see that even for this small database the scripts are complex—certainly more complex than you've seen here.

You've looked at the basics of DDL, and you've seen, for both MSDE and MySQL, how to create, modify, and delete databases and tables. You've also seen how you can create indexes on tables and relationships between the different tables in the database.

Remember the following points when using DDL:

- You usually have multiple ways to do the same thing; you looked at two ways to create primary keys on tables and saw that there was a third. None of the ways to do something is more correct than the others—just use the one you're comfortable using.

- You saw that although the syntax is similar, sometimes different databases handle the same query slightly differently—cast your eyes back over the problem that you encountered when adding the AuthorSSN column to the Author table.

- Be careful when deleting things from the database—it's easy to destroy a table or a database using one line of SQL.

Part Three

The Real World

CHAPTER 11

Application Design and Implementation

IF THE CONTENTS of the book thus far have been teaching you the individual techniques of database access, the remainder of this book aims to start putting all
you've learned into a more real-world light. You may now know how the different
objects in a data provider work together and are put to use, and you may have
learned how to put an ASP.NET page together that will do the tasks you want it to
perform, but taking that next step forward and putting together a whole data-
driven site requires an extra set of skills.

Let's start with what you do know and then think bigger. As you develop more
complex data-driven pages, you start to section database functionality into functions so that they can be called time and time again rather than written out in full.
That good programming practice saves you time and space even on a single page.
If you take the time to design your Web site well, you can make such common
functions available to every page rather than just individual ones—more time,
space, and resources saved. In fact, the benefits are exponential.

Indeed, a well-designed and well-implemented application is easier to maintain, test, debug, and extend than one grown a page at a time, so in this chapter,
you'll look at some of the concepts in the *development life cycle* of a data-driven
application. The point here is to give you an idea of the issues to be aware of and
the questions to ask yourself as you build your application rather than tell you
exactly what to do and when.

From initial ideas to post-release, the main stages of software development
are as follows:

1. **Requirements gathering and analysis**: Defining what functionality an
   application will have, how people and machines will interact with the
   application, and some ways to measure how well your site is performing.

2. **Design**: Drawing up a namespace and class structure for the application
   that's clean, flexible, and easily extendable. Drawing up an equally efficient and extendable database structure (building upon the techniques
   you learned in Chapter 2—you'll spend a fair amount of time on this).

3. **Implementation**: Writing code over the class structure, and taking into account the good practices you've learned thus far in the book and you'll see in the next two chapters. We won't dwell on it in this chapter.

4. **Testing and debugging**: Testing each module to see whether it passes the benchmarks you laid out for it in the analysis phase, and tracking down those annoying bugs.

This chapter will never be the complete reference to the software life cycle, and it isn't intended to be. Every project has its own unique qualities, so there's always something that isn't quite covered anywhere. Indeed, whole books have been written on just the design and analysis stages by themselves, so think of this not as the Encyclopaedia Galactica on the subject but rather as its Hitchhiker's Guide—useful, common information only. So, with the mandatory warning—don't panic!—let's begin.

> **NOTE** *This chapter is intended as a pause for thought before you begin your case study; it contains no actual code or examples. Instead, it introduces many concepts and links to books and Web sites where you can find examples.*

Analysis

It'd be unwise to jump straight into coding an application that could jeopardize the safety of a group of astronauts traveling to Mars without taking some time first to consider what the application needed to do. You should apply that same caution to any application whether or not lives are at stake. If an application doesn't perform to a client's standards, others may think again about contracting you to build something for them, and you certainly won't get any further business from the original client either. Even if you're working on something for yourself—a portfolio piece, if you will—there's no point not coding it well if it will be on display for others to see; this is doubly so if it's an open-source project where the standard of your coding will be judged.

Client Requirements

Your first job will be to sit down and work on a list of requirements for the application. If this is a contracted job, you need to sit down with your clients to draft this. This sounds fine, but what kind of requirements are you after? Well, you can broadly categorize them as described in the following sections.

Site Contents and Functionality

Site contents and functionality includes the following questions: What are the main aims for this application, who is it for, and what tasks should it be performing? Specifically, you should consider the following:

- What kind of application is it? Is it a personal Web site for a friend, a reference site for a business, an e-commerce store for a retail company, a showy site for a rock 'n' roll band?

- Is this application envisaged as an intranet site, an extranet site, or a public site on the Internet?

- How many pages will the site comprise? What will they do? What information is being provided in these pages to the application's users? Can you devise a site map?

- What information is being provided to the site's owners about the site's users? Will the site need to track user habits and logons?

While the clients are trying to describe how they'd like the application to run, your goals are to try to identify the items and events that could be modeled in a database and to pin the clients down on the distinct functionality of the site that you can translate into a class structure. Now, this latter point won't actually happen because unless this application is remarkably trivial, clients will continue to change their minds, adding and removing features as you try to make progress. However, the core functionality of the site should be possible to pin down, as will the way the site should work and how well it should work. These two points come up in the next two sections.

User Roles and Access

User roles and access includes getting to know more about who will use this application and how they will use it. Specifically, you should consider the following:

- Who is going to be using this application? Will the user base be confined to a single company if it's an intranet or a known set of users (if it's an extranet), or can anyone access it (if it's on the Internet)?

- Will this application interface with any other application online or otherwise? How will this interaction be achieved, and to what other applications will it be available?

- Of those users, can you distinguish the roles they may have in the site? For example, in a forum site, guests may only read posts, members may write posts, and moderators may approve and reject posts.

- What are the use cases? Can you determine how people in various roles will try and perform a task and how the application will behave in response? For example, in a forum site, how will a member look for a post on a topic and reply to it? What happens if a guest tries the same thing?

Use cases can be tricky to write, but they become invaluable when it comes to coding pages that are applicable to them. You need to worry as much about what the page does as how to implement it. They also provide a useful double-checking mechanism against the site contents list that the client provides. Can the pages the clients want to see actually perform the tasks the use cases have demarcated?

> **NOTE** *Use cases are typically written in English and then more formally in a graphical notation known as Unified Modeling Language (UML). Read more about UML in* UML Applied: A .NET Perspective *by Martin Shoemaker (Apress, 2004).*

Security issues also raise their head here for the first time. Use cases should include when users without sufficient permissions for a task are knocked back by the application. You also want to establish here how the different roles for an application may map onto its different users and the type of user authentication strategy you may use. If you're working on an intranet, Windows Authentication may be fine. If you're working on an Internet site, forms-based authentication or even Passport-based authentication may be more appropriate.

Available Resources and Performance Targets

You need to ascertain what resources the application will have available to it and whether those resources will be able to perform as the clients would have them do. Specifically, you need to consider the following:

- Who will be hosting this application and where? Will the developers get physical access to the servers? What specification are they using? Which database is running? What is the connection speed?

- What's in the budget for the day-to-day running of the site?

- Will this application use proprietary or open-source software (besides ASP.NET)?

- Roughly how many users are expected to use this application at any one time? How quickly does the client think the number of users will rise, and how fast do they think the amount of data to be stored and retrieved in the database will increase?

The majority of clients will already have a hosting solution in place and presumably .NET, too. If they're already using Java or PHP, now may be a good time to go and get another book, say on Java database programming, and put this one down. Either that, or start extolling the virtues of .NET at them to see if they bite.

The key in this part of the requirements document is to establish the kind of performance and scalability targets they want to achieve and whether their hosting solution will accommodate that. In concert with this, you also need to devise the tests, or metrics, that will allow you to measure whether your code has attained those standards. For example, a friend of ours is working on a project with a SQL Server database containing 200,000 records that will have to be referenced and may be updated every day between 10 p.m. and 6 a.m. An obvious benchmark, then, is the speed with which this database scan can be done.

If your clients are relying on you to provide a hosting solution as well as the application itself, the onus is on you to work with their budget and their performance targets to find the solution that best suits them. Typically, you need to establish a compromise between the price you pay for a database, the size of the connection you can use, the level of support provided for the servers if they're located off-site, and so on. You'll find a quick guide to choosing the right databases you've used later in the section "The Right Data Source" to help with this. If their budget stretches to it, you could investigate using and extending a commercially available piece of software as the backbone of the application. For example, you could use Microsoft Commerce Server for an e-commerce solution.

Future Proofing

Understanding how the client may want to extend the application in the future will have an influence on how you design the application, and you have to answer questions regarding how new site content and functionality is to be added and how maintenance is to be performed after the application's initial delivery. Specifically, you have to consider the following:

- Is this application a one-off, or will it be refactored as a different application with the same purpose but different content, as is the case with dotnetjunkies.com and sqljunkies.com?

- How will this site continue to grow? Will it be a case of existing functionality being refined, or will completely new aspects of the application be added?

- How will content and data be added to the application and maintained? Will a user add it through a Web page or with a Windows application? Will data be updated automatically from system to system (for example, as one application pulls current stock prices from Wall Street)?

- How will application upgrades be applied? Will they be applied from a CD directly on the server or online—perhaps via FTP, via some source versioning control system, or even via a set of Web services?

You should have resolved all the bugs you can find in the application before you release it to the client, but that won't mean there won't be more. Look at Windows. That's been in continuous development for more than ten years, and you can still find bugs all over the place. Maintainability isn't just about considering how the client will keep the application and the data it consumes current, but it's also about how you can make bug fixes and small alterations to the application with the least interference to its uptime.

It's also about leaving yourself with the path of least resistance when it comes to upgrading an application with new features or reapplying it to some new purpose. The key is to design an open class structure so that new functionality can be "plugged into" the application without disrupting anything else. It's also vital to make sure the code is well documented and commented so that developers who come to the code after you can see how it works and write their upgrades in a way to blend with your code. You may also be able to reuse code you've already written for other projects or use code online if it's OK to do so.

Last but not least, it may not be a bad idea here to profile the client yourself and see if there's anything they've missed or may want to add to the application in the second version. Forewarned is forearmed, as they say.

Asking Again

Don't be afraid to ask clients for clarifications to their requirements list, especially when they revise them in the middle of the whole process. If they can bother you, you can bother them—especially if it means you go one way or another with the application's design.

Choosing the Right Tools

With a set of requirements from a client, you can start deciding on the basic build-ing blocks for the application. You've already decided on .NET as the framework of choice, but what about the server hosting it, the database maintaining the appli-cation's data, and even the tools you'll use to create the application? If the client has predetermined the database and hosting solution, that's fine; it leaves you with just your development tools to pick. If not, you should consider the following sections.

The Right Data Source

Although it may sound strange to say it, does this application actually need to use a relational database as its data source? Would it suffice to use an alternative data source such as a set of XML files, Excel spreadsheets, .csv files, or perhaps an alter-native type of database, XML-based or object-oriented? Looking on such open source sites as SourceForge (http://www.sourceforge.net) or even GotDotNet work-spaces (http://workspaces.gotdotnet.com), it's not too difficult to find applications with the same goal but a different approach to data storage. Take the example of two blogging engines, dasBlog and .Text. Both are designed to make blogging easy for users, but dasBlog uses XML files to store recent entries and .Text uses SQL Server. dasBlog is more portable and easier to host; however, .Text can provide blogging for many users once set up, and dasBlog works for one user per installation.

As this example implies, all the decisions you make are trade-offs—one requirement against another. You're inevitably forced to make financial decisions based on your time and their budget, and to balance the issues of performance, scalability, maintainability, and availability based on their requirements and the tools you're using. Your choice of database, if you have one, reflects that. The fol-lowing is a list of some of the factors that may influence your decision:

Price: MSDE is free to download, Access is part of Microsoft Office, and SQL Server varies in price from expensive to very expensive depending on which version you want to use. Oracle does likewise. MySQL is free to download, but phone support costs if you don't fancy using newsgroups.

Performance: Access (*.mdb) files are easy to create and use but are slow compared to actual database servers such as SQL Server or MySQL. MySQL's emphasis is on fast data retrieval, but SQL Server and Oracle both beat it for performance at enterprise levels.

Data provider: Where possible, use a database with its own data provider rather than using the generic OLE DB or ODBC data providers supplied by

Microsoft. For example, ByteFX is currently working on a native data provider for MySQL. When it's finished, use that rather than the ODBC provider you're stuck with at the moment.

Ease of use: All databases work fine with .NET, but some are easier to administer than others, as you've seen. For example, SQL Server and Oracle both have a complete set of administrative tools to work with, but the administrative tools for MySQL aren't out of beta yet (unless you're using PHP). Further, the MSDE Administrator tool is sadly lacking in some features. Similarly, how easy is it to migrate a database across to a new installation or even a new version of the database?

Functionality: Relational databases all have the same core functionality because they're all built according to the 12 rules of relational database design originated back in the late 1970s. What you need to look for are the extensions to the core that the database vendor has decided to add that may help you in building your application. Does it handle XML, transactions, and stored procedures? What extensions to the SQL standard does it support? How does its error handling work? What about user roles, security, and backup tools? You need to establish what functionality you need out of the database and shop around for the one that does it best.

Support: Last but not least, how well is this database supported by the vendor should something go wrong and you have no choice but to ask for help? Newsgroups and FAQs are all very well, but phoning technical support is sometimes the only solution.

The Right Web Server

It may seem like a no-brainer that you have to use Microsoft's Internet Information Services (IIS) as the Web server for your application, but that's not quite accurate. Apache (http://httpd.apache.org) is by far a more popular Web server than IIS and more efficient, too. It can also host ASP and ASP.NET applications thanks to the efforts of Covalent (http://www.covalent.com) and the open-source Mono project (http://www.go-mono.com), both of which provide an ASP.NET extension for your troubles.

The Right Development Tools

You've used the free Web Matrix editor for all the ASP.NET development work in this book thus far. It's a perfectly acceptable tool, works particularly well with C#

and VB .NET, and is built by the ASP.NET team as a free alternative for developers who can't afford Visual Studio .NET. However, it's not the only code editor available, and maybe it hasn't floated your boat so far, particularly if you've come to ASP.NET development with an open-source or Java background. Therefore, the following are some alternatives:

- Emacs (http://www.gnu.org/software/emacs/windows/ntemacs.html) and Vim (http://www.vim.org/) both have bolt-on modules that give you C# development modes you can use to create ASP.NET pages. Indeed, a whole host of open-source .NET tools are available for use; pick up a copy of *Open Source .NET Development* by Brian Nantz (Addison-Wesley, 2004) for more information.

- Java fans will be pleased to know that the Eclipse integrated development environment (IDE) (http://www.eclipse.org/) supports XML and ASP.NET as well as Java.

- Macromedia fans should note that Dreamweaver MX and Dreamweaver MX 2004 (http://www.macromedia.com/software/dreamweaver/) both support building ASP.NET sites.

- Microsoft's Visual Studio .NET (http://msdn.microsoft.com/vstudio/) of course supports ASP.NET development.

If you're new to programming and aren't used to any development tool yet, stick with Web Matrix for the time being and download evaluation copies of a few others. Bluntly put, Visual Studio .NET has by far the best support for .NET development of all these tools, with features such as the class browser, integrated data explorer, and IntelliSense making things a lot easier than they may otherwise be, but it's still your choice.

One gotcha about Visual Studio .NET, though, is that the standard editions of this product (marketed as Visual C# .NET Standard Edition and Visual Basic .NET Standard Edition) are missing some handy features that the Professional and Enterprise Editions, and in one case Web Matrix, contain. Users of the Standard Edition, for example, can't compile classes into DLLs, administer databases, or create stored procedures from their data window. Now admittedly, you can do these things outside Visual Studio .NET, too, but if you're planning on doing these things and can't afford the Professional Edition of the product, it may not be a bad idea to check out the other development tools before settling on the Standard Edition of Visual Studio .NET.

Design

As Web developers, you may tend to regard Web sites as groups of pages. However, it's far wiser to approach them as traditional applications. Indeed, Web applications are the en vogue thing (as if you didn't know). Bearing this in mind then, it's safe to say that ASP.NET sites are subject to the following usual tenets of software engineering:

- A software application, be it Web-based, desktop-based, or even designed for a mobile platform, is implemented by dividing the tasks it must perform into smaller and smaller tasks until they can't be reduced any further. These atomic tasks are represented as a line of code in the application, and where atomic tasks are often called in the same sequence, they're grouped into methods.

- A software application of any size is subject to bugs and the want to upgrade it from the client. Dividing the functionality of an application into classes and namespaces that can be debugged and upgraded individually lessens the downtime for the application as a whole. It also has the added bonus that because several people can work on individual classes and namespaces simultaneously as long as the public application programming interfaces (APIs) are as agreed, development time will be quicker.

The purpose of analyzing the requirements for an application is to identify the common tasks it'll execute, how well they should execute, and the various ways in which you can segregate its functionality into manageable chunks—what you'll implement as namespaces and classes. In the design phase, your goal is to translate those requirements into a class and namespace structure and a supporting database design that will mean your application works efficiently and can be easily maintained. You can then use the metrics you created for the site to check that the various chunks of the application work as well as required.

You can and should split this phase of development into two parts: designing the table structure for the database that underlies the application and then designing its namespace and class structure.

Database Design

Like every other subject in this chapter, we could write a whole book on just this subject. Many people make a very good living from just designing and administering databases, but the salient points are all here. Database design in general is all about efficiency. If you can correctly identify and model the various objects and events this application needs to keep details on, the application will be easier to write, it will run faster because fewer queries need to be made to the database, it will be easier to maintain and upgrade because the SQL will be easier to work with, and it will be easier to add new tables into the database when needed.

At this basic level, you're most concerned with three issues: modeling the application's data correctly, speeding up access to the data, and strengthening the database.

Modeling Data Correctly

As you learned in Chapter 2, a lot of good database design is simply a result of paying attention to the details. However, it all bears repeating here.

Your core job at this stage is to correctly identify the individual types of objects and events you'll model in the database underlying your application. For example, in a blogging application, you'd need to model messages, users, and comments. In the Hypertext Markup Language (HTML) reference case study, you need to provide tables for HTML elements, attributes, events, browsers, and standards. Don't forget the following simple tips toward this end:

- Each table in the database should contain details about one object or event. Don't try to match up two objects that are roughly the same—for example, buildings and companies. The ploy may work at first, but it'll require you to split them later when the application is up and running, which would mean you'd need to take the application offline while this was being done.

- Pay attention to the name of the tables and fields as they're conceived. Using plurals and words such as *or* and *and* could indicate that a field needs to be split into its own table that has a one-to-many or many-to-many relationship with the original. Try to make every field and table name unique.

Of course, you have a more formal way to achieve a streamlined database design, called *normalization*, that you'll look at next.

Normalization

The basic rules of normalization have been around since 1972. They've been tweaked and added to since then, but the same goal remains: to improve the performance of a database by eliminating duplicate data and therefore the chance of any errors occurring when information is added, updated, or deleted. A normalized database will also make searching easier because it won't have to deal with redundant copies of data. Take, for example, the sample database. We chose to include the main topic for each book as text inside each row in the Book database, but as you saw in Chapters 7 and 8, this made some aspects of working with this particular field quite troublesome. It's also a waste of time and a source of potential errors to enter the main topic by hand for each book. Why not just enter the main topics once and then refer to which one of them each book belongs to? This would also remove the possibility of a user misspelling a topic name (C~, c#, or csharp perhaps?). This would make accurate searches trickier. By using normalization, you identify duplicate data that could be stored in separate tables.

Using normalization to improve the design of a database is a three-step process. The result of each step is known as a *normal form*. There are extra steps beyond the first three, but these are rarely used in the real world; we'll stick to the first three in this chapter.

First Normal Form

The goal of the first normal form is to eliminate repeating groups of data in a table. You create a separate table for each related set of data and identify each table with a primary key.

> **NOTE** *A relation is in first normal form (1NF) if and only if all underlying simple domains contain only atomic values.*

In more practical terms, a database table is in 1NF only if all values in all fields can't be split any further into separate fields—in other words, they're *atomic*. Furthermore, atomic values shouldn't be repeated over various fields. For example, Figure 11-1 shows the Book table as it was originally.

ID	Title_Publisher	BookAuthors	BookMainTopic
1	Starting Up C# (Apress)	Dan Maharry, Damien Foggon	C#
. . .			

Figure 11-1. The Book table not in 1NF

Now this isn't in 1NF for a number of reasons, but the most obvious is that Title_Publisher contains two pieces of information that should be split into two separate fields—the title of the book and its publisher. The BookAuthors field also contains more than one piece of information depending on how many authors are associated with a book. To obey the first half of the 1NF rule then, the table should look like Figure 11-2.

ID	Publisher	Title	Author1	Author2	MainTopic
1	Apress	Starting Up C#	Dan Maharry	Damien Foggon	C#
. . .					

Figure 11-2. Splitting atomic values

The only problem is that this table still isn't in 1NF because the second half of the rule states that atomic values shouldn't be repeated over more than a field in the same table. The two columns, Author1 and Author2, violate this, so Figure 11-3 shows another try at splitting them into two tables.

Table Name: Book

ID	Publisher	Title	MainTopic
1	Apress	Starting Up C#	C#
. . .			

Table Name: Author

ID	BookID	BookName	AuthorName
1	1	Starting Up C#	Dan Maharry
2	1	Starting Up C#	Damien Foggon
. . .			

Figure 11-3. 1NF achieved

By creating the Author table, you now have an AuthorName field containing individual author names. Both tables are in 1NF. Note how the tips for accurately naming fields would help in identifying whether a table is in 1NF. A pluralized name indicates that perhaps the field should be separated from the table. Any sign of an *or* or an *and* would indicate that a field may be better as two or more.

Second Normal Form

The second step in the normalization process seeks to identify relationships between entities in a database and to model them correctly.

> **NOTE** *A relation is in second normal form (2NF) if and only if it's in 1NF and every nonkey attribute is fully dependent on the primary key.*

The first part of this definition is a given. You shouldn't be moving onto 2NF if you haven't made your database design 1NF already. The second part of the definition warrants attention, however. In plainer English, if a field isn't uniquely related to the primary key in a table, it should be elsewhere.

Let's take a look at the two tables, which are both in 1NF. The primary key for the Book table is the ID of the book, so you need to establish which of the values for the three other fields are linked directly to that ID. The answer is only the BookName field; both the name of the book's publisher and its main topic aren't dependent on the book having a certain ID. As you've seen, many books may have the same publisher or main topic, so to satisfy 2NF, you'll have to split them into a different table. Neither field relies on the other either, so you'll need to create one table each for them (see Figure 11-4).

Table Name: Book

ID	Publisher	Title	MainTopic
1	1	Starting Up C#	1
. . .			

Table Name: Publisher

ID	Name
1	Apress
. . .	

Table Name: Topics

ID	Name
1	C#
. . .	

Figure 11-4. Putting the Book table in 2NF

Like the Book table, the Author table isn't in 2NF. The AuthorName field is fully dependent on the ID field, which is the primary key, but the BookID and BookName fields aren't—the author Dan Maharry will not only write books called *Starting Up C#*, for example. You need to introduce a third table to express the many-to-many relationship between authors and books and thus satisfy 2NF (see Figure 11-5).

Table Name: Author

ID	AuthorName
1	Dan Maharry
2	Damien Foggon
. . .	

Table Name: Author_Book

BookID	AuthorID
1	1
1	2
. . .	

Figure 11-5. Putting the Author table in 2NF

The Author table is now in 2NF because the AuthorName is dependent on the AuthorID field, and the Author_Book table is in 2NF because it has a compound key comprising both fields. If you wanted to keep a record, say, of how much an author was paid for a given book, the rules of normalization would say that this payment would be recorded in the Author_Book table.

Third Normal Form

The third and final step looks specifically at tables with compound primary keys.

> **NOTE** *A relation is in third normal form (3NF) if and only if it's in 2NF and every nonkey attribute is nontransitively dependent on the primary key.*

In plain English, this rule basically says that a field in a table must depend on all the elements in a primary key. So if a table has a simple primary key (that is, the primary key is only one field) and is in 2NF, it's also in 3NF. If a table has a compound primary key, however, you'll need to take a closer look. For example, what if the Author_Book table had two more fields, as in Figure 11-6?

Table Name: Author_Book

BookID	AuthorID	Royalty	ISBN
1	1	5%	1590591234
1	2	5%	1590591234
. . .			

Figure 11-6. Removing the ISBN field will leave this table in 3NF.

Both the Royalty and the ISBN fields are dependent on the primary key in this table, so it's still in 2NF, but whereas the Royalty field depends on both BookID and AuthorID fields for context, the ISBN field relies only on the BookID field. This partial dependence is also referred to as *transitive dependence*, which means the table isn't in 3NF. The ISBN field should be moved to the Book table for the whole database to now be in 3NF.

Normalizing a database will make it faster to sort and search through by reducing the chance of redundant data being added to/maintained by the database. In particular, the database will need fewer indexes, which will improve the performance of INSERT, UPDATE, and DELETE statements. Note, however, that normalization can increase the complexity of joins required to retrieve the data.

This, in some cases, may hinder performance. Sometimes, databases are denormalized to reduce the complexity of joins and to get quicker query response times (one of the reasons why fourth and fifth normal forms aren't often used). As always, you have to strike a balance between flexibility and speed. This is the first of such juggling acts you'll encounter as you implement the application.

Completing the Model

Normalization is a great tool for laying the groundwork in your database design, but just because your tables are all in 3NF doesn't mean you've modeled the data the best you can for the application. As noted, you may even want to denormalize a few things to get the best performance from the database. The following are a few more tasks to complete before you can move on:

- .NET doesn't care how tables and fields are named as long as they're identified unambiguously in SQL statements. For your own benefit then, you should try to name them all sensibly and uniquely as you did in the sample database. You only have to look at the number of fields that could be called ID in this example to see that it's always a good idea to give them all unique names so you don't get confused as you write your code.

- You've identified the various tables in the database and the relationships they have between each other, but when you're setting up the foreign key constraints, you need to consider each time how a child table should be affected when a row in the parent table is created, updated, and deleted. Are the database's defaults fine, or should the implications cascade down into the child table?

- You've identified the various fields in each table of the database, but what type should they be and what length? Should ID fields be automatically generated integers or globally unique identifiers (GUIDs)? How long should each string be? Should the database store the image or just the image's filename?

- Will it be of any benefit to you to create distinct views over the database for querying? It does mean that you can keep your SQL queries simple but at what cost? Each time a view is queried, the statement to create that view must first be queried so there are actually two statements being used here for the sake of one.

With these questions answered (and you hope no changes in the requirements from the client), you can start to determine how to speed up database access and secure them against both the malevolent and the stupid.

Database Speed and Strength

It may seem a little strange to consider performance issues before any code has been written, but you know from Chapter 2 that adding indexes and, in particular, compound indexes, will speed up searches across the table, especially if they are across the table's primary key. If you can identify at this point the fields most likely to be searched across in the database and apply indexes there as well, you'll be laughing.

Similarly at this point, you may want to start identifying common tasks that will often be performed by the database. For example, will the application often make a search for books? If so, you can create *stored procedures* for these common queries, which will also increase the speed of the database, as you saw in Chapter 9.

You can also start to include measures to handle the deeds of both malicious and naïve users. In the requirements list, we asked for a list of user roles, each of which had a different set of permissions for the database. At this point, you can add the user accounts, user groups, and roles to your design, so you have a reference for any class design behavior you may need to factor in based on whom is using the site.

Last but not least, you can start thinking about whether your interactions with the database should be modeled as transactions. This would make sure that every update either completely works or completely fails, which means that the data in the database will be consistent at all times. Of course, there's always a drawback, and this is no exception. By encapsulating your database operations in transactions, you use more database resources, and you may notice a drop in speed because a table is locked while being accessed by a transaction and because no data can be returned from that table until the transaction is finished and the lock removed.

Application Design

While design of any kind is somewhat in the eye of the beholder and subject to a person's own preference for doing things a certain way, it's good to know that database designs won't vary that much between architects given the same list of requirements. The design of an application's class structure, on the other hand, can be much more divergent.

Not only must you marry functionality to Web page, you must also see that the classes you design reflect the database design you've just achieved and obey the second software tenet. For those of you who missed it earlier, this means that to make it as quick to implement, easy to debug and maintain, and straightforward to upgrade as possible, you need to divide the tasks of the application in clearly defined sections that you can then map to namespaces and classes. So, for example, you can split such easy-to-define sections of a Web site as forums, polls, shopping carts, product browsing, and so on, but it isn't so obvious how to split potential namespaces into individual classes.

Fortunately, a great deal of practice and trial and error by a great many people has taught us that you can think of an application (or a piece of one) as split across several tiers and layers.

Defining the Tiers

Splitting the functionality of the site into separate modules—polls, forums, carts, newsletters, and so on—means that you can add new modules to the site at any time and that individual modules can be shut down for maintenance without affecting the rest of the site. To make things easier, you can split the tasks each module performs into the following three tiers:

Data access tier: Code in the data access tier deals solely with sending commands to and retrieving data from the database, checking that the current user has permissions, and handling errors coming back from the database as it goes along. If code in either of the two other tiers needs to interact with the database, it must do so through the data access tier.

Presentation tier: Code in the presentation tier deals exclusively with the application's user experience and the generation of pages when requested. It will use the business rules and data access tiers to retrieve the content for a page and then use its own code to assemble it on the page. No code from the business rules or data access tier should directly alter the user interface of the application.

Business rules tier: Finally, the business rules tier is where the majority of the work happens. Here is where the application will determine how to react to a user's request, log the request for future reference, start the process of creating a new page by requesting information from the data access layer, and then interpret that new data into something a user will be able to understand.

For example, when a user requests the home page of a site, the business rules tier may take care of such tasks as trying to identify the user by requesting a cookie, retrieving user site preferences, determining what's new on the site since the user last came by, and telling the presentation tier how to react accordingly.

Splitting a code module into tiers and then into classes within those tiers gives you great flexibility. Suppose you were writing an e-commerce cart module and were told to provide front ends for both Web and mobile users. You could write separate classes for the module's presentation tier, one for browsers and one for mobile devices; they would both interface with the business rules tier in the same way, but each would optimize the presentation of content for their respective device. In the same way, you could write individual modules for the different ways to pay for the items in the shopping cart. To the users, this would be invisible, but to the owners of the e-commerce store, this would be invaluable. Should they choose to barter Visa transactions with a different merchant bank, for example, you could take down and revise just the Visa class in the e-commerce module leaving the cash, Mastercard, and so on, modules up and running. Compare this against a situation where all transactions are run through a single class or as a single monolithic piece of code. To update the Visa functions, you'd have to take down the whole shopping cart for the work to take place. Likewise, you could write new classes for working against a new database rather than rewriting the old ones.

As long as the public interface to each parallel class remains the same (it may expand to include new public calls, too) so you don't have to worry about other classes calling functions that no longer exist, you could work with as many different databases, credit cards, banks, and interfaces as you like. Good application design gives you this kind of flexibility, and separating an application into these three tiers is the first step along the way to achieving it.

NOTE *Depending on how complex your site or a module for your site is, its code may split logically into only one or two tiers. Don't worry about this and go searching for the third tier. Three is just the standard number; there are always exceptions to the rule.*

Defining the Structure

Now that you understand how an application may be split into data, business rules, and presentation tiers, a question arises. Say you're building a community Web site and have identified a number of modules you'll eventually want to add to it (see Figure 11-7).

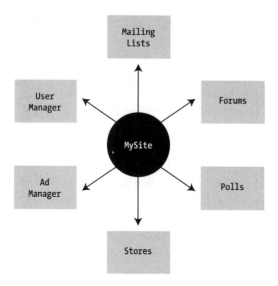

Figure 11-7. A site and its modules, but how to divide it?

What translates into a namespace and the classes inside it? Do you have three namespaces for each tier of the application and a class for each relevant section of forums, polls, and so on, inside those namespaces? Or are the individual modules modeled better as namespaces with the tiers split inside them into classes? The latter. Taking the long view, if you design a uniform class structure and API for working with the core of the application for each—you get a nice plug-in API from which it's easy to add or remove functionality. If you keep the core of the site separate, you can come up with a namespace structure looking something like Figure 11-8.

Depending on how detailed your brief is/how complex the application is, you may want to encapsulate the three tiers within classes rather than namespaces. Note that you'll need to tailor the creation of namespaces to the functionality of the module rather than arbitrarily creating presentation, business rule, and data access namespaces and attempting to wedge all functionality into those. In Figure 11-8, for example, the UserManager module won't return any on-screen information per se, so it won't need a presentation tier. Meanwhile, the NewsManager acquires an additional namespace for configuration to keep track of news feeds being used. In the same way, a shopping cart may have a separate namespace for negotiating sales with merchant banks with each bank being dealt with in a separate class.

With any luck, the requirements list you've already procured will give you plenty of clues as to what the classes within each namespace will encompass, but if not, take the opportunity to go back to the client and ask for more details on any functionality that isn't clear and see if it can make the class structure clearer.

Remember that some classes will reflect the objects and events you're modeling in the database, and some will simply be utility classes, which may not be immediately foreseeable. Work through the use cases for each module in turn. Understand which pieces of data they will require (create, alter, and delete) and the way in which the sequence of events within them will flow. It'd be nice to say that every enumeration and class will come forth in a Zen-like way from the pattern of the application, but they won't initially. Just don't get frustrated when this happens. You can't identify every single facet of the application design until you've implemented and looked at it again in hindsight. That's why you prototype and post-mortem your projects.

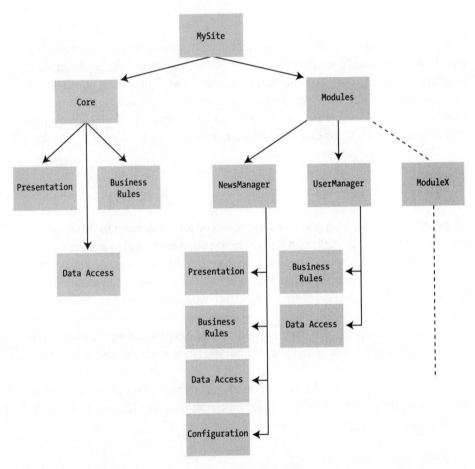

Figure 11-8. A clean namespace structure for MySite

Like every subject in this chapter, good class design is a topic that warrants its own book. Good ones in this case are siblings: the *C# Class Design Handbook* (Apress, 2003) and the *Visual Basic .NET Class Design Handbook* (Apress, 2003). Using techniques such as design patterns to drill down into individual classes also apply at this stage, but although handy, a lot of this step comes down to your own experience and anyone else's experience you can lean on. Remember that however you choose to design (and implement) your application, the whole point of breaking it up into components is to give it a flexible, efficient structure that's easy to program and extend.

Implementation

Lest we forget that this book is aimed squarely at introducing you to developing pages using a database to supply the content, the following sections on implementing your design will be restricted to the basic issues of writing code related to working with the database. How you choose to present information on a page isn't the issue here and neither are any business rules you may be adding according to requirements. You'll focus on data-tier-related issues.

Prototyping

We noted earlier that it's a good idea to prototype an application to prove and refine an initial design. Although it won't help you identify and deal with every problem that seemed reasonable on paper but that doesn't translate across into code, it will catch many. It also has the added advantage of giving you something to show your clients and get their feedback on, which can't be a bad thing. Inevitably, on seeing even the first iteration of their commission, customers often have opinions and questions that may affect the final product, so it's worth building a prototype at least once to validate your design and pacify the client, if nothing else.

Exactly how much detail you include in a prototype is up to you, but from a data access point of view, you definitely want to validate the following pieces of the design:

- The application core

- The database design

- The various SQL statements to the database that are most likely to be made and the classes you'll create to wrap these statements

Security always seems to get put aside in favor of the noticeable functionality of the site, but try to prototype the user registration and log on to make sure that each user role has the correct set of permissions for access to the database. You could even use the metrics you've designed previously to test the prototype and see how far away you are from your performance goals.

Stored Procedures

When you send a SQL query to a database, the database checks that its syntax is correct and then compiles it, making sure that the tables, fields, constraints, and so on that it references actually exist. Finally, it figures out how best to execute the query and then does it. This whole process is repeated for each new query. Even with a small number of concurrent users, it's not difficult to spot how those four steps can quickly mount up and burden the database. Fortunately, there's a solution.

Most relational database management systems (RDBMSs) now offer the ability to create and save stored procedures. As you learned in Chapter 9, a stored procedure is a SQL statement precompiled and saved on the server so that rather than the database working through four steps, the stored procedure requires only one. It's not hard to see then that using stored procedures offers you the promise of a significant performance increase if you use them. Like normalization, not everything works better as a stored procedure, though. There's a small overhead associated with actually retrieving and then executing the stored procedure to the point where simple SQL queries (for example, selecting data from a single table) may actually do better to come from the code directly. In general, though, stored procedures are a good thing to use if the database server supports them.

> **NOTE** *Note that MySQL 4.0.x doesn't support stored procedures. However, the unstable 4.1.x and 5.0.x versions do.*

Stored procedures also give you an extra level of flexibility when it comes to retrieving data. When you get to the inevitable decision of whether to use DataSets or DataReaders to build your pages, you can also use a stored procedure's output parameters to retrieve single values straight into a variable without the need for either. They also give you a more structured way to introduce error handling and transactions into a SQL statement. By using SQL aggregate functions, you can use stored procedures to perform quite a few calculations that you may have thought only .NET could do for you.

Code Issues

Designing an application well will help a project along so far, but it's making informed implementation decisions on the spot based on the design and your experience that really count. The following are some of the most common data-related issues that will crop up:

Choosing a DataReader or DataSet: We've spent a good 100 pages of this book getting you to the point where you can answer this question with a reasonably informed mind. In fact, it will probably crop up in every class in your application's data access tier. We could spend another ten pages recapping what you saw earlier, but rather than that, we'll proffer here a page from the .NET SDK documentation that raises an additional set of issues to inform this choice further. Browse to `ms-help://MS.NETFrameworkSDKv1.1/cpguidenf/html/cpconDecidingOnDataAccessStrategy.htm`, read Chapters 6, 7, and 8 again, and make the choice.

Choosing code beside or code behind: The pages you've built in this book have used Web Matrix to build code-beside pages. That is, the `.aspx` pages have included the various event handlers and classes you've written inside `<script>` elements in the HTML of the page. An alternative to this approach, and one really supported only by Visual Studio .NET, is to split the C# code from the HTML altogether. This approach makes both code and HTML more readable, and it also means that you can alter the layout of a page without needing to recompile it. However, it also introduces more potential for problems. Interestingly enough, Microsoft's alpha release of Visual Studio 2005 hints that it's leaving code behind, well, behind.

Using the right data provider: It sounds obvious, but you do need to consider the actual data provider you use in your code. Take, for example, mySQL. It has a solid, stable ODBC connector, and you can take advantage of that using the ODBC data provider, which is also stable. However, is this the best solution (as opposed to the best stable solution)? ByteFX is writing a native .NET data provider for the database, but it's still in beta. You could also use the OLE DB for ODBC data provider, which is faster than ODBC itself.

Modeling data better in the database: If speed is of the essence, then the amount of data retrieved from a database is surely one of the key factors in keeping the speed up, so finding ways of packing information into smaller pieces is always handy. Reducing the maximum length of a field is always a risk, but take the case of an ISBN. This is a ten-digit string consisting of nine integers and a tenth-check digit that's either another integer or an X. The check digit is always calculated in the same way, so do you store the ISBN as a ten-character string that's held by 10*8 bits = 80 bits or as a nine-digit integer that can be held comfortably in 32 bits and create the check digit programmatically when required?

Keeping data secure: It's easier to write code that does the job required and then add security measures after the fact, but coding securely is an art in itself; in fact, it's something you should always try to do. You've already seen some good practices in earlier chapters. Hide your database connection strings in `web.config` or an application variable to keep them from prying eyes. Try not to use the query string for values being sent to and from the database. Work with multiple SQL server users rather than just one. If using a DataReader, close it with `Close()` as quickly as possible.

Of course, you'll have to make many more trade-offs and decisions as you implement your design, but rather than tread in places that have been well covered by books before, we'll now carry on into the realms of testing and debugging your application. Chapters 12 and 13 discuss many more implementation issues with the examples in the case studies.

Testing and Debugging

Nothing is more annoying than installing a new application and seeing a dialog box pop up as you're doing some work to inform you that an error has occurred and that the application will now shut down. You've now lost all the work you were doing and have to drive to casualty after kicking the desk in frustration (well, someone we know did anyway). If the application had been debugged more thoroughly, that may not have happened.

This phase of the software life cycle is certainly as crucial as the others, yet it's usually written about less because it's almost impossible to describe how to debug specific errors; further, writing for the generic case isn't very helpful. However, without going into the debugging process itself, you can try to factor a handful of useful techniques into your development process.

> **TIP** *For a complete guide to .NET debugging strategies, try* Debugging Strategies for .NET Developers *(Apress, 2003) or (if you can find it)* Visual Basic .NET Debugging Handbook *(Wrox Press, 2002). The latter is out of print but packed with gems of information.*

Unit Testing

As mentioned earlier, one of the benefits of writing code as individual modules is that you can write them in parallel. It goes further than that. You can debug and test them individually as well. Back in the analysis phase of the software life cycle, you devised a set of benchmarks and use cases that could measure the performance of your application as it was built. By isolating the relevant user scenarios and benchmarks and writing some code (a *test harness*) that reflect the metrics you also designed to test the application against those benchmarks, you can prove the utility of this module before you move onto the next. This process is known as *unit testing*.

One of the more frustrating aspects of this process is that as requirements change and targets are realigned, modules that you've already written and tested will need to be altered and retested. Indeed, this cycle of rebuild and retest is quite short, so a few utilities now allow you to automate the unit testing process. The best of these is nUnit (http://www.nUnit.org).

nUnit is the standard unit testing framework for .NET applications and was itself written in C#. By itself, nUnit comes with a choice of rudimentary command-line interface or rudimentary graphical interface, which do the job albeit in a not particularly attractive way. The nUnit site has a great tutorial on installing it (http://www.nunit.org/getStarted.html) and writing test harnesses for your code (http://www.nunit.org/files/QuickStart.doc), so we won't cover them here. But we'll issue a warning: nUnit on its own is great for testing business rules and data access code, but it needs help to test ASP.NET pages because they can't be "run" inside the nUnit framework. In this case, you need to use nUnitASP (http://nunitasp.sourceforge.net/download.html), which essentially hooks into the ASP.NET worker process and gives nUnit a view of the intrinsic objects (Context, Response, Request, and so on) to use. You can find a great introduction to using nUnitASP at http://www.theserverside.net/articles/showarticle.tss?id=TestingASP.

> **TIP** *nUnit is a free, stand-alone application that's great if you continue to use Web Matrix or some other free product. If you use Visual Studio .NET, however, you'll be pleased to note that you can run nUnit as an add-in, using TestRunner for Visual Studio .NET (*http://www.mailframe.net/Products/TestRunner.htm*). This is also free.*

Don't forget that unit testing applies to only single modules, but you need to account for the way modules interact with each other, as well. Do they successfully share session and user information, for instance? If one module makes a call to another, is that call being made for the purpose the method was originally intended, or is it being forced into the engine of another car? If the latter is the case, you may want to investigate why this is being done and how better to achieve the desired results before continuing.

> **NOTE** *The .NET 2.0 version of Visual Studio .NET will include its own unit testing suite under the banner of* Visual Studio 2005 Team System *at the time of this writing. For more information, refer to* `http://msdn.microsoft.com/vstudio/teamsystem/tester/default.aspx`.

Measuring Performance

As is the case with most development, the strategies you use to measure the performance of your Web site are formed by the experience you've had using different techniques in previous jobs and whether they worked for you. You can then define the target metrics for an application and the tests you know will be able to prove that those benchmarks have been achieved. But where to begin? What methods can you use to stress test your application and retrieve results? Can you continue to work on your site without buying an IDE? Of course you can. Microsoft even tells you how.

Refer to the ASP.NET performance page at `http://msdn.microsoft.com/asp.net/using/understanding/perf/default.aspx`. This page links to many articles, each covering a different aspect of performance you may not have considered and the various ways to measure and improve it. These articles cover this topic far more completely and succinctly than this chapter could do. In particular, look first at the articles entitled "Performance Monitoring and When to Alert Administrators," "MyTracer Monitors and Traces ASP.NET Applications," and "Real-World Load Testing Tips." For a great resource on testing and improving the performance of a database, look no further than `http://www.sql-server-performance.com`. It focuses specifically on SQL Server (and therefore MSDE), but a lot of the knowledge therein is applicable to any other database. A good place to start reading is the basics page at `http://www.sql-server-performance.com/performance_introduction.asp`.

You can also find several good books that cover performance issues and testing. Try *Performance Tuning and Optimizing ASP.NET Applications* by Hasan and Tu (Apress, 2003) and *Test-Driven Development in Microsoft .NET* by Newkirk and Vorontsov (Microsoft Press, 2004).

Summary

In this chapter, you looked at some of the issues you have to face each time you start a new project. Working with a client on the specifications can be fruitless if you haven't got a specific agenda. The more information you have, the more sympathetic your design can be to the resources you have available and the tasks you're trying to achieve. You can use the three-tier design to make your application a more flexible and easily maintainable design. You can iron out more wrinkles in both design and specifications by building prototypes to prove the concept and showing those to the client.

When it comes to implementing the design, you need to keep in mind the good practices you've learned in the first half of this book and apply them evenly to improve security and performance. In the rest of this book, you'll look in more depth at some of the implementation issues in this chapter with a case study that shows some of this in action.

CHAPTER 12

The Case Study, Part I

So FAR IN THIS BOOK we've covered many details of building data-aware Web pages. You've seen all these details through quite small and relatively simple examples. In this and the following chapter, you'll use what you've learned and build a more complete application—the BAND HTML Reference.

In this chapter you'll start your look at the BAND HTML Reference by first looking at the complete application and seeing the pertinent parts of the site. We won't go into detail about every page of the application, but we'll present the important pages.

Once you have an understanding of the overall BAND HTML Reference, you'll then learn how to design the application.

The first topic you'll look at is modeling the database you need. Before you even open Web Matrix and create the first line of code, the database design should be complete—if it isn't, you can almost guarantee that there will be a field or relationship you've missed that will require major rewrites of the code that you've already written.

When designing the database, you'll start by looking at the data you need to model—the elements that make up Hypertext Markup Language (HTML). In Chapter 11 you looked at the process of normalization, and you saw how the first normal form (1NF), second normal form (2NF), and third normal form (3NF) rules modify the structure you have and lead you from the initial definition of the data to a database structure that has separate tables and relationships that correctly model the data you require.

You'll then take a moment to build the database you'll need. Rather than building each table manually as in Chapter 2, we'll provide a database script that will allow you to construct the database far more quickly. Although we've designed the entire database, the script will build only the parts of the database you require—you won't create every table and relationship, only those you need to build the examples.

The final thing you'll do in this chapter is build a data access tier and, in particular, a DataAccess class that allows you to abstract the code for accessing the database away from the page developer. Although in the previous chapter you saw that there can be three tiers in the application design, for the BAND HTML Reference you have only two—the data access tier and a combined presentation and business rules tier. Not every application needs to have three tiers separated, and as this is a simple application, having separate presentation and business rules tiers would make the application unnecessarily complex.

We'll then use this DataAccess class to show how easy it is to access the database. You can build data-driven Web pages without worrying whether you've created the correct Connection and Command objects.

In Chapter 13, you'll then build on the foundation you've created and look at error handling, stored procedures, controlling user access, and transactions.

> **NOTE** *The two chapters dedicated to the BAND HTML Reference can't possibly cover every single page and line of code in the application. Throughout the examples in these two chapters, you'll build a cut-down version of the site that looks at the issues identified previously.*

Introducing the Application

The application you'll look at for this case study is a HTML reference called the BAND HTML Reference. This application allows users to select the HTML element that they're interested in and see information about the element. Figure 12-1 shows the home page of the application.

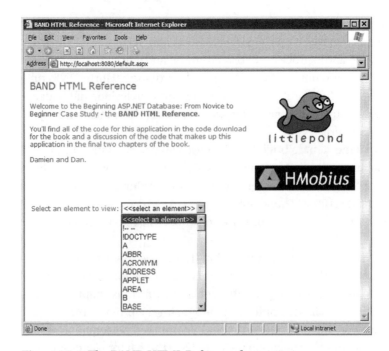

Figure 12-1. The BAND HTML Reference home page

As you can see, the application allows the user to select an element to view more information about the element. The information that can be viewed for an element is as follows:

- Standards that specify the element

- Browsers that support the element

- Attributes that are available on the element and the standards that support the attribute for the element

- Events that are available for the element and the standards that support the event for the element

All of this information is presented on an individual page for the element, as you can see for the DIR element in Figure 12-2.

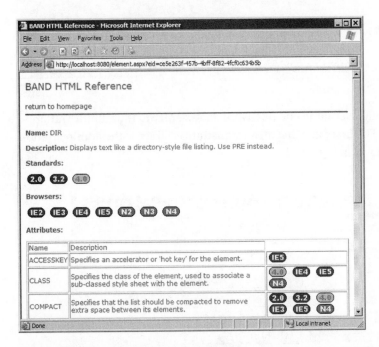

Figure 12-2. The DIR element detail page

The Admin Pages

The majority of the BAND HTML Reference is concerned with maintaining the data within the database. New standards are released and browsers are updated, so the site must allow you to add these new standards and browsers. You must also be able to modify data that's already in the database in case there are any errors.

To access the administration pages, you must provide a username and password; any attempt to access the administration pages will result in the user being asked for a valid username and password, as shown in Figure 12-3.

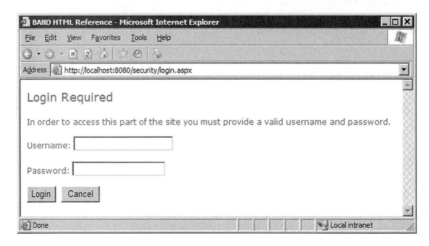

Figure 12-3. The administration pages are password protected.

Entering a valid username and password allows entry to the administration pages of the site. The first page that an administrator will see is the administration home page, as shown in Figure 12-4.

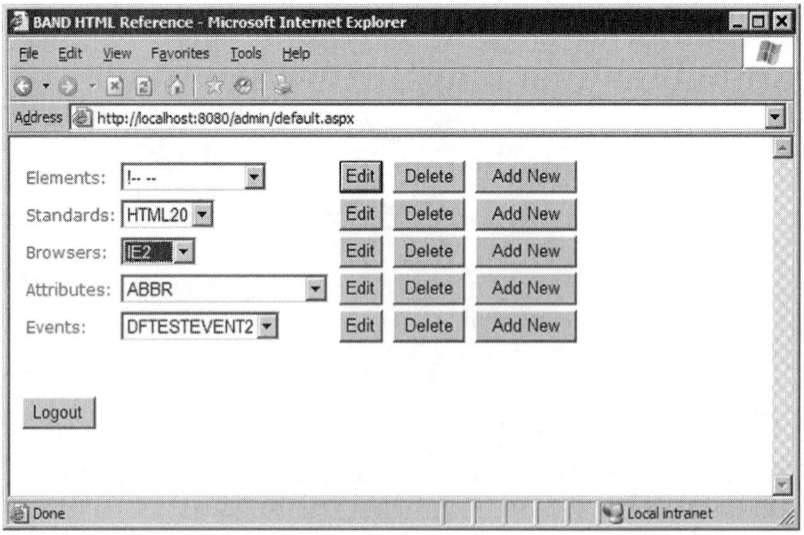

Figure 12-4. The administration home page

From this page you can add, edit, and delete all the different "objects" you need to store in the database.

For standards, browsers, attributes, and events, the information you can enter is limited; you can give them a name and a description. Browsers and standards also have a uniform resource locator (URL) and an image URL, as you can see in Figure 12-5 for browsers.

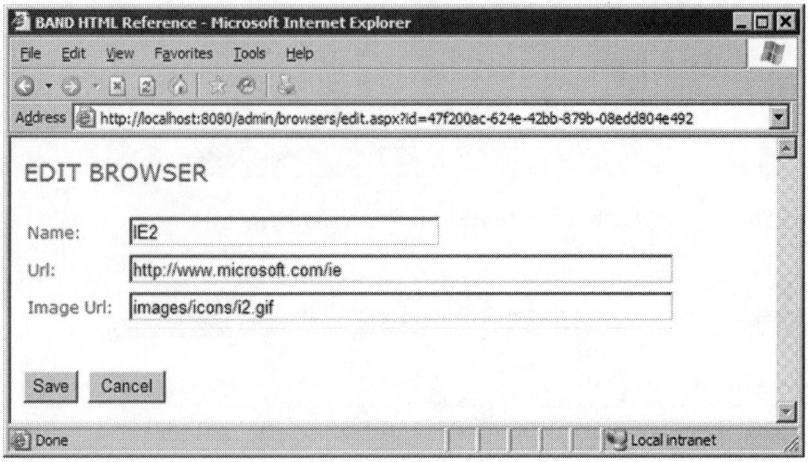

Figure 12-5. Editing a browser

It's the editing of elements where the real power of the application lies. As well as allowing a name and description to be entered, you can specify which standards and browsers support the element as well as the details for the attributes and events the element supports.

This editing is accomplished through a five-step wizard. The first step allows the name and description of the element to be specified in a similar way to browsers, as you saw in Figure 12-5.

The second and third steps of the wizard allow the selection of the different browsers and standards that support the element. Figure 12-6 shows the step for modifying the browser support.

The final two steps of the wizard allow the attributes and events for the element to be specified as well as the standard and browser support. Figure 12-7 shows the step for specifying the attributes.

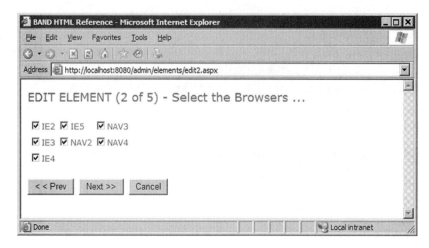

Figure 12-6. Specifying the browsers that support an element

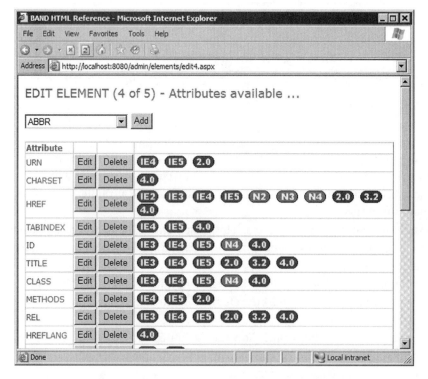

Figure 12-7. Specifying the attributes available for an element

Designing the Database

Before you start writing even a single line of code for the BAND HTML Reference, you need to look at the database for the application. If you start writing the application before you've completely tied down the database design, you're guaranteed to run into problems—there'll be a field or relationship you've missed that will require a rewrite of substantial portions of the code that you've already written.

As you saw in Chapter 11, when designing a database structure, you use several normalization rules to take your initial database design and turn it into an optimum format. As your database experience grows, you'll start applying the normalization rules without knowing you're doing it—they very quickly become second nature. When you're starting out, though, your initial database designs will most likely not be of the optimum format, so you can use the normalization rules to create a more correct database design.

The Initial Design

If you refer to Figure 12-2, you'll see that the main point of the BAND HTML Reference is to allow users to look at HTML elements and see what attributes and events the element supports, the browsers that support the element, and the standards that specify the element.

This can be modeled in the database as a single table, tblElement, that contains everything having to do with the element. If you look at what information is needed for a specific element, such as the DIR element in Figure 12-2, you'd need to store the information shown in Table 12-1. Note that this isn't all the information needed—there are more attributes than the two that are specified here, and the same goes for the events. Listing them all in the table would require an awful lot of space, and showing two still allows us to show why tables need to be normalized.

You can immediately see that this table isn't in 1NF; there are repeating groups of data in the table, and therefore by definition it can't be in 2NF or 3NF. You'll now look at how to move from the initial design shown in Table 12-1 to the normalized final database design.

Table 12-1. The Information Required for the DIR Element

Field Name	Data
ElementDescription	Displays text like a directory-style file listing. Use PRE instead.
ElementName	DIR.
Attributes	CLASS (Internet Explorer 4, Internet Explorer 5, Netscape Navigator 4, HTML 4.0 deprecated). LANGUAGE (Internet Explorer 4, Internet Explorer 5).
Browsers	Internet Explorer 2, Internet Explorer 3, Internet Explorer 4, Internet Explorer 5, Netscape Navigator 2, Netscape Navigator 3, Netscape Navigator 4.
Events	onclick (Internet Explorer 4, Internet Explorer 5, HTML 4.0) onblur (Internet Explorer 5, HTML 4.0)
Standards	HTML 2.0, HTML 3.0, HTML 4.0 (deprecated).

First Normal Form (1NF)

As you'll recall from Chapter 11, a table is in 1NF if, and only if, it contains only atomic values. You can see immediately from Table 12-1 that there are only two atomic values in the table—ElementName and ElementDescription—and separate tables are needed to hold the details that are currently in the Attributes, Browsers, Events, and Standards fields.

A new field could have been added to tblElement to hold each piece of information, but this wouldn't be 1NF because atomic information would be repeated over several columns. Also, there's no guarantee as to the number of columns that are required—an element may be in more than one standard, and the number of standards that it is in depends upon the element.

First normal form requires a different table for the five different entities—elements, attribute, browsers, events, and standards. These tables will be called tblElements, tblAttributes, tblBrowsers, tblEvents, and tblStandards, respectively. Also, each table needs a primary key to identify an individual entry within the table, and for the BAND HTML Reference these are globally unique identifiers (GUIDs).

This primary key is required when you relate the tables together, and its name consists of the table name followed by ID. So, tblElement has a primary key called ElementID, tblBrowser has BrowserID, and so on, for the remaining three tables.

As you can see from Figure 12-8, a few extra fields have also been added to each of the tables.

tblAttribute	
PK	AttributeID
	AttributeName
	AttributeDescription

tblElement	
PK	ElementID
	ElementName
	ElementDescription

tblEvent	
PK	EventID
	EventName
	EventDescription

tblBrowser	
PK	BrowserID
	BrowserName
	BrowserURL

tblStandard	
PK	StandardID
	StandardName
	StandardURL

Figure 12-8. The database tables

Each of the tables also has a name field that's a 32-character varchar, which is used to identify the entity within the application

Three of the tables—tblElement, tblAttribute, and tblEvent—also have a description field that's a 256-character varchar. As you can see from Figure 12-2, you use the description to provide more information to the user.

For tblBrowser and tblStandard, there isn't a description field but a URL field instead. This is again a varchar, but this time it contains up to 128 characters. This field is used to provide a link to the relevant documentation for the standard or browser—for a standard you can use this as a link to the actual specification, and for a browser you can use this to refer to the manufacturer's site for the browser.

One piece of information is still missing from these tables, and that's the details of the icons used to identify the browsers and standards. If you refer to Figure 12-2, you'll see that instead of the name of the browser or standard, an icon identifies them. The way the icon information is stored isn't normalized, so you'll come back and look at this after the database design is completed.

Now that the different entities have been created as five tables in the database, it's time to look at the relationships required for 2NF. With 1NF the relationships between the tables are lost, and 2NF allows these "lost" relationships to be re-created.

Relating the Tables: Second Normal Form (2NF)

As you know, none of the five tables that you've just seen sits alone in a vacuum; from the introduction to the application and the details given in Table 12-1, you saw that you need to model several different relationships. Second normal form seeks to identify the relationships between tables, and you'll look at the relationships here.

The first relationship to model is between Elements and Browsers. From Table 12-1 it may seem that there's a quite simple relationship and a BrowserID can be specified in tblElement so that an Element is supported by a Browser. However, this isn't quite correct—an Element may be supported by many different

Browsers, and this would require multiple columns, one for every possible Browser that supports the Element. And if a new browser is released, a new column would have to be added to tblElement. This would quickly get out of hand.

Modeling the relationship the other way by specifying an ElementID in tblBrowser has the same problem—a Browser supports several different elements, requiring a column for every possible Element that the Browser supports.

This relationship is an example of the many-to-many relationship you saw in Chapter 2—an Element is supported by several different Browsers, and a Browser will support many different Elements. This type of relationship requires a link table to model the relationship correctly.

As you can see in Figure 12-9, a link table, tblDoesBrowserSupportElement, has been added to link tblElement to tblBrowser.

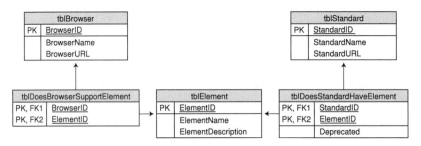

Figure 12-9. Elements, Browsers, and Standards

Not only have we added tblDoesBrowserSupportElement to link tblElement and tblBrowser, we've also related tblElement to tblStandard in the same way. An Element may exist in many different Standards, and a Standard will support many different Elements. This relationship is modeled in tblDoesStandardHaveElement.

The two tables, tblDoesBrowserSupportElement and tblDoesStandardHave-Element, join tblElement to tblBrowser and tblStandard, respectively. The tables have two foreign keys that refer to the two tables that are joined, and these make up a composite primary key.

You'll also see that tblDoesStandardHaveElement has an extra field, Deprecated. This is a boolean field that's used to show that although the Standard does indeed have the Element, its use is being "phased out," so you shouldn't rely on the Element being available in subsequent versions of the standard.

A similar relationship exists for Elements to Attributes—an Element can have many Attributes, and the same Attribute may be available on several different Elements. The same is also true for the relationship between Elements and Events—an Element can have many events, and the same Event may be available on several different Elements.

These, again, are many-to-many relationships and require two new link tables, as shown in Figure 12-10.

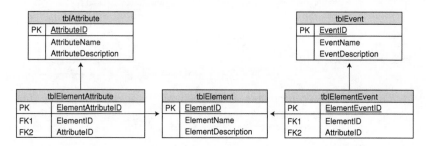

Figure 12-10. Elements, Attributes, and Events

Again, the two new tables, tblElementAttribute and tblElementEvent, are simply used to join tblElement to tblAttribute and tblEvent, respectively. Two foreign keys refer to the two tables that are joined, but this time there's a new field for the primary key.

The primary key, as with all keys in the database, is a GUID. A new primary key is required because the Element-to-Attribute relationship is needed when looking at which Browsers and Standards support using the Attribute with a given Element. A composite primary key, consisting of ElementID and AttributeID, could have been used, but having a new key, ElementAttributeID, makes the database design slightly easier to manage.

This leads nicely into the next relationship that is required—which Browsers and Standards support using an Attribute by an Element. It's easy to say that an Element is available in a given Standard or supported by a particular Browser, but doing the same for Attributes isn't as simple. An Attribute isn't simply supported by a Standard or Browser, because for one Element it may be supported but for another Element it may not.

If you refer to Table 12-1, you'll see that although an Element supports an Attribute or an Event, the support is specific to a Browser or Standard—for the DIR element, the CLASS attribute is supported only in Internet Explorer 4 and Internet Explorer 5 browsers and in the HTML 4.0 standard. No other browsers or standards support the CLASS attribute when used on the DIR element.

Figure 12-11 shows the relationships between tblElementAttribute and tblBrowser and tblStandard.

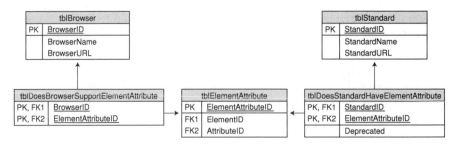

Figure 12-11. ElementAttribute, Browsers, and Standards

Again, there's a link table between the two tables of interest, and these are identical to the way the Element-to-Browser and Element-to-Standard relationships were modeled earlier. A composite primary key contains the two foreign keys that identify the tables that are being linked. As in tblDoesStandardHaveElement, there's also a Deprecated field in tblDoesStandardHaveElementAttribute to enable you to specify that the Attribute may not be valid for that Element in future versions of the standard.

The same relationship exists for tblElementEvent to tblBrowser and tblStandard, as shown in Figure 12-12.

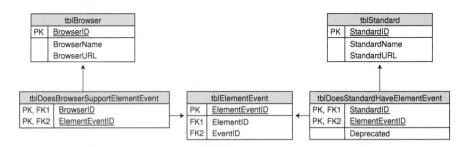

Figure 12-12. ElementEvent, Browsers, and Standards

Third Normal Form (3NF)

Third normal form, as you may recall from Chapter 11, deals exclusively with the relationships between tables in the database.

A table is in 3NF if all the fields in the table depend exclusively upon all the parts of the primary key. For those tables that have a single element in the primary key, if they're in 2NF, then they're also in 3NF, so that removes quite a lot of the tables in the database and leaves only the tables involved in the many-to-many relationships.

The first group of tables to consider are the tables that relate Elements, Attributes, and Events to Browsers. Figure 12-13 shows these three tables.

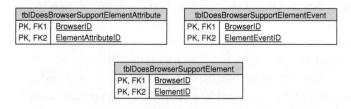

tblDoesBrowserSupportElementAttribute	
PK, FK1	BrowserID
PK, FK2	ElementAttributeID

tblDoesBrowserSupportElementEvent	
PK, FK1	BrowserID
PK, FK2	ElementEventID

tblDoesBrowserSupportElement	
PK, FK1	BrowserID
PK, FK2	ElementID

Figure 12-13. No nonkey fields exist, so 3NF rules don't apply.

These tables are already in 3NF because they don't contain any columns that aren't in the primary key and are therefore automatically in 3NF.

For the tables relating to Standards, as shown in Figure 12-14, the 3NF rules do apply.

tblDoesStandardHaveElementAttribute	
PK, FK1	StandardID
PK, FK2	ElementEventID
	Deprecated

tblDoesStandardHaveElementAttribute	
PK, FK1	StandardID
PK, FK2	ElementEventID
	Deprecated

tblDoesStandardHaveElement	
PK, FK1	StandardID
PK, FK2	ElementEventID
	Deprecated

Figure 12-14. Nonkey fields exist, so 3NF rules apply.

Because there's extra information stored in these tables, the 3NF rule applies—does the Deprecated field depend completely on the composite primary key?

The entire point of the Deprecated field in tblDoesStandardHaveElement is to say that an Element is supported by a Standard and the field can't be placed in any other table. In tblDoesStandardHaveElement, we're saying that an Element is deprecated in that particular version of the Standard, so the Deprecated field can't be moved to tblElement or tblStandard. The same is also true in tblDoesStandardHaveElementAttribute and tblDoesStandardHaveElementEvent—we're talking only about that particular entity being Deprecated in the specified standard.

Because Deprecated can't be moved to any other table without changing its meaning, tblDoesStandardHaveElement, tblDoesStandardHaveElementAttribute, and tblDoesStandardHaveElementEvent are in 3NF.

The Remaining Entities

Now that we've covered 13 tables and their relationships, you may be forgiven for thinking that we've covered everything. However, this isn't the case; you need to consider two more tables. We haven't covered these tables in the main discussion previously because the first table isn't normalized and the second sits on its own, unrelated to anything else in the database. You'll look at both of these here.

The first of the extra tables stores the details for the images that are going to be displayed to indicate the browser and standard support. If you look at Figure 12-2, you'll see that instead of using text to indicate which of the Browsers and Standards that support the Element (and Attribute and Event), an icon is used.

This information could have been stored in tblBrowser and tblStandard, but a new table, tblImage, has been created to store just the image details. Figure 12-15 shows this table and its relationships to tblBrowser and tblStandard.

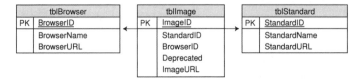

Figure 12-15. Storing the image details

For the Browser icons, the ImageUrl field could be stored in tblBrowser without any problems because for a Browser there's only one image—the browser supports something, or it doesn't. For every entry in tblBrowser, there's one entry in tblImage, with the BrowserID field in tblImage matching the entry in tblBrowser.

But for the Standard icons there's the added complication that the Standard can deprecate an Element (or an Attribute or Event). One image shows Standard support, and a different image shows that the support is deprecated in this version of the Standard. The Deprecated field in tblImage shows support for this facility, and for every entry in tblStandard there are two entries in tblImage—one with the Deprecated field set to false and the other with the Deprecated field set to true.

The final table that needs to be modeled in the database is the details for the administration user. This is done in a table exclusively for the login details, tblUser (see Figure 12-16). The table contains Username and Password fields as well as a UserID field that contains a GUID unique to that user.

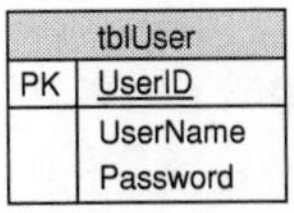

tblUser	
PK	UserID
	UserName
	Password

Figure 12-16. User details are stored in the database.

Creating the Database

To work through the examples in this and the next chapter, you'll need to build the database we've just detailed. We could have an example that walks through constructing every table and relationship in Web Matrix or SQL Web Data Administrator, but we showed how to create tables this way in Chapter 2, so you may recall that it was quite time consuming. You'll use some of the techniques you learned in Chapter 10 and use a Data Definition Language (DDL) script to create the database you need.

However, you won't build the entire database; you'll create only a subset of the database that contains enough information to enable you to look at the pertinent parts of the BAND HTML Reference to illustrate the points we need to cover.

Try It Out: Using the Database Script

You'll use the provided database script to create the database for the rest of this chapter and the following chapter.

1. Open a command prompt, and navigate to the folder containing the database scripts within the code download. If you've extracted the code download to the default location, this will be `C:\BAND\Database`.

2. Enter the following command to start `osql.exe`, and enter **secpas** at the prompt for the password:

   ```
   osql -U sa -S (local)\BAND
   ```

3. Once `osql.exe` has started, enter the following commands to create the database:

   ```
   CREATE DATABASE BANDCASE
   GO
   ```

4. Exit the command-line tool by typing **EXIT** and hitting Return.

5. At the command prompt, enter the following to execute the database creation script and create the database. Enter a password of **secpas** when prompted.

```
osql -i case.sql -U sa -S (local)\BAND
```

6. This will create the tables and stored procedures you'll need. Figure 12-17 shows the partial output from executing the script.

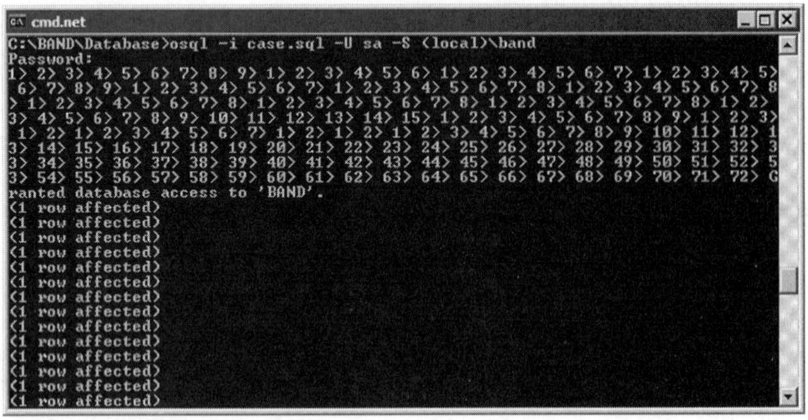

Figure 12-17. Executing a script to create the database

How It Works

You've already looked at the different DDL queries to create databases and tables in Chapter 10 and for stored procedures in Chapter 9, so we won't cover what the scripts actually do in any detail.

The script creates the five database tables and the stored procedures that are required for the examples. The script also gives the band user execute permissions on all the stored procedures within the database.

As well as creating the database structure, the script also adds some data to the database—not everything that's in the real application but enough to work through the examples.

- The A, ACRONYM, ADDRESS, APPLET, and AREA elements are added to tblElement.

- Seven different browsers—Internet Explorer 2 to Internet Explorer 5 and Netscape Navigator 2 to Netscape Navigator 4—are added to tblBrowser.

- The relationship between the elements and browsers are added to tblDoesBrowserSupportElement.

- The icons details for the browsers are added to tblImage.

- The details for a single user are added to tblUser.

Creating the Data Access Tier

Now that you have a database for the BAND HTML Reference, you can start to build the application. Before you look at any pages that the user will see, you'll briefly return to the tiered architecture you saw in Chapter 11.

All the examples you've seen in the book so far contain the same basic code on each page.

```
string ConnectionString = ↵
  @"server=(local)\BAND;database=Books;uid=band;pwd=letmein";
string CommandText = "select * from Publisher";
SqlConnection myConnection = new SqlConnection(ConnectionString);
SqlCommand myCommand = new SqlCommand(CommandText, myConnection);

myConnection.Open();

DataGrid1.DataSource = myCommand.ExecuteReader(CommandBehavior.CloseConnection);
DataGrid1.DataBind();

myConnection.Close();
```

Although this works fine—and for small sites is a perfectly acceptable solution—it isn't recommended for any but the smallest of sites. As you saw in Chapter 11, you can separate your application into several different tiers that perform individual tasks. One of these is the data access tier.

By having a data access tier that deals solely with sending queries to and retrieving data from the database, you can shield the page developer from the intricacies of the database—you can provide simple methods that allow the full set of database operations to be performed without having to worry about creating the correct Connection, Command, and Parameter objects.

Having a data access tier allows you to make changes to the tier—such as moving from using a Microsoft SQL Server 2000 Desktop Engine (MSDE) database to using a MySQL database—without having to modify every single page that uses the data access code. The actual objects that are being used to connect to the database are hidden from the other tiers, and you can change those objects without causing any problems.

> **NOTE** *Even with a data access tier hiding the database implementation, you may still need to change the code that the page developer has written in one particular instance. If, as in most applications, you're using DataReader and DataAdapter objects, then you're going to be using a specific version of these objects, such as* SqlDataReader *and* SqlDataAdapter. *If you change the type of database that the application is using (say, from MSDE to MySQL), you're going to be using different versions of these objects such as* OdbcDataReader *and* OdbcDataAdapter. *In this case, you'd need to make a change to the declaration of the variable on the page to use the correct version of the object.*

Designing the Data Access Tier

The data access tier must allow you to do everything you need to do with the database. Before you can think about the physical design of the tier, you need to consider the things you need the data access tier to accomplish.

As mentioned, the main point of the data access tier is to shield the page developer from the details of the different ADO.NET objects (SqlConnection, SqlCommand, and so on) and provide them with easy methods that do the things they need.

The functions you need the data access tier to accomplish are as follows:

- You need methods to execute the different types of queries you're going to want to make against the database. In Chapter 4, you saw that there are three different ways of executing queries against the database—ExecuteNon-Query(), ExecuteReader(), and ExecuteScalar().

- When you looked at DataSets in Chapter 7, you saw that you needed a DataAdapter object to correctly populate a DataSet and you need some way of retreiving a valid SqlDataAdapter.

- When you looked at queries in Chapter 4 and stored procedures in Chapter 9, you saw sometimes you need to add parameters to modify the functionality of the query or stored procedure. You'll need methods to allow parameters to be used.

- You'll also need some way of dealing with transactions within the database. By using transactions, you can ensure that several different queries either all succeed or all fail.

The previous is a complete list of all the functionality you require in the data access tier. In several instances, you can model the data access tier in a single class, and for the BAND HTML Reference the DataAccess class will contain all the required functionality.

The functionality required will be supported by the DataAccess class as follows:

1. The Execute methods of the Command object will be available using methods of the same name—ExecuteNonQuery(), ExecuteReader(), and ExecuteScalar(). As you'll see shortly, though, the signature for these methods is a lot different from the methods that the SqlCommand object exposes.

2. To provide a consistent interface to the database, we'll provide an Execute-DataAdapter() method that returns a SqlDataAdapter.

3. Parameters to the queries are handled by four methods that allow full control over the parameters passed to the database:

   - AddParameter(): This will be used to add a parameter to the parameters that will be passed to the database.

   - GetParameter(): This method will return the value of the specified parameter.

   - ModifyParameter(): If you need to change the value of a parameter, you can use this method to specify the new value.

   - RemoveParameter(): Once you've added a parameter, there shouldn't be any reason for wanting to remove the parameter from the query that you're going to make, but just in case you'll add a method to remove a parameter from the parameters that will be passed to the database.

4. Transactions will be handled by allowing the DataAccess class to be created as either transactional or nontransactional.

Rather than build the complete class here and overload you with lots of code, we'll start with just the basics and introduce further functionality as it's required.

You'll add the methods and properties for dealing with stored procedures and transactions in the next chapter. For now we'll cover the points raised in the first two bullets. Figure 12-18 shows the entity diagram for the basic DataAccess class.

```
DataAccess

+New()
+Dispose()
-OpenConnection()
-CloseConnection()
+ExecuteAdapter(in strCommand) : SqlDataAdapter
+ExecuteAdapter(in strCommnad, in objType : SqlDataAdapter
+ExecuteNonQuery(in strCommand) : int
+ExecuteNonQuery(in strCommand, in objType) : int
+ExecuteReader(in strCommand) : SqlDataReader
+ExecuteReader(in strCommand, in objType : SqlDataReader
+ExecuteReader(in strCommand, in objType, in objBehaviour) : SqlDataReader
+ExecuteScalar(in strCommand) : object
+ExecuteScalar(in strCommand, in objType) : object
```

Figure 12-18. Entity diagram for the basic DataAccess class

> **NOTE** *You won't see any detailed discussion of entity diagrams here. What you do need to know about the previous diagram is that the plus (+) sign before the method name indicates that it's a public method and the minus (-) sign indicates that it's a private method.*

Of the 13 methods you've suddenly been exposed to, nine of these methods can be accounted for by the methods identified in the first bullet point earlier.

That still leaves four methods that are unaccounted for; you'll look at these methods in turn before returning to look at the overloaded Execute methods in more detail.

Constructing the DataAccess Class

When a class is created in .NET, a constructor method is always called; it's here you initialize whatever you need to for the class. The constructor for DataAccess will be responsible for creating the SqlConnection and SqlCommand objects that you need and for storing these within class variables for use elsewhere in the class.

```
public DataAccess()
{
    // setup the connection object
    m_Connection = new SqlConnection();
    m_Connection.ConnectionString = ConfigurationSettings.AppSettings["Database"];

    // setup the command object
    m_Command = new SqlCommand();
    m_Command.Connection = m_Connection;
}
```

As you know, you want to store the database connection string in the web.config file, and you use this to create the SqlConnection object. This is then used to specify the connection for the SqlCommand object. Because you don't want database connections open any longer than is absolutely necessary, the database connection is not opened in the constructor—you'll leave this to the last possible moment.

Opening and Closing the Database Connection

As you saw in Chapter 4, you want to open the database connection only just before you need it and close it as soon as you're finished with it. You could open the database connection in the constructor, but this may open the connection quite a long time before any of the Execute methods are called.

Instead of this, you'll open the database connections in the Execute method, as you'll shortly see, immediately before an open database connection is required. You could open the connection using the Open() method of the SqlConnection object within the various Execute methods, but having a private method, Open-Connection(), provides you with only one location where the database connection is opened. If you want to run any other common code when you open the database connection, you can add it to this method rather than having to add it to every instance of the Open() method being called.

Similarly, you have a private CloseConnection() method that you call when you want to close the database connection. However, closing the connection to the database connection isn't as straightforward as opening it.

Disposing of the DataAccess Class

One of the main considerations you need to look at when designing DataAccess is how you're going to deal with the connections to the database. You open the database connection at the last possible minute, but when do you close the database connection? Are you going to leave it up to the page developer to close the database connection, or do you close this connection as soon as you can?

This is easy for "one-shot" queries that you can run using the `ExecuteNonQuery` or `ExecuteScalar` methods; you'll always close the database connection after the query has been executed as a connection to the database is no longer required. But what happens when want to use a `SqlDataAdapter` or `SqlDataReader` object? Both of these require an open connection to the database, and you therefore can't immediately call the `CloseConnection()` method.

You could make the `CloseConnection()` method public and allow the page developer to call this method directly to close the database connection, but .NET provides a more elegant (and standard!) way of doing this by using the `IDisposable` interface.

We won't go into the whys-and-wherefores of the `IDisposable` interface other than to say that if you make your class use this interface, you must then implement a public `Dispose()` method. In here you can call the `CloseConnection()` method to close the database connection.

The Execute Methods

Now that all the "housekeeping" methods are out of the way, it's time to look at the overloaded Execute methods you've implemented on the class.

If you start by looking at the `ExecuteNonQuery()` methods, you'll see that the other methods follow a similar pattern.

As you'll recall from Figure 12-18, there are two `ExecuteNonQuery()` methods of the DataAccess class, and these wrap a call to the `ExecuteNonQuery()` method of the `SqlCommand` object. The two `ExecuteNonQuery()` methods on the DataAccess class have the following signatures:

```
public int ExecuteNonQuery(string strCommand)
public int ExecuteNonQuery(string strCommand, CommandType objType)
```

You have two versions because you need to deal with the different types of command that you can execute against the database—in other words, are you passing a query to the database or the name of a stored procedure? You've already seen that stored procedures are the preferred way of accessing what's in the database, and the first version of this method assumes that the command you're passing in is indeed a stored procedure. Sometimes, however, you want to execute a query that isn't a stored procedure, so you provide the second version of the method to allow the specification of what you're executing by specifying a `CommandType`.

> **NOTE** *In the entire application we only ever use the first versions of the Execute methods because we're always going to use stored procedures to query the database. We've added the methods in the manner that we have to provide a more complete data access tier that you should be able to take and use in a wide variety of places—not just in applications that rely on stored procedures!*

Having two methods that do the same thing presents you with a little bit of a problem. If all that's different between the two methods is the type of command that you want to execute, then you don't really need two versions of the method—two methods with nearly identical code means that you have two places where you can have an error. You can get around this problem by having the first version of the ExecuteNonQuery() method call the second, specifying that the command that's being executed is a stored procedure.

```
public int ExecuteNonQuery(string strCommand)
{
   return(ExecuteNonQuery(strCommand, CommandType.StoredProcedure));
}
```

This is the same as when you implement the overloaded versions of the ExecuteScalar() method—one version of the method simply calls the other.

The ExecuteReader() Methods

The same overloading process is in action for the ExecuteReader() methods except that there are three different methods.

```
public SqlDataReader ExecuteReader(string strCommand)
public SqlDataReader ExecuteReader(string strCommand, ⤷
   CommandType objType)
public SqlDataReader ExecuteReader(string strCommand, ⤷
   CommandType objType, CommandBehavior objBehaviour)
```

The first version of the method assumes that it's a stored procedure you want to execute and calls the second version of the method, specifying CommandType.StoredProcedure as the second parameter. This is the same as you've seen for ExecuteNonQuery() and ExecuteNonScalar().

However, you have a third version of the ExecuteReader() method.

As you'll recall from Chapter 4, when calling the ExecuteReader() method, you also specify how the SqlConnection is closed, and it's this you control with the third version of the ExecuteReader() method. You can pass in any of the defined CommandBehavior types to the third version of the ExecuteReader() method, and this will be used when the SqlDataReader object is created.

So, for the first two ExecuteReader() methods of the DataAccess class, you actually have the following:

```
public SqlDataReader ExecuteReader(string strCommand)
{
  return(ExecuteReader(strCommand, CommandType.StoredProcedure));
}
public SqlDataReader ExecuteReader(string strCommand, ⏎
  CommandType objType)
{
  return(ExecuteReader(strCommand, objType, ⏎
    CommandBehavior.CloseConnection));
}
```

By default we're always going to force the DataAccess class to use the CommandBehavior.CloseConnection behavior for creating SqlDataReader objects, so you specify this in the call to the third ExecuteReader() method.

It's only within the third version of ExecuteReader() that any interaction with the database occurs.

The ExecuteAdapter() Methods

When working with DataSets you need to use a DataAdapter to populate the DataSet and enable changes to the DataSet to be reflected in the database. Unlike the three Execute methods you've seen so far, there's no Execute method for creating a SqlDataAdapter; you must create one directly. For completeness, the method to construct the SqlDataAdapter is named in the same manner as the other Execute methods.

```
public SqlDataAdapter ExecuteAdapter(string strCommand, ⏎
  CommandType objType)
{
  // set the properties correctly
  m_Command.CommandText = strCommand;
  m_Command.CommandType = objType;

  // open the database connection
  OpenConnection();
```

```
// create the data adapter object
SqlDataAdapter objAdapter = new SqlDataAdapter(m_Command);

// return the adapter
return(objAdapter);
}
```

Within the ExecuteAdapter() method you create a new SqlDataAdapter using the correct SqlCommand object and return this from the method. The page developer is free to use the returned SqlDataAdapter however they want as long as they remember to call the Dispose() method of DataAccess once they're finished with SqlDataAdapter.

If you refer to Figure 12-18, you'll see that you have two overloaded versions of the ExecuteAdapter() method; it will come as no surprise that the first version calls the second, specifying that you want to use a stored procedure to construct the SqlDataAdapter.

```
public SqlDataAdapter ExecuteAdapter(string strCommand)
{
  return(ExecuteAdapter(strCommand, CommandType.StoredProcedure));
}
```

Try It Out: Building the DataAccess Class

Now that you've learned why you need a data access tier and seen the methods that you need on the DataAccess class, it's time to build the class itself. In this example, you'll build only the DataAccess class; you won't see it in operation—you need to wait until the following example for that.

As you saw earlier, you can add a lot more methods to the class than those that you've seen so far—you haven't yet looked at support for stored procedures and transactions. You'll take your time over the class and look at the basic Data-Access class before moving on in the next chapter to look at extending this class to support stored procedures and transactions.

1. Open Web Matrix, and navigate to the C:\BAND\Chapter12 folder.

2. Add a new file to the application, and, as shown in Figure 12-19, select Class as the type of file to create and call the file code.cs. Also, specify the class name as DataAccess and the namespace for the class as notashop.band.

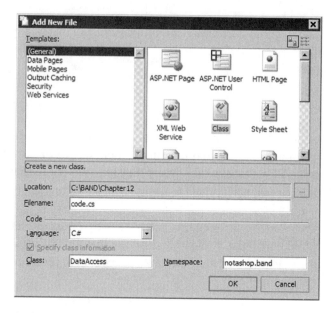

Figure 12-19. Adding a class to the application

3. Remove all the comments from the template that's generated, and add definitions for all the namespaces you're going to need.

```
namespace notashop.band {
    using System;
    using System.Configuration;
    using System.Data;
    using System.Data.SqlClient;
    using System.Web;
```

4. Now make the class implement the IDisposable interface by modifying the class definition, and add the two private variables you're going to need.

```
public class DataAccess : IDisposable {
    SqlCommand m_Command;
    SqlConnection m_Connection;
```

5. Change the constructor of the class so that it sets up the SqlCommand and SqlConnection objects as required.

```
public DataAccess()
{
    // setup the connection object
    m_Connection = new SqlConnection();
```

```
m_Connection.ConnectionString = ⤶
    ConfigurationSettings.AppSettings["Database"];

// setup the command object
m_Command = new SqlCommand();
m_Command.Connection = m_Connection;
}
```

6. Add the Dispose() method that you must now provide.

```
public void Dispose()
{
    // close the database connection
    CloseConnection();

    // don't want the GC to clean up
    GC.SuppressFinalize(this);
}
```

7. Add the private OpenConnection() and CloseConnection() methods.

```
private void OpenConnection()
{
    if (m_Connection.State == ConnectionState.Closed)
    {
        m_Connection.Open();
    }
}
private void CloseConnection()
{
    if (m_Connection.State == ConnectionState.Open)
    {
        m_Connection.Close();
    }
}
```

8. Add the ExecuteAdapter() methods.

```
public SqlDataAdapter ExecuteAdapter(string strCommand)
{
    return(ExecuteAdapter(strCommand, CommandType.StoredProcedure));
}
public SqlDataAdapter ExecuteAdapter(string strCommand, ⤶
    CommandType objType)
```

```
{
    // set the properties correctly
    m_Command.CommandText = strCommand;
    m_Command.CommandType = objType;

    // open the database connection
    OpenConnection();

    // create the data adapater object
    SqlDataAdapter objAdapter = new SqlDataAdapter(m_Command);

    // return the adapter
    return(objAdapter);
}
```

9. Add the ExecuteNonQuery() methods.

```
public int ExecuteNonQuery(string strCommand)
{
    return(ExecuteNonQuery(strCommand, CommandType.StoredProcedure));
}
public int ExecuteNonQuery(string strCommand, CommandType objType)
{

    // set the properties correctly
    m_Command.CommandText = strCommand;
    m_Command.CommandType = objType;

    // open the database connection
    OpenConnection();

    // execute the query and return the correct result
    int intReturn = m_Command.ExecuteNonQuery();

    // close the connection
    CloseConnection();

    // return the result
    return(intReturn);
}
```

10. Add the ExecuteReader() methods.

```
public SqlDataReader ExecuteReader(string strCommand)
{
   return(ExecuteReader(strCommand, CommandType.StoredProcedure));
}
public SqlDataReader ExecuteReader(string strCommand, ⏎
   CommandType objType)
{
   return(ExecuteReader(strCommand, objType, ⏎
     CommandBehavior.CloseConnection));
}
public SqlDataReader ExecuteReader(string strCommand, ⏎
   CommandType objType, CommandBehavior objBehaviour)
{
   // set the properties correctly
   m_Command.CommandText = strCommand;
   m_Command.CommandType = objType;

   // open the database connection
   OpenConnection();

   // execute the query and return the correct result
   SqlDataReader objReader = m_Command.ExecuteReader(objBehaviour);

   // return the reader
   return(objReader);
}
```

11. Add the ExecuteScalar() methods.

```
public object ExecuteScalar(string strCommand)
{
   return(ExecuteScalar(strCommand, CommandType.StoredProcedure));
}
public object ExecuteScalar(string strCommand, CommandType objType)
{
   // set the properties correctly
   m_Command.CommandText = strCommand;
   m_Command.CommandType = objType;

   // open the database connection
   OpenConnection();
```

```
        // execute the query and return the correct result
        object objReturn = m_Command.ExecuteScalar();

        // close the connection
        CloseConnection();

        // return the result
        return (objReturn);
    }
```

12. Save the class.

How It Works

Phew—that was quite a lot of code! You've already looked at the reasoning behind the choices that we made in the design of the class, so we'll cover only the way that the code works here.

The first thing you do is make your class implement the `IDisposable` interface.

```
public class DataAccess : IDisposable {
```

This forces you to implement the `Dispose()` method, and you'll use this to close the database connection, as you'll shortly see.

The first method of the class you need to look at is the constructor. Here you create the `SqlConnection` and `SqlCommand` objects that you need and assign these to the class variables `m_Connection` and `m_Command`, respectively.

```
public DataAccess() {
    // setup the connection object
    m_Connection = new SqlConnection();
    m_Connection.ConnectionString = ⏎
        ConfigurationSettings.AppSettings["Database"];

    // setup the command object
    m_Command = new SqlCommand();
    m_Command.Connection = m_Connection;
}
```

You've specified the connection string as the `Database` configuration variable, so you extract this and set the `ConnectionString` of the `SqlConnection` object to use it. You then use this object to set what database the `SqlCommand` object uses.

You'll notice that you haven't opened the connection to the database yet. As we pointed out earlier, you'll do this at the last possible moment.

You then added the `Dispose()` method.

```
public void Dispose()
{
  // close the database connection
  CloseConnection();

  // don't want the GC to clean you up
  GC.SuppressFinalize(this);
}
```

You close the connection to the database by calling the (soon to be discussed) `CloseConnection()` method, and then you call the `GC.SupressFinalize(this)` method. Although not required, the `GC.SupressFinalize(this)` call tells the .NET garbage collector that it doesn't need to clean up this class before it's destroyed. You could remove this call without any problems, but it will make the class marginally slower in operation.

You then have the `OpenConnection()` and `CloseConnection()` methods. If you look at the `OpenConnection()` method, you'll see that you check to ensure that the connection is closed before you attempt to open it.

```
private void OpenConnection()
{
  if (m_Connection.State == ConnectionState.Closed)
  {
    m_Connection.Open();
  }
}
```

You do the same for the `CloseConnection()` method except that you check that the connection is open before closing it.

Then you come to the four groups of methods used to query the database. Rather than look at all nine methods individually, you'll see the `ExecuteNonQuery()` methods in detail because all four groups follow the same paradigm.

As you saw when we introduced the overloading of the Execute methods, you have two versions of the `ExecuteNonQuery()` method, with one method calling the other to perform the query.

The first version of the `ExecuteNonQuery()` method that you have simply accepts a command and calls the second method, specifying that you're trying to execute a stored procedure.

```
public int ExecuteNonQuery(string strCommand)
{
  return(ExecuteNonQuery(strCommand, CommandType.StoredProcedure));
}
```

It's in the second version of the `ExecuteNonQuery()` method that the work to execute the query actually occurs.

```
public int ExecuteNonQuery(string strCommand, CommandType objType)
{
  // set the properties correctly
  m_Command.CommandText = strCommand;
  m_Command.CommandType = objType;

  // open the database connection
  OpenConnection();

  // execute the query and return the correct result
  int intReturn = m_Command.ExecuteNonQuery();

  // close the connection
  CloseConnection();

  // return the result
  return(intReturn);
}
```

The first thing you do is set the `CommandText` and `CommandType` properties on the `SqlCommand` object you're using to the values of the parameters passed into the method.

Now that the `SqlCommand` is fully formed, you're ready to perform the query against the database, so you open the database connection by calling the `Open-Connection()` method.

Once the connection is open, you perform the query against the database and return the data in the format you require. In this case, you return an integer count of the number of rows that were affected by the query as `intReturn`.

The database connection is then closed by calling the `CloseConnection()` method and the count of the number of rows, `intReturn`, returned from the method.

The `ExecuteScalar()` methods follow this same paradigm, but there's a slight difference when you look at the `ExecuteReader()` method. When returning a `SqlDataReader`, you don't want to close the connection to the database. If you look at the `ExecuteReader()` method, you'll see that the only real difference is that you don't close the connection to the database.

```
public SqlDataReader ExecuteReader(string strCommand,
  CommandType objType, CommandBehavior objBehaviour)
{
  // set the properties correctly
  m_Command.CommandText = strCommand;
  m_Command.CommandType = objType;

  // open the database connection
  OpenConnection();

  // execute the query and return the correct result
  SqlDataReader objReader = m_Command.ExecuteReader(objBehaviour);

  // return the reader
  return(objReader);
}
```

The ExecuteAdapter() methods are also different because you must create the SqlDataAdapter rather than generate it by calling an Execute method on the SqlCommand object.

```
public SqlDataAdapter ExecuteAdapter(string strCommand, ↵
  CommandType objType)
{
  // set the properties correctly
  m_Command.CommandText = strCommand;
  m_Command.CommandType = objType;

  // open the database connection
  OpenConnection();

  // create the data adapater object
  SqlDataAdapter objAdapter = new SqlDataAdapter(m_Command);

  // return the adapter
  return(objAdapter);
}
```

You open the connection to the database shortly before creating the SqlData-Adapter, and, as with the ExecuteReader() methods, you leave it up to the page developer to close the connection to the database by calling Dispose().

Try It Out: Using the DataAccess Class

It's all well and good having a DataAccess class, but you really need to use it to see the advantage of it. You'll build a simple page that mimics the home page of the BAND HTML Reference and presents all the elements that are available without any of the graphical "tarting up" that's visible in the final application.

1. Open Web Matrix, and navigate to the C:\BAND\Chapter12 folder.

2. Create a web.config file for the application, and replace the contents of the autogenerated file with the following:

    ```
    <?xml version="1.0" encoding="utf-8" ?>
    <configuration>
      <appSettings>
        <add key="database" value="server=(local)\BAND;
          database=BANDCASE;uid=band;pwd=letmein;" />
      </appSettings>
    </configuration>
    ```

3. Add a new page to the application, and call it default.aspx.

4. Switch to the All view of the page, and add the following import and assembly statements to the top of the page immediately after the <@ Page > element.

    ```
    <%@ import Namespace="System.Data" %>
    <%@ import Namespace="notashop.band" %>
    <%@ assembly Src="code.cs" %>
    ```

5. Switch to the Design view of the page, add the text **Select an element to view** to the start of the page, drag a DropDownList control onto the page, and call it lstElements. The page should look as shown in Figure 12-20.

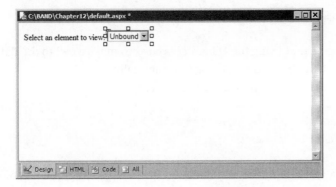

Figure 12-20. Adding a list box to show the elements that are available

6. Add the Load event to the page, adding the following code to the event handler that's created:

```
// create the data object
DataAccess objData = new DataAccess();

// get a DataReader and bind it to the listbox
lstElements.DataSource = objData.ExecuteReader("stpGetAllElements");
lstElements.DataTextField = "ElementName";
lstElements.DataValueField = "ElementID";
lstElements.DataBind();

// finished with the data object
objData.Dispose();
```

7. Run the page, and you should see that the list is populated with five elements, as shown in Figure 12-21.

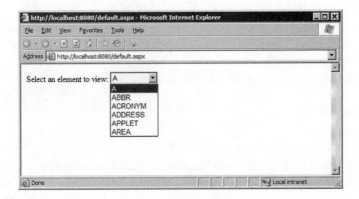

Figure 12-21. The first use of the DataAccess class

How It Works

You'll probably agree that using the DataAccess class to make a call to the database is definitely easier than coding the access manually.

You first create the necessary DataAccess object.

```
// create the data object
DataAccess objData = new DataAccess();
```

To use the DataAccess object, all you have to do is call the method you require and specify the query or stored procedure you want to execute. Although you won't look at parameters to stored procedures until the next chapter, you can actually use stored procedures now—provided they don't require any parameters. The stored procedure that you want to execute, returning the ElementID and ElementName for every element in the database, is as follows:

```
CREATE PROCEDURE dbo.stpGetAllElements
AS

-- list the names and IDs of the elements
SELECT ElementID, ElementName FROM tblElement ORDER BY ElementName
```

You call the ExecuteReader() method, passing in the name of the stored procedure, and bind the SqlDataReader that's returned to lstElements, setting the Data-TextField and DataValueField so that the correct information is displayed.

```
// get a DataReader and bind it to the listbox
lstElements.DataSource = objData.ExecuteReader("stpGetAllElements");
lstElements.DataTextField = "ElementName";
lstElements.DataValueField = "ElementID";
lstElements.DataBind();
```

Once you're finished with the DataAccess object, you call the Dispose() method to ensure that the connection to the database is closed.

```
// finished with the data object
objData.Dispose();
```

That's how easy it is to use the new DataAccess class you've built—create the DataAccess object, call the correct Execute method specifying the query or stored procedure to execute, and dispose of the DataAccess object once you're finished with it.

Summary

In this chapter, you've started to look at the BAND HTML Reference. After taking a quick look at the application itself, you looked at the design of the database.

- The tables you need to model the requirements of the application correctly

- The relationships that exist between the tables

Rather than build the database you require by hand, you used a DDL script to create everything you need automatically.

You then built a basic version of the DataAccess class that allows you to execute queries and stored procedures that don't require parameters against the database using the most appropriate Execute method. You then looked at using this DataAccess class to return the elements that are in the database and present these to the user.

In the next chapter, you'll look at several different topics for the BAND HTML Reference: error handling, stored procedures, security, and transactions.

Error handling: You briefly looked at error handling as far back as Chapter 3 and saw how you can log errors that occur in the application. For the BAND HTML Reference, you'll change this slightly and e-mail the site administrator whenever an error occurs. You'll also look at how you can present a friendly error message to the user rather than the standard ASP.NET error message.

Stored procedures: You'll expand the DataAccess class to allow parameters to be added to the queries and stored procedures you're executing.

Security: As you saw in the introduction to the BAND HTML Reference, the administration pages of the site are security protected, so you'll build a basic Security class to allow access to the administration pages to be restricted.

Transactions: Transactions allow you to "package" several different database queries together and ensure that all the different parts fail if any one part of the package fails. You'll look at why you'd want this behavior to occur and extend the DataAccess class to allow it to handle transactions.

The Case Study, Part II

IN THE PREVIOUS CHAPTER, you looked at the basics of the BAND HTML Reference.
You started with a look at the structure of the application, and we talked about
what we wanted the application to accomplish. You then looked at the database
and the DataAccess class that you'll use to access it. At the end of the chapter, you
built a cut-down version of the application home page that allowed you to view
the list of elements that were added to the database by the database creation
script.

You'll now look at the remaining pieces of the puzzle and see how you can
take the parts of what you've learned and piece them all together to build a subset
of the functionality available in the complete BAND HTML Reference.

The different pieces you'll look at in this chapter are as follows:

Error handling: You'll briefly look at the various options you have for handling
errors that can occur within your application and then see how the BAND
HTML Reference handles any errors.

Stored procedures: You already saw that in the previous chapter you can execute stored procedures using the DataAccess class as it currently exists, but to
use parameters you'll need to modify the DataAccess class.

Controlling user access: On a data-driven Web site, access to parts of the site
usually needs to be restricted—after all, you don't want any Tom, Dick, or
Harry to change the data that drives the site. You'll see how to handle this for
the BAND HTML Reference by providing a Security class that you can use to
control access to individual pages.

Using transactions: When you're performing one query that modifies the data
(in other words, a DELETE, INSERT, or UPDATE statement) and it fails, the
database isn't left in a corrupt state. If you have three statements that needed
to be executed together in a single action and the last one fails, you don't want
the first two to be executed because this most likely will leave you with a database that contains data that's incorrect. This is where transactions come to
your aid by allowing you to group several different queries together—either
they all work or they all fail.

We can't possibly teach you how to build the BAND HTML Reference in its entirety in these two chapters, so we'll concentrate on presenting the major topics outlined previously and show you how to construct a subset of the BAND HTML Reference. At the end of this chapter, you'll have built the two user-facing pages and have started on constructing the wizard that will allow you to add and modify the HTML elements within the database.

Error Handling

When building an application, you can guarantee that at some point an error is going to occur. Whether it's the code you've written, a hardware problem preventing database access, or any number of other reasons, presenting the user with the standard ASP.NET error message, as shown in Figure 13-1, doesn't really give a good impression about the site.

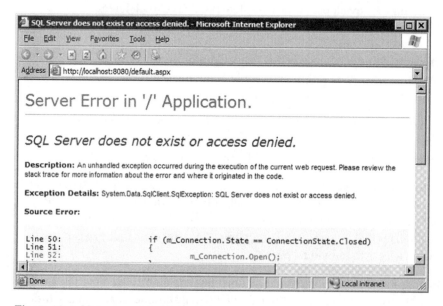

Figure 13-1. Not a very good impression

What you really want to do when an error occurs is to hide any information that may be useful to hackers (such as the database name) and present the user with a friendlier error message. You can handle errors in an application in a number of ways. We'll briefly show each in turn before adding the required error handling to the BAND HTML Reference.

Catching Errors in Code Using try..catch..finally

The try..catch..finally syntax used throughout the book allows you to catch any errors that occur on a page and will usually be your first line of defense against errors occurring.

Before we recap how you handle errors, it's worth taking a moment to emphasize that you shouldn't rely too much on try..catch..finally to catch errors in your code. If you know that a particular condition may occur, don't rely on the error handler picking it up—code for the possible condition. Checking for a specific condition that may occur will always be quicker than relying on a try..catch..finally construct to handle the error.

If in your code you have a particular range of values that you can deal with, don't rely on the incorrect values causing an exception to be raised. If a string may be empty, check that it's not empty before attempting to use the empty string and perhaps causing an error.

Sometimes, however, an error is unavoidable, and you need to use try..catch..finally—for instance, someone unplugging the database server is something you can't foresee, and you need to gracefully handle it rather than presenting the "nasty" error message in Figure 13-1.

In the BAND HTML Reference, you use a try..catch..finally block to ensure that the DataAccess object you've created is disposed of correctly. You always create the DataAccess object before the start of the try..catch..finally block so that it's available in all parts of the block.

```
// create the data object you need
DataAccess objData = new DataAccess();

try{
  // do the work that we want to
}
catch
{
  // do any error handling you need
}
finally
{
  // clean up the data object
  objData.Dispose();
}
```

You do all the work you need to do within the try block; if there are any errors, you trap these in the catch block and perform any error handling that's necessary. In most cases within the BAND HTML Reference you don't have any extra steps to take, and the majority of the code won't have a catch block—you'll see shortly that you can define actions to be taken if you have an error on a sitewide basis, and you'll use this method because it allows you to keep the error handling in one place rather than spreading out across every page within the application.

In the finally block that will always be executed you dispose of the DataAccess object by calling the Dispose() method.

Database Errors and @@ERROR

As well as handling errors that are raised within the C# code that you're writing, it's also possible to trap errors that occur within the database directly using the @@ERROR global variable in MSDE.

The @@ERROR global variable is set whenever a SQL statement causes an error, and you can check the value of this variable to see if the last statement caused an error and recover from the error in as graceful a way as possible.

Using the following example SQL statement to insert a new element into tblElement will work fine if you're trying to insert a new element:

```
INSERT INTO tblElement (ElementID, Name, Description)
  VALUES (@elementid, @name, @description)
```

However, if you try to insert the same element again, you'll get an error (in particular error code 2627, "Violation of PRIMARY KEY constraint ...") because you can't have two elements in tblElement with the same ElementID.

Using the @@ERROR global variable, you can check if an error has occurred and attempt to update the record instead, like so:

```
INSERT INTO tblElement (ElementID, Name, Description)
  VALUES (@elementid, @name, @description)
IF @@ERROR<>0 BEGIN
  UPDATE tblElement SET Name = @name, Description = @description
    WHERE ElementID = @element
END
```

We find this method of error handling dreadful and have stayed away from implementing it in every application we've ever built and advise that you do the same. We'll explain why.

MSDE has two types of errors: fatal and nonfatal.

- *Fatal errors* are those errors that mean you can't continue and cover things such as internal server errors, hardware problems accessing the database files, and so on.

- *Nonfatal errors* are errors that the database thinks you should be able to recover from. The "Violation of PRIMARY KEY constraint..." error is an example of a nonfatal error.

If you have a fatal error, then you obviously need to pass this out to the calling code. Further, as fatal errors always cause execution to stop, these are always passed to the calling code, and you have no opportunity to handle the error within the database.

For nonfatal errors, you can, in nearly all cases, catch the error before it occurs just by thinking about what you're trying to do. In this example, it stands to reason that you may have an existing element with the same ElementID. You can code for this and not rely on the error being raised.

```
IF EXISTS (SELECT * FROM tblElement WHERE ElementID = @element) BEGIN
  INSERT INTO tblElement (ElementID, Name, Description)
    VALUES (@elementid, @name, @description)
END ELSE BEGIN
  UPDATE tblElement SET Name = @name, Description = @description
    WHERE ElementID = @element
END
```

If you equate using @@ERROR to handling errors in a try..catch..finally structure, then you should handle potential errors in the same way—you never want to rely on @@ERROR to check if something is correct. Always code for every eventuality you can think of.

Catching Errors for an Entire Site

Although you've seen how you can handle errors for a particular page and clean up any objects you need using try..catch..finally, this isn't the end of the story; you don't want to present the user with the type of message shown in Figure 13-1. Instead, you want to give them a friendlier error message that shows you're doing something about the error. Thankfully, ASP.NET provides the means to do this as well as a whole lot more.

Try It Out: Handling Errors

In this example, you'll add error handling to the home page you created in Chapter 12 to ensure that if an error does occur, you close the connection to the database correctly. You'll then extend the example to present a friendlier error message to the user and send an e-mail to the site administrator saying that an error has occurred.

1. In Windows Explorer, navigate to C:\BAND and copy the Chapter12 folder, naming the copy Chapter13.

2. Start Web Matrix, and open default.aspx from the Chapter13 folder.

3. Switch to the Code view of the page, and change the code within the Page_Load event handler to the following:

```
// populate the page on first load
if (!Page.IsPostBack)
{
  // create the data object that we need
  DataAccess objData = new DataAccess();

  try{
    // get a DataReader and bind it to the listbox
    lstElements.DataSource = objData.ExecuteReader("stpGetAllElemens");
    lstElements.DataTextField = "ElementName";
    lstElements.DataValueField = "ElementID";
    lstElements.DataBind();

    // add a default entry
    lstElements.Items.Insert(0, ⏎
      new ListItem("<<select an element>>", ""));
  }
  finally
  {
    // clean up the data object
    objData.Dispose();
  }
}
```

4. Execute the page, and if necessary start the Web Matrix Web server. The page should generate an error similar to the one shown in Figure 13-2.

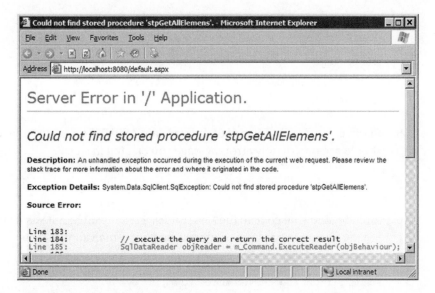

Figure 13-2. Unhelpful error messages are still presented to the user.

5. Switch to Web Matrix, and add a new HTML page to the application called error.htm.

6. In the Design view of error.htm, add the error message, as shown in Figure 13-3.

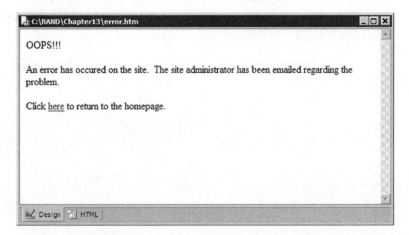

Figure 13-3. The friendly error message

The hyperlink on the last line (shown underlined) is a link back to default.aspx and can be dragged onto the page from the HTML Elements section of the Web Matrix toolbox.

7. Open the `web.config` file, and add the following to the `<configuration>` section of the file:

```
<system.web>
   <customErrors mode="On" defaultRedirect="error.htm" />
</system.web>
```

8. Rerun `default.aspx`. Instead of the standard ASP.NET error message, you should see the friendly error message you created in step 6.

9. Add a new `Global.asax` file to the solution, and call it `global.asax`.

10. Add the following code to the `Application_Error` event handler, substituting the `webmaster@apress.com` address for your e-mail address:

```
// set the content of the e-mail
string strFrom = "webmaster@apress.com";
string strTo = "webmaster@apress.com";
string strSubject = "Error in " + Request.Url.AbsoluteUri + " page";
string strMessage = Server.GetLastError().InnerException.ToString();

// send the mail
System.Web.Mail.SmtpMail.Send(strFrom, strTo, strSubject, strMessage);
```

11. Rerun `default.aspx`, and, as well as the friendly error message from step 6, you should also receive an e-mail containing the complete error details, as shown in Figure 13-4.

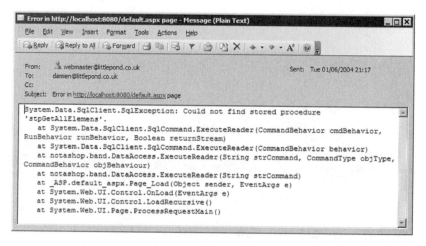

Figure 13-4. Error messages are now e-mailed.

12. Open default.aspx, and change the stored procedure name back to the correct value so that you no longer generate the error.

```
lstElements.DataSource = objData.ExecuteReader("stpGetAllElements");
```

13. Open web.config, and change the mode attribute of customErrors to RemoteOnly.

```
<customErrors mode="RemoteOnly" defaultRedirect="error.htm" />
```

How It Works

In this example, you've modified the home page for the BAND HTML Reference, default.aspx, by adding the required error handling to it. All your interactions with the DataAccess object occur within a try..catch..finally block, and if an error is raised, you dispose of the DataAccess object within the finally part of the block.

However, we've introduced a deliberate mistake into the page by calling a stored procedure that doesn't exist—we've misspelled the name of the stored procedure as stpGetAllElemens instead of stpGetAllElements. This will always throw an error—just what we need for the rest of the example.

Rather than present the user with the unhelpful error page that ASP.NET will generate, as shown in Figure 13-2, you've created a more helpful error message in step 6 that will be used instead.

With a friendly error page created, you can tell the application to use this error message whenever an error is raised. You do this using the <customErrors> element within the <system.web> section of web.config.

```
<system.web>
  <customErrors mode="On" defaultRedirect="error.htm" />
</system.web>
```

By specifying a defaultRedirect you're telling ASP.NET that whenever an error occurs, you want to be shown a specific page, error.htm, rather than being presented with the ASP.NET error.

This isn't the end of the story; you can determine when the error message is actually shown by using the mode attribute.

The mode attribute can take one of three possible values: on, off, and RemoteOnly. A value of on always redirects to the specified error page, and off, not surprisingly, never redirects to the error page and gives the full error message to the user.

The remaining value, RemoteOnly, is a combination of on and off. If accessing the page from the local machine, then it appears as though error handling is turned off; if accessing from a remote machine (for example, across the Internet), the error handling appears to be turned on and all errors redirect to the friendly error message.

You've had to use a value of on for mode in this example because you want to see the error page. Because you're running on the local machine, a value of RemoteOnly would act the same as a value of off, and you wouldn't see the friendly error page.

> **NOTE** *When developing you'll use either the* off *or the* RemoteOnly *values because you want to see the real error messages immediately. The best one to use, if possible, is the* RemoteOnly *value because you can leave this as the same value for both the development and live sites—it's easy to forget to change this value, and* RemoteOnly *will not allow real errors to be displayed across the Internet.*

It's all well and good dealing with the error and presenting the user with a friendly error message, but unless you, as the site developer, actually know about the error, you're no further forward—you need to know about the error before you can fix it. The clue to how you do this is in the friendly error message that's presented to the user—yes, you'll be automatically emailed every time an error is generated. If nothing else, the deluge of e-mails in your inbox will prompt you to fix the problem!

To enable e-mail messages to be generated for every error that's raised for the application, you can take advantage of the Error event of the Application object in global.asax.

```
public void Application_Error(Object sender, EventArgs e) {
    // set the content of the e-mail
    string strFrom = "webmaster@apress.com";
    string strTo = " webmaster@apress.com";
    string strSubject = "Error in " + Request.Url.AbsoluteUri + " page";
    string strMessage = Server.GetLastError().InnerException.ToString();

    // send the mail
    System.Web.Mail.SmtpMail.Send(strFrom, strTo, strSubject, strMessage);
}
```

The `Application_Error` event is raised whenever an error is generated anywhere in the application. You use the `InnerException` property of the `Server.GetLastError()` method to return the details of the error. The `SmtpMail.Send()` method accepts the fairly self-explanatory parameters and sends the message to the recipient.

As you saw in Figure 13-4, the error message contains a quite detailed error trace that should help track down the error.

Although you're sending an e-mail containing only the error that has been raised, you can perform any number of tasks in the `Application_Error` event handler. You could write an entry to the event log, log the error to the database, or log the error to a text file.

Stored Procedures and the DataAccess Class

You've already seen that the DataAccess class allows you to execute stored procedures within the database. There's one drawback, though—you can't, at the moment, pass any parameters to the stored procedure.

To pass parameters to stored procedures, you could require a fully formed `SqlParameter` object to be passed to the DataAccess class, but the whole point of the class is to shield the interaction with the database and specific database objects. By requiring them to create `SqlParameter` objects, you've removed one of the main reasons for the class.

You'll now add several new methods to the class in order to add parameters to the database call. Figure 13-5 shows these methods in the updated entity diagram.

```
+-----------------------------------------------------------------------------+
|                              DataAccess                                      |
+-----------------------------------------------------------------------------+
|                                                                             |
+-----------------------------------------------------------------------------+
| +New()                                                                      |
| +Dispose()                                                                  |
| -OpenConnection()                                                           |
| -CloseConnection()                                                          |
| +AddParameter(in strName, in objType, in objDirection) : void               |
| +AddParameter(in strName, in objType, in objDirection, in ojbValue) : void  |
| +GetParameter(in strName) : object                                          |
| +ModifyParameter(in strName, in objValue) : void                            |
| +RemoveParameter(in strName)                                                |
| +ExecuteAdapter(in strCommand) : SqlDataAdapter                             |
| +ExecuteAdapter(in strCommnad, in objType : SqlDataAdapter                  |
| +ExecuteNonQuery(in strCommand) : int                                       |
| +ExecuteNonQuery(in strCommand, in objType) : int                           |
| +ExecuteReader(in strCommand) : SqlDataReader                               |
| +ExecuteReader(in strCommand, in objType : SqlDataReader                    |
| +ExecuteReader(in strCommand, in objType, in objBehaviour) : SqlDataReader  |
| +ExecuteScalar(in strCommand) : object                                      |
| +ExecuteScalar(in strCommand, in objType) : object                         |
+-----------------------------------------------------------------------------+
```

Figure 13-5. The DataAccess class with the parameter methods added

As you can see, you have five new methods (the two overloaded AddParameter() methods and another three that allow you to manipulate the parameters) that allow you to control what parameters are passed to the query.

- **AddParameter**: The overloaded AddParameter() methods allow a new parameter to be added. The versions differ only in that the second version allows a value to be set for the parameter (which you won't need if the parameter is an output parameter).

- **GetParameter**: This method returns the current value of the parameter and can be used to retrieve the values of output parameters once the database call has been made.

- **ModifyParameter**: The ModifyParameter() method allows the value of the specified parameter to be changed.

- **RemoveParameter**: If for some reason you no longer require the parameter that you've added, you can use RemoveParameter() to remove it.

Try It Out: Updating the DataAccess Class

You'll now add the five new methods for handling parameters to the DataAccess object.

1. Start Web Matrix, and open code.cs in the C\BAND\Chapter13 folder.

2. Add the following two AddParameter() methods to the DataAccess class:

```
public void AddParameter(string strName, SqlDbType objType, ⏎
  ParameterDirection objDirection)
{
  SqlParameter l_Param = new SqlParameter();
  l_Param.ParameterName = strName;
  l_Param.SqlDbType = objType;
  l_Param.Direction = objDirection;
  m_Command.Parameters.Add (l_Param);
}

public void AddParameter(string strName, SqlDbType objType, ⏎
  ParameterDirection objDirection, object objValue)
{
  AddParameter(strName, objType, objDirection);
  ModifyParameter(strName, objValue);
}
```

3. Add the GetParameter() method.

```
public object GetParameter(string strName)
{
  // does the parameter exist
  if (m_Command.Parameters.IndexOf(strName) != 0)
  {
    return(m_Command.Parameters[strName].Value);
  }
  else
  {
    return(null);
  }
}
```

4. Add the ModifyParameter() method.

```
public void ModifyParameter(string strName, object objValue)
{
  // we need to play nice with GUIDs
  if (m_Command.Parameters[strName].SqlDbType == ⏎
    SqlDbType.UniqueIdentifier){
    // if a string then need to create a new GUID object
    if (objValue.GetType() == typeof(System.String)){
      objValue = new System.Guid(objValue.ToString());
    }
  }

  // modify the value of the parameter
  m_Command.Parameters[strName].Value = objValue;
}
```

5. Add the RemoveParameter() method.

```
public void RemoveParameter(string strName)
{
  // does the parameter exist
  if (m_Command.Parameters.IndexOf(strName) != 0)
  {
    m_Command.Parameters.RemoveAt( ⏎
      m_Command.Parameters.IndexOf(strName));
  }
}
```

How It Works

The five methods you've added aren't that complex, and they quite nicely shield the page developer from some of the complexities of dealing with parameters. Granted, you still need to know the different SqlDbType and ParameterDirection values for the parameter, but you can provide documentation for each stored procedure that details what values are required.

The first two methods to look at are RemoveParameter() and GetParameter(). These are the two simplest methods that you've added, so it makes sense to start here.

RemoveParameter() removes the parameter from the Parameters collection of the m_Command object, which you'll recall is the SqlCommand object that you use to interact with the database. Before you do this, you must first check that the parameter exists using the IndexOf() method of the collection. If the parameter exists, it's a simple matter to use RemoveAt() to remove it.

```
if (m_Command.Parameters.IndexOf(strName) != 0)
{
  m_Command.Parameters.RemoveAt( ↵
    m_Command.Parameters.IndexOf(strName));
}
```

The GetParameter() method is similar to RemoveParameter(). You first check to see if the parameter exists. If it does, you return its value; if it doesn't, you return null.

```
if (m_Command.Parameters.IndexOf(strName) != 0)
{
  return(m_Command.Parameters[strName].Value);
}
else
{
  return(null);
}
```

Modifying the value of a parameter, as you do in the ModifyParameter() method, is slightly more complex than the two methods you've already looked at because you need to be careful when dealing with global unique identifier (GUID) values.

In most cases, dealing with GUIDs using the System.Guid structure is long winded, and using a string is by far easier. You can perform comparisons on strings a lot easier than you can with the System.Guid structure, and for this reason alone we're using a string rather than a System.Guid.

However, if you try to use a string as the value of a parameter that has a type of SqlDbType.UniqueIdentifier, an error will be generated as a string cannot automatically be converted to a System.Guid. You must check for this condition and create the correct System.Guid if required.

You can do this by first checking that the type of the parameter is SqlDbType.UniqueIdentifier and that the type of the value you're using is String. If it is, you change the value you're trying to add into a System.Guid.

```
// we need to play nice with GUIDs
if (m_Command.Parameters[strName].SqlDbType == ⏎
  SqlDbType.UniqueIdentifier){
  // if a string then need to create a new GUID object
  if (objValue.GetType() == typeof(System.String)){
    objValue = new System.Guid(objValue.ToString());
  }
}
```

You can then set the value of the parameter correctly:

```
m_Command.Parameters[strName].Value = objValue;
```

Although the AddParameter() methods are the two you're likely to use first, you're looking at them last because they rely on the functionality provided by ModifyParameter().

The first AddParameter() method doesn't accept a value for the parameter and simply creates a new instance of SqlParameter; sets its name, type, and direction; and then adds it to the Parameters collection of m_Command.

```
public void AddParameter(string strName, SqlDbType objType, ⏎
  ParameterDirection objDirection)
{
  SqlParameter l_Param = new SqlParameter();
  l_Param.ParameterName = strName;
  l_Param.SqlDbType = objType;
  l_Param.Direction = objDirection;
  m_Command.Parameters.Add (l_Param);
}
```

The second AddParameter() method also accepts the value that you want to set for the parameter. You could write a method that creates a new SqlParameter, sets the necessary properties, and then adds the parameter to m_Command. However, you don't want to write any more code than is necessary, and you can use the existing AddParameter() and ModifyParameter() methods to do the same task.

```
public void AddParameter(string strName, SqlDbType objType, ⌮
  ParameterDirection objDirection, object objValue)
{
  AddParameter(strName, objType, objDirection);
  ModifyParameter(strName, objValue);
}
```

You use the first AddParameter() method to add the parameter to the Parameters collection, and then you use ModifyParameter() to set its value.

Try It Out: Adding Parameters to Database Calls

In this exercise, you'll build a page that allows you to view the details for the selected element. You'll first need to modify default.aspx to allow you to select which of the elements you want to view.

1. Copy the icons folder from the images folder in the code download for the case study to the C:\BAND\Chapter13\images folder.

2. Start Web Matrix, and open default.aspx in the C:\BAND\Chapter13 folder.

3. In the Design view, add a button after the drop-down list. Enter **GO>>** for Text and **btnGo** for its ID. The page should look like Figure 13-6.

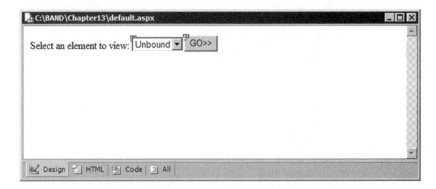

Figure 13-6. Adding the dynamic elements to the home page

4. Double-click the GO>> button to add the click event handler. Within the `btnGo_Click` event handler, add the following code:

```
// only if the first entry isn't selected
if(lstElements.SelectedIndex != 0)
{
    // navigate to the element page
    Response.Redirect("element.aspx?eid=" + lstElements.SelectedValue);
}
```

5. Create a new ASP.NET Page called `element.aspx`. In the Design view of the page, add the text and controls as shown in Figure 13-7.

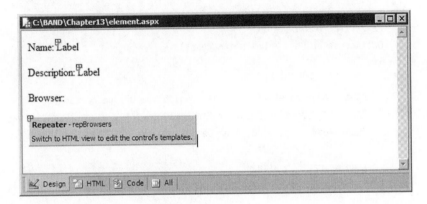

Figure 13-7. The layout of `element.aspx`

The two Label controls have names of `lblName` and `lblDescription`, and the Repeater, as you can see, has a name of `repBrowsers`.

6. Switch to the All view of the page, and add the following before the first `<script>` tag:

```
<%@ import Namespace="System.Data" %>
<%@ import Namespace="System.Data.SqlClient" %>
<%@ import Namespace="notashop.band" %>
<%@ assembly Src="code.cs" %>
```

7. Switch to HTML view, and add the following `<ItemTemplate>` to the repBrowsers Repeater control:

```
<ItemTemplate>
  <asp:Image id="imgBrowserImage" width="39" height="18" ⏎
    runat="server"></asp:Image>
</ItemTemplate>
```

8. Add a Load event for the page, and place the following code in the Page_Load event handler:

```
// get the id from the query string
string m_ElementID = Request.QueryString["eid"];

// get the basic details
DataAccess objData = new DataAccess();
try
{
  objData.AddParameter("@element", SqlDbType.UniqueIdentifier, ⏎
   ParameterDirection.Input, m_ElementID);
  SqlDataReader objReader = objData.ExecuteReader("stpLoadElement");

  // do we have an element
  if (objReader.Read())
  {
    // display the basic details
    lblName.Text = objReader["ElementName"].ToString();
    lblDescription.Text = objReader["ElementDescription"].ToString();

    // get the browser details
    DataAccess objDataBrowsers = new DataAccess();
    try
    {
      objDataBrowsers.AddParameter("@element", ⏎
        SqlDbType.UniqueIdentifier, ParameterDirection.Input, ⏎
        m_ElementID);
      repBrowsers.DataSource = ⏎
        objDataBrowsers.ExecuteReader("stpLoadElementInBrowser");
      repBrowsers.DataBind();
    }
    finally
    {
      objDataBrowsers.Dispose();
```

```
      }
    }
  }
  finally
  {
      objData.Dispose();
  }
```

9. Add an ItemDataBound event to repBrowsers, and place the following in
    the repBrowsers_ItemDataBound event handler:

    ```
    ((Image)e.Item.FindControl("imgBrowserImage")).ImageUrl = ⤶
      DataBinder.Eval(e.Item.DataItem, "ImageUrl").ToString();
    ```

10. Execute default.aspx, and select the A element in the drop-down list.
    Click the GO>> button to open element.aspx.

11. The details for the A element will be returned, as shown in Figure 13-8.

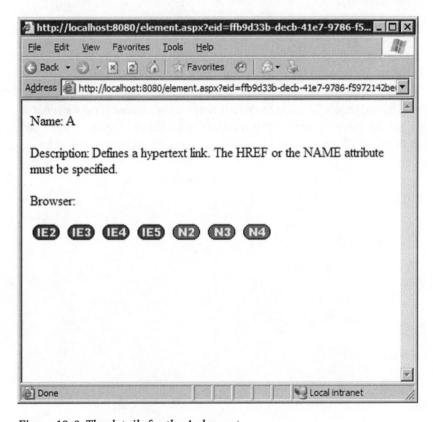

Figure 13-8. The details for the A element

How It Works

The first thing you must ensure is that when you have some details for an element to show, you have the correct icons available. Rather than creating new ones, you copy the ones from the code download. You can still run the example without the icons, but instead of the easy-to-use icons as shown in Figure 13-8, you'll get the "image not found" icon, and any information that you're trying to convey will be lost.

Before you moved on to look at adding the parameters in element.aspx, you modified the home page, default.aspx, to allow you to select an element to view. You do this by adding a button control and adding a Repsonse.Redirect to the click event handler, first checking that an element has been selected.

```
// only if the first entry isn't selected
if(lstElements.SelectedIndex != 0)
{
    // navigate to the element page
    Response.Redirect("element.aspx?eid=" + lstElements.SelectedValue);
}
```

The redirect takes you to element.aspx with the value of the element you've selected appended to the querystring as the eid variable.

Moving onto element.aspx, you'll see that you're using a couple of Label controls to hold the name and the description for the element and a Repeater control to hold the browser support information. You'll shortly populate these controls, but first you'll look at the way you deal with error handling within the Page_Load event.

If you look at Page_Load, you'll see that you have two try..catch..finally blocks with one nested inside the other.

```
try
{
    // some work is done here
    try
    {
        // some work is done here
    }
    finally
    {
        objDataBrowsers.Dispose();
    }
}
```

```
finally
{
  objData.Dispose();
}
```

Having the try..catch..finally blocks nested in this manner allows you to gracefully handle errors no matter where they occur. If an error occurs within the inner try..catch..finally block, the inner finally statement will execute and dispose of objDataBrowsers correctly. Because you haven't handled the error using a catch statement within the inner try..catch..finally block, the outer finally statement will also be executed and will dispose of objData.

You'll also notice that you use two different DataAccess objects. The DataAccess class is, at the moment, a "one-shot" class—you can use it for one access to the database, and then you can't use it again. This stops you getting into all sorts of problems with having the wrong parameters passed to stored procedures and also makes for more readable code. In this example, you can see that you use objData to get the details for the element and then use objDataBrowsers to get the browser support details; you can immediately see which object contains what data from the name of the object. If you had used only one object, it would be difficult to see what the object was currently being used for.

With the first use of DataAccess, objData, you use the stpLoadElement stored procedure to return the name and description for the selected element. Before you can call the stored procedure, you must add the @element parameter. You can do this using the AddParameter() method and specifying the correct name, type, direction, and value for the parameter.

```
objData.AddParameter("@element", SqlDbType.UniqueIdentifier, ⤶
 ParameterDirection.Input, m_ElementID);
```

You then execute the stored procedure and display the name and description for the element if you've returned a record.

```
SqlDataReaer objReader = objData.ExecuteReader("stpLoadElement");

// do we have an element
if (objReader.Read())
{
  // display the basic details
  lblName.Text = objReader["ElementName"].ToString();
  lblDescription.Text = objReader["ElementDescription"].ToString();
```

If you've retrieved an element, you also want to show the details of what browsers support the element. You do this by using the second DataAccess object, objDataBrowsers, to execute the stpLoadElementInBrowser stored procedure.

The stpLoadElementInBrowser stored procedure returns the BrowserID and ImageUrl for all the browsers that support the element. It accomplishes this by performing a join across tblBrowser, tblDoesBrowserSupportElement, and tblImage.

```
SELECT tblDoesBrowserSupportElement.BrowserID, tblImage.ImageUrl
FROM tblBrowser
  INNER JOIN tblDoesBrowserSupportElement ON
    tblBrowser.BrowserID = tblDoesBrowserSupportElement.BrowserID
  INNER JOIN tblImage ON tblBrowser.BrowserID = tblImage.BrowserID
WHERE tblDoesBrowserSupportElement.ElementID = @element
ORDER BY tblBrowser.BrowserName
```

Before you can call stpLoadElementInBrowser, you again need to set the @element parameter. Instead of returning the results into a SqlDataReader object, you pass it into the DataSource property of repBrowsers before binding the data using the DataBind() method.

```
// get the browser details
DataAccess objDataBrowsers = new DataAccess();
try
{
  objDataBrowsers.AddParameter("@element", ⤸
    SqlDbType.UniqueIdentifier, ParameterDirection.Input, ⤸
    m_ElementID);
  repBrowsers.DataSource = ⤸
    objDataBrowsers.ExecuteReader("stpLoadElementInBrowser");
  repBrowsers.DataBind();
```

Because you've defined an ItemDataBound event for repBrowsers, this will be executed for every record that's returned from stpLoadElementInBrowser, and you use the ImageUrl field to set the ImageUrl property for the Image control within the Repeater control's ItemTemplate.

```
((Image)e.Item.FindControl("imgBrowserImage")).ImageUrl = ⤸
  DataBinder.Eval(e.Item.DataItem, "ImageUrl").ToString();
```

Controlling User Access

Although the user-facing parts of a Web site are important, what the user sees isn't the only part of the Web site. For all data-driven Web sites, you'll also have an administration section of the site to which you need to restrict access.

To control access to the site, you must authenticate the users who attempt to access the protected areas to ensure they are who they say they are. After all, you don't want any Tom, Dick, or Harry accessing the site and changing your data.

You have several options for authenticating users. You could use integrated Windows security and require that a valid Windows username and password is used to access the site, or you could require that all users have a Microsoft Passport account to access the site. You could even go as far as requiring that an X509 certificate is required before the administration side of the site can be accessed.

> **NOTE** *You have a lot more options for security and authentication using .NET than covered here. Entire books have been written regarding Web site security, and we can't even begin to scratch the surface of what's available. For a good start, refer to* http://msdn.microsoft.com/library/en-us/cpguide/html/cpconASPNETWebApplicationSecurity.asp.

Most of the topics for securing Web sites are beyond the scope of this book. For the BAND HMTL Reference, you'll implement your own Security class that will allow you to control, relatively simply, whether a user can access the site.

To log in, you'll require that a username and password be entered before reaching the administration section. You obviously need to store this username and password somewhere, so you store this in tblUser within the database. Figure 13-9 shows the structure of this table.

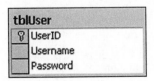

Figure 13-9. The user table

To implement security in the BAND HTML Reference, you'll build another class, called Security. This class has three methods that allow you to check whether a user is logged in, log in a user using the username and password they've specified, or log out a currently logged-in user.

Try It Out: Building the Security Class

In this example, you'll build the Security class and add the three methods that will allow you to restrict access to the parts of the site that you desire.

1. Start Web Matrix, and open code.cs in the C:\BAND\Chapter13 folder.

2. Add a new class definition for Security at the bottom of the file as follows:

```
public class Security
{
}
```

3. Add the static IsLoggedIn() method.

```
// function to check if the user is logged in
public static bool IsLoggedIn(bool boolRedirect)
{
  bool l_Return = true;

  // if no user id then we're not logged in
  if (HttpContext.Current.Session["UserID"] == null)
  {
    l_Return = false;
  }

  // do we want to do the redirect
  if (boolRedirect == true && l_Return == false)
  {
    // now redirect to the login page
    HttpContext.Current.Response.Redirect(HttpContext.Current.Request.
    ApplicationPath.TrimEnd('/') + "/security/login.aspx");
  }

  // now return the correct value
  return(l_Return);
}
```

4. Add the Login() method.

```
public static bool Login(string strUsername, string strPassword)
{
    // create the necessary objects
    DataAccess l_Data = new DataAccess();
    bool l_Return;

    try
    {
        // add the parameters
        l_Data.AddParameter("@username", SqlDbType.VarChar ↵
            ParameterDirection.Input, strUsername);
        l_Data.AddParameter("@password", SqlDbType.VarChar ↵
            ParameterDirection.Input, strPassword);

        // store the user id in the session
        HttpContext.Current.Session["UserID"] = ↵
            l_Data.ExecuteScalar("stpSecurityLogin");

        // return correct value of true or false
        if (HttpContext.Current.Session["UserID"] != null)
        {
            // we've logged in so return true
            l_Return = true;
        }
        else
        {
            // we've not logged in so return false
            l_Return = false;
        }
    }
    finally
    {
        // close the data connection
        l_Data.Dispose();
    }

    // return the results
    return (l_Return);
}
```

5. Add the Logout() method.

```
public static void Logout()
{
    // simply abandon the session
    HttpContext.Current.Session.Abandon();
}
```

How It Works

The first method you looked at is the IsLoggedIn() method, and this is the most critical method within the Security class.

As you can see, you're relying on a UserID being stored in the session object. As you'll soon see, once a user logs in correctly, you store the UserID from tblUser in the session object, and you can use this to determine if the user is logged in.

If there's a UserID, the user is logged in, and you can return true from the function. If there isn't a UserID in the session, then the user isn't logged in, and you can either return false from the method or, if you've requested it by specifying true as the sole parameter to the method, redirect to the login page at security/login.aspx.

You've provided the optional redirection to the login page so that you can use the IsLoggedIn() method to perform two roles within the Security class. You can use it to check if a user is logged in and, if they're not, redirect to the login page by specifying a parameter of true to the method call.

However, you may also want to simply check if a user is logged in—you may want to change the user interface of the site (perhaps to decide if you need to show a login or a logout button), and you can perform this action by passing false as the parameter. If the user is logged in, the method will return true, and if they're not logged in, the method will return false.

As you'll see in the next example, you can use this method as the first call in the Page_Load event for all the pages in the administration section of the site, and they will require a valid username and password to be granted access. You'll look at this in more detail, but it's as easy as adding the following to the top of the Page_Load event handler:

```
Security.IsLoggedIn(true);
```

To set the UserID in the session variable, you can use the Login() method and pass in the username and the password that the user has entered. These are added as parameters to a DataAccess object, and the stpSecurityLogin stored procedure

494

is called. This stored procedure uses the provided username and password to
return the corresponding UserID:

```
SELECT tblUser.UserID
FROM tblUser
WHERE tblUser.Username = @username and tblUser.Password = @password
```

The stored procedure will return a record containing a single field if the username and password match an entry in the database. You store this value directly
in the UserID session variable by using the ExecuteScalar() method to call the
stored procedure.

```
HttpContext.Current.Session["UserID"] = ⏎
  l_Data.ExecuteScalar("stpSecurityLogin", ⏎
  CommandType.StoredProcedure);
```

Storing the result of the ExecuteScalar() method directly in a session object
will result in either a correct UserID being stored or a value of null. You can use this
fact to return the correct value of true or false from the Login() method.

```
if (HttpContext.Current.Session["UserID"] != null)
{
  // we've logged in so return true
  l_Return = true;
}
else
{
  // we've not logged in so return false
  l_Return = false;
}
```

The value returned from the Login() method can then be used to determine
whether the login was successful. If it was successful, you can redirect to the correct
place, and if unsuccessful, you can display a suitable error message to the user.

If you have a Login() method, it stands to reason you'll need an associated
Logout() method. Although the user's session will expire, by default, after 20 min-
utes, you still want to give them the option of manually logging out from the site.
You do this in the Logout() method by simply abandoning the current session.

```
HttpContext.Current.Session.Abandon();
```

Try It Out: Using the Security Class

You'll now build the pages that are required to allow you to control access to the site. You'll build a basic login page and the corresponding logout page before looking at the first page in the administration section and blocking access to this page if the user can't supply a valid username and password.

1. Open Web Matrix, and create a new security folder in the C:\BAND\Chapter13 folder.

2. To this new folder, add an ASP.NET page called login.aspx.

3. Add the two pieces of text, the corresponding text boxes, two buttons, and a label to the page as shown in Figure 13-10.

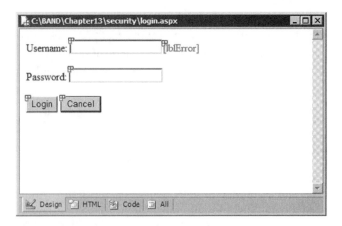

Figure 13-10. The login page

4. Change the IDs of the two text boxes to txtUsername and txtPassword and set the TextMode property of txtPassword to Password. The two buttons should have their Text property changed to Login and Cancel, respectively, and have their ID values set to the matching btnLogin and btnCancel. The Label control has an ID of lblError, its Text property is set to an empty string, and its ForeColor property is set to Red.

5. Double-click the Login button to create the btnLogin_Click event handler and add the following code:

```
// check if the details are correct
if (Security.Login(txtUsername.Text, txtPassword.Text)) {
  // redirect to admin home page
```

```
    Response.Redirect("../admin/default.aspx");
}else{
    // set the error message
    lblError.Text = "Invalid username/password";
}
```

6. Switch back to Design view, double-click the Cancel button to add the btnCancel_Click event handler, and add the following to it:

```
// redirect to the home page
Response.Redirect("../default.aspx");
```

7. Switch to the All view of the page, and add the following before the first `<script>` tag:

```
<%@ assembly Src="../code.cs" %>
<%@ import Namespace="notashop.band" %>
```

8. Add a new ASP.NET page to the security folder, and call it logout.aspx. Add a Page_Load event with the following definition:

```
void Page_Load(object sender, EventArgs e) {
    // call the logout method
    Security.Logout();

    // redirect to the home page
    Response.Redirect("../default.aspx");
}
```

9. Switch to the All view of the page, and add the following before the first `<script>` tag:

```
<%@ assembly Src="../code.cs" %>
<%@ import Namespace="notashop.band" %>
```

10. Create a new folder in C:\BAND\Chapter13 called admin.

11. Open Windows Explorer, and copy C:\BAND\Chapter13\default.aspx to C:\BAND\Chapter13\admin\default.aspx.

12. Switch to Web Matrix, and open the `default.aspx` file in the admin folder. Modify the page so that it looks like Figure 13-11.

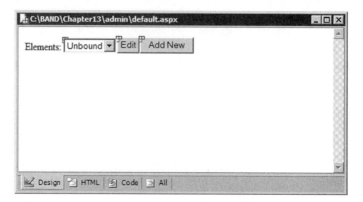

Figure 13-11. The administration home page

13. The `Edit` button is actually the GO>> button from the original page and has had its ID changed to btnElementEdit and its `Text` property changed to Edit. The Add New button is a new control and has a name of btnElementAdd.

14. Select btnElementEdit, and switch to the Events view in the Properties window. Remove `btnGo_Click` from the click event, and double-click the drop-down list to add the new `btnElementEdit_Click` event handler.

15. Add the following to the `btnElementEdit_Click` event handler:

```
// redirect to the edit page and specify the ID
Response.Redirect("elements/edit.aspx?id=" + lstElements.SelectedValue);
```

16. Remove the event handler for `btnGo_Click` completely from the code.

17. Add a new click event handler for btnElementAdd, and add the following code to the `btnElementAdd_Click` event handler:

```
// redirect to the edit page without and id
Response.Redirect("elements/edit.aspx");
```

18. Add the following as the first lines of the `Page_Load` event handler:

```
// must be logged in to get here
Security.IsLoggedIn(true);
```

19. Switch to the All view of the page, and change the assembly directive for `code.cs` to the following:

```
<%@ assembly Src="../code.cs" %>
```

20. Switch to the Design view of the page, and add a new button to the page called btnLogout with a Text property of Logout.

21. Double-click btnLogout to add a new click handler, and add the following code to the btnLogout_Click event handler:

```
// redirect to the logout page
Response.Redirect("../security/logout.aspx");
```

22. Execute the page, making sure that the application directory is `C:\BAND\Chapter13`, not `C:\BAND\Chapter13\admin`.

23. Rather than the page you expect, you're taken to the login page. Enter a username of **admin** and a password of **letmein**, and click the Login button.

24. You'll be presented with an error, shown in Figure 13-12, because the details that you've entered aren't correct.

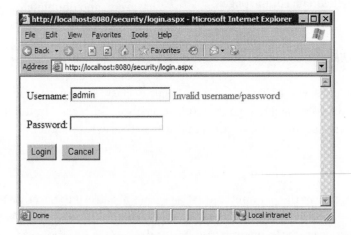

Figure 13-12. You must have a valid username and password to log in.

25. Enter the correct details—this time entering the password of **password**—and click the Login button.

26. Instead of an error message, you'll be shown the administration home page in Figure 13-13.

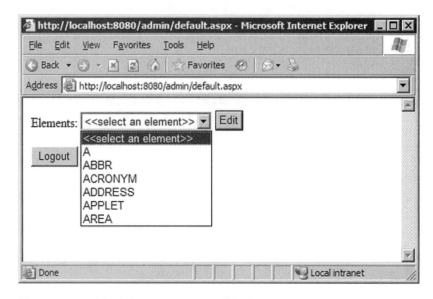

Figure 13-13. Administrators can modify elements

27. Click the Logout button to log out of the site and return to the BAND HTML Reference home page.

How It Works

That wasn't too hard, was it? You've used the Security class, and you've seen that you can block access to pages, as you've done in admin/default.aspx, by adding a call to IsLoggedIn() as the first statement in the Page_Load event handler.

```
Security.IsLoggedIn(true);
```

You pass in true as the parameter to IsLoggedIn() because if the user isn't logged in, you want them to be forced to enter a username and password. As you saw in the previous example, passing true causes the security/login.aspx page to be displayed—allowing the user to enter their username and password.

If you look at the code for login.aspx, you'll see that the majority of the work required to check for a valid username and password is contained within the Login() method of the Security class.

```
// check if the details are correct
if (Security.Login(txtUsername.Text, txtPassword.Text)) {
    // redirect to admin home page
    Response.Redirect("../admin/default.aspx");
}else{
    // set the error message
    lblError.Text = "Invalid username/password";
}
```

You pass the username and password that are entered by the user to Security.Login(); if it returns true, you redirect to the administration home page at admin/default.aspx. If the login fails, you display an error message using lblError.

On the administration home page, you've added buttons that allow existing elements to be edited and new elements to be added. You'll look at editing elements shortly when you look at transactions.

Also on the administration home page is a Logout button. To log out, you redirect the user to security/logout.aspx. This page calls the Logout() method on the Security class to abandon the current session and then redirects to the BAND HTML Reference home page at default.aspx.

Using Transactions

Transactions, as you learned in Chapter 11, are a way to group different database commands so that they all complete or they all fail—you can't have some of them completing and some of them failing. It's all or nothing.

To use the correct terminology, you BEGIN a transaction and then perform whatever steps you need to take as part of the transaction. If everything went as you wanted it to, you then COMMIT the transaction, and all modifications are saved to the database. If something has gone wrong, you ROLLBACK the transaction, and the database isn't modified—it'll appear as though the SQL statements you executed never took place.

Transactions, as with most things in the computing world, have their own acronym: ACID. It's not some throwback to the 1960s but the first letters of the four properties that all transactions must exhibit.

Atomic: All statements within the transaction should succeed or fail. The archetypal example that's always used is a bank transfer scenario. If money is being transferred between two bank accounts, taking the money from the source account and putting the money in the destination account both must succeed, or they both must fail. You can't have money removed from the source account but not added to the destination, and you can't have money appearing in the destination account without the money being removed from the source account.

Consistent: A transaction transforms the database from one consistent state to another consistent state.

Isolated: A transaction that's currently executing will not see the results of any other transaction until the other transaction has completed.

Durable: A committed transaction should remain committed in the database even if a failure occurs after the transaction has been committed.

Using MSDE and .NET, transactions can be handled in the following three places:

- **Database**: MSDE makes it possible to implement transactions within stored procedures and ensure that all the statements that are to be executed are indeed executed.

- **Code**: Using ADO.NET you can enlist different commands within the same connection to be part of a transaction. This allows you, as you'll shortly see, to execute several different stored procedures and only commit the results to the database if all the stored procedures execute correctly.

- **COM+ and System.EnterpriseServices**: .NET makes it possible to use the facilities of COM+ to run transactions across several different machines. These distributed transactions aren't a beginner's topic and are beyond the scope of this book.

> **NOTE** *If you want to know more about distributed transactions, refer to "Distributed Transactions Overview" on MSDN at* http://msdn.microsoft.com/library/ en-us/cossdk/htm/pgdtc_dev_3lrn.asp.

One thing to bear in mind when using transactions is that they impart a performance penalty on execution. During the lifetime of the transaction, any resources that are used are locked until the transaction is completed or rolled back. Any other stored procedures trying to access those resources will be blocked and will have to wait until the transaction is over before the resource can be used.

If you're going to use transactions, think carefully about it. Obviously sometimes you must use transactions to ensure that the data is correct and can't be left

in a state that you don't want it in. Don't, however, assume that every SQL statement you're executing must be wrapped in BEGIN TRANSACTION and COMMIT
TRANSACTION statements—this will slow the database down an awful lot.

Transactions in the Database

The simplest transaction type you have is a transaction that is "complete" within
one stored procedure—either everything you're trying to do is committed to the
database or it's rolled back.

The BAND HTML Reference contains several places where you want this to
happen. Whenever you want to delete something from the database, it is quite
likely that it's referenced in more than one place.

If you're deleting an element, for instance, then you want to delete the details
from tblElement, but you also need to delete any reference to the element from all
the other tables that it may be in. If you look at the stpDeleteElement stored procedure, you'll see that although the version in the complete BAND HTML Reference
contains a few more DELETE statements, the current version still has two.

```
-- transaction as we don't want to delete half
BEGIN TRANSACTION

-- delete from ATTRIBUTE link details
DELETE FROM tblDoesBrowserSupportElement WHERE ElementID = @element

-- now finally delete the ELEMENT
DELETE FROM tblElementWHERE ElementID = @element

-- now commit this to the database
COMMIT TRANSACTION
```

The first thing you do is use the BEGIN TRANSACTION statement to instruct
the database that you want to execute a transaction. After you execute the two
DELETE statements, you then call the COMMIT TRANSACTION statement to
commit the changes to the database. It's only at this point that the data is actually
deleted from the database.

You'll notice that you don't have a ROLLBACK TRANSACTION statement in
the stored procedure. If a transaction is started and a fatal error is raised, the
ROLLBACK TRANSACTION statement is executed automatically by the database,
which causes any changes to be rolled back. In this case, you wouldn't have an element that was partially deleted.

Although you don't need a ROLLBACK TRANSACTION if you have an error, you do need the COMMIT TRANSACTION statement at the end of the stored procedure. Although the database calls ROLLBACK TRANSACTION automatically if an error has occurred, it won't automatically call COMMIT TRANSACTION if the stored procedure executes successfully.

Failure to commit or roll back a transaction that has been started will result in an error being raised, as shown in the error e-mail in Figure 13-14, which was received as the site was being developed.

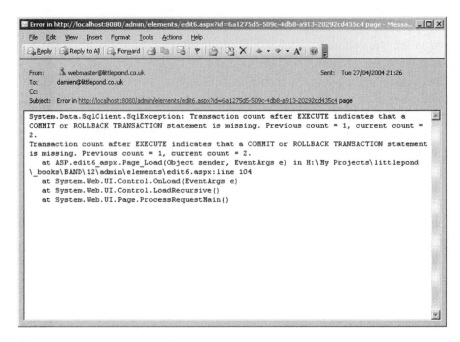

Figure 13-14. You must always commit or roll back a transaction.

As you can see from the first line in the e-mail, your error indicates exactly what the problem is—you haven't called COMMIT or ROLLBACK TRANSACTION to complete the transaction you started.

Using Transactions in Code

Although you've seen how easy it is to use transactions within a single stored procedure, you sometimes need to include several different stored procedures in a transaction. This isn't something you're likely to do an awful lot; you'll find that transactions within a single stored procedure are by far more common.

To illustrate this point, we have one instance of code-based transactions, which you're about to see, in the BAND HTML Reference whereas you have transactions within stored procedures on nearly every edit or delete that you need to make against the database.

That's not to say that code-based transactions aren't of value. Sometimes, such as the example you're about to look at, their use can be a godsend and can reduce the amount of code that needs to be written substantially.

However, as with transactions in stored procedures, code-based transactions add an overhead to the database interactions, so use them only if you absolutely must.

Adding a Transaction to the SqlCommand Object

To use transactions within code, you must use a SqlTransaction object to tell the SqlCommand object that it's part of the transaction.

You'll recall from Chapter 4 that you had a constructor to the SqlCommand object that took a SqlTransaction object as a parameter.

```
SqlCommand(string, SqlConnection, SqlTransaction)
```

Once you have a SqlTransaction object, it's simple to enlist a SqlCommand object in the transaction by passing the object to the SqlCommand constructor, or you can set the Transaction property after you've created the SqlCommand. However, starting the transaction is not as simple as creating a new SqlTransaction object.

To create a SqlTransaction object, you must use the BeginTransaction() method of the SqlConnection object because you cannot directly create a SqlTransaction object. Calling this method creates the necessary SqlTransaction object and tells the SqlConnection that it needs to be transactional.

You can then use the created SqlTransaction object with all the SqlCommand objects that you want to include in the transaction before calling Commit() on the SqlTransaction to commit the transaction to the database or before calling Rollback() to abort the transaction.

The process for using transactions in code is simple and can be broken down into the following six steps:

1. Open the connection to the database.

2. Call the BeginTransaction() method on the SqlConnection to start the transaction, and store the SqlTransaction object for later use.

3. Create a `SqlCommand` object, and specify the `SqlTransaction` object that you want to use.

4. Use the `SqlCommand` object as you normally would.

5. Loop steps 3 and 4 as often as required.

6. Either commit or roll back the transaction by calling the `Commit()` or `Rollback()` method on the `SqlTransaction` object.

Changes to the DataAccess Class

You could create all the necessary code for the previous six steps on every page that you want to make transactional, but as you're trying to hide the page developer from any direct interaction with the database, you can't do this. You can accomplish the same functionality by making a few changes to the DataAccess class.

To implement transactions, you need to add a new constructor as well as three new methods to the DataAccess class.

- **DataAccess(boolean):** If you create the DataAccess class and specify true as the parameter to this constructor, you want to use transactions.

- **Reset():** By the design of the DataAccess class, to this point it has been a "one-shot" class that you could use to access the database only once. The `Reset()` method resets the class while keeping the same connection to the database. Using this method, you can execute multiple queries against the database with the same connection and, if transactional, enlist all the queries within the same transaction.

- **CommitTransaction():** This will wrap the `Commit()` method of the hidden `SqlTransaction` object.

- **RollbackTransaction():** This will wrap the `Rollback()` method of the hidden `SqlTransaction` object.

Figure 13-15 shows the complete entity diagram for the DataAccess class.

```
┌─────────────────────────────────────────────────────────────────┐
│                         DataAccess                                │
├─────────────────────────────────────────────────────────────────┤
│                                                                   │
├─────────────────────────────────────────────────────────────────┤
│ +New()                                                            │
│ +New(in blnTransactional)                                         │
│ +Dispose()                                                        │
│ -OpenConnection()                                                 │
│ -CloseConnection()                                                │
│ +AddParameter(in strName, in objType, in objDirection) : void     │
│ +AddParameter(in strName, in objType, in objDirection, in ojbValue) : void │
│ +GetParameter(in strName) : object                                │
│ +ModifyParameter(in strName, in objValue) : void                  │
│ +RemoveParameter(in strName)                                      │
│ +ExecuteAdapter(in strCommand) : SqlDataAdapter                   │
│ +ExecuteAdapter(in strCommnad, in objType : SqlDataAdapter        │
│ +ExecuteNonQuery(in strCommand) : int                             │
│ +ExecuteNonQuery(in strCommand, in objType) : int                 │
│ +ExecuteReader(in strCommand) : SqlDataReader                     │
│ +ExecuteReader(in strCommand, in objType : SqlDataReader          │
│ +ExecuteReader(in strCommand, in objType, in objBehaviour) : SqlDataReader │
│ +ExecuteScalar(in strCommand) : object                            │
│ +ExecuteScalar(in strCommand, in objType) : object                │
│ +Reset() : void                                                   │
│ +CommitTransaction() : void                                       │
│ +RollbackTransaction() : void                                     │
└─────────────────────────────────────────────────────────────────┘
```

Figure 13-15. The completed DataAccess class entity diagram

Try It Out: Adding Transactions to the DataAccess Class

You'll now make the changes to the DataAccess class to support transactions. In the following example, you'll then look at using the completed class.

1. Start Web Matrix, and open code.cs in the C:\BAND\Chapter13 folder.

2. Add a new member variable to the start of the DataAccess class.

   ```
   SqlTransaction m_Transaction;
   ```

3. Change the existing constructor to the following:

   ```
   public DataAccess() : this(false)
   {
   }
   ```

4. Add the new transactional constructor.

   ```
   public DataAccess(bool IsTransaction)
   {
       // setup the connection object
       m_Connection = new SqlConnection();
   ```

```
m_Connection.ConnectionString = ⤦
  ConfigurationSettings.AppSettings["Database"];

// begin the transaction (if required)
if (IsTransaction == true)
{
  // open the connection
  OpenConnection();

  m_Transaction = m_Connection.BeginTransaction();
}

// reset the state of the object
Reset();
}
```

5. Add the Reset() method.

```
public void Reset(){
  // setup the command object
  m_Command = new SqlCommand();
  m_Command.Connection = m_Connection;

  // add the transaction if we need to
  if (m_Transaction != null){
    m_Command.Transaction = m_Transaction;
  }
}
```

6. Add the CommitTransaction() and RollbackTransaction() methods.

```
public void CommitTransaction()
{
  m_Transaction.Commit();
}

public void RollbackTransaction()
{
  m_Transaction.Rollback();
}
```

How It Works

The first change you'll notice to the DataAccess class is that you've removed the existing constructor and replaced it with two new ones.

The default constructor has no implementation and simply makes a call to the "real" constructor, specifying that you don't want to make this instance of the DataAccess object transactional by passing false as the parameter.

```
Public DataAccess () : this (false)
```

You could have written two different constructors, but the only difference between the two would be that one uses transactions and the other doesn't. You need to pass true to use transactions so it makes sense that passing false, as you do for the default constructor, won't use transactions.

The second constructor is the one where you do all the setup work; the first two lines should be familiar—you create the SqlConnection object and set the ConnectionString property correctly.

```
m_Connection = new SqlConnection();
m_Connection.ConnectionString = ↵
 ConfigurationSettings.AppSettings["Database"];
```

You then check to see if you want to use transactions for the DataAccess object by checking the parameter that you passed to the constructor. If it's true, then you want to make this instance of DataAccess transactional.

```
// begin the transaction (if required)
if (IsTransaction == true)
{
```

If you've requested a transaction, the first thing you need to do is open the connection to the database, because you can't start a transaction without an open database connection. As you'll recall from Chapter 4, the only real rule was "don't open the connection to the database until the last possible moment." Doing so here breaks that rule. Unfortunately, you must have an open connection to the database, and this is another indicator of why you should use transactions in code only when you need to do so.

```
// open the database connection
m_Connection.Open();
```

Once the connection to the database has been opened, you can then call the BeginTransaction() method of the SqlConnection object. This starts a transaction and returns the SqlTransaction object that you need to store as m_Transaction for use later.

```
// start the transaction
m_Transaction = m_Connection.BeginTransaction();
}
```

Irrespective of whether you're using transactions, you then call the Reset() method to initialize the SqlCommand object.

```
public void Reset(){
    // setup the command object
    m_Command = new SqlCommand();
    m_Command.Connection = m_Connection;

    // add the transaction if we need to
    if (m_Transaction != null){
        m_Command.Transaction = m_Transaction;
    }
}
```

The Reset() method creates the new SqlCommand object and tells it to use the existing connection. If a SqlTransaction object exists, you're in a transaction, and you set the Transaction property of the SqlCommand object to the stored SqlTransaction object.

As well as using the Reset() method to initialize the SqlCommand object, you can also use the Reset() method to make the DataAccess object a "multishot" class. Calling Reset() allows you to use the same object and connection to the database for multiple queries, all with different parameter sets. When you're using transactions, all the queries you execute must use the same connection, so you must call Reset() between each query to ensure that you don't have any problems with the parameters that have been set for the previous command.

Once you've created the DataAccess object and specified that it's transactional, executing queries is no different from the way you've already used the class. You have to ensure only that you call Reset() between each different query.

Once you've completed all the stages of the transaction, you must then call the Commit() method of the SqlTransaction object to commit all the changes to the database. Because the SqlTransaction object is hidden from the page developer, you provide a CommitTransaction() method that simply makes the necessary call for you.

```
public void CommitTransaction()
{
  m_Transaction.Commit();
}
```

Similarly, if for some reason you've encountered a problem and you need to roll back the changes, you must call the Rollback() method of the SqlTransaction object. To enable you to call this method, you wrap it in the RollbackTransaction() method of the DataAccess class.

```
public void RollbackTransaction()
{
  m_Transaction.Rollback();
}
```

We'll offer one word of warning regarding code-based transactions and what happens if you don't commit or roll back the transaction once it's completed: Whereas with database-controlled transactions you receive an error if you haven't completed the transaction, when using COMMIT TRANSACTION or ROLLBACK TRANSACTION, a code-controlled transaction will not raise an error if you don't complete it. If you don't complete the transaction, ADO.NET assumes that the transaction has failed and automatically causes the transaction to be rolled back.

Always remember to handle the completion of the transaction and don't rely on ADO.NET to complete it. As you'll see in the next example, it's easy to handle this using try..catch..finally, so you have no excuse for not doing it.

> NOTE *The* SqlTransaction *object, along with the corresponding transaction objects for the other data providers, has a few more properties and methods than those you're looking at here. In most situations you'll never use these other properties and methods. If you're really keen, have a look at the MSDN documentation at* http://msdn.microsoft.com/llibrary/en-us/cpref/html/ frlrfsystemdatasqlclientsqltransactionclasstopic.asp.

Editing an Element

As mentioned, BAND HTML Reference has only one place where you use code-based transactions—adding or editing elements.

As you'll recall, the element is the cornerstone of the BAND HTML Reference and relates to every other element in the database—it may be supported by a browser or a standard, and it can have various attributes and elements. It'd be difficult (if not impossible) to save all these details in one stored procedure call—it's much easier if you can make several database calls and commit or roll back all the changes as a single transaction. Thankfully, ADO.NET allows you to do just that easily!

Before you look at the pages that you need to build to edit an element, you'll take a moment to look at the "wizard" you'll use.

When you're editing attributes, events, browsers, or standards, the process is relatively simple—load the data, edit the data, save the data. You're concerned only with editing a single piece of data in the database—for instance, you modify the attributes details, but you're not interested in the relationship of the attribute to an element or to the standards that apply or any browser support that may exist.

When editing an element, you're concerned with these relationships. For the element, you need to know what browsers support it, what standards apply, and which attributes and elements it supports. This is a multistage process and requires a multistage "wizard" to make editing the element easy.

The steps you need to take when editing an element are as follows:

1. Allow the basic element details to be edited, as shown in Figure 13-16.

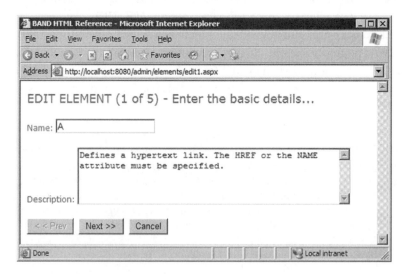

Figure 13-16. Editing the basic details for an element

2. Clicking the Next button will proceed to step 2 of the wizard and allow the selection of the browser that supports the element, as shown in Figure 13-17.

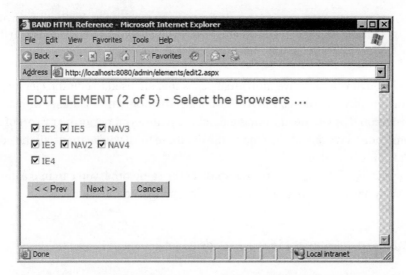

Figure 13-17. Specifying the standards that apply for an element

3. The third stage allows the selection, in the same way as you select the browser that supports the element, of the standards that apply.

4. The fourth step of the wizard allows the attributes that the element supports to be selected using a list box to add the element to those that are available, as shown in Figure 13-18.

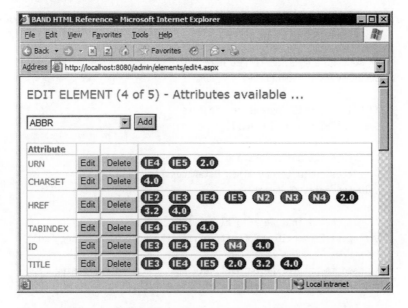

Figure 13-18. Specifying the attributes that the element supports

5. Once you've specified the attributes, you move onto the final stage of the editing and specify the events that are available. You do this, as you do for the attributes, using a list box to specify the event.

Although you have five individual pages that are used to edit the element, you interact in only two places with the database. You populate a DataSet with all the information that you need from the database before you perform any sort of editing and don't save any of the data to the database until you've made all the edits you're going to make.

By saving all the data to the database at the same time, you can make the save transactional and remove any risk of partial changes to the data.

Try It Out: Transactions in Code

The entire wizard you've just looked at is quite complex and not something we can cover adequately in the space available. Instead of building the entire wizard, you'll build the first two steps, which will give you enough information to require the use of a transaction when updating the database.

1. Start Web Matrix, and navigate to the C:\BAND\Chapter13 folder.

2. Add a new folder to the admin folder and call it elements.

3. Add a new ASP.NET Page called edit.aspx, and add the following code to the Page_Load event handler:

```
// must be logged in to get here
Security.IsLoggedIn(true);

// kill any existing session objects
Session["ElementDS"] = null;

// create the DataAccess and SqlDataAdapter objects
DataAccess objDataLoad = new DataAccess();
SqlDataAdapter objAdapter;

// get the ID that we're dealing with
string strElementID = Convert.ToString(Request.QueryString["id"]);

// need to create the DataSet here that contains everything
DataSet objDataSet = new DataSet("ElementDS");

// ********************
// * GET THE BROWSERS *
// ********************
```

```
objAdapter = objDataLoad.ExecuteAdapter("stpGetAllBrowsers");
objAdapter.Fill(objDataSet, "tblBrowser");

// **************************
// * GET/CREATE THE ELEMENT *
// **************************
if (strElementID != null){
  // add the parameter (same for all queries)
  objDataLoad.AddParameter("@element", SqlDbType.UniqueIdentifier, ⏎
    ParameterDirection.Input, strElementID);

  // tblElement
  objAdapter = objDataLoad.ExecuteAdapter("stpLoadElement");
  objAdapter.Fill(objDataSet, "tblElement");

  // tblDoesBrowserSupportElement
  objAdapter = objDataLoad.ExecuteAdapter("stpLoadElementInBrowser");
  objAdapter.Fill(objDataSet, "tblDoesBrowserSupportElement");
}else{
  // adding a new element so create an id
  strElementID = System.Guid.NewGuid().ToString();

  // create tblElement (as we're not getting it from the database)
  DataTable objDataTable = new DataTable("tblElement");
  objDataTable.Columns.Add("ElementID", Type.GetType("System.Guid"));
  objDataTable.Columns.Add("ElementName", ⏎
    Type.GetType("System.String"));
  objDataTable.Columns.Add("ElementDescription", ⏎
    Type.GetType("System.String"));

  // add the row that we're going to need (and create ID)
  DataRow objDataRow = objDataTable.NewRow();
  objDataRow["ElementID"] = strElementID;
  objDataTable.Rows.Add(objDataRow);

  // add the table to the DataSet
  objDataSet.Tables.Add(objDataTable);
}

// dispose of the data object
objDataLoad.Dispose();

// **********************************
// * CREATE ANY TABLES THAT WE NEED TO *
// **********************************
// we may not have all the tables that we need...
// 1) we're adding a new element so no join tables
// 2) we're editing but element doesn't have anything in that table
```

```
// tblDoesBrowserSupportElement
if(objDataSet.Tables.Contains("tblDoesBrowserSupportElement")==false){
 DataTable objDataTable = new DataTable("tblDoesBrowserSupportElement");
 objDataTable.Columns.Add("ElementID", Type.GetType("System.Guid"));
 objDataTable.Columns.Add("BrowserID", Type.GetType("System.Guid"));

  // add the table to the DataSet
  objDataSet.Tables.Add(objDataTable);
}

// save the DataSet to the Session
Session["ElementDS"] = objDataSet;

// now redirect to the first edit page
Response.Redirect("edit1.aspx");
```

4. Switch to the All view of the page, and add the following before the
    <script> tag:

```
<%@ assembly Src="../../code.cs" %>
<%@ import Namespace="System.Data" %>
<%@ import Namespace="System.Data.SqlClient" %>
<%@ import Namespace="notashop.band" %>
```

5. Create a new ASP.NET page in the admin\elements folder called edit1.aspx.

6. Add two text boxes and three buttons to the page, as shown in Figure 13-19.

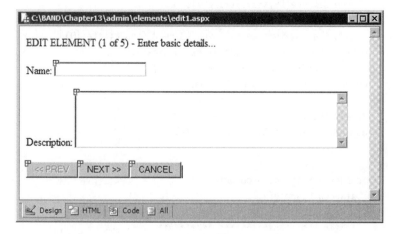

Figure 13-19. Design of the first page of the wizard

7. The two text boxes are called txtName and txtDescription, and the buttons are called btnPrev, btnNext, and btnCancel. The txtDescription text box has its `TextMode` property set to MultiLine, Rows to 5, and Columns to 50; the btnPrev button has its `Enabled` property set to False.

8. Add a `Page_Load` event to the page, and add the following code to the event handler:

```
// must be logged in to get here
Security.IsLoggedIn(true);

// load the DataSet from the Session
objDataSet = (DataSet)Session["ElementDS"];

// only populate the page on the first go
if (Page.IsPostBack == false){
  // populate what we need to
  txtName.Text =
    objDataSet.Tables["tblElement"].Rows[0]["ElementName"].ToString();
  txtDescription.Text =
    objDataSet.Tables["tblElement"].Rows[0]
    ["ElementDescription"].ToString();
}
```

9. Add a click handler for btnNext, and add the following code to the btnNext_Click event handler:

```
// save the page before we navigate
SavePage();

// redirect to the next page
Response.Redirect("edit2.aspx");
```

10. Add a click event handler for btnCancel, and add the following code to the btnCancel_Click event handler:

```
// simply redirect to the correct page
Response.Redirect("../default.aspx");
```

11. Add the following declaration to the top of the Code view for the page:

```
DataSet objDataSet;
```

12. Add the SavePage() method.

```
void SavePage(){
  // save what we need to the correct table
  objDataSet.Tables["tblElement"].Rows[0]["ElementName"] = ⤸
    txtName.Text;
  objDataSet.Tables["tblElement"].Rows[0]["ElementDescription"] = ⤸
    txtDescription.Text;

  // save the DataSet to the Session
  Session["ElementDS"] = objDataSet;
}
```

13. Switch to the All view of the page, and add the required declarations before the <script> tag.

```
<%@ assembly Src="../../code.cs" %>
<%@ import Namespace="System.Data" %>
<%@ import Namespace="System.Data.SqlClient" %>
<%@ import Namespace="notashop.band" %>
```

14. Create the second page of the wizard as edit2.aspx in the admin\elements folder.

15. Add the text "EDIT ELEMENT (2 of 5) - Select the browsers..." to the start of the page.

16. Add a CheckBoxList control on to the form and call it lstBrowsers. Set its RepeatColumns property to 3.

17. Add three buttons to the page called btnPrev, btnNext, and btnCancel and set their Text properties to <<PREV, NEXT>>, and Cancel, respectively.

18. The page should look like Figure 13-20.

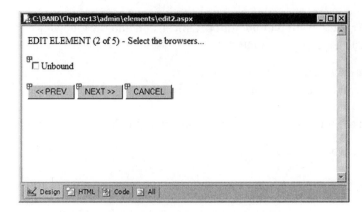

Figure 13-20. Design of the second page of the wizard

19. Add a `Page_Load` event to the page, and add the following code to the event handler:

```
// must be logged in to get here
Security.IsLoggedIn(true);

// load the DataSet from the Session
objDataSet = (DataSet)Session["ElementDS"];

// only populate the page on the first go
if (Page.IsPostBack == false){
  // create the checkbox list
  lstBrowsers.DataSource = objDataSet.Tables["tblBrowser"];
  lstBrowsers.DataTextField = "BrowserName";
  lstBrowsers.DataValueField = "BrowserID";
  lstBrowsers.DataBind();

  // set all the currently selected values
  foreach (DataRow objRow in ⤷
    objDataSet.Tables["tblDoesBrowserSupportElement"].Rows)
  {
    // do we have a matching list item
    ListItem objItem = ⤷
      lstBrowsers.Items.FindByValue(objRow["BrowserID"].ToString());

    // do we need to set it's value
    if (objItem != null) objItem.Selected = true;
  }
}
```

20. Add a click handler for btnPrev, and add the following code to the `btnPrev_Click` event handler:

```
// save the page before we navigate
SavePage();

// now redirect
Response.Redirect("edit1.aspx");
```

21. Add a click handler for btnNext, and add the following code to the btnNext_Click event handler:

```
// save the page before we navigate
SavePage();

// redirect to the next page
Response.Redirect("edit6.aspx");
```

22. Add a click event handler for btnCancel, and add the following code to the btnCancel_Click event handler:

```
// simply redirect to the correct page
Response.Redirect("../default.aspx");
```

23. Add the following declaration to the top of the Code view for the page:

```
DataSet objDataSet;
```

24. Add the SavePage() method.

```
void SavePage(){
  // clear the values from the table
  objDataSet.Tables["tblDoesBrowserSupportElement"].Clear();

  // need to loop for all elements in the check list box
  foreach (ListItem lstItem in lstBrowsers.Items){
    // only add those that are selected
    if (lstItem.Selected == true) {
      // create the new row
      DataRow objDataRow = ⏎
        objDataSet.Tables["tblDoesBrowserSupportElement"].NewRow();

      // set the necessary details
      objDataRow["ElementID"] = ⏎
        objDataSet.Tables["tblElement"].Rows[0]["ElementID"].ToString();
      objDataRow["BrowserID"] = lstItem.Value;

      // add the row to the table
      objDataSet.Tables["tblDoesBrowserSupportElement"] ⏎
        .Rows.Add(objDataRow);
    }
  }

  // save the DataSet to the Session
  Session["ElementDS"] = objDataSet;
}
```

25. Switch to the All view of the page, and add the required declarations before the `<script>` tag.

```
<%@ assembly Src="../../code.cs" %>
<%@ import Namespace="System.Data" %>
<%@ import Namespace="System.Data.SqlClient" %>
<%@ import Namespace="notashop.band" %>
```

26. Add the final page, `edit6.aspx`, to the `admin\elements` folder.

27. Add a `Load` event handler to the page, and add the following code to the Page_Load event:

```
// must be logged in to get here
Security.IsLoggedIn(true);

// load what we need from the session
DataSet objDataSet = (DataSet)Session["ElementDS"];

// accept all changes (we're only interested in the final versions)
DataSet objDataSet.AcceptChanges();

// create the object that we need
DataAccess objDataSave = new DataAccess(true);

// in a transaction so error handle
try{
  // ELEMENT (we will only ever have one)
  objDataSave.AddParameter("@element", SqlDbType.UniqueIdentifier, ↵
    ParameterDirection.Input, ↵
    objDataSet.Tables["tblElement"].Rows[0]["ElementID"]);
  objDataSave.AddParameter("@name", SqlDbType.NVarChar, ↵
    ParameterDirection.Input, ↵
    objDataSet.Tables["tblElement"].Rows[0]["ElementName"]);
  objDataSave.AddParameter("@description", SqlDbType.NVarChar, ↵
    ParameterDirection.Input, ↵
    objDataSet.Tables["tblElement"].Rows[0]["ElementDescription"]);
  objDataSave.ExecuteNonQuery("stpSaveElement");

  // ELEMENT TO BROWSER (need to do this once for each row)
  if (objDataSet.Tables["tblDoesBrowserSupportElement"].Rows.Count > 0){
    objDataSave.Reset();
    objDataSave.AddParameter("@element", SqlDbType.UniqueIdentifier, ↵
      ParameterDirection.Input);
    objDataSave.AddParameter("@browser", SqlDbType.UniqueIdentifier, ↵
      ParameterDirection.Input);
    foreach (DataRow objRow in ↵
```

```
        objDataSet.Tables["tblDoesBrowserSupportElement"].Rows)
      {
        // set the two parameter values
        objDataSave.ModifyParameter("@element", objRow["ElementID"]);
        objDataSave.ModifyParameter("@browser", objRow["BrowserID"]);
        objDataSave.ExecuteNonQuery("stpSaveElementInBrowser");
      }
    }


    // must commit the transaction that we started
    objDataSave.CommitTransaction();
}catch (Exception ex){
    // failed so rollback
    objDataSave.RollbackTransaction();

    // now throw the error out so it's caught by the page handler
    throw(ex);
}finally{
    // dispose of the data object
    objDataSave.Dispose();
}

    // redirect to the admin page
    Response.Redirect("../default.aspx");
```

28. Add the following declaration to the top of the Code view for the page:

    ```
    DataSet objDataSet;
    ```

29. Switch to the All view of the page, and add the required declarations before the `<script>` tag:

    ```
    <%@ assembly Src="../../code.cs" %>
    <%@ import Namespace="System.Data" %>
    <%@ import Namespace="System.Data.SqlClient" %>
    <%@ import Namespace="notashop.band" %>
    ```

30. Open `admin/default.aspx`, and execute it. If you need to start the Web Matrix Web server, ensure that the application directory is `C:\BAND\Chapter13`.

31. After logging into the application, select the A element from the drop-down list and click the Edit button. This will open the first page of the wizard and allow the name and description of the element to be changed if required.

32. Clicking the NEXT>> button will move to the second page of the wizard, as shown in Figure 13-21, and from here you can select which browsers support the element.

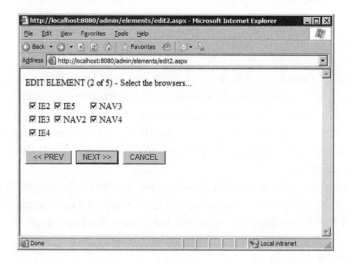

Figure 13-21. Editing the browser support for the A element

33. Uncheck NAV2, NAV3, and NAV4, and click the NEXT>> button.

34. You'll be taken back to the administrative home page, and you can view the changes by navigating to the BAND HTML Reference home page (at /default.aspx) and opting to view the A element. You'll see that the element no longer has any Netscape support, as shown in Figure 13-22.

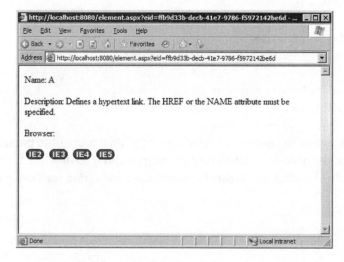

Figure 13-22. You've removed support for the A element for Netscape browsers.

35. If you go back to /admin/default.aspx in Internet Explorer, you'll see the Add New button; clicking it will allow you to add a new element to the database, which will then appear in the drop-down list on the BAND HTML Reference home page.

How It Works

In the first "hidden" page of the wizard, edit.aspx, you populate a DataSet with all the information you require to edit the element without making any further trips to the database. You've already looked at populating a DataSet in Chapter 8.

All the code for edit.aspx is contained within the Page_Load event. You always want this code to run, and putting it in this method ensures that it will always run when the page is loaded.

The first thing you do is to check that the person accessing the page is logged into the site using the Security.IsLoggedIn() method, passing a parameter of true to ensure that if they're not logged in you redirect them to the login page.

```
// must be logged in to get here
Security.IsLoggedIn(true);
```

You then create the four objects you're going to need: the DataAccess and SqlDataAdapter objects you use to interact with the database, a string to hold the ElementID you're editing, and a DataSet that you're going to populate.

```
// create the DataAccess and SqlDataAdapter objects that we'll need
DataAccess objDataLoad = new DataAccess();
SqlDataAdapter objAdapter;

// get the ID that we're dealing with
string strElementID = Convert.ToString(Request.QueryString["id"]);

// need to create the DataSet here that contains everything
DataSet objDataSet = new DataSet("ElementDS");
```

Once you've set up the necessary objects, you can then move onto populating the DataSet with the necessary data. The first thing you do is retrieve the list of browsers from the database and create the matching table within the DataSet.

```
// ********************
// * GET THE BROWSERS *
// ********************
objAdapter = objDataLoad.ExecuteAdapter("stpGetAllBrowsers");
objAdapter.Fill(objDataSet, "tblBrowser");
```

As you'll recall, you use the Fill() method of the SqlDataAdapter to create a DataTable within a DataSet, and you can use the ExecuteAdapter() method of the DataAccess object to return a SqlDataAdapter. Combining these two methods you can create the required DataTable in two lines.

As you can see, you name the table in the DataSet the same as the table in the database. This isn't necessary, but it does make things a little easier as the relationship between the tables in the database and the DataSet is immediately obvious.

Once you've retrieved the list of browsers, what you do next depends upon whether you're editing or adding an element.

If you're editing an element, you'll have an ElementID, which you can use to load everything having to do with the element from the database. You do this by adding the ElementID as a parameter to the DataAccess object and then calling various stored procedures to populate the tables you need.

```
if (strElementID != null){
  // add the parameter (same for all queries)
  objDataLoad.AddParameter("@element", SqlDbType.UniqueIdentifier,
   ParameterDirection.Input, strElementID);

  // tblElement
  objAdapter = objDataLoad.ExecuteAdapter("stpLoadElement");
  objAdapter.Fill(objDataSet, "tblElement");

  // tblDoesBrowserSupportElement
  objAdapter = objDataLoad.ExecuteAdapter("stpLoadElementInBrowser");
  objAdapter.Fill(objDataSet, "tblDoesBrowserSupportElement");
}else{
```

If you don't have an element, then you must create the tables you need. However, if you're editing, you can see from the previous code that you populate two tables. If you're adding an element, you'll create only one table, tblElement, here. You'll look at tblDoesBrowserSupportElement shortly.

Before creating tblElement, you must create a new ID for the element. As all the elements in the BAND HTML Reference are GUIDs, you can create a new ID using the static NewGuid() method of System.Guid, storing this so you can use it later.

```
  // adding a new element so create an id
  strElementID = System.Guid.NewGuid().ToString();
```

You then create the table you need and specify the three fields—ElementID, ElementName, and ElementDescription—that make up the DataTable:

```
// create tblElement (as we're not getting it from the database)
DataTable objDataTable = new DataTable("tblElement");
objDataTable.Columns.Add("ElementID", Type.GetType("System.Guid"));
objDataTable.Columns.Add("ElementName", ⤸
Type.GetType("System.String"));
objDataTable.Columns.Add("ElementDescription", ⤸
Type.GetType("System.String"));
```

Once you've created the table, you need to add the new element to it so that it's available for editing. As you don't have a name of a description of the element yet, you simply create a new row and set the ElementID to the new ID you've created. When you come to modify the DataSet, you'll set the ElementName and ElementDescription fields.

```
// add the row that we're going to need (and create ID)
DataRow objDataRow = objDataTable.NewRow();
objDataRow["ElementID"] = strElementID;
objDataTable.Rows.Add(objDataRow);
```

You then add the table to the DataSet.

```
// add the table to the DataSet
objDataSet.Tables.Add(objDataTable);
}
```

You still need to execute more code to fully set up the DataSet, but you don't need anything else from the database. There's no point having an open connection to the database if you don't need one, so you dispose of the DataAccess object.

```
// dispose of the data object
objDataLoad.Dispose();
```

Although you've disposed of the DataSet, you still may not have a DataSet that contains everything you need to modify an element. The following are two possible reasons for this:

- If you're adding a new element, you have no data to retrieve from the database for the relationship between the element and the browsers.

- If you're editing an element, you won't have created the necessary tables if there's no relationship between the element and the browsers. If no browsers support the element, the stpLoadElementInBrowser stored procedure won't return any information, and the Fill() method of the SqlDataAdapter won't be able to create the tblDoesBrowserSupportElement table.

Whatever the reason for not creating the table earlier, you must create it before you go any further. You've already seen how you create a table—as you did for tblElement if you're adding a new element—and you simply repeat the process here for the remaining table.

Before creating the DataTable, you check that it doesn't exist using the Contains() method of the Tables collection of the DataSet. This returns true or false, and you only want to create the table if doesn't exist.

```
// tblDoesBrowserSupportElement
if (objDataSet.Tables.Contains("tblDoesBrowserSupportElement")==false){
    DataTable objDataTable = new DataTable("tblDoesBrowserSupportElement");
    objDataTable.Columns.Add("ElementID", Type.GetType("System.Guid"));
    objDataTable.Columns.Add("BrowserID", Type.GetType("System.Guid"));

    // add the table to the DataSet
    objDataSet.Tables.Add(objDataTable);
}
```

Once you've ensured that you have all the necessary tables, you can save the DataSet to the session and navigate to the first page of the wizard.

```
// save the DataSet to the Session
Session["ElementDS"] = objDataSet;

// now redirect to the first edit page
Response.Redirect("edit1.aspx");
```

The First Page of the Wizard

The first page of the wizard, edit1.aspx, allows the user to modify the name and description for the element. You've constructed pages that perform this same task in earlier chapters, and all you'll look at here is how you populate the values in the text boxes and then save the values to the DataSet.

The code to populate the two text boxes on the form is contained, as usual, in the Page_Load event for the page. After checking that you're logged in and allowed to view the page, you get the DataSet from the session and assign this to the objDataSet class variable.

```
void Page_Load(object sender, EventArgs e) {
    // must be logged in to get here
    Security.IsLoggedIn(true);

    // load what we need from the session
    objDataSet = (DataSet)Session["ElementDS"];
```

If you're not posting the page back (as you'll do when you want to move to the next page or cancel the edit of the element), you can then populate the two text boxes.

You retrieve the first row from the tblElement table in the DataSet and specify which column you require, convert this to a string, and then assign it to the Text property of the text box.

```
    // only populate the page on the first go
    if (Page.IsPostBack == false){
        // populate what we need to
        txtName.Text = ⏎
            objDataSet.Tables["tblElement"].Rows[0]["ElementName"].ToString();
        txtDescription.Text = ⏎
            objDataSet.Tables["tblElement"].Rows[0]["ElementDescription"].ToString();
    }
}
```

To move to the next page of the wizard, you click the Next button, and you call the btnNext_Click event handler. This calls the SavePage() method and redirects to the second page of the wizard, edit2.aspx.

The SavePage() method is, not surprisingly given its name, where you save the details before moving onto the next stage.

```
void SavePage(){
    // save what we need to the correct table
    objDataSet.Tables["tblElement"].Rows[0]["ElementName"] = ⏎
        txtName.Text;
    objDataSet.Tables["tblElement"].Rows[0]["ElementDescription"] = ⏎
        txtDescription.Text;

    // save the DataSet to the Session
    Session["ElementDS"] = objDataSet;
}
```

You simply do the reverse of the page population process—you set the correct column of the first row of the tblElement table to be the value that's currently in the corresponding text box.

Once all the changes have been made to objDataSet, you then put this back into the session so that the changes are stored if you come back to this page by clicking the Previous button on the next page of the wizard.

The Second Page of the Wizard

The second page of the wizard follows the same process as the first page. You populate the controls on the page with the correct data from the DataSet in the Page_Load event, and you save the new data to the DataSet in the SavePage() method that's called before you navigate to another page within the wizard.

In this page you're using a CheckBoxList to display the information, and you can use the data binding techniques you saw in Chapter 7 to populate this with the information from the correct table, tblBrowser, in the DataSet.

```
// create the checkbox list
lstBrowsers.DataSource = objDataSet.Tables["tblBrowser"];
lstBrowsers.DataTextField = "BrowserName";
lstBrowsers.DataValueField = "BrowserID";
lstBrowsers.DataBind();
```

Populating the CheckBoxList is only half the story; you also need to show which of the browsers are currently supported. You do this by iterating through each of the rows in tblDoesBrowserSupportElement and setting the Selected property to true for the corresponding check box.

```
// set all the currently selected values
foreach (DataRow objRow in ⤴
  objDataSet.Tables["tblDoesBrowserSupportElement"].Rows)
{
  // do we have a matching list item
  ListItem objItem = ⤴
    lstBrowsers.Items.FindByValue(objRow["BrowserID"].ToString());

  // do we need to set it's value
  if (objItem != null) objItem.Selected = true;
}
```

Once the user elects to go to another page of the wizard, the SavePage() method is called, and you then add the currently selected browsers to tblDoes-BrowserSupportElement.

The list of browsers that's currently in the table is removed because you'll add all the selected ones again. You can do this using the Clear() method of the DataTable.

```
// clear the values from the table
objDataSet.Tables["tblDoesBrowserSupportElement"].Clear();
```

You then loop through all the items in the check box list and, if they're selected, add a new row to tblDoesBrowserSupportElement.

```
// need to loop for all elements in the check list box
foreach (ListItem lstItem in lstBrowsers.Items){
  // only add those that are selected
  if (lstItem.Selected == true) {
    // create the new row
    DataRow objDataRow = ⤸
      objDataSet.Tables["tblDoesBrowserSupportElement"].NewRow();

    // set the necessary details
    objDataRow["ElementID"] = ⤸
      objDataSet.Tables["tblElement"].Rows[0]["ElementID"].ToString();
    objDataRow["BrowserID"] = lstItem.Value;

    // add the row to the table
    objDataSet.Tables["tblDoesBrowserSupportElement"] ⤸
      .Rows.Add(objDataRow);
  }
}
```

Save the DataSet to the Database

Once you've made all the changes that are required to the data, you then need to populate this back to the database. As you're using a DataSet, you could use its automatic features to populate some of the information back to the database. However, you're using the DataSet simply as a data storage area, so you're going to manually put everything back into the database.

As with the page to populate the DataSet, the code to save to the database is included in the Page_Load event. You again check that the user is logged in before you retrieve the DataSet from the session object.

```
// must be logged in to get here
Security.IsLoggedIn(true);

// load what we need from the session
DataSet objDataSet = (DataSet)Session["ElementDS"];
```

Now that you have the DataSet, you're nearly ready to save the data to the database. As you'll recall, the DataSet contains several different versions of the data, but you're interested in only the final version of the data, so you call the AcceptChanges() method on the DataSet to remove all the other versions from the DataSet.

```
// accept all changes (we're only interested in the final versions)
objDataSet.AcceptChanges();
```

You then need to save all the tables back to the database. Before you can start saving to the database, you need to create a DataAccess object. You do this as you've always done, but this time you specify that you want it to be transactional by passing true into the constructor.

```
// create the object that we need
DataAccess objDataSave = new DataAccess(true);
```

You're wrapping the entire code to save the data to the database inside a try..catch..finally block because you need to catch any errors within the code. If there's a problem, you need to roll back all the changes that have been made.

Within the try block, the first thing you'll save is the element, and you simply add the three parameters you need and call the ExecuteNonQuery() method of the DataAccess object.

```
// ELEMENT (we will only ever have one)
objDataSave.AddParameter("@element", SqlDbType.UniqueIdentifier,
  ParameterDirection.Input,
  objDataSet.Tables["tblElement"].Rows[0]["ElementID"]);
objDataSave.AddParameter("@name", SqlDbType.NVarChar, ⏎
  ParameterDirection.Input, ⏎
  objDataSet.Tables["tblElement"].Rows[0]["ElementName"]);
objDataSave.AddParameter("@description", SqlDbType.NVarChar, ⏎
  ParameterDirection.Input, ⏎
  objDataSet.Tables["tblElement"].Rows[0]["ElementDescription"]);
objDataSave.ExecuteNonQuery("stpSaveElement");
```

The only difference between this and any code you've seen previously is that you're specifying the values of the stored procedures from the DataSet rather than controls on the form. You'll notice that there's no difference to the code even though you're in a transaction.

The stpSaveElement stored procedure is quite simple.

```
-- delete the element as we're about to replace everything
EXEC dbo.stpDeleteElement @element

-- now insert it
INSERT INTO tblElement (ElementID, ElementName, ElementDescription)
  VALUES (@element, @name, @description)
```

You use the stpDeleteElement procedure you've already seen to remove any details for the element from the database because you'll replace them with values specified within the wizard. You then insert the element into tblElement, specifying its ID, name, and description.

To save the browsers that support the element, you first check to see that there are some browsers that support the element. There isn't an awful lot of point trying to save data that doesn't exist.

```
// ELEMENT TO BROWSER (need to do this once for each row)
if (objDataSet.Tables["tblDoesBrowserSupportElement"].Rows.Count > 0){
```

If you have some data to save, you first reset the DataAccess object to clear the existing parameters before adding the two parameters you're going to need:

```
objDataSave.Reset();
objDataSave.AddParameter("@element", SqlDbType.UniqueIdentifier, ↵
ParameterDirection.Input);
objDataSave.AddParameter("@browser", SqlDbType.UniqueIdentifier, ↵
ParameterDirection.Input);
```

You'll notice that although you add the parameters, you don't specify a value. You need to loop through every row in the table, and for each row every parameter will take a different value.

```
foreach (DataRow objRow in ↵
  objDataSet.Tables["tblDoesBrowserSupportElement"].Rows){
  // set the two parameter values
  objDataSave.ModifyParameter("@element", objRow["ElementID"]);
  objDataSave.ModifyParameter("@browser", objRow["BrowserID"]);
```

```
    objDataSave.ExecuteNonQuery("stpSaveElementInBrowser");
  }
}
```

You loop through each row, setting the two parameters to the correct value and using ExecuteNonQuery() to save the details to the database.

If you save everything to the database without encountering any problems, you can then commit the transaction using the CommitTransaction() method of the DataAccess object.

```
// must commit the transaction that we started
objDataSave.CommitTransaction();
```

However, if an error has occurred, this will be caught by the catch statement, and the transaction will be rolled back.

```
}catch (Exception ex){
  // failed so rollback
  objDataSave.RollbackTransaction();
```

Because you've handled the error using the catch statement, you've told ASP.NET that the error is no longer of consequence. Further, because you're handling errors at the application level, you need to rethrow the error so that the friendly error page is shown to the user and the e-mail is sent to the site administrator.

```
  // now throw the error out so it's caught by the page handler
  throw(ex);
```

Whether the transaction has been committed or rolled back, you must dispose of the DataAccess object to close the connection to the database.

```
}finally{
  // dispose of the data object
  objDataSave.Dispose();
}
```

If you've gotten to this point, the element has been modified, and you can redirect the user to the administration home page.

```
// redirect to the admin page
Response.Redirect("../default.aspx");
```

Summary

In the previous two chapters, we've presented the BAND HTML Reference and discussed several different topics, all of which fit together to provide a working application. Through a series of hands-on examples, you've done the following:

- Built a DataAccess class to hide the nitty-gritty of the interaction with the database. The DataAccess class provides a higher-level means of accessing the database, and nondatabase programmers will be able to use the class.

- Looked at how you can deal with errors that occur on the site. You firstly ensured that any resources that you open were closed using a try..catch..finally block, and then you looked at providing a friendly error message to the user. You also looked at how you can log errors that occur by e-mailing the details to the site administrator.

- Looked at how the basic DataAccess class can be expanded to add parameters to the queries and stored procedures that you're executing against the database.

- Looked at transactions and saw how to handle transactions in two places— in the database or in the code. You looked at how you can use the BEGIN TRANSACTION and COMMIT TRANSACTION statements to control transactions in the database before looking at using transactions in code. Again, you shielded most of the transaction details from the page developer within the DataAccess class. The final example in the chapter introduced the most complex part of the BAND HTML Reference by providing a cut-down version of the Edit Element wizard, and you used some quite advanced techniques to manage the data for the wizard.

This isn't the end of the story, though; there's more to the BAND HTML Reference than you've seen here. Although you looked at adding and editing elements in the last example, in this chapter you haven't seen how you deal with attributes, browsers, events, and standards.

In the code download for the book, you'll find a CaseStudy folder that contains the entire BAND HTML Reference. This includes the parts of the application you haven't seen. Although it gets a little more complex, all the code is fully commented. In other words, you should, with a little digging, be able to follow it.

Part Four

Appendixes

APPENDIX A

Installation

IN THIS APPENDIX you'll find installation instructions for the following applications:

- .NET 1.1

- .NET ODBC Data Provider

- Web Matrix

- MSDE

- SQL Web Data Administrator

- MySQL

- MySQL Control Center

- MySQL Administrator

- MySQL ODBC connector

All of these are used at some point in the book. .NET 1.1 and Web Matrix are core items and should be installed with whatever database you're using. Which of the remaining six you install depends on whether you're going to work with MSDE or MySQL throughout the book.

.NET 1.1

The .NET 1.1 Framework is installed by default in Windows Server 2003. It runs only on Windows Server 2003, Windows XP, and Windows 2000 Service Pack 3 (SP3). You can visit http://windowsupdate.microsoft.com and install it from there, or you can follow these steps:

1. Download the .NET 1.1 Redistributable Package installer from http://msdn.microsoft.com/netframework/technologyinfo/howtoget/default.aspx. The link to the download is at the bottom of this Web page. If you prefer to type it in directly, the link is http://www.microsoft.com/downloads/details.aspx?FamilyId=262D25E3-F589-4842-8157-034D1E7CF3A3.

2. Once downloaded (the file `dotnetfx.exe` is 24MB), simply double-click it and let the installer run.

.NET ODBC Data Provider

The .NET ODBC Data Provider provides an alternate, and sometimes the only, way to connect to a data source. With respect to this book, ODBC is the only stable way to connect to the MySQL database (through MySQL's ODBC connector) because MySQL doesn't work with the OLE DB or SqlClient data providers.

You must download and install the .NET ODBC Data Provider in addition to the .NET software development kit (SDK). Follow these steps:

1. Download the .NET ODBC Data Provider installer `http://msdn.microsoft` `.com/netframework/downloads/updates/default.aspx`. The link to the download is in the .NET 1.0 Framework Downloads section. If you prefer to type it in directly, the URL is `http://www.microsoft.com/downloads/details` `.aspx?familyid=6ccd8427-1017-4f33-a062-d165078e32b1`.

2. Once downloaded (the file `odbc_net.msi` is 848 KB), double-click it and let the installer run using the default values it suggests.

Web Matrix

The ASP.NET team's Web Matrix integrated development environment (IDE) is a small (1MB) but powerful IDE, also written in .NET, that caters specifically to ASP.NET programmers. Officially it's still a beta product, but the team is unlikely to release it as a finished product; indeed, it's more than stable for the tasks you'll need it to do.

To install it, follow these steps:

1. Open a browser, navigate to `http://www.asp.net/webmatrix/download.aspx`, and click the Download and Install ASP.NET Web Matrix link.

2. You have to register to download this software, so enter your e-mail address as requested and hit Next.

3. If you want to sign up for the ASP.NET Forums at http://www.asp.net/forums, then give your proposed sign-in name on the following screen and click Next. If not, just click Next.

4. On the next screen, click the link to start downloading Web Matrix.

5. Once downloaded (the file WebMatrix.msi is 1.3MB), double-click it and let the installer run using the default values it suggests.

MSDE

The Microsoft SQL Server 2000 Desktop Engine (MSDE) is a freely available, cut-down version of Microsoft's SQL Server 2000 Enterprise Database Server. Use the SqlClient data provider to access it from your ASP.NET pages.

To install it, follow these steps:

1. Download the MSDE installer from http://msdn.microsoft.com/netframework/downloads/sdkmsde/default.aspx.

2. Once downloaded (the file SQL2KDeskSP3.exe is 68MB, so make sure you have enough space on your hard drive and a nice cup of tea handy), double-click it, and the files needed to install MSDE will be extracted to c:\sql2ksp3. However, you can change this if you need to do so.

3. Make sure you're logged on as a user with administrative privileges and then open a command prompt window. Change the directory to the one containing the install files you've just extracted from sql2ksp3.exe. Start the installer by typing the following:

```
Setup.exe /qb+ INSTANCENAME="BAND" SAPWD="secpas" SECURITYMODE="SQL"
```

Installation will take about a minute.

4. You may need to restart your machine once the installer has finished. Now check that MSDE has been installed and is working. The way to do this differs across platforms, but for Windows XP, you can find it by selecting Start Menu ➤ Control Panel ➤ Administrative Tools ➤ Services.

5. Look for a service named MSSQL$BAND in the list (see Figure A-1). This is your installation of MSDE. Make sure the Status and Startup Type options are set to Started and Automatic, respectively. The Startup Type setting will ensure that MSDE starts automatically whenever your computer is rebooted.

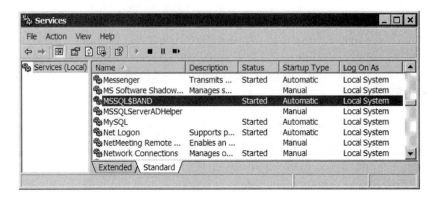

Figure A-1. The Services control panel shows the new instance of MSDE.

Note that you can install several instances of MSDE side by side on one machine. Hence, we called ours BAND (Beginning Asp.Net Databases—geddit?). An instance of MSDE/SQL Server installed with no instance name would be called MSSQLSERVER.

SQL Web Data Administrator

The MSDE team provides a graphical front end for administering MSDE. Like MSDE, this is a free and cut-down set of administration tools based on those that come with SQL Server. To install SQL Web Data Administrator, follow these steps:

1. Download the SQL Web Data Administrator installer from `http://www.microsoft.com/sql/msde/downloads/default.asp`. The link to the download is clearly marked as Web Data Administrator. If you prefer to type it in directly, the URL is `http://www.microsoft.com/downloads/details.aspx?FamilyId=C039A798-C57A-419E-ACBC-2A332CB7F959`.

2. Once downloaded (the file `setup.msi` is 3.33MB), double-click it and let the installer run using the default values it suggests.

MySQL

The MySQL database is freely available under the GNU General Public License (GPL) from MySQL AB at http://www.mysql.com. It's powerful and used widely at the enterprise level but is also good for beginners because of the level of user support as a paid service and because of the free mailing lists at http://lists.mysql.com/. Use the MySQL ODBC connector and the .NET ODBC Data Provider to access it from your ASP.NET pages.

To install the latest stable version of the MySQL Database—4.0.18 at the time of this writing—follow these steps:

1. Download the latest MySQL installer from http://www.mysql.com/downloads/ mysql-4.0.html. The correct link to the download (shown in Figure A-2) is marked Windows 95/98/NT/2000/XP/2003 in the Windows Downloads section. Don't select the option marked Without Installer.

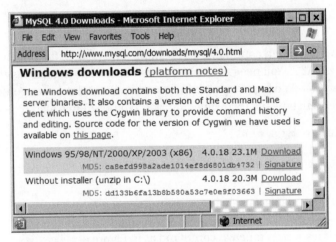

Figure A-2. The MySQL download choices

2. Once downloaded (the file mysql-4.0.18-win.zip is 23.1MB), extract all the files inside to a temporary directory of your choice.

3. Change the directory to the one containing the install files you've just extracted. Start the installer by double-clicking setup.exe, and let it install into the default directory of C:\MySQL.

    At this point, the code to run MySQL is installed but needs to be initialized. That is, its system tables need to be created and the root user account needs to be secured. This was done automatically in MSDE, but you must do it manually in MySQL.

4. Open a command-line window, and change the directory to C:\MySQL\bin. Now type **mysqld --console**, and press Return. MySQL enters its startup sequence, writing some information to the command line. When it finishes, you'll see a line saying that MySQL is ready for connections (see Figure A-3). Its system tables have now been created.

```
C:\WINDOWS\System32\cmd.exe - mysqld --console
C:\mysql\bin>mysqld --console
InnoDB: The first specified data file .\ibdata1 did not exist:
InnoDB: a new database to be created!
040421 14:47:21  InnoDB: Setting file .\ibdata1 size to 10 MB
InnoDB: Database physically writes the file full: wait...
040421 14:47:22  InnoDB: Log file .\ib_logfile0 did not exist: new to be created

InnoDB: Setting log file .\ib_logfile0 size to 5 MB
InnoDB: Database physically writes the file full: wait...
040421 14:47:23  InnoDB: Log file .\ib_logfile1 did not exist: new to be created

InnoDB: Setting log file .\ib_logfile1 size to 5 MB
InnoDB: Database physically writes the file full: wait...
InnoDB: Doublewrite buffer not found: creating new
InnoDB: Doublewrite buffer created
InnoDB: Creating foreign key constraint system tables
InnoDB: Foreign key constraint system tables created
040421 14:47:31  InnoDB: Started
mysqld: ready for connections.
Version: '4.0.18-max-debug'  socket: ''  port: 3306
```

Figure A-3. Running mysqld --console

5. Now open a second command-line window, and change the directory to C:\MySQL\bin. You need to secure the root user by giving it a password. You'll also stop giving every user full control of your databases. At the prompt then, type the following (and, yes, type mysql twice):

```
C:\mysql\bin> mysql mysql
mysql> DELETE FROM user WHERE Host='localhost' AND User='';
mysql> FLUSH PRIVILEGES;
mysql> QUIT
C:\mysql\bin> mysqladmin -u root password secpas
```

You'll get responses for each command as in Figure A-4. Leave the command prompt window open.

```
C:\WINDOWS\System32\cmd.exe
C:\mysql\bin>mysql mysql
Welcome to the MySQL monitor.  Commands end with ; or \g.
Your MySQL connection id is 1 to server version: 4.0.18-max-debug

Type 'help;' or '\h' for help. Type '\c' to clear the buffer.

mysql> DELETE FROM user WHERE Host='localhost' AND User='';
Query OK, 1 row affected (0.11 sec)

mysql> FLUSH PRIVILEGES;
Query OK, 0 rows affected (0.03 sec)

mysql> QUIT
Bye
C:\mysql\bin>mysqladmin -u root password secpas
C:\mysql\bin>
```

Figure A-4. Securing the MySQL root account

At this point, MySQL is fully installed, but you need to start it manually when you need to use it. It makes sense then to install it as a Windows service like MSDE and have Windows start it automatically.

6. You need to shut MySQL down before you install it as a Windows service. In the command prompt window you left open, type the following and press Return:

```
C:\mysql\bin> mysqladmin --user=root --password=secpas shutdown
```

In the first command-line window, you'll see messages from MySQL saying that it's shutting down.

7. Now install MySQL as a service by typing mysqld --install. If you open the Services control panel, you'll find an entry named MySQL. Select it with the mouse, and then click the entry to start the service. Now right-click the MySQL entry, and check that the Startup Type option is Automatic (see Figure A-5). This will ensure that MySQL starts and closes down when Windows does.

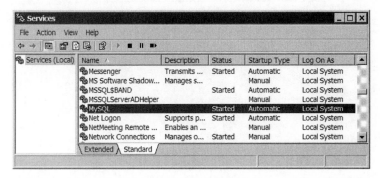

Figure A-5. The Services control panel shows the new instance of MSDE.

MySQL Control Center

MySQL Control Center is the official graphical user interface (GUI) client—still in beta—for MySQL from MySQL AB. It makes creating databases and tables and entering data much easier—much like you can access MSDE graphically through MSDE Web Data Administrator or Web Matrix's data window.

To install the latest version of MySQL Control Center—0.9.4 beta at the time of this writing—follow these steps:

1. Download the latest MySQL Control Center installer from http://www.mysql .com/downloads/mysqlcc.html. The link to the download is the only entry in the Windows Downloads section.

2. Once downloaded (the file `mysqlcc-0.9.4-win32.zip` is 3.4MB) extract all the files inside to a temporary directory of your choice.

3. Change the directory to the one containing the install files you've just extracted. Start the installer by double-clicking `setup.exe`, and let it install using the default settings.

4. In order for your installation of MySQL to work with MySQL Control Center, you need to register its presence. Run MySQL Control Center. The Register Server dialog box will appear and ask you to register MySQL. In the dialog box, set Name to BAND, Host Name to localhost, User Name to root, and Password to secpas (or whatever you set your root password to), as shown in Figure A-6. Click Test to make sure you've entered the correct settings, and then click Add if the test is successful.

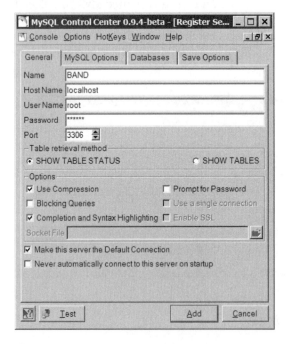

Figure A-6. Registering MySQL in MySQL Control Center

MySQL Administrator

Whereas MySQL Control Center lets you get down and dirty creating tables and databases, MySQL Administrator helps you perform day-to-day administration duties such as monitoring users, making backups, and so on.

To download and install the latest version of MySQL Administrator—1.0.3alpha at the time of this writing—follow these steps:

1. Download the latest MySQL Administrator installer from http://www.mysql .com/downloads/administrator/. The correct link to the download (shown in Figure A-7) is marked as Windows 95/98/NT/2000/XP/2003 in the Windows Downloads section. Don't select the option marked Without Installer.

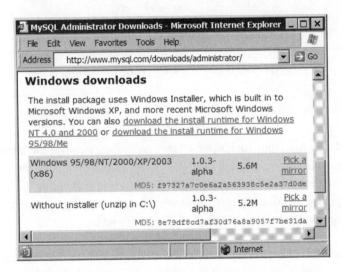

Figure A-7. The MySQL Administrator download choices

2. Once downloaded (the file mysql-administrator-1.0.3alpha-win.zip is 5.6MB), extract all the files inside to a temporary directory of your choice.

3. Change the directory to the one containing the install files you've just extracted. Start the installer by double-clicking setup.exe, and let it install using the default settings.

4. To get your installation of MySQL working with MySQL Administrator, you need to register its presence, so run MySQL Administrator. A dialog box appears and asks you for connection details. Set Username to root, Password to secpas (or whatever you set your root password to), and Hostname to localhost, as shown in Figure A-8. Then click OK.

Figure A-8. Connecting to MySQL in MySQL Administrator

MySQL ODBC Connector

The MySQL ODBC connector provides an ODBC-compliant exterior for MySQL, which means that .NET users can use the .NET ODBC Data Provider to interact with MySQL. Note that MySQL must be installed before you install this.

To download and install the latest stable version of the MySQL connector/ODBC—3.51.06 at the time of this writing—follow these steps:

1. Download the latest MySQL connector/ODBC from http://www.mysql .com/downloads/connector/odbc/3.51.html. The correct link to the download (shown in Figure A-9) is marked as Driver Installer in the Windows Downloads section. Don't select the Driver DLLs Only option.

Figure A-9. The MySQL connector/ODBC download choices

2. Once downloaded (the file MyODBC-3.51.06.exe is 731KB), double-click it and let the installer run.

SQL Primer

IN THIS APPENDIX, you'll find a recap of all the syntax used for the SQL statements covered in this book. In order of appearance, we'll cover the following:

- SELECT

- INSERT

- DELETE

- UPDATE

- CREATE DATABASE

- CREATE TABLE

- DROP DATABASE

- DROP TABLE

- ALTER DATABASE

- ALTER TABLE

Note that SQL statements don't need to be separated over many lines, and the SQL keywords don't need to be in capitals. It just makes it easier to read and understand them. SQL is case insensitive except for cases where the database server insists that table names *are* case sensitive.

KEY *SQL keywords are in capitals. Optional elements of a statement are surrounded by brackets. User-defined elements of a statement are in* italics.

> **TIP** *Don't forget that MDB files return an error if you use quotes around literal values and if you use field aliases in ORDER BY statements. See Chapter 7 for more information.*

You can find Microsoft's T-SQL reference online at `http://msdn.microsoft.com /library/en-us/tsqlref/ts_tsqlcon_6lyk.asp`. You can find MySQL's SQL reference online at `http://dev.mysql.com/doc/mysql/en/SQL_Syntax.html`. Each section in this appendix will also include links relevant to the specific statement from these references. If you'd like a book on SQL in general, try either *The Programmer's Guide To SQL* by Darie and Watson (Apress, 2004) or *Teach Yourself SQL in 10 Minutes* by Ben Forta (SAMS, 2004). Both are good introductory guides to the subtleties of SQL not covered here.

SELECT

The purpose of a SELECT statement is to return some information from the database. This information may be any of the following:

- A single scalar value returned as an object by a call to `ExecuteScalar()`

- A table of values returned as a single result inside a DataReader object by a call to `ExecuteReader()`

- A set of tables of values returned as multiple results inside a DataReader object

The syntax of the SELECT statement looks like this:

```
SELECT desired_results
FROM main_table
   [join_expression]
[WHERE set_of_conditions]
[ORDER BY list_of_fields [DESC]]
```

This statement has the following five pieces:

- A list of *desired_results* to be retrieved from the database. Generally this is either a comma-separated list of field names from the database, the * wildcard (meaning every field in the given table should be returned), or an aggregate function on a set of columns such as `COUNT()` or `TOP()`.

- The name of the main *table* from which the selection should originate.

- An optional *join_expression* determining how other tables should be linked to the information in the *main_table*. There can be as many *join_expressions* as needed to retrieve the required data from other tables in the database.

- An optional *set_of_conditions* prefixed by the keyword WHERE that allow you to filter out data not to be returned. The *set_of_conditions* isn't a comma-separated list. Each condition is joined by one of the three boolean conditions OR, AND, or NOT and is a comparison of a field to either a literal value or another field.

- An optional comma-separated *list_of_fields* indicating which fields the results of the SELECT statement should be ordered by. By default, they're organized into ascending order. Adding the keyword DESC to the end of the *list_of_fields* will organize the results in descending order.

For example, if you wanted to retrieve the names of all the family members in a genealogy database, you'd use the following statement:

```
SELECT MemberName FROM familymember
```

If you wanted to retrieve all the details about the dogs in the family, you'd use the following statement:

```
SELECT * FROM familymember
WHERE MemberSpecies = 'dog'
```

If you wanted to retrieve the Social Security number for every member of the family older than 18, you could use the following statement:

```
SELECT familymember.MemberName, financialdetail.SSN FROM familymember
INNER JOIN financialdetail
    ON financialdetail.MemberID = familymember.MemberID
WHERE Memberbirthdate < '01/04/1986'
```

Note that some of the elements of SELECT have been left out for simplicity's sake and because they aren't covered in the book. For a complete look at SELECT, check out the following links or pick up a copy of *SQL Queries for Mere Mortals* by Hernandez and Viescas (Addison-Wesley, 2002):

- `http://msdn.microsoft.com/library/en-us/tsqlref/ts_sa-ses_9sfo.asp`

- `http://dev.mysql.com/doc/mysql/en/SELECT.html`

- `http://dev.mysql.com/doc/mysql/en/JOIN.html`

INSERT

The purpose of an INSERT statement is to add some new information to a table in a database. This new data must conform to the rules and constraints already laid out on the table or else an error will be returned. INSERT statements are called either through a DataAdapter's Update() method or by calling ExecuteNonQuery() on a Command object, which returns the number of rows in the table the command has added (you hope just the one).

The syntax of the INSERT statement looks like this:

```
INSERT [INTO] table_name
    (field_list)
    VALUES (field_value_list)
```

This statement has the following five pieces:

- The optional keyword INTO to make the statement more readable.

- The *table_name* that determines the table to be added to.

- The optional (comma-separated) *field_list* that names the fields in the new row to which you're giving values. This list must be surrounded by parentheses.

- The keyword VALUES that separates the *field_list* from the *field_value_list*.

- The (comma-separated) *field_value_list* that contains a value for each of the fields in the *field_list* for the new row. Each value can be a literal, an expression saying how a value is to be determined from the values of other fields (firstname + ' ' + surname, for example), the keyword DEFAULT indicating that the field should take its default value as defined in the database, or NULL. This list must be surrounded by parentheses.

- The number of the items in the *field_list* should equal the number of items in the *field_value_list* and be ordered in the same way. Thus, the first field named in the *field_list* will be filled with the first value in the *field_value_list*, the second with the second, and so on. If a *field_list* isn't supplied, the *field_value_list* must supply a new value for every field in the table.

For example, if you wanted to add a newcomer to the family database, you'd use the following command:

```
INSERT INTO familymember
(MemberID, MemberName, MemberBirthdate, MemberSpecies)
VALUES (25, 'Spot', 14/04/04, 'Cat')
```

For more information about INSERT in T-SQL/ANSI SQL, try these links:

- http://msdn.microsoft.com/library/en-us/tsqlref/ts_ia-iz_5cl0.asp

- http://dev.mysql.com/doc/mysql/en/INSERT.html

DELETE

The purpose of a DELETE statement is to remove one or more rows of information from a table in a database. DELETE statements are called either through a Data-Adapter's Update() method or by calling ExecuteNonQuery() on a Command object, which returns the number of rows in the table the command has deleted.

The syntax of the DELETE statement looks like this:

```
DELETE [FROM] table_name
[WHERE list_of_conditions]
```

This statement has the following three pieces:

- The optional keyword FROM to make the statement more readable.

- The *table_name* that determines the table data will be deleted from.

- An optional *list_of_conditions* to identify the target rows preceded by the keyword WHERE. If more than one condition is being used, each condition should either be ANDed or ORed together.

For example, if you decided to remove all cats from the family database, you'd use the following command:

```
DELETE FROM familymember
WHERE MemberSpecies = 'Cat'
```

Note that calling DELETE without a *condition_list* would remove all the rows of information from a table but wouldn't remove the table itself. Also, you should check whether your databases will DELETE data regardless of whether the DELETE statement breaks referential integrity constraints. Some do, some don't.

```
DELETE familymember
```

For more information about DELETE in T-SQL/MySQL, try these links:

- `http://msdn.microsoft.com/library/en-us/tsqlref/ts_de-dz_9lut.asp`

- `http://dev.mysql.com/doc/mysql/en/DELETE.html`

UPDATE

The purpose of an UPDATE statement is to modify some already existing information in a table in the database. UPDATE statements are called either through a DataAdapter's `Update()` method or by calling `ExecuteNonQuery()` on a Command object, which returns the number of rows in the table the command has modified.

The syntax of the UPDATE statement looks like this:

```
UPDATE table_name
SET column1_name = expression1,
    column2_name = expression2,

          .

          .

          .

    columnM_name = expressionM
[WHERE condition_list]
```

This statement has the following four pieces:

- The *table_name* that identifies the table in which data will be updated.

- The keyword SET to denote the start of the *set_list*.

- A comma-separated list of assignments where individual fields are set to given values.

- An optional *condition_list* to identify the target rows preceded by the keyword WHERE. If more than one condition is being used, each condition should either be ANDed or ORed together.

For example, if you wanted to change a female family member's name because she's getting married, you'd use the following command.

```
UPDATE familymember
SET MemberName = 'Jane Maharry' WHERE MemberName='Jane Randall'
```

For more information about UPDATE in T-SQL/MySQL, try these links:

- http://msdn.microsoft.com/library/en-us/tsqlref/ts_ua-uz_82n9.asp

- http://dev.mysql.com/doc/mysql/en/UPDATE.html

CREATE DATABASE

The purpose of a CREATE DATABASE statement is to create a new database to be hosted by the database server software. Generally, this command is issued as part of either a back-up script or indirectly through a graphical user interface (GUI) administration client. It may be called directly through a database server's command-line tool—for example, osql.exe or mysql.exe—or by calling ExecuteNonQuery() on a Command object.

The common syntax of the CREATE DATABASE statement looks like this:

```
CREATE DATABASE database_name
```

where *database_name* is the name of the new database to be created.

For example, if you wanted to create a database to hold family information called Genealogy, you'd use the following command:

```
CREATE DATABASE Genealogy
```

Note that there's a lot more to this command but that the syntax is almost completely different in T-SQL to MySQL. For a full reference, check out the following links:

- http://msdn.microsoft.com/library/en-us/tsqlref/ts_create_1up1.asp

- http://dev.mysql.com/doc/mysql/en/CREATE_DATABASE.html

CREATE TABLE

The purpose of a CREATE TABLE statement is to create a new table and columns within that table for a given database. It may be called directly through a database server's command-line tool—for example, `osql.exe` or `mysql.exe`—or by calling `ExecuteNonQuery()` on a Command object.

The syntax of the CREATE TABLE statement looks like this:

```
CREATE TABLE name
[(
    column1-name column1-type column1-options,
    column2-name column2-type column2-options,
    ...
    columnN-name columnN-type columnN-options,
    [table-options]
)]
```

This statement has the following three pieces:

- The *name* of the table to be created.

- An optional comma-separated list of columns to be added to the new table, surrounded by parentheses. Each column may be given a name, a data type (with length in parentheses), and any other properties it may have—constraints or key details for instance.

- An optional list of space-separated *table_options* that govern the properties of all the rows in the table and how the table is stored in the file directory.

For example, if you wanted to add a new table to contain details of family members to a database, you'd use the following command:

```
CREATE TABLE familymember
(
    MemberID int IDENTITY NOT NULL PRIMARY KEY,
    MemberName varchar (75) NOT NULL,
    MemberBirthdate date,
    MemberSpecies varchar (20) NOT NULL
)
```

Note that some of the elements of CREATE TABLE have been left out for simplicity's sake. For a complete look at CREATE TABLE, check out the following links:

- `http://msdn.microsoft.com/library/en-us/tsqlref/ts_create2_8g9x.asp`

- `http://www.mysql.com/doc/en/CREATE_TABLE.html`

DROP DATABASE

The purpose of a DROP DATABASE statement is to completely remove a database and all its tables and data from a database server. **Be careful using this statement!** Generally, this command is issued as part of either a back-up script or indirectly through a GUI administration client. It may be called directly through a database server's command-line tool—for example, `osql.exe` or `mysql.exe`—or by calling `ExecuteNonQuery()` on a Command object.

The common syntax of the DROP DATABASE statement looks like this:

```
DROP DATABASE database_name
```

where *database_name* is the name of the database to be deleted from the server.

For example, if you wanted to delete the database holding the family information, you'd use the following command:

```
DROP DATABASE Genealogy
```

For more information about DROP DATABASE in T-SQL/ANSI SQL, try these links:

- `http://msdn.microsoft.com/library/en-us/tsqlref/ts_de-dz_82lh.asp`

- `http://www.mysql.com/doc/en/DROP_DATABASE.html`

DROP TABLE

The purpose of a DROP TABLE statement is to completely remove a table and all its data from a database. **Be careful using this statement!** In T-SQL, this statement can't remove a table that's referenced by a foreign key; that foreign key must be removed first. However, this isn't the case in MySQL. DROP TABLE may be called directly through a database server's command-line tool—for example, `osql.exe` or `mysql.exe`—or by calling `ExecuteNonQuery()` on a Command object.

The common syntax of the DROP TABLE statement looks like this:

```
DROP TABLE table_name
```

where *table_name* is the name of the table to be deleted from the database.

For example, if you wanted to delete the database holding the family member information, you'd use the following command:

```
DROP TABLE familymember
```

You can find more information on DROP TABLE at the following links:

- http://msdn.microsoft.com/library/en-us/tsqlref/ts_de-dz_7uud.asp

- http://www.mysql.com/doc/en/DROP_TABLE.html

ALTER DATABASE

The purpose of an ALTER DATABASE statement is to change some overall aspect of a database on a server. In MySQL, you can change the database's character set and collation options. In T-SQL, you can change the database name and physical storage options. ALTER DATABASE may be called directly through a database server's command-line tool—for example, osql.exe or mysql.exe—or by calling ExecuteNonQuery() on a Command object.

The syntax of the ALTER DATABASE statement looks like this:

```
ALTER DATABASE name
alteration
```

This statement has the following three pieces:

- The keywords ALTER DATABASE denoting the action to the database server

- The *name* of the database to be altered

- The exact *alteration* to be made to the database

Note that the exact types of alteration are completely different for T-SQL and for MySQL. Also, T-SQL allows you to make several alterations in one go as long as each alteration is separated by a comma from the next one. To get a full list of the options for T-SQL and MySQL, check out the following links:

- http://msdn.microsoft.com/library/en-us/tsqlref/ts_aa-az_4e5h.asp

- http://www.mysql.com/doc/en/ALTER_DATABASE.html

ALTER TABLE

The purpose of an ALTER TABLE statement is to change some aspect of a given table in a database. This usually means one of the following three things:

- Adding, modifying. or removing the properties or constraints on a column in the table

- Adding or removing a column from the table

- Adding or removing an index or constraint on the table

Exactly what you can do within each of these three options varies between T-SQL and MySQL. See the links to the online reference for exactly how they work. ALTER TABLE may be called directly through a database server's command-line tool—for example, osql.exe or mysql.exe—or by calling ExecuteNonQuery() on a Command object.

The syntax of the ALTER TABLE statement looks like this:

```
ALTER TABLE name
[ALTER COLUMN column_name new_column_type [new_column_properties]]
[ADD new_column_name [new_column_type new_column_properties]]
[DROP item_to_be_dropped]
```

Only the first line here is mandatory, and only one of the three following lines may be used in any one ALTER TABLE statement. The four pieces to this statement are as follows:

- The *name* of the table to be altered.

- An ALTER COLUMN statement that allows you to change details on a column that already exists in the named table, specifying the *column_name*, *new_column_type* and a few additional properties (for example, NULL, NOT NULL) that you need to add to it.

- An ADD statement that allows you to add a completely new column to the named table. Note that the optional *new_column_properties* section allows you to define default values, autonumber, and constraints on this column.

- A DROP statement that allows you to either remove a constraint from a column in the named table or to remove the whole column. *item_to_be_dropped* is thus either CONSTRAINT *constraint_name* or COLUMN *column_name*.

For example, if you wanted to add a new column for eye color to the family-member table, you'd use the following command:

```
ALTER TABLE familymember
ADD MemberEyeColor varchar(20) NULL
```

If you then decided you didn't want it after all, you'd use the following:

```
ALTER TABLE familymember
DROP COLUMN MemberEyeColor
```

Be careful when modifying columns because it's easy to lose data if you don't think things through fully—whether this is from a data type conversion that was unintended or because a character column has had its length reduced. Neither MSDE nor MySQL will warn that this is about to occur; both will just assume you know what you're doing. For more information on what you can change and what you can't in T-SQL and MySQL, check out the following:

- http://msdn.microsoft.com/library/en-us/tsqlref/ts_aa-az_3ied.asp

- http://www.mysql.com/doc/en/ALTER_TABLE.html

NOTE *The differences between the MSDE and MySQL syntax for modifying columns is because this functionality isn't defined in the SQL specification. Most databases allow this functionality, and their implementations are all slightly different.*

SQL Data Types

Databases support the same core set of data types as defined in the SQL standard but annoyingly call them different things. The following sections of the appendix provide easy references to those types as defined in SQL Server (MSDE), Jet (Access), and MySQL. We've split them up into the following four groups:

- Text types

- Numeric types

- Date and Time types

- Miscellaneous types

Note that Web Matrix doesn't allow you to specify all the types in the Jet engine like Access does.

Text Types

Several text-based types are defined in SQL, as given in Table 2-15, and are distinguished by the following two main characteristics:

- Does it support Unicode?

- Does it have a fixed length or a variable length?

Unicode support is fairly straightforward, but it's worth qualifying what we mean by *fixed* and *variable length*. If you choose a fixed-length type for a field and the string it contains is smaller than that length, the string is padded with spaces to make it the right length. This padding won't occur if you use a variable-length data type, but you must specify a maximum length for the string using the Length/Size property for the field.

char

The char type is as follows:

- In SQL Server, char represents a fixed-length string of up to 8,000 non-Unicode characters.

- In Jet, char represents a variable-length string of up to 255 Unicode characters.

- In MySQL, char represents a fixed-length string of up to 255 non-Unicode characters.

longtext

The longtext type is as follows:

- In MySQL, longtext represents a variable-length string of up to $2^{32} - 1$ (4,294,967,295) non-Unicode characters.

- There is no direct equivalent in SQL Server or Jet.

mediumtext

The mediumtext type is as follows:

- In MySQL, mediumtext represents a variable-length string of up to $2^{24} - 1$ (16,777,215) non-Unicode characters.

- There's no direct equivalent in SQL Server or Jet.

nchar/national char

The nchar/national char type is as follows:

- In SQL Server, nchar represents a fixed-length string of up to 4,000 Unicode characters.

- The closest equivalent to nchar in Jet is the char data type.

- In MySQL, national char represents a fixed-length string of up to 255 Unicode characters.

nvarchar/national varchar

The nvarchar/national varchar type is as follows:

- In SQL Server, nvarchar represents a variable-length string of up to 4,000 Unicode characters.

- The closest equivalent to nvarchar in Jet is the char data type.

- In MySQL, national varchar represents a variable-length string of up to 255 Unicode characters.

ntext/national text

The ntext/national text type is as follows:

- In SQL Server, ntext represents a variable-length string of up to $2^{30} - 1$ (1,073,741,823) Unicode characters.

- The closest equivalent to ntext in JET is the text data type.

- In MySQL, ntext, or national text, represents a variable-length string of up to 2^{16} - 1 (65.535) Unicode characters.

text

The text type is as follows:

- In SQL Server, text represents a variable-length string of up to 2^{31} - 1 (2,147,483,647) non-Unicode characters.

- In Jet, text represents a variable-length string of up to 2^{31} - 1 (2,147,483,647) Unicode characters. This type is also known as memo in Jet.

- In MySQL, ntext represents a variable-length string of up to 2^{16} - 1 (65.535) non-Unicode characters.

tinytext

The tinytext type is as follows:

- In MySQL, tinytext represents a variable-length string of up to 2^8 - 1 (255) non-Unicode characters.

- There's no direct equivalent in SQL Server or Jet.

varchar

The varchar type is as follows:

- In SQL Server, varchar represents a variable-length string of up to 8,000 non-Unicode characters.

- The closest equivalent to varchar in Jet is the char data type.

- In MySQL, varchar represents a variable-length string of up to 255 non-Unicode characters.

Numeric Types

Like .NET types, data types are available in MSDE and MySQL for both integer and floating-point values. However, there's a difference in implementation. Both databases assume by default that these types are signed—that is, they have negative values—but only MySQLCC gives you the option to make a type unsigned (by clicking the UNSIGNED check box) and thus give the field a range from zero to double the previous positive value plus one.

In addition, all numeric types are fixed-length data types. If a field contains a value that doesn't use all its allocated value, it's padded with spaces. In MySQL, if you check the ZEROFILL switch, numeric values are padded with zeroes instead of spaces.

Autonumbers

Supporting the notion that primary key fields must contain unique values, all three database types can autogenerate unique integer values for ID (primary key) fields. They can also generate globally unique ID fields (GUIDs)—128-bit hexadecimal numbers that are both random and unique. The following are the various ways to do this:

- To autogenerate integers in SQL Server, set the field's data type to int and then IsIdentity to true. The properties IdentitySeed and IdentityIncrement then let you set the first value to be generated for the field and the difference between each subsequent value, respectively.

- To autogenerate GUIDs in SQL Server, set the field's data type to uniqueidentifier and DefaultValue to newid().

- To autogenerate integers in JET, set the field's data type to autonumber. If you own a copy of Access, you can also generate random integer values.

- To autogenerate GUIDs in JET, set the field's data type to ReplicationID and then Autogenerate to true.

- MySQL supports only autogenerated integers. Set the field's data type to one of the integer data types and set AUTO_INCREMENT to true.

bigint

You should use Bigint only if you're absolutely sure that the integers you need to store can't fit in an int data field. The bigint type is as follows:

- In SQL Server, bigint represents an 8-byte integer that can take values between -2^{63} (-9,223,372,036,854,775,808) and 2^{63} - 1 (9,223,372,036,854,775,807).

- There's no Jet equivalent to bigint.

- In MySQL, bigint means the same as in SQL Server.

bit

bit is typically used as the data type to store boolean values. Columns of type bit can't have indexes on them. The bit type is as follows:

- In SQL Server, bit is an integer type that can take three values: 0, 1, or NULL.

- In Jet, bit is an integer type that can take three values: 0, 1, or NULL. It's also known as yes/no, where the values yes and no are equivalent to 1 and 0.

- In MySQL, bit is an integer type that can take three values: 0, 1, or NULL. It's also known as bool and, in MySQL 4.1 and onward, boolean.

decimal

decimal represents a number range defined by a maximum number of digits (its *precision*) and the maximum number of digits that can be used to the right of the decimal point (its *scale*). The decimal type is also known as numeric in all three databases. The decimal type is as follows:

- In SQL Server, the decimal type can have a maximum precision of 38, and the default scale is 0.

- In Jet, the decimal type can have a maximum precision of 28. The default precision is 18, and the default scale is 0.

- In MySQL, the decimal type can have a maximum precision of 38, and the default scale is 0. This type is also known as dec and fixed as well as numeric.

float

The float type is as follows:

- In SQL Server, float represents a variable range of floating-point numbers. You have to specify the number of bits used to store the mantissa of the number during its declaration, up to a maximum value of 0 and 53. At maximum precision, float can store a value between $1.79E^{308}$ to $-4.94E^{-324}$ for negative values, zero, and $4.94E^{-324}$ to $1.79E^{308}$ for positive values. float(53) is also known as double precision.

- In JET, float represents the same range of numbers as in SQL Server.

- In MySQL, float works in the same way as SQL server, but if you specify a precision of 24 or higher, it uses the synonym double.

int

The int type is as follows:

- In SQL Server, int represents a range of integers between -2^{31} (-2,147,483,648) and $2^{31}-1$ (2,147,483,647). It's also known as integer.

- MySQL and Jet also use the same definition of integer.

mediumint

The mediumint type is as follows:

- In MySQL, mediumint represents a range of integers between -2^{23} (-8,388,608) and $2^{23}-1$ (8,388,607)

- There are no equivalents of mediumint in SQL Server or Jet.

number

The number type is as follows:

- In Jet, users may use this generic type for integers and floating-point values. It detects the largest value for the field and uses that as the basis to decide how many bytes each field value should be stored in.

- In SQL Server, a close, but not exact, equivalent is sql_variant.

- There's no equivalent in MySQL.

real

The real type is as follows:

- In SQL Server, real represents a fixed range of floating-point numbers of -3.40E^{38} to - 1.40E^{-45} for negative values, zero, and 1.40E^{-45} to 3.40E^{38} for positive values. It's the functional equivalent of float(24).

- In Jet, real represents the same range of numbers as in SQL Server.

- In MySQL, real is another name for double, which equates to float(n) where n is between 24 and 53.

smallint

The smallint type is as follows:

- In SQL Server, smallint represents a range of integers between -2^{15} (-32,768) and 2^{15}-1 (32,767).

- MySQL and Jet also use the same definition of smallint.

tinyint

The tinyint type is as follows:

- In SQL Server, tinyint represents a range of integers between -128 and 127.

- MySQL and Jet also use the same definition of tinyint.

Date and Time Types

All three databases support "instance-in-time" fields, but only MySQL supports time unit types.

date

The date type is as follows:

- In MySQL, date represents a date between 1000-01-01 and 9999-12-31.

- There's no equivalent to date in SQL Server or Jet.

datetime

The datetime type is as follows:

- In SQL Server, datetime represents a date and time combination between midnight on Jan. 1, 1753, through to 23:59:59 on Dec. 31, 9999.

- In Jet, datetime represents a date and time combination between midnight on Jan. 1, 1000, through to 23:59:59 on Dec. 31, 9999

- In MySQL, datetime represents a date and time combination between midnight on Jan. 1, 1000, through to 23:59:59 on Dec. 31, 9999

smalldatetime

The smalldatetime type is as follows:

- In SQL Server, datetime represents a date and time combination between midnight on Jan. 1, 1900, through to 23:59:59 on June 6, 2079.

- There's no equivalent to smalldatetime in Jet or MySQL.

time

The time type is as follows:

- In MySQL, time represents a period of time in the format HH:MM:SS between -838:59:59 and 838:59:59.

- There's no equivalent to time in SQL Server or Jet.

timestamp

The timestamp type is as follows:

- In SQL Server, timestamp represents an automatically generated 8-byte binary number, which is guaranteed to be unique within a database.

- There is no equivalent to timestamp in Jet.

- In MySQL, timestamp is a date and time value automatically generated and given to the field when its row is added to the table or modified. Note that exactly how timestamp works differs between MySQL versions 4.0 and before and versions 4.1 onward. Please check the online documentation at http://dev.mysql.com/doc/mysql/en/TIMESTAMP_pre-4.1.html and http://dev.mysql.com/doc/mysql/en/TIMESTAMP_4.1.html, respectively, for full details.

year

The year type is as follows:

- In MySQL, year represents a range of years from 1901 to 2155 if you're using four digits and 1970 to 2066 if you're using two digits.

- There's no equivalent to year in SQL Server or Jet.

Binary Types

All databases define a few data types for the storage of binary data for storing such things as compiled programs, images, and audio. Look out for the rather unflattering acronym for binary data in general—Binary Large OBjects (BLOBs).

binary

The binary type is as follows:

- In SQL Server, binary represents a fixed-length binary sequence of up to 8,000 bytes.

- In Jet, binary represents a fixed-length binary sequence of up to 8,000 bytes.

- The closest equivalent to binary in MySQL is BLOB.

blob

The blob type is as follows:

- In MySQL, blob represents a variable-length binary sequence of up to 2^{16}-1 (65,535) bytes.

- There's no direct equivalent to blob in SQL Server or Jet.

image

The image type is as follows:

- In SQL Server, image represents a variable-length binary sequence of up to 2^{31}-1 (2,147,483,647) bytes.

- In Jet, image represents a variable-length binary sequence of up to 2^{31}-1 (2,147,483,647) bytes.

- The closest equivalent to image in MySQL is longblob.

longblob

The longblob type is as follows:

- In MySQL, longblob represents a variable-length binary sequence of up to $2^{32} - 1$ (4,294,967,295) bytes.

- There's no direct equivalent to longblob in SQL Server or Jet.

mediumblob

The mediumblob type is as follows:

- In MySQL, mediumblob represents a variable-length binary sequence of up to $2^{24} - 1$ (16,777,215) bytes.

- There's no direct equivalent to mediumblob in SQL Server or Jet.

tinyblob

The tinyblob type is as follows:

- In MySQL, tinyblob represents a variable-length binary sequence of up to $2^8 - 1$ (255) bytes.

- There's no direct equivalent to tinyblob in SQL Server or Jet.

varbinary

The varbinary type is as follows:

- In SQL Server, varbinary represents a variable-length binary sequence of up to 8,000 bytes.

- The closest equivalent to varbinary in Jet is the binary data type.

- The closest equivalent to varbinary in MySQL is BLOB.

Miscellaneous Types

Finally, the last group of types aren't easily classifiable into any one category other than miscellaneous.

cursor

The cursor type is as follows:

- In SQL Server, cursor represents a data type for variables or for stored procedures' OUTPUT parameters that contain a reference to a cursor. Any variables created with the cursor data type are nullable.

- There's no equivalent to cursor in Jet or MySQL.

enum('value1','value2',...)

This type is as follows:

- In MySQL, an enumeration containing a number of different strings (up to 65,535) can be defined using enum. The field can contain only one of these values, which are represented internally as integers.

- There's no equivalent to enum in SQL Server or Jet.

money

The money type is as follows:

- In SQL Server, money represents a range of monetary values from -2^{63} (-922,337,203,685,477.5808) through to $2^{63} - 1$ (+922,337,203,685,477.5807), with accuracy to a ten-thousandth of a monetary unit.

- In Jet, the money type does the same thing as in SQL Server.

- There's no direct equivalent type to money in MySQL.

```
set('value1','value2',...)
```

This type is as follows:

- In MySQL, a set of up to 65,535 different strings can be defined using `set`. The field can then contain up to 64 of these values, which are represented internally as integers.

- There's no equivalent to `set` in SQL Server or Jet.

smallmoney

The `smallmoney` type is as follows:

- In SQL Server, `smallmoney` represents a range of monetary values from -2^{31} (-214,748.3648) to 2^{31} - 1 (+214,748.3647), with accuracy to a ten-thousandth of a monetary unit.

- There's no direct equivalent to `smallmoney` in Jet or MySQL.

sql_variant

The `sql_variant` type is as follows:

- In SQL Server, a column of type `sql_variant` may contain rows of different data types. For example, a column defined as `sql_variant` can store `int`, `binary`, and `char` values. The only types of values that can't be stored using `sql_variant` are `text`, `ntext`, `image`, `timestamp`, and `sql_variant`.

- There's no equivalent for either Jet or MySQL.

table

The `table` type is as follows:

- In SQL Server, `table` is a special data type that can store the results of a query for later processing.

- There's no equivalent to `table` in Jet or MySQL.

uniqueidentifier

The uniqueidentifier type is as follows:

- In SQL Server, uniqueidentifier denotes that the field will hold a GUID.

- In Jet, uniqueidentifier works in the same way as SQL Server.

- There's no equivalent to uniqueidentifier in MySQL.

APPENDIX C

Sample Database Tables

THIS APPENDIX CONTAINS the complete structure of and data for the four tables in the sample database used in the examples in Chapters 3–8. Use it in conjunction with the instructions given in Chapter 2 to build the sample database. Alternately, use the instructions at the end of this appendix for generating the databases automatically.

To begin with, we'll mention the following:

- If you're creating a MySQL database, all tables must be InnoDB-type tables.

- This sample database has a user account attached to it called BAND. Please refer to Chapter 2 to see how to add this user account to the database.

The Publisher Table

The Publisher table contains the fields listed in Table C-1. This table also lists the properties of each field that should be altered from their defaults.

Table C-1. Fields in the Publisher Table

Field Name	MDB/Web Matrix	MSDE/Admin	MySQL/MySQLCC
PublisherID	DataType: Autonumber InPrimaryKey: True IsUniqueKey: True	DataType: int PrimaryKey: true Length: 4 Allow Null: false Identity: true	DataType: int PrimaryKey: true AUTO_INCREMENT: true
PublisherName	DataType: Text Size: 50 AllowNulls: False InPrimaryKey: False IsUniqueKey: False	DataType: varchar Length: 50 Allow Null: true	DataType: varchar Length: 50
PublisherCity	DataType: Text Size: 50 AllowNulls: False InPrimaryKey: False IsUniqueKey: False	DataType: varchar Length: 50 Allow Null: true	DataType: varchar Length: 50
PublisherContact_Email	DataType: Text Size: 100 AllowNulls: False InPrimaryKey: False IsUniqueKey: False	DataType: varchar Length: 100 Allow Null: true	DataType: varchar Length: 100
PublisherWebsite	DataType: Text Size: 100 AllowNulls: False InPrimaryKey: False IsUniqueKey: False	DataType: varchar Length: 100 Allow Null: true	DataType: varchar Length: 100

Table C-2 shows the data for the Publisher table.

Table C-2. Data in the Publisher Table

PublisherID	PublisherName	PublisherCity	PublisherContact_Email	PublisherWebsite
1	Apress	Berkeley	someguy@apress.com	http://www.apress.com
2	Friends Of Ed	Birmingham	aneditor@friendsofed.com	http://www.friendsofed.com
3	SAMS	Indianapolis	helper@samspublishing.com	http://www.samspublishing.com
4	Addison-Wesley	Boston	manager@aw.com	http://www.awprofessional.com
5	Manning	Greenwich	theboss@manning.com	http://www.manning.com

The Author Table

The Author table contains the fields listed in Table C-3. This table also lists the properties of each field that should be altered from their defaults.

Table C-3. Fields in the Author Table

Field Name	MDB/Web Matrix	MSDE/Admin	MySQL/MySQLCC
AuthorID	DataType: Autonumber InPrimaryKey: True IsUniqueKey: True	DataType: int PrimaryKey: true Length: 4 Allow Null: false Identity: true	DataType: int PrimaryKey: true AUTO_INCREMENT: true
AuthorFirstName	DataType: Text Size: 50 AllowNulls: False InPrimaryKey: False IsUniqueKey: False	DataType: varchar Length: 50 Allow Null: true	DataType: varchar Length: 50
AuthorSurname	DataType: Text Size: 50 AllowNulls: False InPrimaryKey: False IsUniqueKey: False	DataType: varchar Length: 50 Allow Null: true	DataType: varchar Length: 50
AuthorSSN	DataType: Text Size: 11 AllowNulls: False InPrimaryKey: False IsUniqueKey: False	DataType: char Length: 11 Allow Null: true	DataType: varchar Length: 11
AuthorLastContact	DataType: DateTime AllowNulls: True InPrimaryKey: False IsUniqueKey: False	DataType: smalldatetime Length: 0 Allow Null: true	defaultDataType: datetime Allow Null: true

The Author table contains the data shown in Table C-4.

Table C-4. Data in the Author Table

AuthorID	AuthorFirstName	AuthorSurname	AuthorSSN	AuthorLastContact
1	Dan	Maharry	123-55-6254	01/02/2004
2	Damien	Foggon	123-55-7651	12/02/2004
3	Dave	Sussman	123-55-9164	13/12/2003
4	Jane	Randall	123-55-1743	14/02/2004
5	Dominic	Briffa	123-55-8632	24/04/2003
6	Megan	Rothwell	123-55-2134	15/11/2003
7	Dan	Squier	123-55-4122	30/09/2003
8	James	Hart	123-55-0723	13/02/2004

The Book Table

The Book table contains the fields listed in Table C-5. This table also lists the properties of each field that should be altered from their defaults. In addition, the Book table has the following indexes and constraints on it:

- A simple index called IX_BookMainTopic on the BookMainTopic field

- The foreign key constraint FK_PublisherID_BookPublisherID that links the field BookPublisherID to the primary key field PublisherID in the Publisher table

    If you're using MySQL, you'll need to add a second simple index (called IX_BookPublisherID in the example) on the BookPublisherID field before adding the foreign key constraint.

Table C-5. Fields in the Book Table

Field Name	MDB/Web Matrix	MSDE/Admin	MySQL/MySQLCC
BookID	DataType: Autonumber InPrimaryKey: True IsUniqueKey: True	DataType: int PrimaryKey: true Length: 4 Allow Null: false Identity: true	DataType: int PrimaryKey: true AUTO_INCREMENT: true
BookTitle	DataType: Text Size: 100 AllowNulls: False InPrimaryKey: False IsUniqueKey: False	DataType: varchar Length: 100 Allow Null: true	DataType: varchar Length: 100
BookPublisherID	DataType: Integer AllowNulls: False InPrimaryKey: False IsUniqueKey: False	DataType: int Length: 4 Allow Null: false	DataType: int
BookMainTopic	DataType: Text Size: 25 AllowNulls: False InPrimaryKey: False IsUniqueKey: False	DataType: varchar Length: 25 Allow Null: true	DataType: varchar Length: 25

The Book table contains the data shown in Table C-6.

Table C-6. Data in the Book Table

BookID	BookTitle	BookPublisherID	BookMainTopic
1	Starting Up C#	2	C#
2	Beginning ASP.NET	1	ASP.NET
3	Waking up to .NET	3	.NET Framework
4	Starting Up VB .NET	2	VB.NET
5	Beginning ASP.NET Databases	1	ASP.NET
6	Journeyman Webforms	4	ASP.NET
7	Journeyman Winforms	4	C#
8	Starting Up ADO.NET with C#	2	ADO.NET
9	Jumping from VB6 to VB.NET	5	VB.NET
10	Jumping from Java to C#	5	C#
11	Dive Into Databases with ASP.NET and VB .NET	1	VB.NET
12	Professional .NET Application Design	3	C#
13	Games .NET	5	C#
14	Journeyman E-Commerce	2	ASP.NET
15	Deep Down ASP.NET	4	ASP.NET
16	Deep Down C#	4	C#
17	Deep Down VB .NET	4	VB.NET
18	System.Net Class Library Reference	2	.NET
19	MySQL in .NET	1	.NET
20	Open-Source .NET	5	.NET
21	VB .NET Reflection Handbook	1	VB.NET
22	Secure Programming	3	C#
23	Crypto .NET	5	C#
24	Delve into Intermediate Language	1	IL
25	Professional .NET Assemblies	2	.NET
26	Beginning ASP.NET 2.0 Preview	3	Whidbey
27	C# 2.0 Programmers Reference	3	Whidbey
28	Discovering WinFS	2	Longhorn
29	Discovering Avalon	2	Longhorn
30	Discovering Indigo	2	Longhorn

The WhoWroteWhat Table

The WhoWroteWhat table contains the fields listed in Table C-7. This table also lists the properties of each field that should be altered from their defaults. In addition, the WhoWroteWhat table has the following constraints on it:

- The foreign key constraint FK_BookID_WWWBookID that links the field WWWBookID to the primary key field BookID in the Book table

- The foreign key constraint FK_AuthorID_WWWAuthorID that links the field WWWAuthorID to the primary key field AuthorID in the Author table

If you're using MySQL, you'll need to add a second simple index (called IX_WWWAuthorID in the example) on the WWWAuthorID field before adding the foreign key constraint.

Table C-7. Fields in the Book Table

Field Name	MDB/Web Matrix	MSDE/Admin	MySQL/MySQLCC
WWWBookID	DataType: Integer InPrimaryKey: True IsUniqueKey: False	DataType: int PrimaryKey: true Length: 4 Allow Null: false Default: 0	DataType: int Primary Key: true
WWWAuthorID	DataType: Integer InPrimaryKey: True IsUniqueKey: False	DataType: int PrimaryKey: true Length: 4 Allow Null: false Default: 0	DataType: int Primary Key: true

The Book table contains the data shown in Table C-8.

Table C-8. Data in the WhoWroteWhat Table

WWWBookID	WWWAuthorID	WWWBookID	WWWAuthorID
1	1	16	8
1	2	17	1
2	3	18	2
3	1	19	1
3	3	19	3
4	5	19	4
5	3	20	4
6	6	21	5
7	1	22	6
7	7	23	5
7	8	23	7
8	8	24	8
9	1	25	1
10	2	26	2
11	2	27	3
11	3	27	4
12	4	27	6
13	5	28	4
14	6	29	5
15	3	30	6
15	7	30	7

Using the Database Scripts

In the code download for this book, you'll find a Database folder. Inside you'll find five items. Three of these are the clean, control versions of the sample database described here and built in Chapter 2. Obviously, you can make a copy of the Access/MDB file and use it straightaway, but the other two files—Generate_Books_MSDE.sql and Generate_Books_MySQL.sql—are SQL scripts that must be run by the appropriate database application before you can use the database.

> **NOTE** *By running these scripts, you erase any changes made to the contents of the database since its creation. Therefore, save any changes you may want to keep before running these scripts.*

To refresh the MSDE database, follow these steps:

1. Open a command prompt window, and navigate to X:\Program Files\ Microsoft SQL Server\80\Tools\Binn where X is your Windows partition.

2. Type the following command (with no line breaks):

   ```
   osql -i [path to Generate_Books_MSDE.sql] -U sa -P secpas
     -S "(local)\BAND" -e
   ```

To refresh the MySQL database, follow these steps:

1. Open MySQL Control Center, and then click File ➤ Query (Ctrl+Q).

2. Now click File ➤ Open, and navigate to Generate_Books_MySQL.sql. Double-click to select it. The text of it will appear in the window.

3. Run the script by hitting Query ➤ Execute (Ctrl+E).

The other two files in the Database folder are an Excel spreadsheet and .csv file for use in Chapter 3.

Webliography

THIS APPENDIX LISTS useful Web sites that focus on databases and related issues, as well as all the Web sites referenced in the book. Where appropriate, URLs are given more than once for easy reference.

Installation Links

The following are helpful links related to installation of the products mentioned in this book:

- .NET 1.1: `http://www.microsoft.com/downloads/details.aspx?FamilyId=262D25E3-F589-4842-8157-034D1E7CF3A3`

- .NET ODBC Data Provider: `http://www.microsoft.com/downloads/details.aspx?familyid=6ccd8427-1017-4f33-a062-d165078e32b1`

- Web Matrix: `http://www.asp.net/webmatrix/download.aspx`

- Microsoft Excel and Access: `http://office.microsoft.com`

- Microsoft SQL Server 2000 Desktop Engine: `http://msdn.microsoft.com/netframework/downloads/sdkmsde/default.aspx`

- SQL Web Data Administrator: `http://www.microsoft.com/downloads/details.aspx?FamilyId=C039A798-C57A-419E-ACBC-2A332CB7F959`

- MySQL: `http://www.mysql.com/downloads/mysql-4.0.html`

- MySQL Control Center: `http://www.mysql.com/downloads/mysqlcc.html`

- MySQL Administrator: `http://www.mysql.com/downloads/administrator/`

- MySQL ODBC connector: `http://www.mysql.com/downloads/connector/odbc/3.51.html`

Data Source Product Web Sites

The following sections give URLs for the data source products mentioned in this book.

Object-Oriented Data Stores

The following are object-oriented data stores:

- Objectstore: http://www.objectstore.net/products/objectstore/index.ssp

- Objectivity/DB: http://www.objectivity.com

- Versant enJin: http://www.versant.com/

- Gemstone: http://www.gemstone.com/

- Poet Software: http://www.poet.com/en/indexjs.html

XML Databases

The following are XML databases:

- Snapbridge: http://www.snapbridge.com/products/fdx_xml_server.html

- Ipedo: http://www.ipedo.com/html/ipedo_xml_database.html

- Berkeley DB XML: http://www.sleepycat.com/

- Tamino: http://www.softwareag.com/tamino/

Relational Databases

The following are relational databases:

- Microsoft SQL Server: http://msdn.microsoft.com/sql/

- Microsoft SQL Server 2000 Database Engine:
  http://msdn.microsoft.com/sql/msde/

- Microsoft SQL Server CE: `http://msdn.microsoft.com/sql/sqlce/default.aspx`

- Microsoft Access: `http://office.microsoft.com`

- PostgreSQL: `http://www.postgresql.org`

- MySQL: `http://www.mysql.org`

- Sybase Adaptive Server: `http://www.sybase.com/products/databaseservers`

- Oracle: `http://www.oracle.com`

- IBM Informix: `http://www-306.ibm.com/software/data/informix/`

- Teradata: `http://www.teradata.com/t/`

- IBM DB2: `http://www-306.ibm.com/software/data/db2/`

- GNU SQL Server: `http://www.ispras.ru/~gsql/`

- Firebird SQL: `http://firebird.sourceforge.net/`

Community-Based Development Sites

The following are community-based ASP.NET development sites worth checking out for more information on the topics found in this book:

- ASP.NET Homepage: `http://www.asp.net`

- dotNet Junkies: `http://www.dotnetjunkies.com`

- SQL Junkies: `http://www.sqljunkies.com`

- ASP Advice: `http://www.aspadvice.com`

- 4 Guys From Rolla: `http://www.4guysfromrolla.com`

- ASP Alliance: `http://www.aspalliance.com`

- ASP Today: `http://www.asptoday.com`

Chapter 2

The following are mentioned in Chapter 2:

- .NET Support in Yukon (SQL Server 2005): `http://www.microsoft.com/sql/yukon/productinfo/top30features.asp#B`

- World Wide Web Consortium (W3C): `http://www.w3c.org`

- W3C XQuery 1.0 Specification: `http://www.w3.org/XML/Query`

Chapter 3

The following are mentioned in Chapter 3:

- Connection string samples: `http://www.able-consulting.com/ADO_Conn.htm`

- Accessing SQL Server using Windows Authentication: `http://msdn.microsoft.com/library/en-us/vbcon/html/vbtskaccessingsqlserverusingwindowsintegratedsecurity.asp`

- Jet Engine Service Pack 8: `http://support.microsoft.com/?kbid=239114`

- `SqlConnection` class: `htp://msdn.microsoft.com/ library/en-us/cpref/html/frlrfsystemdatasqlclientsqlconnectionclasstopic.asp`

- `OdbcConnection` class: `http://msdn.microsoft.com/lbrary/en-us/cpref/html/frlrfsystemdatasqlclientsqlconnectionclasstopic.asp`

- `OleDbConnection`: `http://msdn.microsoft.com/library/en-us/cpref/html/frlrfsystemdatasqlclientsqlconnectionclasstopic.asp`

- Introducing `web.config`: `http://msdn.microsoft.com/library/en-us/cpguide/html/cpconaspnetconfiguration.asp`

- The `System.Diagnostics.EventLog` class: `http://msdn.microsoft.com/library/en-us/cpref/html/frlrfsystemexceptionclasstopic.asp`

Chapter 6

The following is mentioned in Chapter 6:

- The DataAdapter.Fill() method variations: `http://msdn.microsoft.com/library/`
  `en-us/cpref/html/frlrfSystemDataCommonDbDataAdapterClassFillTopic.asp`

Chapter 7

The following are mentioned in Chapter 7:

- The difference between DataGrid, DataList, and Repeater controls:
  `http://msdn.microsoft.com/library/en-us/vbcon/html/`
  `vbcondisplayinglistsusingwebcontrols.asp`

- Good articles on the Repeater control: `http://www.sitepoint.com/article/`
  `1014` and `http://www.dotnetjohn.com/articles/articleid58.aspx`

Chapter 9

The following is mentioned in Chapter 9:

- "Output Parameters Are Not Returned When You Run an ADO.NET
  Command in Visual C# .NET": `http://support.microsoft.com/`
  `default.aspx?scid=kb;en-us;Q308621`

Chapter 10

The following are mentioned in Chapter 10:

- `osql.exe` flags: `http://msdn.microsoft.com/library/en-us/coprompt/`
  `cp_osql_1wxl.asp`

- `mysql.exe` flags: `http://www.mysql.com/doc/en/mysql.html`

- Create database syntax (T-SQL): `http://msdn.microsoft.com/library/en-us/`
  `tsqlref/ts_create_1up1.asp`

- Create database syntax (MySQL): http://www.mysql.com/doc/en/
  CREATE_DATABASE.html

- Create table syntax (T-SQL): http://msdn.microsoft.com/library/en-us/
  tsqlref/ts_create2_8g9x.asp

- Create table syntax (MySQL): http://www.mysql.com/doc/en/CREATE_TABLE.html

- Alter table syntax (T-SQL): http://msdn.microsoft.com/library/en-us/
  tsqlref/ts_aa-az_3ied.asp

- Alter table syntax (MySQL): http://www.mysql.com/doc/en/ALTER_TABLE.html

- Enabling MySQL to support table relationships:
  http://www.mysql.com/doc/en/InnoDB.html

Chapter 11

The following are mentioned in Chapter 11:

- SourceForge: http://www.sourceforge.net

- GotDotNet workspaces: http://workspaces.gotdotnet.com

- Apache Web server home page: http://httpd.apache.org

- Covalent ASP.NET plug-in for Apache: http://www.covalent.com

- Mono project. .NET on Linux: http://www.go-mono.com

- Emacs: http://www.gnu.org/software/emacs/windows/ntemacs.html

- Vim: http://www.vim.org

- Eclipse IDE: http://www.eclipse.org/

- Dreamweaver MX 2004: http://www.macromedia.com/software/dreamweaver/

- Visual Studio .NET: http://msdn.microsoft.com/vstudio/

- nUnit: http://www.nUnit.org

- Installing nUnit: `http://www.nunit.org/getStarted.html`

- Writing test harnesses for nUnit: `http://www.nunit.org/files/QuickStart.doc`

- nUnitASP: `http://nunitasp.sourceforge.net/download.html`

- An introduction to using nUnitASP: `http://www.theserverside.net/articles/showarticle.tss?id=TestingASP`

- TestRunner for Visual Studio .NET: `http://www.mailframe.net/Products/TestRunner.htm`

- Visual Studio 2005 Team System: `http://msdn.microsoft.com/vstudio/teamsystem/tester/default.aspx`

- ASP.NET performance home page: `http://msdn.microsoft.com/asp.net/using/understanding/perf/default.aspx`

Index

forums.apress.com

FOR PROFESSIONALS BY PROFESSIONALS™

JOIN THE APRESS FORUMS AND BE PART OF OUR COMMUNITY. You'll find discussions that cover topics of interest to IT professionals, programmers, and enthusiasts just like you. If you post a query to one of our forums, you can expect that some of the best minds in the business—especially Apress authors, who all write with *The Expert's Voice*™—will chime in to help you. Why not aim to become one of our most valuable participants (MVPs) and win cool stuff? Here's a sampling of what you'll find:

DATABASES
Data drives everything.

Share information, exchange ideas, and discuss any database programming or administration issues.

PROGRAMMING/BUSINESS
Unfortunately, it is.

Talk about the Apress line of books that cover software methodology, best practices, and how programmers interact with the "suits."

INTERNET TECHNOLOGIES AND NETWORKING
Try living without plumbing (and eventually IPv6).

Talk about networking topics including protocols, design, administration, wireless, wired, storage, backup, certifications, trends, and new technologies.

WEB DEVELOPMENT/DESIGN
Ugly doesn't cut it anymore, and CGI is absurd.

Help is in sight for your site. Find design solutions for your projects and get ideas for building an interactive Web site.

JAVA
We've come a long way from the old Oak tree.

Hang out and discuss Java in whatever flavor you choose: J2SE, J2EE, J2ME, Jakarta, and so on.

SECURITY
Lots of bad guys out there—the good guys need help.

Discuss computer and network security issues here. Just don't let anyone else know the answers!

MAC OS X
All about the Zen of OS X.

OS X is both the present and the future for Mac apps. Make suggestions, offer up ideas, or boast about your new hardware.

TECHNOLOGY IN ACTION
Cool things. Fun things.

It's after hours. It's time to play. Whether you're into LEGO® MINDSTORMS™ or turning an old PC into a DVR, this is where technology turns into fun.

OPEN SOURCE
Source code is good; understanding (open) source is better.

Discuss open source technologies and related topics such as PHP, MySQL, Linux, Perl, Apache, Python, and more.

WINDOWS
No defenestration here.

Ask questions about all aspects of Windows programming, get help on Microsoft technologies covered in Apress books, or provide feedback on any Apress Windows book.

HOW TO PARTICIPATE:

Go to the Apress Forums site at **http://forums.apress.com/**.
Click the New User link.